The new Far East

Arthur Diósy

THE YELLOW PERIL.

(THE GERMAN VERSION.)

Drawn, in 1895, by H. Knackfuss, from a Design by His Majesty William II., German Emperor
King of Prussia.

THE
NEW FAR EAST

BY

ARTHUR DIÓSY

CHAIRMAN OF COUNCIL OF THE JAPAN SOCIETY, LONDON

WITH ILLUSTRATIONS FROM SPECIAL DESIGNS

By KUBOTA Beisen, of Tōkio

A Reproduction of a CARTOON *designed by* H.M. *the* GERMAN EMPEROR,
and a specially-drawn MAP

Fourth Edition

CASSELL AND COMPANY, LIMITED
LONDON, PARIS, NEW YORK & MELBOURNE. MCMIV

First Edition *November* 1898.
Second Edition *July* 1900.   Third Edition 1900.
Fourth Edition *March* 1904.

TO

THE MEMORY OF

MY FATHER

PREFACE

TO THE FOURTH EDITION.

THE intense interest aroused by the outbreak of the war between Japan and Russia has caused an immediate demand for a fourth edition of this book. It has been thought advisable to re-issue it absolutely without alteration and I venture to think that these pages, written in 1898, will rather gain in interest when read by the light of the stirring events which have occurred since that year.

To what I have written in the Preface to the Second Edition (to be found in the next few pages) I have nothing to add, save to call attention to the three great historical changes that have since come about :—

THE ALLIANCE OF BRITAIN AND JAPAN, whereby British policy in the Far East has, at last, entered on the "Clear Course" which I have so long strenuously advocated, and which is treated of in Chapter X.

THE WAR BETWEEN RUSSIA AND JAPAN, the inevitable struggle for preponderance in the Far East, and Japan's immediate exposure of the hollowness of Muscovite bluff.

The unmistakable symptoms of the gradual AWAKENING OF CHINA under Japanese impulse, the Chinese turning, in their extremity, more and more towards their late foes, whose just and humane conduct in the repression of the "Boxer" outbreak of 1900 so deeply impressed the Celestial mind.

ARTHUR DIÓSY.

LONDON, *March*, 1904.

PREFACE

TO THE SECOND EDITION.

THE events now convulsing the Chinese Empire, and threatening the peace not only of the Far East but of the whole world, are the inevitable outcome of the conditions it was my object to describe in the following pages.

I have discussed the various chapters of this book, last summer, in the Far East with the statesmen who guide the policy of New Japan, and with Chinese and Koreans representative of the spirit that animates their nations, with Mandarins of the typical, ultra-conservative sort, with leaders of the lamentably small Chinese Reform Party, with chiefs of Chinese Secret Societies, and with Korean Princes and exiles, banished for their reforming tendencies—and I find no necessity for altering a single statement.

The reader, bearing in mind that the book was written in 1898, will be able to judge, by the light of recent portentous developments, the accuracy of my views on the forces at work in Eastern Asia. I have no desire to assume an attitude or "I told you so!" I simply invite a comparison of my statement of the position of the different Powers interested as it was in 1898, of their aims, their methods and their relative strength, with the situation at the present moment, which is the logical development of the causes I have striven to indicate and to explain. Nothing has occurred within the last two years to change the aspirations of the nations of Eastern Asia and of the Occidental Powers in contact with them. The nations have proceeded along the lines marked out for them by the spirit animating their policies. Nothing has taken place but what the nature of those various policies rendered inevitable. Russia's power in the Far East has increased apace—Manchuria is in her iron grip, the great Trans-Siberian Railway is approaching completion, and in Korea she is steadily pushing her way once more to the position of influence she had abandoned when more important matters demanded her undivided attention elsewhere and made it unadvisable for her to risk a conflict, at that time, with Japan. France has continued to give her dear "friend and ally," Russia, her valuable and energetic support in her Far Eastern policy. Germany has firmly established herself at Kiao-chau, and claims to be considered as a factor of prime importance in the politics of Eastern Asia. The United States of America make a similar claim, based chiefly on their prickly possession of the Philippine Islands. Italy, still smarting from the snub administered to her by China when she sought a "Sphere of Influence" in Che-kiang, takes a lively and active interest in the great drama on which the curtain has just been raised. Britain has improved her strategical position by her possession of Wei-hai-wei (pronounced "Way-high-way")—an occupation I was the first publicly to forecast, as far back as 30th December, 1897, as mentioned on p. 309—and of the *Hinterland*, or, as I prefer to call it (why use the German term?), the "backland" of Kow-loon, or Kau-lung, opposite Hong-kong.

The latter increase of territory was rendered absolutely necessary in order to protect our great and flourishing seaport from the fire of modern long-range guns. Wei-hai-wei might, with considerable expenditure and the application of some of the energy shown by the Germans at Kiao-chau, have been made once more into a formidable place of arms. As it is, the most notable sign of British occupation was, a year after the hoisting of the flag, a well-situated cricket-pitch. Certainly, some surveys have been made and a Report has been ordered on the works and armaments necessary in order to restore the powerful stronghold destroyed by the Japanese, but, at the present rate of progress, war will probably be conducted by means of navigable balloons by the time the fortress has been rebuilt and re-armed. Something important has, however, been done at Wei-hai-wei ; a native regiment, "Her Majesty's First Chinese," has been raised from amongst the sturdy villagers, and has been trained, with apparently excellent results, by British officers and drill-sergeants, forming a force well adapted for police duties and for operations against Chinese, but probably incapable of successfully encountering European troops in regular warfare.

The improvement, within the last two years, in Britain's strategical position in the Far East has not kept pace with the rapid advance in Russia's military strength in those regions since the Muscovites entered into possession of Port Arthur and began to pour a never-ending stream of troops and armaments into the formidable place of arms they have also turned into one of the world's largest storehouses of steam coal. Whatever gain, and it is small enough, may have accrued to Britain in a military sense is more than counterbalanced by the continued loss of prestige, that most important factor in Far Eastern affairs. Deeply impressed by Russia's relentless advance, the Chinese authorities were already only too much disposed to make light of Britain's power when the news of our early disasters in South Africa, much exaggerated in transmission, and distorted to our further disadvantage by unfriendly Occidental channels of information, came to convince them that as a Great Power Britain was "played out" And they acted accordingly, snubbing British diplomacy at every turn, and calmly ignoring, for months together, its claims, its representations, its protests and its threats. Even in Japan, a country so predisposed to cordial relations with Britain, the echoes of the news from South Africa in the earlier part of the war shook the belief of many in Britain's ability to defend her interests in the Far East. The want of military foresight, to put it mildly, displayed at the outset, made a deep impression on the Japanese mind. There were not wanting unfriendly critics amongst the Non-British foreign residents in Japan who spared no efforts to increase this impression, and it is greatly to the credit of Japanese common-sense that the majority of the people suspended their ultimate judgment until the news of the turn of the tide in South Africa came to justify the attitude of the Japanese press, which sided, with few and unimportant exceptions, with Britain from the commencement of the struggle.

Korea is still, as in 1898, a prey to conflicting factions, an "Empire"—save the mark !—torn by dissensions and misgoverned to an almost incredible degree. As for Japan, pursuing her onward march in the path of civilisation according to Western methods, adapted to her needs, she is daily gaining in strength. That Japan, with her powerful navy and her excellent army, holds the key of the Far Eastern Question is even more evident now than when this book was written. Her navy and her army have vastly increased in power since Chapter VII. ("Fighting Power") was penned, but their development has proceeded along the lines indicated in that chapter. I was able, last summer, thanks to the special opportunities so courteously given to me by the Japanese naval and military authorities, to satisfy myself, by careful personal investigation, of the absolute

*

efficiency of Japan's forces by sea and land. At this moment Japan possesses the most powerful battleship afloat—a sister-ship is almost ready for sea—and her admirably-conceived Naval Programme is approaching completion, whilst the value of her perfectly-organised and sensibly-equipped army has been immensely increased by the re-armament of the Field Artillery with *quick-firing*, "non-recoiling" guns, immeasurably superior to the obsolete field ordnance taken out to South Africa by our own Royal Artillery.

And what of China? The Chinese people, entertaining a strong and not unnatural objection to the virtual absorption of parts of their country by foreign Powers, have determined on making a bold attempt to put an end to the continual grabbing of "Leased Territories" and "Spheres of Influence." "China for the Chinese!" is now the national cry, and they mean thereby "China for the Chinese *only!*" To ensure this end, they are making a desperate effort to remove the hated foreigners from within the borders of the Celestial Empire. Perusal of Chapter IV. ("The Men of Old China") will give an insight into the Chinese spirit and will show the reasons that make it so easy for the ruling classes to inflame the passions of the populace against the "Foreign Devils" whose subversive influence threatens the whole system of administrative corruption on which the officials, with few exceptions, fatten. The Mandarins have done their fell work but too thoroughly. Hell is let loose in a great part of China, and more than one of the Great Powers looks not unfavourably upon the idea of furnishing Japan with an International Mandate to act as the World's Police in restoring peace and order in the distracted Empire. This course appeals strongly to those Powers that realise most clearly the great dangers and the enormous difficulties attendant on operations carried on by combined International Forces. One of these difficulties, and it is indeed a serious one, presents itself at once in the fact that the eight Powers whose armed forces have been landed in China use eight different rifles, and, consequently, eight different patterns of cartridges. It is easy to imagine the difficulty of keeping an International Column properly supplied with ammunition in these circumstances.

The giving of an International Mandate to Japan, the Power most favourably situated for the performance of such a gigantic task, meets with two serious obstacles: the objection of Russia to anything tending to increase Japan's importance, and to diminish her own, in Eastern Asia, and the natural disinclination of Japan—" once bitten, twice shy!"—to undertake the onerous duty of World's Police in China without first obtaining the most satisfactory guarantees that her national interests would gain substantially in return for the blood and the treasure she would be called upon to expend. Japan has not forgotten, nor is she likely to forget, her treatment by the "Long Firm," Russia France and Germany, immediately after her victory over China. The intervention of the three Great Powers that forced her to give up Port Arthur, so that Russia might seize that coveted place of arms, and Britain's and America's neglect, at that critical moment, of the interests of Japan, *that are also their interests in the Far East*—these are a crime and a blunder the memory of which rankles in the Japanese heart. The blunder on the part of the English-speaking nations is forgiven — they are suffering heavily enough for it now—but it is not forgotten. The Japanese recognise that espousal of their cause at the time of the intervention of the Three Powers might have led Britain, and perhaps America, into a conflict with Russia, France and Germany for which the ever-unready English-speaking nations were unprepared, and the cautious statesmen who direct Japan's policy hesitate to face a repetition of the situation. They are unwilling to commit their country to a course that might lead to its being once more left in the lurch by its natural friends.

What compensation *could* Europe and America guarantee to Japan were she, as the World's Constable, entrusted with a warrant for the pacification of China? It has been suggested that her reward should be territorial, that the Province of Fu-kien (opposite to her new dependency, Formosa) should be handed over to her by the grateful Powers for her "Sphere of Influence." Japan would reply, "Thank you for nothing!" for she has already secured, by arrangement with China, Fu-kien as her prospective "Sphere," not to be alienated to any other Power. Japan's guerdon must be of a different kind to induce her to run the great risks involved. We may obtain some idea of its probable nature if we bear in mind that the ideal of the Japanese is the regeneration of China by Japanese agency. They aspire to lead their tottering "Elder Brother" away from the brink of the precipice into the safe road of modern enlightenment along which Japan has so rapidly marched within the last thirty years of the nineteenth century.

That Japan is better fitted to undertake this stupendous task

than any other Power is, I trust, clearly indicated in the following
pages. That she would undertake it from purely disinterested
motives is not to be expected ; a certain amount of exploitation
seems inseparable from the task of regenerating a nation. Should
Japan assume the enormous responsibility of pacifying and
cleansing, of regulating and educating China, she would deserve
to reap very substantial profit from her efforts. In the immediate
future the whole world would be the gainer, and the Powers
could well afford to let Japan obtain a very large share of the
benefits accruing from her labours

Whether the situation to be created in the remote future
by an awakening of China's millions, quickened into new life
under Japanese, or, indeed, *under any civilised guidance*,
would present dangers, the magnitude of which can hardly be
estimated, to the interests of the white race—that is one of
the greatest, probably the greatest problem before the Occidental world to-day. In order to consider this " Yellow Peril "
(treated of in Chapter VIII.) with the necessary calm, the
statesmen of the West must await the extinction of the present
conflagration in China, a blaze that threatens to extend far beyond
the borders of the Celestial Empire. It is when the flames have
been put out in China that the greatest danger may arise. The
International Fire Brigade, a very mixed body, may not be unanimous as to the best means to adopt to prevent a renewal of the
catastrophe. Their ideas as to preventive measures may differ,
and dissensions may easily arise as to the proper remuneration
some, if not all, of the Firemen will claim for their services. A
grouping of the Powers may take place, in which it is fervently
to be hoped, for the sake of peace, that Britain, America, and
Japan, perhaps also Italy—whose interests are, in the main,
identical—may have the wisdom to stand steadfastly together.
That this is the desire of the vast majority of the Japanese nation
I know from personal experience, for I had, last summer, unusual
opportunities of ascertaining the feelings towards the English-
speaking nations of Japanese of all classes, from the Emperor in
his palace at Tōkio to the humblest of His Majesty's subjects in
remote mountain villages. But this feeling of friendship for
Britain and America, based on mutual interests, will not lead the
shrewd Japanese into a policy of adventure. They will fight, and
fight heroically, if their national interests absolutely demand it ;
but what they require above all is Peace—a few years, at least, of
Peace to further the development of their rising industries and

to attract the foreign capital of which those enterprises stand so much in need.

Will the English-speaking nations entrust the chief share in the regeneration of China to Japan? Will they combine to protect Japan from the possible, nay, probable, interference of other Powers in the execution of her task? Can they persuade Germany to give them her support, or, at least, assurances of her neutrality? Will they guarantee to Japan a reasonable return for her labours? These are questions demanding close study. If the English-speaking nations really desire to approach the solution of the tremendous Chinese problem—a Chinese puzzle if ever there was one!—with clear comprehension of the facts they must first make up their minds to ignore the mischievous political catch-words that have come into such prominence of late, terms that are mere words, obscuring the real issues at stake. Let us think less of "Treaty Rights" in a country whose Government has no adequate means (and no will to do so if it had the means) to enforce the treaties wrung from it by force and threats; let us think less of "Spheres of Influence"—in plain English: "Spheres of Exploitation"— vaguely defined, like that hazy notion of the "Yang-tsze Valley," so glibly used by thousands who have no idea of its exact whereabouts. Let us cease to consider the removal from power of the Dowager Empress of China, or even of the still more rabidly anti-foreign Prince Tūan, as the panacea for all the ills that China is heir to; the masterful old lady and the rabid Prince must go, indeed, but their disappearance from the scene will by no means solve the question, for they respectively wield their immense influence chiefly because each of them is, in different degrees, the incarnation of the anti-foreign spirit that pervades the minds of the majority of the Chinese. Let us remember that the "Righteous Harmonists," whom English journalists in the Treaty Ports have so conveniently dubbed "The Boxers," are not merely one of the numerous Secret Societies with which China is honeycombed, but that they represent the feelings of the vast majority of the pig tailed hundreds of millions in their war-cry: "Expel the Foreigners!" (The same cry heralded the dawn of the New Era in Japan; may it be a like portent in China!) Above all, let us bear in mind that the "Open Door," excellent watchword though it be, admits of various loose interpretations. It is quite possible for an astute Power to keep the door widely open, yet to spread across it a strong, but almost invisible, net that will effectually shut out the commerce of her rivals.

Whilst we, as a nation, are just beginning to study these great problems, Japan has long devoted the closest attention to them. She has applied her wonderful energies to making herself ready for their solution, in conjunction, at least at first, with other interested Powers. She has proudly taken her place in the comity of civilised nations now that her Revised Treaties with other Powers have come into operation—contrary to the predictions of Occidental croakers in Japan; without causing any very serious friction—and have abolished the humiliating foreign jurisdiction within her borders and made her, at last, mistress in her own land. The Japanese are ready. They have learned the great lesson of latter-day history, of all history, right well, the lesson that if they want to secure the Peace so necessary to their development they must be nationally *strong.* The Gospel according to Sandow? Not quite, for national power is strength of character, of body and of resources, prudently directed by intellect and knowledge. These combined constitute Might, and since the days of Bismarck, more than ever, Might has been Right all over the globe. Is it too much to hope that in the not too distant future those that are in the Right may be the only ones who wield the Might? So may it be, in the Far East and throughout the world!

ARTHUR DIÓSY.

LONDON, *July*, 1900.

PREFACE TO THE FIRST EDITION.

THIS book is not intended for the expert. It has been written for the many who, knowing a little about the Far East, are anxious to know more.

It has been my earnest endeavour to write impartially; if any bias be noticeable in the expression of my opinions it is due to the standpoint from which I consider the subject—the standpoint of one who believes that Britain is called upon to play a part of supreme importance in the future of Eastern Asia

Profoundly as I esteem and admire Japan, warmly as I rejoice in her rising fortunes, *I love Britain*, my native country, *best;* and I am convinced that I am serving her in the best way open to me by endeavouring to contribute to the formation of a sound Public Opinion upon the Far Eastern Question, based on knowledge of the Truth.

The Inscriptions on the Cover of the volume call for a few words of explanation :—

The three Inscriptions in Oriental characters, to be read from top to bottom, are translations of the title : *The New Far East.*

The Inscription on the right is in Chinese, written with the rather square form of ideograms used for titles of books. It is due to the deft brush of a distinguished Chinese diplomatist, one of the few Mandarins who place love of country before love of self, a true patriot, an erudite scholar, an ardent reformer— and, of course, powerless in the face of the stolid opposition of the ignorant and the corrupt who are stifling China. The beautifully formed characters read : *Hsin Yuen Tong* (" New Far East "). The Japanese pronunciation of these Chinese characters is : *Shin Yen To.*

The Inscription in the centre is in Korean *Ön-mun* alphabetic character, and reads : *Sai Tong Pang.* The bold, clear characters were written for me by the brush of a notable Korean, the *Sak-sa* Yi Chun-yong, a nephew of the reigning Emperor and a grandson of that redoubtable personage, His late Highness the *Tai-wen-kun*, the father of the present Sovereign. Accomplished and earnest, Yi Chun-yong adds to his exquisite courtesy and calm dignity— qualities that are general amongst the Korean aristocracy—a keen, receptive intelligence, a thirst for knowledge, a capacity for work, and a concern for his country's welfare, that are, alas ! rarely found amongst his compatriots of high rank.

The Inscription on the left is in Japanese *Hiragana*, or cursive syllabic character, written, in a fine flowing hand, by Professor TAKAHASHI Sakuyé, of the Imperial Naval Staff College (some- times called " The Naval University ") at Tōkio, a Corresponding Member of the Japan Society. It reads : *Arata-naru Higashi-no Haté*, but the meaning is the same as that of *Shin Yen To* (" New Far East ").

All three nationalities can read, and understand, the Inscrip- tion in Chinese character; although each one would give the words, as I have just shown, a different sound, the ideograms, well known to every fairly well-educated man amongst them, would at once represent, to their minds, the words " New Far East." But the other two inscriptions can be read only by com- patriots of those who wrote them—or by the few of other nationalities who have, by dint of much study, acquired the requisite knowledge—neither Chinese nor Korean can read Japanese *Hiragana ;* neither Chinese nor Japanese can read Korean *Ŏn-mun.* Both these systems of writing being phonetic they express *sounds,* varying widely in the different tongues : the Chinese characters, which all three Far Eastern nations use, being ideographic, express *thoughts,* that the reader can render in the sounds of his own language.

With the exception of the reproduction of the celebrated cartoon drawn by Herr H. Knackfuss from a design by H.M· William II., German Emperor and King of Prussia, the Illustrations have all been drawn specially for this book by KUBOTA Beisen, of Tōkio. I append some particulars regarding this interesting artist, in the very words used, in a recent letter to me, by my friend Mr. Fukai—one of the leading journalists and authors in New Japan—joint editor, with Mr. Tokutomi, of the *Kokumin Shimbun* ("The Nation"), an important Tōkio daily, and of the *Kokumin-no Tomo* ("The Nation's Friend"), a monthly Review , and editor of the highly-interesting monthly, in *English,* entitled *The Far East.* Mr. Fukai's English letter deserves to be quoted unabridged, as evidence of remarkable linguistic talent on the part of a Japanese who spent but a very short time in English-speaking countries. He writes :—

"KUBOTA Beisen was born in 1852, in the City of Kiōto, the ancient capital, famed for the beauty of its natural scenery and the excellence of its fine arts. He early made up his mind to devote himself to art, in spite of the objection of his father, who wished to let his son succeed him in business. To copy pictures from story-books was all the practice that he could make, until, at the age of sixteen, he began to study drawing under SUZUKI Hyakunen, one of the celebrated masters of the time But, even then, his devotion to art was not approved of by his parents, and he had to pursue his studies during the night time, when they were asleep.

"His father, once discovering the secret pursuits of the uture artist, went so far as to throw his brushes, and other materials for drawing, into a river near by. The career of one of the masters of pictoral " (*sic*) " art in Japan was begun under these unfavourable circumstances, and it was only after his parents perceived the failing health of their son KUBOTA Beisen was allowed by them to follow his inclination freely.

"Kubota Beisen is a self-made artist, and his style of drawing is entirely his own. His works are characterised by vivacity, force, originality of conception and boldness of stroke. His fame spreads year by year. As early as in 1878 he was called upon to take part in establishing the School of Art at Kiōto. In 1886, he was ordered to decorate the ceiling and doors of one of the rooms in the Imperial palace, which was then newly building. He has been twice abroad; in 1889, he visited Paris, where he made a careful study of European masters. Though his style remains strictly Japanese, there can be no doubt that he has greatly profited by his knowledge of Western principles and methods.* Since 1890 Kubota Beisen has been attached to the *Kokumin Shimbun*, one of the most influential and enterprising daily newspapers in Tōkio. As the Artist-Correspondent of that Journal, he attended the World's Columbian Exhibition at Chicago, in 1893, and accompanied the Japanese army at the time of the war with China. His vivid illustration of the scenes of the battlefields was very highly appreciated by the public.

"On Kubota Beisen's return from the front, the Emperor was pleased to summon him to the General Headquarters, and to order him to draw pictures in the Imperial presence. In Japan, such an honour is very rarely accorded to artists, and the fact that Kubota Beisen was favoured in this way testifies to the high position occupied by him."

Thus, *verbatim et literatim*, a Japanese journalist who learnt English *in Japan*, and whose letter bears traces of having been written on the spur of the moment, without the slightest hesitation. I may add that a painting by Kubota Beisen was amongst the presents from Japan to Her Majesty the Queen on the occasion of her "Diamond" Jubilee.

In transliterating proper nouns, and other words, from Chinese, Japanese, and Korean into the Roman character, I have followed the method adopted by the Japan Society in its publications, namely: the vowels to be pronounced as in Italian, the consonants as in English. The Chinese *ü* is identical with the German *ü*, and the French *u;* the Korean *ŏ* is equivalent to the same letter in German, and to the French *eu*. In Japanese

---

* This is not apparent in the illustrations to this book, as he was directed to draw them in *purely Japanese* style. It will be remarked that he is much happier in his representations of thoroughly Far Eastern scenes than in depicting figures in Occidental costumes

the final *n* has a nasal *ng* sound ; in the case of double consonants *both* must be sounded—as in *amma*, a shampooer, pronounced *am-ma*—and the distinction between the *short* vowels, *i, o,* and *u,* and the *long* vowels, *ī, ō, ū,* must be carefully observed, as the meaning often depends upon the slight difference The Japanese *e* is always pronounced as in the English word *set.* I have thought it necessary to accentuate it (*é*) when it forms the terminal sound of a Japanese word, as in *saké,* rice-wine, the tendency of the English tongue being to treat the final *e* as mute

The hyphen is used, in the transliteration of Far Eastern compound words, to indicate the parts represented in the original by separate Chinese ideograms. I have refrained, however, from using the hyphen in the geographical names in frequent use, such as Peking and Tōkio (really . Pé-king, Tō-kio, each of these names being written with *two* Chinese characters), and in Japanese personal names. Although the names of the present capital of Japan, formerly Yedo, and of the ancient Imperial Court City, are now often transliterated : Tōkyō (" Eastern Capital "), and Kyōtō (the latter also : Sai-kyō, " Western Capital "), I have kept to the orthography adopted by the Japanese Post Office : Tōkio and Kiōto.

In the names of Far Eastern persons, the word in BOLD type is the family name, corresponding to our surname. As will be noticed, it comes *before* the personal appellation, answering to our Christian name—the Chinese, the Japanese and the Koreans (and, in Europe, a nation originally of the same stock, the Magyars, whose names are placed in the same order), arguing, with considerable logical force, that an individual owns the family name from birth, the other name, or names, being bestowed later. Our opposite method has so accustomed us to look upon the *last* name as the one indicating the family, that I have thought it advisable to adopt the course pursued in the publications of the Japan Society, and to distinguish the family name, where it appears in conjunction with a " given name," by using bolder type.

I need hardly state that the Japan Society is in no way responsible for the views expressed in this book, which are entirely my own personal opinions.

ARTHUR DIÓSY.

LONDON, *November,* 1898.

CONTENTS.

LIST OF ILLUSTRATIONS.

THE NEW FAR EAST

CHAPTER I.

THE BIRTH OF THE NEW FAR EAST.

ON the seventeenth of September, 1894, from noon to sunset, the thunder of great guns rolled over the waters of Korea Bay, between the Island of Hai-yang and the mouth of the Yalu River, proclaiming to an amazed world the birth of the New Far East.

In that fierce sea-fight, by its consequences the most important naval action since Trafalgar, Japan had completely broken China's maritime power. The hotly-contested battle between the fleets of the two great yellow peoples, using, for the first time in warfare, the latest death-dealing devices of the white men, had resulted in a victory for Japan so decisive that from that moment no doubt as to the ultimate issue of the struggle could arise in the minds of those who understood the modern science of war.

The Japanese fleet, consisting chiefly of unarmoured cruisers (not one of its three ironclads falling within the category of modern armoured battleships), had sunk, or burnt, without very serious damage to any of its own vessels, one of the five armoured ships (two of them powerful battleships) and four of the cruisers of the Chinese squadron. Those of Vice-Admiral Ting's battleships and cruisers that escaped destruction off the mouth of the Yalu were to meet their fate later at Wei-hai-wei; those the Japanese torpedos did not sink proving welcome additions to the fleet of Japan.

B

The victory in Korea Bay had given Japan the command of the sea. Her squadrons could, thenceforward, range freely over the China seas, her admirably-equipped armies could land, almost unopposed, at the points offering the greatest advantages for those combined operations by sea and land that placed the gateways of Northern China —Port Arthur and Wei-hai-wei—in her possession, and, most important fact of all, her communications with the base at home were secure from any danger. The Dragon Flag had disappeared from the Eastern seas, and the perfect security with which Japan could forward reinforcements and supplies to her armies in the field rendered her ultimate triumph merely a matter of time.

Vice-Admiral Itō's victory over his gallant adversary, Vice-Admiral Ting, had secured for Japan a moral success no less important than the great material advantages reaped. It had proved conclusively to the world the fact, hardly realised up to that time by the Japanese themselves, that the sailors of New Japan were fully capable of using to the best advantage, with a cool, calculating skill for which even their own countrymen had not hitherto given them credit, the complicated engines of destruction devised by Western men of science, the effects of which were, until then, still matter for speculation. Moreover, the Japanese had now proved that they could achieve these results alone, unaided by foreign supervision, even against an enemy assisted by many brave and experienced European and American officers.

The importance of the Yalu sea-fight was quickly appreciated throughout the world. It revealed suddenly, as if by magic, the existence of an entirely new, hitherto barely suspected, condition of affairs in Eastern Asia. That huge Chinese Empire, which the Western world, ever ready to mistake bigness for greatness, had credited with boundless stores of latent strength, was shown to be an inert mass of corruption, feebly drifting towards disintegration, whilst Japan stood revealed in the full glare of a new light as a nation no longer in leading-strings, but capable of being, and fully determined to be, a dominant factor in Eastern Asia—a power to be reckoned with, in future, in any political combination affecting the countries which face the rising sun. Pre-conceived notions, deeply implanted in the minds of Western statesmen, were uprooted, popular misconceptions received a rude shock ; and, as the battle-smoke drifted away over the waves of the China Sea, the astonished eyes of Occidentals beheld the Old Far East sinking in the flood, along with the boasted naval power of China, and, in its stead, rising steadily from "the Edge of Asia," the New Far East came into view.

The revelation of the new order of things in Eastern Asia caused surprise, bordering on amazement, not only amongst the peoples of Europe, but even in the councils of their statesmen. Sufficient prescience might have been expected from the Cabinets to render impossible the unseemly state of flurry into which the victory of Japan threw the Governments of all the European states having Asiatic interests, *with the exception of one.* The imperturbable statesmen, unhampered by Parliament or Press, who steadfastly direct the unchanging policy of the colossal Russian Empire, were, as usual, prepared for any emergency. The conflict between China and Japan, with its inevitable result, had come to pass, owing to the sagacity of Japan's military advisers, a few years too soon to fit accurately into Russia's plans. The far-sighted, scientific soldiers who direct Japan's military policy had fully realised that the decisive blow must be struck at China before the completion of the great railway across Siberia made the Tsar the arbiter of Northern and North-Eastern Asia, and gave him a preponderating influence throughout the vast realm of China. The statesmen of St. Petersburg gave their closest attention to the struggle by land and sea, inwardly regretting, no doubt, what was for them its premature occurrence. They noted the facts, registered the birth of the New Far East, and prepared to shape their course accordingly, making the necessary minor alterations in a policy the main outlines whereof had been laid down in the last century and unceasingly kept in view ever since.

Quite otherwise was the situation faced in other European countries, and especially by the British nation, whose interests in the Far East vastly outweigh those of all other Powers. In order to appreciate the great difficulties which stand in the way of a clear comprehension of the problems of the Far East, it is necessary to investigate the causes of the surprise prevailing amongst the nations, and of the unpreparedness of most of the Governments, in presence of a situation that should not have been unexpected. The state of things implied by the term "the New Far East," had, indeed, been gradually, and steadily, coming into existence ever since, in 1841, the echoes of the British guns, battering down the forts in the Canton River, had reached the shores of Japan ; but it was only now that Europe in general, and Britain in particular, became aware of the stupendous results of that first collision between the iron pot of Modern Europe and the earthen jar of the Old Far East. An examination of the causes that retarded Occidental, and especially British, recognition of the true facts relating to the great change in Eastern Asia, will give us some idea of the sources of information regarding the Far East generally available prior to the war between China and Japan, and of the relative value of these sources. It will also, incidentally, reveal the causes of many grievous blunders committed by European statesmen in their Far Eastern policy. It will explain certain aspects of the question not easily understood at first sight, and it should prove full of warning as to the necessity for being well posted in the matter, whilst exercising the greatest caution in the selection of sources of information.

The opening lines of an old German students' song,

by Wollheim, aptly describe the state of Occidental feeling when the New Far East first stood revealed :—

> "*Ganz Europa wundert sich nicht wenig,*
> *Welch' ein neues Reich entstanden ist*"

As the old *Studentenlied* prophetically puts it :—

> "All Europe wonders not a little
> At the new Empire that has arisen."

Why this astonishment on the part of the Western nations? Surely, it was not for want of channels of information, presumably trustworthy and easy of access. The West had long been represented in the Far East by a numerous body of trained diplomatists and consular officers; its warships and its merchant vessels flocked to the Eastern Seas; many of its most able men of science had been engaged for years in teaching the youth of New Japan or in exploring the vast interior of China; hundreds of devoted men and women were spending their lives amongst the people of the yellow races, preaching the religion of Christ; commercial intercourse, vastly facilitated by steam navigation and telegraphic communication, was daily forming new links between the continents, and the narratives of travellers into Far Cathay and into the Land of the Rising Sun filled many bulky volumes. Yet, what was the general opinion of the West at the commencement of the struggle that was so completely to revolutionise Eastern Asia, to upset the balance of power in the East, to affect it seriously in the West, and to produce the actual political situation, fraught with such momentous consequences in the near future?

When, in the summer of 1894, the news of Japan's declaration of war against China was received, the feeling all over the civilised world, except in the British Empire, was one of sympathy with Japan. Hopes were loudly expressed that she would prevail over her huge adversary, but, in almost every country, doubts were entertained as to her ability to do so. In Germany alone did public opinion from the outset predict the victory of the Japanese armies, knowing them to have been organised on a system skilfully adapted to Japanese requirements from the German model. The German Staff Officers, who had acted for years as advisers in the organisation and training for war of the Japanese army, had returned to Berlin well satisfied with the progress made by their apt pupils. As usual, the Germans possessed sound information on all the points of the approaching conflict. They were not only aware of the military efficiency of the Japanese and of their perfect readiness for war, but they also knew from those German officers who were engaged as instructors by various Chinese Viceroys how hopeless was the attempt to overcome the ill-will, the ignorance, and the corruption of the Military Mandarins, who at every turn frustrated their heroic efforts to make an army out of the raw material abounding in China.

The Russian press waited to see which way British opinion would incline, and as soon as its tendency showed, at the very outset of the war, a leaning towards China, what passes for " public opinion " in Russia took the opposite view. This did not, of course, affect the attitude of the Russian Government; that made no pronouncement of its views until the moment of the crisis, when it stepped into the arena, calm, cool, ready with a well-defined policy, and supported by allied Governments helping Russia to carry out that policy, utterly regardless of what had been, up to that very time, the loudly-expressed public opinion of their own nations.

The attitude of the British nation, whose vast interests in Asia made it, of right, the most nearly concerned of the neutral Powers, was at the outset matter for pained surprise to all those who really understood the position of affairs and the magnitude of the issues. As soon as it became known that Japan had resolved upon challenging China to a trial of strength on sea and land—nominally as a solution of their conflict of interests in Korea, really in order to determine, once for all, which was to be the predominant empire in the Mongolian East—a wave of indignation swept over Britain. "What!" cried the average Briton, represented by his principal newspapers and magazines, with few exceptions, "What! Those impertinent little 'Japs' going wantonly to attack our natural ally, China, to disturb the balance of power, to jeopardise trade! They will have to pay dearly for their presumption. They may score a success or two just at first, but when China brings into play her enormous latent strength, when her huge population, her unlimited resources, her boundless staying power, begin to tell, Japan must needs be crushed in the unequal conflict."

Thus spoke John Bull in his wrath against the presumptuous "Japs," as he has, unfortunately, got into the habit of calling the natives of Japan, not only colloquially, but also in print—in "smart," and would - be "smart," books of travel and in the organs of the New Journalism. Let me here make a friendly protest against the use of this slipshod vulgarism, an importation from across the Atlantic that is highly offensive to the Japanese. They do not realise the craving for abbreviations characteristic of the lazy Anglo-Saxon tongue, whose indolence has well-nigh killed the art of conversation in English. They fail to appreciate the fact that the term "Jap" is often employed in perfect good humour, implying a feeling of sympathetic familiarity, for in Japan the rules of a strict etiquette, of hoary antiquity, are punctiliously observed in the daily intercourse of all classes, even between the nearest relations. Familiarity, as we know it, between parent and child, husband and wife, brother and sister, or between friends, appears ill-bred to the Japanese mind. However intimate a Japanese may be with a friend, he never slaps him on the back nor calls him "old man!" Hence the feeling of irritation experienced by them when we, however cheerily, call them by the distasteful abbreviation. A Japanese once said to me: "If your people call us 'Japs,' we shall"—he paused before gravely uttering the dire threat — "we shall have to call you 'Brits'!" It is to be feared that even this menace may not deter Britons from using a term in which they can see no harm. Their own good feeling will, I hope, prompt them to abandon it as soon as they know it to be offensive to the Japanese—the most sensitive, the most punctilious of nations, whose exquisite courtesy surely deserves some return on our part.

At the time of which I am writing, however, John Bull used the word "Japs" in a contemptuous sense, for he was very angry indeed at the Japanese attack on his supposed "ally," China. The history of Britain's relations with the Far East is full of myths (we have all heard of "the legend of Ta-lien-wan"), and the myth of the Chinese alliance is one of the most curious. In spite of all the symptoms of creeping paralysis and of senile decay the Chinese Empire had manifested for years past, a belief had taken root in the British mind that imprisoned in the form of the decrepit Chinese dragon lay an enchanted Princess, awaiting deliverance at the hands of a British Prince Charming. The meekness with which successive British Governments had, of late years, endured the many outrages on their subjects in China, the obstacles —openly or secretly—opposed to legitimate commerce, and the continual slights put upon Britain's representatives, was supposed to be part of an astute policy. The Chinese were to see in this forbearance the clearest proof that Britain was their only true friend, generous and forgiving to a fault; and, in return, when the day of their awakening came, it was from Britain they were to obtain their new civilisation, including, of course, largely increased quantities of Manchester goods, and of the products of Birmingham and of Sheffield, as its necessary adjuncts. Another priceless boon was to be ours in consequence of our friendship with China—her teeming

millions were to supply us, in time of need, with a huge
army, trained and led by British officers, an army whose
mere existence would reduce Russia to inactivity in Asia
and render India safe from any attack.

This delusion was fostered in high places. No less an
authority than Field-Marshal Viscount Wolseley had testified, in print, to the excellent military qualities to be
found in the Chinese, foretelling the dire distress of Europe,
overrun by millions of Celestials, armed, drilled, and dis-
ciplined on Western principles. Other military experts had
foreshadowed the raising of that enormous host, under
British command, which was, some day, to checkmate
Russia. The Chinese navy, too, was supposed to have been
brought to a high state of efficiency under the guidance
of Captain Lang and the British instructors associated
with him. And now those restless Japanese, for no
apparent valid reason, were about to imperil the realisation
of these magnificent schemes by a wanton aggression, sure
to result in their own undoing, but equally certain to
destroy, for a time at least, Britain's great Far Eastern
trade. Japan would, without doubt, pay heavily for her
temerity. Such was the trend of British public opinion,
and it is just possible that, at all events, in the minds of
the British commercial settlers in the Far East, a slightly
malicious pleasure entered into the prospect of Japan's
discomfiture.

When Japan's overweening pride was thoroughly
humbled by defeat—there was no "if" about it in the
minds of these prophets of evil—the new Revised Treaty
just concluded between Britain and Japan, whereby Japan
had, for the first time, been recognised as a nation to be
treated on the footing of an equal, would easily be
rendered inoperative, and British subjects would be spared
the indignity of having to abandon their privileged position, and of becoming amenable to Japanese jurisdiction.
Moreover, Britain would, no doubt, step in at the right
moment to save Japan from utter annihilation by China—

the contingency of such ultimate intervention was seriously discussed in several newspapers—and Japan would, of course, be eternally grateful to her rescuer, and would show her gratitude in tangible form.   There was also, in the minds of some, a vague feeling that it might not be to Britain's disadvantage were Japan's rising naval power, now emancipated from British tutelage, to meet with a serious check, as was sure to be the case when her ships —commanded, officered, and manned entirely by natives— met China's fleet, directed by the numerous European and American officers serving, as advisers and instructors, under the Dragon Flag.

How strangely the leading articles, the long and solemn contributions to the newspapers and magazines, of those summer months of 1894, now read !

Naturally, *all* Britons did not share the views just stated. The members of the Japan Society, for instance, about six hundred in number at that period (the number is now very much larger), thought otherwise, and foretold Japan's victory. The accuracy of their prophecy is easily accounted for. The American humourist's warning explains it : " Never prophesy unless you know." They had access to trustworthy information, and *they knew*.

The great majority of the nation were not in possession of the facts regarding the Far East, and the British Government was but little better informed. At all events, if the Government knew more about the situation than the general public—and it would naturally know more—it shared, to a great extent, the erroneous views of the majority as to the likely outcome of the struggle. People and Government continued in their error until the logic of facts convinced them, very shortly after the outbreak of hostilities, that they were "backing the wrong horse." As soon as they realised this, a sudden and total change took place in public opinion and in the attitude of the Government, the change in the Cabinet's policy *following*, in truly British fashion, the alteration in the views of the nation. In France and in Germany, on the contrary, the apparently sudden change in the policy of the Cabinets that placed those powers in alliance with Russia for the purpose of coercing victorious Japan, caused a complete revulsion in the opinions and sympathies of the people, turning them from ardent " Japanophiles " into stern opponents of the aspirations of Japan. In Russia, what does duty for public opinion is supplied, strictly according to regulation pattern, by a paternal government.

I have stated that the majority of Occidentals, and especially of Britons, were misinformed as to the forces operating to produce the New Far East. It is of great importance that the causes of this lamentable ignorance, and of the prejudiced views that resulted from it, should be ascertained, because it seems but too probable that they are still, to a certain extent, in existence. The danger still confronts us that this ignorance—modified, it is true, but not dispelled—of the real factors at work in the Far East, may lead us, in the future, into errors fraught with consequences even more disastrous to our interests than those which followed on our blunders in the past.

For a quarter of a century the sun of New Japan had been steadily rising over the horizon, whilst China continued to sink deeper and deeper into the slough of corruption, losing, one tributary state after another through the incompetence and venality of her officials, the inefficiency of her diplomatists, and the contemptible weakness of her forces. To most Occidentals the contrast presented by the two nations unfortunately failed to convey its lesson. In their eyes, and especially in those of British people, China still loomed mysterious, huge, possessed of vast latent power and of untold resources. It seemed impossible that such a large proportion of the human race should remain absolutely deaf to the voice of progress, perfectly blind to the advantages of modern civilisation. The slightest sign of movement in a forward direction, although it was chiefly aimed at the possession of modern armaments, was hailed by the West as an indication that China was really on the eve of her awakening. The wish was father to the thought, and much sympathy was wasted on what were erroneously held to be symptoms of China's resurrection.

As for Japan, it was still, in the opinion of the great majority of Europeans and of Americans, what it had always been,—a pleasant land of beautiful scenery, bright with lovely flowers ; a country inhabited by an interesting race with charming, gentle manners, imbued with delicate artistic taste, and showing, in recent times, a marvellous aptitude for assimilating Western civilisation, often in a manner producing quaint, even grotesque, results. In short, Japan was, to the Western world, that strange medley of the beautiful and the comical described in the narratives of scores of travellers in the Land of the Rising Sun.

Until the battle of Ping-yang (in Korean, "Phyòng-yang"), the first in which the army of New Japan proved its complete efficiency, and the naval victory off the mouth of the Yalu, testified to her attainment of her majority as a modern nation, the Western peoples had never taken Japan seriously. The wonderful intelligence and spirit of adaptability of the Japanese had long been recognised, they had been patted on the head and smilingly praised for their successful " imitation," as it was thought to be—it was really *adaptation*— of certain phases of European civilisation, and in some quarters, and those laying claim to be the best informed, they had been solemnly warned of their inherent weakness, of the futility of any attempt on their part to enter into serious rivalry with European Powers. The West, having delivered its praise and its homily, turned its attention to the lacquer and the carvings, the bronzes and the coloured prints, of Old Japan, and, with a pitying smile, left the New to struggle through its political teething, its attempt at Parliamentary Government.

A few months changed all this. The *Risen* Sun of Japan, shining on her victorious armies and fleet, cast its rays into every diplomatic *Chancellerie* in Europe, and produced in all of them, except amongst the ice-cool heads in the Ministry of Foreign Affairs on the banks of the Neva, a remarkable effect. A sort of "Japan sunstroke" affected the entire *personnel*, not excepting even those who steered the various ships of state. Such a fluttering of diplomatic dovecotes, such a general "setting to partners," such an almost universal re-casting of parts in the great historical drama, had, in all probability, not occurred since those sultry days, twenty-five years before, when the Napoleonic Empire succumbed to the sledge-hammer blows of the Germans. The confusion and bewilderment, the upsetting of preconceived notions, was not limited to diplomatic circles; in the journalistic world the flurry was, if possible, still greater. Whilst Ministers of Foreign Affairs hastily called for half-forgotten despatches from the Far East, slumbering in dusty pigeon-holes, and Under-Secretaries of State "got up" the subject feverishly, with the help of large maps, there was much sharpening of editorial pencils and a great exercise of editorial ingenuity in the attempt to explain away those inconvenient leading articles, but a few weeks old, in which Japan's endeavour against her colossal foe had been foredoomed to utter failure. The editors might have spared themselves much trouble had they borne in mind the fact that the public seldom have a retentive memory for the contents of leading articles.

The question naturally arises, how happened it that those presumably in the best position to forecast the course of events were so entirely at fault?

Their want of prescience must appear all the more remarkable when the manifold opportunities are considered that Europe and America had for some years enjoyed, enabling them, one would think, to ascertain the truth about New Japan. Thanks to the Canadian Pacific route, Tōkio had already for some time been within little more than a month's journey from London. Japan was already included in the "Grand Tour," considered indispensable as giving the finishing touch to higher education. Not only had hundreds of "globe-trotters" (now increased to thousands), been piloted safely through Japan, thanks chiefly to the ubiquitous dynasty of Cook and to its active emissaries, but scores of eminent personages as well. Several of these had been lavishly entertained at the expense of the Japanese Government, a fact a few of them seemed to forget in after years; others, not quite so eminent, had landed in Japan provided with the particular kind of useful letter of introduction known as "the Diplomatic Soup-ticket," ensuring an invitation to the hospitable board of their country's representative, and, consequently, opportunities of acquiring much local information from the best sources. Moreover, large numbers of Japanese—officials, students, and merchants—had been living for years in the principal cities of Europe and America. For at least five years before the outbreak of the war, hardly a month, nay, hardly a week, passed without the appearance of some work on Japan, until the reviewers loudly complained that Japan had been "overdone." Within the three years previous to the conflict, the Japan Society had been firmly established in London, and met with unprecedented success, counting its members by hundreds, and holding frequent meetings, at which experts, European and Japanese, addressed crowded audiences on every variety of subject connected with Japan, the papers read being published, in due course, in the Society's *Transactions and Proceedings*.

In spite of all this dissemination of information, the power latent in Japan remained unknown, save to a few far-seeing individuals, earnest students of Far Eastern affairs, and these were not heeded when, at the com-

mencement of hostilities, they proclaimed their belief in
the strength of Japan and in the utter rottenness of
China. The European public, and more particularly the
people of Great Britain, set these *cognoscenti* down as
misguided visionaries, and blindly followed the lead of
those who were considered most likely to know, and
whose prognostications were so completely stultified by
the events of the war.

In America, those who foretold Japan's victory found
a more sympathetic public, the relations between the
United States and Japan having been for years on a
footing of mutual respect and esteem that was too often
in sharp contrast to the relations of Japan with the
European Powers. For there is something in the "go-
ahead" spirit, the vigour and energy of New Japan, that
is particularly fascinating to the Americans, who admire
"a real-live nation" as much as they love "a real live
man." To this must be added the hatred of the average
American towards the Chinese, whom he judges from the
specimens of the race—emigrants of the lowest class from
Southern China—he sees in his own land, even when he
is not inflamed against them by the consideration that
they work for wages he could not live on, though mostly
at occupations he considers beneath his own dignity.
These facts, coupled with the memories of Commodore
Perry's expedition in 1853-4, by which America, knocking
loudly at the gates of Japan, already creaking on their
hinges, had first swung them open to the Western world,
account for the clearer grip of the Far Eastern situation
held by the people of the United States, who were
unanimously in favour of Japan during the conflict.

But if the great mass of British public opinion was
hopelessly at fault in its estimate of the relative strength
and capacity of the Empires of the Far East, unfortunately, those who should have led that opinion to
accurate conclusions and to wise resolves were themselves
lamentably ignorant of the truth, and, in their blindness,

committed errors of judgment, some of which appear
irreparable. Incredible as it may seem, their successors at
the helm did not profit by their experience, and made
but futile efforts to repair the mischief wrought by the
astonishing want of foresight of those who, in 1894, should
have known, almost to certainty, what course events
would take.

There is, however, some slight excuse for the 'statesmen who did not foresee, and for the writers who proved
false prophets; it is to be found in the fact that they
depended for their information on sources apparently trustworthy, but, in reality, the least to be relied upon.

The able, genial and courteous gentlemen who, at that
time, represented the Western Powers at the Courts of
Tōkio and of Peking, are not entirely to be blamed if
they failed to convince their respective Governments, long
beforehand, of the importance of the events that were in
preparation. Some of them gave their Governments an
inkling of what would, sooner or later, inevitably occur;
but Ministers of Foreign Affairs did not, as a rule, in
those days, focus their attention on reports from far-off
lands, dealing with apparently remote contingencies. This
does not, of course, apply to Russia, where a special
Asiatic Department of the Foreign Office had, for years,
been kept accurately informed of every phase of the Far
Eastern Question, and had laid its plans accordingly.
Besides, Russia is so essentially a semi-Asiatic state that
it is incorrect to include her, as is too frequently done,
in the term "the Western Powers." Just at the outbreak
of hostilities, the Foreign Offices of all the Powers, as
well as their Legations at Tōkio, were fully occupied with
the important question of the Revision of the Treaties,
in which Great Britain nobly took the lead, in spite of
the vehement opposition of her subjects dwelling in Japan.
The clamour raised by the majority of the Europeans
trading in the Far East in their angry protests against
Treaty Revision caused the low rumblings, premonitory

NEW JAPAN

Ginza, a Main Street of Tôkio, in 1898

Drawn by KUBOTA Beisen.

of the approaching conflict, to pass unnoticed by the statesmen of the West.

The Legations at Peking were also busy at the time, especially the notoriously undermanned British Legation. The astute pettifoggers who compose the Chinese Board of Foreign Affairs, the far-famed *Tsung-li Yamên*, took good care that the worried and overworked foreign diplomatists and consular officers should have but little leisure to devote to probing the rotten condition of China. They kept them incessantly busy with the thousand and one details of the every-day routine of diplomatic work at Peking, which had, for years past, consisted in an uphill struggle to keep the Celestial authorities to the fulfilment of treaties, duly signed and ratified, but never carried out to the full extent of their provisions—a struggle occasionally diversified by claims for indemnities in reparation of outrages on missionaries, and, in the case of the representatives of the more active Powers of Continental Europe, by strenuous efforts to obtain "concessions" for enterprising financiers, or manufacturers, recommended to them by their Governments. Thus fully occupied with the transaction of their ordinary business, the Western representatives in the Far East had neither time nor sufficient opportunity to study the grave situation that was developing around them. Had they done so, it is questionable whether their reports would have received the attention due to their importance. Bitter experience has taught the Western diplomatist that dissertations on the actual condition and future prospects of the country he is accredited to, when they do not happen to square with the views held by his chief at home, are not conducive to promotion.

As to the non-diplomatic sources from which the West expected sound information about the strength of the belligerents in Eastern Asia, they were to be found amongst the European and American communities in the Far East, as represented by their newspapers. It may be

c

said, in sober truth, that no less trustworthy guides could have been found.

There are, probably, no communities, residing out of their own countries, so absolutely isolated from the people amongst whom they live, so completely out of touch with native feeling and aspirations, as the European, and, to a lesser extent, the American, colonies in the Far East.

Hundreds, nay, thousands, of Occidentals have spent the best part of their lives in China, accumulating, in many cases, great wealth derived from trading with the natives, and have left the Flowery Land almost as ignorant of the real character of its inhabitants, of their language, their beliefs and their feelings, as on the day of their first landing in Far Cathay. Their notions of the national characteristics have been derived from their *Compradores* (it is by this Portuguese word, meaning "Buyers," that the Chinese *employés* are designated, who act as the foreign merchants' intermediaries in their dealings with native firms), from their "Boys," those imperturbable, attentive, noiseless body-servants, from the *Ama*, the faithful maids and the devoted nurses who bring up their children; and the information that has reached them through these channels has been conveyed through the medium of "*Pidjin* - English," the most curious jargon in the world. What they know of the character of the Chinese official class, of the thoughts and feelings of the Mandarins, has been chiefly gathered from the table-talk of Consuls and of Occidental officers in the service of the Imperial Chinese Maritime Customs, or otherwise in Chinese employment. Even such knowledge is, of necessity, superficial, and consists, principally, of information, at second-hand, relating to various quaint instances of Chinese official wrong-headedness, of Mandarin wiles and arrogance. Hardly any attempt is made by the Western commercial settler to fathom the true meaning of these instances. They furnish him with material for entertaining after-dinner stories, especially when he returns

to his native land, they supply topics for leisurely discussion, over cheroots and "pegs," in well-appointed Far-
Eastern clubs ; but they seldom stimulate an earnest
attempt to understand the causes underlying these manifestations of the Chinese spirit. "Queer lot, these
Chinamen !" says the average European merchant in
China, and rests satisfied that research into the reasons
for their queerness would be fruitless, or, at all events, a
task to be left to the "Mish," as he colloquially terms
the Missionary.

The latter has unusual opportunities for studying the
people most closely ; unfortunately those with whom he
is habitually in contact rarely belong to the official class,
which is paramount in China. Moreover, his views are,
very naturally, tinged with a large amount of prejudice
against the ancient beliefs and moral codes it is his aim
to destroy, in order to make room for the particular
creed and the particular ethical system he has brought
from far beyond the seas. These remarks do not, be it
well understood, apply to *all* Missionaries, nor do the
foregoing observations hold good of *all* Occidental merchants in China, for there are, in both classes, notable
exceptions, who really know the workings of the Chinese
mind, and can impartially judge the actions and the
motives of Chinese, high or low, cultured official or lowly
"coolie." What I have said of the isolation of the
foreign communities from the people of the land, of their
lack of deep interest in their surroundings, and of their
ignorance of the forces at work around them, remains
true of the great majority of Western commercial
settlers in China, and, to a considerable extent, of those
in Japan.

Many Occidentals who have spent the greater part or
their lives in Japan have, it is true, acquired considerable
fluency in the colloquial tongue (quite distinct from the
literary language), and an extensive acquaintance with the
manners and customs and the mode of thought of the

classes of natives with which they have come in contact. Unfortunately, these are seldom the classes that direct the country's policy. The few foreigners in the employment of the Japanese Government as Technical Advisers, and their number is now reduced to a mere handful, do, indeed, come into daily contact with Japanese of the governing classes ; but it must be borne in mind that these Europeans and Americans, whose services to Japan are beyond all praise, and merit her eternal gratitude, are never Japanese Government *Officers*, but are strictly confined to their limited sphere as advisers and instructors —invaluable guides to be made use of, not responsible officials to be entrusted with secrets of State.

It was hardly, therefore, from these Advisers that information could be looked for which might have enabled the West to forecast the probable course of events in the Far East, especially as the nature of their duties keeps them busily engaged in their several special departments, the Japanese not being at all anxious to afford them assistance in extending their investigations into the field of Japanese policy.

A few, very few, Occidentals have succeeded, after years of patient research—making use of a natural gift of sympathetic insight—in lifting the veil behind which the Far East thinks and hopes and wishes, but their revelations of the workings of the Oriental mind have been either inaccessible to the general public—who do not, as a rule, read the publications of learned societies, nor works with grimly forbidding scientific titles—or else they have been looked upon as the views of enthusiasts, carried away by their own pet hobbies.

One or two of those who had really penetrated into the innermost recesses of the Japanese heart laboured under the disadvantage of being imbued with the poetic spirit, which, harmonising naturally with the fascinating subject of their study, led them to clothe their thoughts in language that impaired the scientific value of their work. Their readers enjoyed a rare literary treat, and laid their books aside with the reflection that all this was very beautiful and highly inspiring, but that, after all, it was poetry, or hyperbolic prose, as the case might be, and, consequently, untrustworthy as a guide to the truth about the Far East.

As to the members of the European and American mercantile community in Japan, what has been stated about the foreign commercial settlers in China applies, in great measure, to them. The totally erroneous nature of their estimate of the capabilities of the people amongst whom they live is clearly demonstrated by a perusal of articles in their organs in the foreign press of Japan, published in the early days of the war. These articles were full of the gloomiest forebodings as to the upshot of the conflict; they eagerly magnified every rumour of a Japanese reverse, however apocryphal; they minimised every report of a Japanese success, and their animus was but too plainly apparent. If not in so many words, yet in perfectly unmistakable terms, these newspapers, written in English for the general foreign community in Japan, and evidently catering for their tastes, predicted defeat to the Japanese arms, and scarcely concealed their satisfaction at the prospect. This sufficiently characterises their value, at that time, as channels of impartial information on Japanese matters. In order rightly to understand the extraordinary behaviour, in the early stages of the war, of certain newspapers published in Japan, which have some claim to be considered as English periodicals, it may be useful to put a hypothetical case on parallel lines, in order to illustrate a highly creditable phase of the Japanese character.

Let us suppose Britain at war with Russia, and several French newspapers published in London, by Frenchmen, circulating widely not only amongst the French colony, but also amongst all the strangers within our gates, and supplying, through the medium of journalistic " exchanges," a large proportion of the news from England appearing in the Continental press. Let us, further, assume that the French colony in London is a large, active, and wealthy community, enjoying special immunities and privileges, and subject only to the French Code, administered by French judges.

Let us imagine that, at the very outset of the war, when Britain's fate is hanging in the balance — all seemingly depending on the result of one or two pitched battles on land and a great sea-fight — that, at this moment of national anxiety, the French organs in London, known to represent the views of the great majority of the foreign residents, publish article after article predicting disaster to the British armies and fleets, chuckling maliciously at every rumour of a reverse to a British column or a mishap to a British ship, and treating the news of every British victory with sarcastic incredulity until unable to deny it any longer. What would be the attitude of the citizens of London towards those newspapers, their editors and publishers, and towards the French colony in general?

Is it wholly improbable that, law-abiding as Londoners are, the provocation would prove too strong, and that a riotous London mob, or, possibly, an organised *posse* of irate citizens, would summarily and effectually suppress the offending journals?

What was the conduct of the Japanese in circumstances precisely similar to those imagined?

Their vernacular press, naturally, evinced the greatest indignation; the same feeling was displayed in the leading English newspaper of Japan—*The Japan Mail*—known to be in close connection with Japanese official circles, and, at that time, in marked antagonism to the other foreign journals in the country (*The Japan Times*, a newspaper in English, owned, and admirably edited, by Japanese, had not yet appeared), but not a stone was thrown at the office of any of the periodicals that published the provocative articles, and their editors and contributors remained absolutely unmolested.

Since the events of the war stultified the prophets of evil, a marked improvement has taken place in the tone of the formerly anti-Japanese English press in Japan. To read their columns, full of appreciative references to Japanese affairs, one would hardly think it possible that from the same editorial pens gall and wormwood had so recently flowed over everything Japanese. Perhaps the rapid approach of the time when, under the operation of the Revised Treaties, foreigners in Japan will become amenable to the laws of the land, and alien editors will, consequently, be subject to stringent Press Laws, may have had its share in bringing about this gratifying change of front. It is suggestive that certain editors of English newspapers in Japan visited several Japanese gaols (in the winter of 1897–8), with a view, so they announced, of ascertaining what kind of prison life awaited Occidentals who might be convicted by a Japanese judge under the provisions of the new Treaties. On the editorial staff of those very outspoken native Japanese newspapers that most frequently come into collision with the Press Laws, a "Prison Editor" is kept, who, instead of going out to combat—not necessarily fatal, or even dangerous—for his journal, like the "Fighting Editor" of the Parisian press, meekly goes into durance vile whenever the Public Prosecutor secures a conviction against the periodical on which his name figures as "Responsible Editor." The appointment of such a "man of straw" may be under consideration, with a view to future contingencies, in more than one English editorial office in Japan; but it will scarcely be necessary if the Japanese authorities, with their usual tact, recognise, as they probably will, that an unfettered foreign press provides a useful safety-valve for the grumbling of the alien settlers, and cannot seriously affect the mass of the population, unable to read a newspaper in a foreign language.

Enough has been said to indicate the difficulties encountered by Occidentals before the war and, to a certain extent, since, in the attempt to obtain absolutely unbiassed information as to the real condition of Japan, the predominant factor in the New Far East, and the true spirit of its people ; but, in corroboration, a conversation may be recalled that took place in London, a little more than two years *before* the war, over postprandial coffee and cigars, at the table of a prominent member of the Japan Society, then newly constituted.

Half-a-dozen Englishmen, all intimately connected with Japan, some of them having spent the best years of their lives in the country, were discussing its future. One foresaw that Japan *might*, some day, manufacture a very considerable quantity of the coarser kinds of cotton goods. Another admitted that Japan *might*, also in that remote future indicated by "some day," produce physicians, but more probably surgeons, whose skill would astonish the world, and who *might* greatly further the healing arts. He believed that Japanese investigators *might* make important discoveries in biology, or in chemistry, owing to their painstaking, minutely precise, methods of research. A third conceded that the skill of her craftsmen, the frugality of their mode of living, and the consequent low rate of wages, *might* divert certain European industries to Japan.

One alone, the writer of these pages, sketched in glowing colours the future of Japan as he foresaw it ; the sea-power, and its attendant commercial and industrial activity ; the military efficiency, the patriotic spirit, enabling the nation to crush its huge rival, China ; then the influx of capital from abroad, the development of natural resources, the advance in all the sciences ; the great shipbuilding industry and the carrying trade—in short, Japan powerful, prosperous, progressive, and rich—the Great Britain of the East !

At once there arose a chorus of dissentient voices,

raising weighty objections. It was evident, they said, that I was a visionary, carried away by my enthusiasm into dreams of the utterly impossible. To begin with, Japan was a poor country, with a larger population than her natural resources could maintain. Every available acre of arable land was cultivated, the country was unsuited for pasture, the forests had been recklessly destroyed in times past, and many years must elapse before the new Forestry Laws could show beneficial results. Japan could never become a great shipbuilding country, as she did not possess iron in sufficiently large quantities. Her mineral wealth in general had been much exaggerated; the gold mines, for instance, were almost exhausted. Europe and America need never fear the industrial rivalry of Japan, whose working classes would, with new wants creating a higher standard of living, soon combine and strike for higher wages.

Moreover, urged the objectors, intellectual, quick at learning, and wonderfully imitative as the Japanese undoubtedly were, their mental powers were strictly limited. Ask anyone, they said, who had instructed Japanese in large numbers, and you would hear that, with a few brilliant exceptions, they seemed unable to rise above a dead level of respectable mediocrity. (This was said as if it were true of the Japanese only, as if such mental conditions were not to be found amongst the youth of every Occidental country!)

Read, they urged, translations of State Papers written by Japanese statesmen, peruse the despatches of their diplomatists, the arguments in their courts of law, the debates in their Parliament, and one must recognise that there was a factor wanting in the Japanese intellect, an element of logic lacking, so that their reasoning could never be brought into line with that of Occidentals. The sorry spectacle presented by the attempt at Parliamentary Government was a sufficient indication of the unfitness of the Japanese for the most advanced institutions of the

West, at least for many years to come. Party strife might ruin the country before it had time to grow up to its new Constitution.

As to the capacity of the Japanese for war, it was admitted by my opponents that they would certainly fight well, for they were brave to a fault, and skilful in the use of arms; but it was a moot point whether their military organisation, "copied, even to minute details, from the German model, and thus entirely foreign to their national spirit," would stand the strain of a war.

Here the objectors were not only wrong in their surmises, but inaccurate in their "facts." The admirable organisation of the Japanese army was never slavishly copied, *en bloc*, from the German pattern. It was skilfully *adapted* to meet Japanese requirements and to suit Japanese national peculiarities. Accuracy in such matters is hardly to be expected from the average British civilian in the Far East, when we consider how little his compatriots at home know about the organisation of their own naval and military forces.

Then the objectors turned to my forecast of Japan's future power at sea. The Japanese, they said, were plucky, even daring, sailors, and their naval officers were able to perform routine duties quite creditably, and to handle their ships, their guns and torpedos, in ordinary circumstances, but it was more than likely that, without European supervision, they would lose their heads under stress of storm, or in the excitement of action.

"Japan defeat China in the long run!" The thought, it was said, was preposterous! Why, China, in spite of undoubted official corruption, had a splendid navy and a large number of troops well armed and drilled on the Prussian system, with colossal resources in men, material of war, and money; and, above all, she enjoyed the enormous advantage of having in her employ a large number of capable European and American officers to train and lead her troops, to take her ships into action,

and to superintend the defence of the strongholds their
science had made impregnable (Port Arthur and Wei-
hai-wei !).

Thus spoke men who were, apparently, in a position
to know the Far East as well as any foreigners could—
men who delighted in the beauty and charm of Japan,
who were devoted admirers of its glorious art, who really
liked, almost loved, its people, but who suffered from the
disadvantage of having, unconsciously, allowed the great
wall of racial prejudice to bar their way to the right
understanding of the true Japanese spirit, and of the
possibilities of New Japan.

They were men of light and leading, whose names are
household words amongst Occidentals in the Far East,
and in wider circles at home, yet the prejudice of race
had warped their views—had obscured their otherwise
keen sense of observation. Almost every one of their
positive assertions has been either totally contradicted,
or greatly modified, by the stern evidence of subsequent
facts, whilst the predictions of their one opponent are
partly realised, partly on the way to early fulfilment.

If men so intimately connected with Japan erred thus
grossly in their estimate of the powers of her people,
others, who ought to have known China thoroughly, were
quite as much at fault in their forecasts of the issue of
the struggle. Often, during the conflict, did I have to
listen to well-meant, but erroneous, advice from men who
had lived many years in the Flowery Land, urging me
to "look facts in the face." The alleged "facts" that
were brought forward, in order to shake my belief in
Japan's ultimate triumph, were of the kind I have already
indicated in the attempt to depict John Bull's leanings
towards China at the commencement of the war—"vast
resources, immense territory, great force of passive resistance, enormous population supplying excellent fighting
material for the numerous Occidental instructors to train
into first-rate soldiers and sailors, boundless staying-power"

—all these advantages on the side of the huge Empire were paraded, time after time, accompanied by loud condemnation of Japan, as was only natural on the part of the red-hot partisans of China. The British public was supplied with these pro-Chinese arguments, *ad nauseam*, one would have thought, and adopted them, at the first report of hostilities, with wonderful alacrity. The logic of events soon caused a complete revulsion of British feeling, but the arguments that were then abandoned had, at first, been so readily accepted that one cannot but think there must have been something in them particularly agreeable to the average Briton's mind.

This was, indeed, the case. Most of the advantages claimed for China were identical with those the average Briton points out as amongst the principal conditions which render his own Empire invincible. For this reason, if for no others, the people of Britain were predisposed to wish success to the Chinese arms. The utter collapse of the huge nation with the "vast resources, unlimited staying-power," and so forth, could not but provide food for unpleasant reflection to the people, and their name is Legion, who relied—and, it is to be feared, still rely—on those very conditions of magnitude of population, of territory, and of accumulated wealth, to make up for the lack of preparation for war. One of the most important—perhaps the most important—of the many lessons to be derived by the English-speaking nations from the victory of Japan is the practical demonstration of the inability of unprepared, untrained, *unmilitary* millions to cope with forces vastly inferior in numbers, but organised, trained, and equipped to perfection, and *ready* at a given signal to utilise the warlike spirit with which they are imbued.

The complete success of the Japanese showed once more that in modern warfare events move in such rapid sequence that the unready nation, however numerous, however rich, cannot bring its resources into play before the conqueror, following up his first success by a quick repetition of well-directed blows, has got his iron heel on his foe's neck.   The thoughtful on both sides of the Atlantic may have noted the lesson ; the bulk of the English-speaking races did not heed it.   The unreadiness of the land forces of the great North American Republic at the outset of the war with Spain plainly indicated that the lesson of the Far Eastern conflict was not sufficiently appreciated in the United States.   The truth inculcated by that lesson had been realised twenty years previously by the statesmen of Japan.   They set to work in their usual thorough fashion, and they had their reward when their nation of *forty-two millions* broke the power of their huge neighbour, the nation of nearly *four hundred millions*—almost a third of the population of the globe, according to some statisticians —and humbled its pride in the dust.

The British public, misled by untrustworthy guides, was not only wrong in its estimate of the relative strength of the contending Empires of the Far East, it was completely mistaken as to the real causes that had brought on the conflict.   In the early days of the war, perplexed citizens asked one another—on that morning journey office-wards which is the busy Briton's chief opportunity of discussing, newspaper in hand, the grave problems of international politics—"what all the trouble in the Far East was about ? "   The invariable answer came from that usually dogmatic, and often dangerous, guide, the Well-informed Person.   From his coign of vantage in the corner-seat of the railway compartment, the tram-car, or the omnibus the Well-informed One spoke :—"Oh ! It's all about Korea.   Japan wants to rule over Korea, and China, whose tributary Korea is, has a prior claim.   So the Japanese are going to fight the Chinese about it, and are sure to be beaten in the end."

The Well-informed Person was superficially right, but radically wrong.   The dispute about the right to send troops into Korea, in order to put an end to the civil war which was devastating that distressful country—the Japanese

complaining that China had broken the Convention of
Tientsin, made with her in May, 1885, by not giving
sufficiently timely notice of her military action—this was,
indeed, the nominal cause of the war, but it was a mere
pretext for the commencement of hostilities.   History
teaches us that nearly all the great wars which have
shaped the destinies of nations arose, *apparently*, from
petty international squabbles that any two men, possessing
an average amount of common-sense, could have settled
satisfactorily in an hour or two, but that the real causes
of the struggles that have rent humanity lie much deeper.
The world notes, and remembers, the trivial pretext. A
monarch's hasty word, the whim of a royal mistress,
a statesman's blunder, an admiral's high-handed action,
an agitator's lurid speech, the momentary fury of a riotous
mob, a square yard of parti-coloured bunting hoisted on
a negro chief's hut, the exclusive right to sell poisonous
potato-spirit and cheap muskets to the inhabitants of some
square miles of pestilential swamp—these, and a score
of other futile reasons, are the causes the schoolboy is
taught to consider as sufficiently accounting for international slaughter on a grand scale. The real, deep-
rooted causes of the struggles between nations remain
hidden to the eyes of the majority, or, if disclosed, are
soon overlooked.

The great duel between France and Germany, in 1870-71,
had for its ostensible reason a dispute of a purely dynastic
character. The throne of Spain was vacant; a German
princeling had applied for the situation—not an unusual
proceeding on the part of one of a class that has provided
occupants for many vacant thrones—Napoleon III. objected
to the candidature; it was reluctantly withdrawn; sharp
notes were exchanged between Paris and Berlin; the King
of Prussia, at Ems, turned his back on the importunate
French Ambassador, and the two greatest nations of
Continental Europe flew at each other's throats. Yet
we know that the titanic struggle would have taken

place, sooner or later, even had there been no Hohen-.
zollern Prince on the look-out for a crown, and no vacant
throne of ·Spain for him to aspire ·to. The German
Empire had to be built up, and "blood and iron" were to
cement and support its foundations. The Second French
Empire was tottering from internal corruption—a war, if
successful, appeared to be its last chance, and the die
had to be cast.

Even so was it with China and Japan. Had there
been no civil strife raging in Korea, and endangering
the important commercial interests Japanese intelligence,
industry, and energy had created in that country ; had
China not sent the troops asked for by the Korean King
to keep him on his shaky throne ; had such a state as
Korea never existed, the struggle between China and
Japan would still have taken place, sooner or later, and
the result would have been the same.

Many, and widely divergent, are the other reasons that
have been alleged for the conflict in the Far East—reasons
ranging from such a magnificently vast scheme as the
contemplated annexation of the whole Chinese Empire,
sans phrase, by ·Japan, to the paltry, childish desire,
attributed to the Japanese, to see how their new and
expensive toys—their spick-and-span cruisers, their great
Armstrong and Canet guns, their torpedos, their quick-
firing ordnance, and their long-range rifles—would work in
actual warfare ; in fact, an infantile craving to "see the
wheels go round." Between these two extremes lay
various less fantastic, or less puerile, surmises. The one
that was most generally accepted, and still counts numerous
supporters, found the cause of the conflict in the alleged
embarrassments of the Japanese Cabinet, seeking in a
desperate warlike venture abroad relief from an intolerable
political crisis at home, just as Occidental governments
had done, time after time, when confronted by an unruly
legislature, or a populace on the verge of revolution. The
sorry spectacle presented, just before the war, by the

brand - new Japanese Parliament, rife with disorderly
"scenes"—although these never approached in violence
the scandalous riots that have disgraced the · French
Chamber of Deputies, the House of Representatives at
Washington, or that legislative bear-garden, the Austrian
Reichsrath—certainly lent an air of probability to this
allegation.

The truth is that the struggle for which both the
Empires had been preparing, each·in its own characteristic
way, for years, was inevitable. China had, long ago,
determined to seek the first favourable opportunity of
reducing Japan, the "Upstart Nation of Dwarfs," as she
called her, to that condition of vassalage Chinese tradition
had assigned as Japan's proper position. The Chinese
official classes, blind votaries of stagnation, gloated over
the disastrous fate in store for "the Dwarfs" who had,
in their opinion, turned traitors to the Yellow Race, those
"Monkeys," who strutted about in Western dress, and
who had the audacity to prosper in their imitation of the
ways of the hated "Western Foreign Devils." As far
back as 1882, the famous Li Hung-chang had memorialised
the Throne, advising the postponement of the invasion of
Japan, the plan for which the Emperor had "graciously
ordered him to prepare," until the Chinese navy could be
brought to a high condition of strength and efficiency,
"meanwhile," wrote the wily old Viceroy, "carefully con-
cealing our object" until a convenient opportunity of
"bringing about a rupture with Japan." Whilst biding
her time, China carried on, for years, without intermission,
a war of needle-pricks against Japan, slighting, baffling,
snubbing the Power which had set the whole Yellow Race
the shockingly subversive example of reform and progress,
and which had lit a torch the rays of which might some
day shine across the sea and dazzle the hordes of sluggish
Celestials.

The knowledge of China's malevolent intentions, the
accumulated resentment of years—at various times re-

pressed, with the greatest difficulty, by wise statesmen
awaiting the right moment for action—these were, undoubtedly, potent factors in causing Japan to draw the
sword against China. Another strong incentive lay in
the necessity for Japan, a thickly-populated country,
mountainous and narrow, of finding a ready market in
China for the products of her rapidly-rising industries,
that give employment to those whom agriculture or the
fisheries cannot support. The Treaty of Peace of Shimonoseki (1895) opened new ports in China to the trade
of the victorious Japanese, but also, owing to the operation of the Most-Favoured-Nation Clause in the various
treaties with China, to the trade of the world—a fact too
often ignored by Occidentals when considering the results
of the war.

Of the manifold influences which were at work to
impel the Japanese towards the struggle, none was more
important than the necessity, often painfully impressed on
Japanese statesmen, of convincing the fiery spirits amongst
the *Shi-zoku,** and especially those of the great fighting
Clan of feudal times, the men of Satsuma, that the new
civilisation had not emasculated the race. The war conclusively proved to them, and to the thousands whose
hearts still hankered, in secret, after the old order of
things, that Western science and foreign ways had not,
as they feared, diminished the true Spirit of Old Japan.
The old "*Yamato Damashi-i*" burnt as brightly as ever
in Japanese hearts. The Japanese sword was still keen,
the Japanese arm still strong, the Japanese heart still
fearless. All was well with Japan; the new civilisation
had not tarnished her honour. It had added lustre to her
glory. Henceforward the new civilisation would have no
opponents, would cause no regrets.

The wise men who guided the destinies of Japan foresaw what a war, which they knew must be successful,

---

* Formerly called *Samurai;* the Gentry, who formed the governing and
military class in Old Japan.

D

would mean as regards their country's position in the
world. With that quick, sharp perception of what is
insincere that is peculiarly their own, they had seen
through the sham of Occidental international ethics. For
thirty years the West had been urging the Japanese onward in their adaptation of · Occidental civilisation, ever
replying to their claim to be treated as equals: "Not
yet! Go on building railways, erect more schools, establish
new hospitals. Study, work, trade, become learned, peaceful, rich—in one word, a civilised nation—and we will
admit you willingly into our midst on an equal footing."

The Japanese took the advice to heart. They built
railways in every direction, established a national educational system second to none, opened hospitals that aroused
the admiration of foreign medical men; they studied, they
worked, they traded; the nation became well-educated,
peaceful, and wonderfully prosperous. But all this was of
no avail. Until Britain, to her everlasting honour, gave
the others a noble lead by the Treaty Revision which
admitted Japan into the comity of nations as an equal,
the Powers had continued to treat her like an interesting, clever child, not to be taken seriously for a moment.
Japan went to war, she conquered by land and sea, and
—hey, presto!—the scene changed. The great, civilised
Christian Powers stood in a line, bowing courteously to the
victor and exclaiming in unison: "Here is a nation that
has cruisers and guns, and torpedos and long-range rifles,
and that knows how to use them so as to kill a great number
of people with small loss to herself. Truly, this is a great
nation and one worthy of our respect!"

In a few months, "frivolous, superficial, grotesquely
imitative, little Japan" had become "the predominant
factor in the Far East"—"a nation to be reckoned with
in all future international combinations affecting Eastern
Asia"—"a rising naval Power," and "the modern Jack
the Giant-Killer." The statesmen and the warriors of
Japan smiled grimly as they noted the complete success

of their efforts to prove Japan a nation. They had rightly gauged the relative value of the triumphs of peace and of those of war in the estimation of the great Powers of the West. Governments that had, in the past, treated Japan with scant courtesy now seriously considered the question of an alliance with her. Other Great Powers paid her the almost equally great compliment of looking upon her as a dangerous rival, and formed a monstrous, unnatural coalition for the purpose of coercing her. Friends and foes alike had begun to grasp the changed situation. The New Far East was born.

Those British statesmen who, of all people, should have foreseen its birth, and the circumstances surrounding it, were either totally misinformed, or did not sufficiently believe in the little knowledge they had to base a firm, consistent policy on it. In the following pages an attempt will be made to impart a knowledge of the truth about the New Far East in some of its principal aspects, especially those in which the nations of the West, and particularly the English-speaking peoples, are the most interested.

The knowledge I shall strive to impart will, I hope, facilitate the appreciation of the enormously important problems now being worked out in Eastern Asia. I trust the information thus conveyed will throw some light on the conditions under which many millions of our fellow men live, the spirit which moves them, and their relations with Occidental nations.

Thus may the Reader, I sincerely hope, be placed in a position to form a sound judgment in the matter, and to contribute a valuable share to a public opinion based not, as too often, on ignorance, passion, and prejudice, but on knowledge, justice, and common-sense.

CHAPTER II.

PARTING, PIGTAIL, AND TOPKNOT.

THE wayward climate of the British Isles plays strange pranks. To compensate for blizzards in June, it occasionally vouchsafes us a few days of sunshine in November. This was the case on the southern and western coasts of England in the first week of November, 1893. The brilliancy of the sun's rays, glistening on the blue waters of Plymouth Sound, phenomenally calm for the time of the year, seemed to the good people of the Three Towns in the nature of a special compliment to the brave tars from far Japan sojourning in their midst, the officers and crew of His Imperial Japanese Majesty's ship *Yoshino** lying off Plymouth. I have good cause to remember those sunny days, when our English November assumed, for the nonce, the brightness and crispness of the atmosphere of Japan at the same season, for I was, during that glorious week, enjoying the delightful hospitality of my friend Captain Y. Kawara, who had recently relinquished his position as Naval *Attaché* to the Imperial Japanese Legation in London on his appointment to the command of the *Yoshino*, at that time the swiftest cruiser in the world. Every moment spent on board of that splendid warship was full of interest, not only to the naval student, who saw in her the combination, in the highest degree, of all the qualities required in the ideal

---

* Yoshino is the name of a mountainous tract in Yamato, celebrated in Japanese history and poetry, and renowned for its cherry-trees, whose delicate, pale pink blossoms are a vision of beauty in late April.

first-class cruiser of the period, but also to the civilian observer.

The ship was the latest expression of what Elswick could do. No vessel had ever left that celebrated Tyneside "Cradle of Fleets" accompanied by greater hopes of good service, and the splendid work done, in the war with China, by the *Yoshino* fully realised the anticipations of her well-wishers. But *the men* who had navigated her from the Tyne to Plymouth, and who, but a few months later brought glory to her flag—*the men* were the greatest of the many wonders of the *Yoshino.* Of their skill and daring as seamen, of their capacity in the management of complicated machinery and of accurately stoked furnaces, of their excellence as gunners and as torpedo-men, their courage and their coolness under fire, I need not speak; they are writ large in the history of the war. What was most noticeable at Plymouth was their exemplary conduct, afloat and ashore. The courteous, polished gentlemen under whose orders they served had good reason to feel proud of their crew, whose gentle manners and polite speech won golden opinions from all who came in contact with them during their stay in English waters. "A ship's company of gentlemen!" was the expression heard on all sides, and one might add: "a ship's company of artists," for, on the third of November, when the Birthday of His Imperial Majesty was celebrated on board with all the pomp and solemnity for which the deck of a great war-ship offers such fitting surroundings, the *Yoshino* was the scene of an exhibition of works of art, made by her crew, entirely out of the ship's stores (all duly restored, un-injured, to their respective uses on the morrow). All the innate artistic feeling, the wonderful manual dexterity, the exquisitely delicate touch, the eye for colour, the imitative skill, the sly sense of humour, which are such truly Japanese characteristics, had been brought to bear on the objects formed by the deft fingers, hardened though they were by the seaman's or the stoker's rough work,

out of such unpromising materials as rope's-ends and
spun-yarn, coloured paper and bunting, engineers' span-
ners and carpenters' chisels, and even cooking utensils from
the galley, coloured rice, split peas, and strings of onions !

On the day after this celebration of the Emperor's
Birthday, towards six o'clock in the evening, the *Yoshino's*
trim steam-pinnace rose and fell gently on the wavelets
off Barbican Pier, in Plymouth Harbour, waiting for the
"liberty men" who had been given their last run on
shore on the eve of the ship's departure for Portland Bay,
where she was to make trial of her torpedo armament
before sailing for Japan. I had been spending the afternoon on shore with a party of the officers, and, as we
took our seats in the stern-sheets of the pinnace, I
expressed to one of them the hope that all the men
would reach the Pier by the appointed time, six o'clock.
"Our men are very punctual," he said, with a quiet smile,
pointing to the group, increasing every moment, of sturdy
little brown sailors, assembling in silence on the quay.
Presently they began to drop into the boat, one by one,
each man carrying a small bundle, wrapped in a gay
coloured handkerchief; bundles neatly made up as only
Japanese bundles are, and containing the little keepsakes
they had amassed on shore—photographs of local views,
cigars, little odds and ends, chiefly small domestic labour-
saving appliances, hair-oil, brushes, maps of England, in
many cases books, especially illustrated guide-books, and—
in more than one bundle—tokens of affection, a handkerchief or a portrait, testifying to sympathetic relations
established with some bright-eyed daughter of the West
Country.

Six o'clock boomed from the great clock on shore, and
the Chief Petty Officer in charge of the "liberty men"
began to call the roll. Smartly the men answered to
their names, and when the forty, or thereabout, had
signified their presence, the report was quietly made:
"*All* present !" The officer by my side smiled again,

and, as the order was given to "shove off," he gave me
a look of justifiable pride. I congratulated him sincerely,
for visions arose before me of far different scenes witnessed at the embarkation of "liberty men" of other,
and older, navies, visions of hulking, six-foot Finns, furiously
drunk, fighting desperately with whole squads of local
policemen, bringing them by main force to the boat in
which a calm Russian officer stood, with a steely gleam
in his eyes foretelling cruel punishment for the unruly on
the Tsar's ship. My mind recalled other sad scenes of
a similar nature; men of almost every nation under the
sun, clad in the uniform of Uncle Sam's navy, brought,
helplessly intoxicated, back to their "total abstinence"
ships; and French man-of-war's men, hardy fishermen from
the Brittany coasts, making night hideous with drunken
uproar, tumbling into the cutter that was to convey them
to the tender mercies of the *Capitaine d'Armes.* And I
thought of the anxious Master-at-Arms on board many a
Queen's ship, making ready the heavy list of "leave-
breakers," which is still too often the sequel to a "run
on shore."

As the steam-pinnace sped along on her way to the
Yoshino, I noticed a certain measure of subdued excitement amongst the Bluejackets. A general and animated
conversation was being carried on in low tones, and I
could, now and then, hear my name whispered. At last,
the Chief Petty Officer evidently gave his assent to something that was submitted for his approval, and a bright-
eyed young Able Seaman, who had evidently been deputed
to act as spokesman, addressed me, saluting:—" *Sen-sei
San** ! My shipmates and I, being sore perplexed, respect-

---

* *Sen-sei San,* a title of respect used in addressing a scholar, a physician,
or an elderly man Frequently employed by Japanese in speaking to a
foreigner in respectful terms It may be translated: " Mr Teacher," or
" Professor " *San* is the colloquial contraction of *Sama,* the usual title of
respect ; it is affixed to names of persons of both sexes, to nouns indicating
rank or calling. and is used in speaking respectfully even of animals.

fully beg for your august advice. All the people on shore have been very kind to us, and for this we humbly return thanks; but one class of the shore-going folk, although they probably meant well, have greatly offended us. The people in the back-streets near the Dockyard, especially the boys, pointed at us as we passed, calling after us: 'Hallo! John Chinaman!' and '*Chin-chin*, Chinaman!' Now, we respectfully request that you will condescend to advise us in this matter. How are we—that is, those of us who cannot speak English—to make the people of the next port we put into understand that we are not *Tō-jin* * *?"* There was a contemptuous ring in his voice as he spoke the word *Tō-jin*, that meant much to one who knew the state of tension in the Far East, where such great events were soon to take place. The young Blue-jacket saluted again and awaited my answer. It was brief. I said:—"*Bōshi-wo toré !*" ("Take your caps off !").

In a moment every cap was doffed, and a quick look of intelligence lit up the Bluejackets' eyes as they saw one another's polls, those luxuriant heads of coarse, absolutely black, hair, cut to regulation shortness; in some cases clipped so close to the head as to give the appearance of a skull-cap of black velvet, but, in most instances, carefully brushed and combed on either side of a well-defined *parting*, redolent of hair-oil, "Florida water," and other toilet luxuries with which the Bluejacket of every nation anoints his locks preparatory to a "run on shore." The long breath, causing a sound resembling a sigh, the Japanese take when they have just heard something which appeals strongly to their feelings, or to their sense of reason, was distinctly audible, and showed that my suggestion was a happy one.† The Bluejackets evidently

---

* *Tō-jin*, Chinamen Europeans and Americans are sometimes called, by the populace, *Ke-Tō-jin*, "Hairy" (or "Bearded") Chinamen.

† This sound must not be confounded with the long in-drawing of the breath that accompanies the low Japanese bow, as a mark of deepest respect.

considered I had hit upon the readiest means of immediately distinguishing between the Chinese and the other
members of the Turanian races of Eastern Asia. The
Chinaman's shaven pate and the long plait of hair hanging
down his back—or coiled, turban-wise, round his head, for
convenience during physical exertion—are the most noticeable, unvarying badges of his nationality. The most
ignorant loafer in the purlieus of an European sea-port,
the wildest urchin of its back-streets, knows that the
"*pigtail*" is the distinctive mark of the native of the
Flowery Land.

The national mode of wearing the hair is, indeed,
strikingly different amongst the Yellow Peoples of the
New Far East, and is, in some respects, typical of their
mental characteristics. Let us consider the appearance of
three typical yellow men—a Japanese, a Chinese, and a
Korean—all three in the prime of early manhood, between
twenty and thirty years of age, and chosen from the
ruling classes of their respective nations. The Japanese
is one of the *Shi-zoku*, the Military Class, formerly called
Samurai, and also *Bu-ké*, who had a monopoly of the
Bum-bu-no Michi, "the Arts of Literature and of War," in
Old Japan's feudal times, and who govern New Japan.
The abolition, in 1871, of the feudal system, and of the
privileges and immunities enjoyed by the *Samurai*, the
wearers of two swords, brought with it the removal of
the disabilities, amounting almost to a denial of all
political rights, under which the bulk of the Japanese
people, those below the Military Class in rank, suffered.
All Japanese became equal before the law, but the
governing power remained, virtually, in the same hands,
and to this day the vast majority of the administrative
offices, the naval and military commissions, the judicial
and educational appointments, are held by *Shi-zoku*, men
of the old gentry of Japan.

The Chinese whom we will consider as a type of the
teeming millions of the Middle Empire also belongs to a

ruling class ; however his character may differ in particular points from that of his compatriot of the masses, the leading features are the same. He is what Occidentals, clinging to the old Portuguese designation, call a " Mandarin," one of the " Literati," the men who, by dint of infinite mental labour, have passed a severe competitive examination in classical knowledge, perfectly useless, from our Western point of view, and have gained degrees which alone entitle to appointments in the public service. In principle, this system of open competitive examination as the sole road to the Civil Service of China- is purely democratic. With the exception of a few classes of persons—those convicted of crime against the State, actors, executioners and others who inflict punishment ordered by the law, undertakers, waiters, and body-servants —and their descendants unto the fourth generation, every male Chinese subject may present himself for examination as often as he pleases, unless debarred therefrom in consequence of malpractices at a former attempt.* Chinese history, even in quite recent times, is full of instances of men, born of very poor and obscure parents, rising to the highest posts in the State ; but the fact remains that, in China as in every other country, the candidate whose wealth enables him to obtain the assistance of a skilled tutor—the " coach " and the " crammer " have flourished for centuries in Far Cathay—enters the Examination Hall with many chances in his favour. Such as his studies of fossilised classics, and the conditions of his service, have made him, the Mandarin is China. Without his active co-operation, or, at least, his goodwill, nothing can ever be brought to a successful issue in the

---

* Barbers and their sons were, until recent times, included amongst those debarred from competing. This disability was removed by the Emperor on the representations of the Governor of Cheh-Kiang, who was *induced* by the powerful Barbers' Guild to plead their cause. Trades' Unions have flourished in China from time immemorial. This is but one instance of their wide-spreading influence in our days.

Middle Empire. Hence the Mandarin is pre-eminently the Chinese whose character it behoves us to study if we would fathom the great problems of the Far East.

The Korean who is to serve as a type of the ruling class of his country is a *Yang-ban*, as those are colloquially termed who belong to the *Nyang-pan*, the "Two Orders," Civil and Military, forming the aristocracy that holds the people of Korea enthralled. The social fabric of Korea has experienced a succession of rude shocks of late years, since the regeneration of the decrepit "Hermit Kingdom," now raised to the brevet rank of a pinchbeck "Empire," was undertaken by powerful neighbours and interested "friends" from far beyond the seas; but the one thing that has remained practically unshaken is the ascendancy of the *Yang-ban*, the aristocracy of birth, originally an aristocracy of office, who hold every government post of any importance and, with rare exceptions, use their predominant position to "grind the faces" of the wretchedly poor, down-trodden masses.

A glance at the three men before us satisfies us as to their racial affinity. Differing considerably in minor points, their faces yet present a marked family likeness. Although the colour of the face varies remarkably in individuals of the same race in Japan, in China, and in Korea, running through the whole scale of tints, from a clear waxen complexion, often with rosy cheeks in childhood and in adolescence, to a coppery brown—according to the district and, still more, to the amount of exposure to the weather rendered necessary by the individual's occupation—the ground-colour is always of a yellowish hue. So striking is this peculiarity to Western eyes that we, the White (or should it not rather be the Pale Pink?) Folk, dub our fellow men of the Far East "the Yellow Races." In stature and in build Japanese, Chinese, and Koreans differ greatly. The Japanese are, with notable exceptions, a small-sized race, the average height of the *men—*

5.02 feet—being about the same as the average stature of European *females*, and that of the women proportionately less. To define the stature and build of the Chinese nation is rendered very difficult by the fact of the great difference in this respect, and in the matter of colour, and of several mental characteristics as well, between the natives of Northern and of Southern China. The people to the north of Shanghai are, speaking generally, much taller and of heavier build than the natives of the Southern Provinces. Many of the Northern Chinese are fine specimens of well-developed humanity; some of them would be noticeable amongst the tall men of Northern Europe and the long-limbed North Americans and Australians, with the advantage of heavier build than is usually found amongst the two races last mentioned. The stately bearing and dignified, flowing robes of the Northern Chinaman add to the impressiveness of his appearance, and make him look taller than he really is. Strangely enough, both in Japan and in China, the natives of the North are darker than those of the South, a fact that would seem to indicate descent from different branches of the great Mongolian parent stock. The Korean is, often, almost as tall as his cousin of Northern China, and is well set-up, robust and stately in his demeanour.

The Occidental who comes into contact for the first time with a number of natives of the Far East generally experiences some difficulty in identifying individuals, especially amongst the younger men, whose smooth faces —for beards grow late, and then but sparsely, on Mongolian chins—seem to his unaccustomed eye as like one another as buttons on a coat. As soon as more frequent intercourse with Turanian Orientals has familiarised him with their appearance, he begins to note the points of divergence in physical conformation, the differences of features and of facial expression, which are, however, undoubtedly not nearly so numerous as between individuals of the same nationality in Europe or in America, where

the intermingling of races has been taking place for
centuries to a degree unknown, within historic times,
amongst the exclusive peoples of Eastern Asia.   It is a
fact, not, I believe, generally known, that the people of
the Far East, when first coming into communication with
Occidentals, experience the same difficulty in distinguishing one white man from another, except by noticing the
colour of the hair, the trim of the hair worn on the
face, and the colour and cut of the clothes.   A Japanese
once told me that in the early days of his intercourse
with foreigners, he experienced the greatest difficulty in
recognising anyone of his Occidental acquaintances who
had made any change in his manner of trimming his
whiskers, or his beard, or who had donned a suit of
clothes in which he had never seen him before.   He
failed utterly to trace any difference in features between
smooth-faced men and women, and was thankful, he said,
that the difference of costume was so marked between
the sexes, amongst Occidentals, as to save him from many
an awkward mistake.   Fortunately for my Japanese friend,
he has since so largely widened the circle of his Western
acquaintances that, far from being unable to identify them,
he has become quite an expert physiognomist.   One
shudders to think of the mistakes of identity he would
have made had he first encountered Occidentals in these
days of "rational" dress for ladies.   He would, to a
certainty, have failed to distinguish the New Woman from
the inferior creature, Man.

   Differing notably in stature, in build, in some features,
and especially in facial expression, Japanese, Chinese, and
Koreans all have certain strongly-marked physical characteristics common to the three nations, besides the yellowish
colour already mentioned.   Their kinship as members of
the Mongolian branch of the great Turanian race is made
manifest by the shape of their large skulls, with broad,
prominent cheek-bones, so broad and prominent that the
skin is stretched tightly across them, over the almost flat

upper part of the nose, which has hardly any "bridge," even those Japanese noses of strikingly aquiline shape, to be found amongst the upper classes, especially in Kiōto and its neighbourhood, beginning to curve much lower down than on the "Caucasian," the Semitic, or the American-Indian face.*   But the colour of the skin and the shape of the skull are not the only marks of race common to Japanese, Chinese and Koreans.   The dark eyes of all three are set more or less obliquely, making them appear as if they were slightly turned up at the outer corners.   This peculiarity varies considerably in degree.   In some individuals the eye is so narrow as to appear like a mere oblique slit ; in others, especially amongst the Japanese, it is large and full, even prominent, but in all cases there is a peculiarity that at once arrests attention, although it is, at first, difficult to define.   It arises from the shape of the rather "puffy" eyelids, scantily provided with eye-lashes, and having, apparently, no borders, or only a slight indication of a thickening at the rims. The "Caucasian" eye-lid has a "hem," the Mongolian eye-lid has, as a rule, none ; its edge looks as if slit with a knife in the tightly-stretched skin.   This smoothness of the skin about the eyes accounts, in great measure, for the mildness of expression in young Mongolian faces.   It is, of course, less noticeable when age has begun to furrow the countenance with wrinkles, and the relaxation of the facial muscles causes the eyes to appear sunken, and, consequently, more nearly approaching to the position they occupy in the "Caucasian" face.

That a slight obliquity in the set of the eyes is anything but displeasing to our tastes is easily proved by a glance at the winsome face of a pretty Japanese girl, the fine, dignified countenance of a comely Chinese Mandarin (for there are such), or the handsome features of many a Korean *Yang-ban.* We all know the peculiar charm

* I employ the incorrect term "Caucasian" for want of a better one in general use

imparted to the faces of some European and American women by the possession of piquantly bright eyes "*à la Chinoise.*" These slightly slanting eyes are not uncommon in our days; we have only to look at the portraits of contemporary beauties by the great English painters of the eighteenth century to notice that they existed in many instances, and were evidently admired, at a time when the craze for everything Chinese had spread from Paris to London.

I have already alluded to the late appearance and scanty growth of the Mongolian beard. This applies also to the hair on the arms, legs, and chest, far less abundant than in the Western races, and often almost totally absent. There are, of course, exceptions to this, as to every rule. Amongst the Japanese we occasionally find men with heavy beards, giving their owners a most uncanny appearance in our eyes, accustomed to the sight of smooth Mongolian faces, and many Japanese grow, in mature years, very creditable moustaches; still the fact remains that such hirsute tendencies are looked upon by Mongolians themselves as abnormal. The sight of a Japanese with a heavy beard irresistibly reminds his compatriots of the Aino, the hairiest race in the world, the non-Mongolian people whom the smooth-skinned Japanese drove northwards when they settled in what is now Japan.

I have heard Japanese "chaffing" an abnormal fellow-countryman, "bearded like the pard," by suggesting that he would, no doubt, soon require a "*saké*-stick," after the fashion of the hairy Aino. The remnants of the hairy race, reduced to about fifteen thousand, inhabit the great northern Island of Yezo, and are gradually dwindling away, in spite of the humane efforts to regenerate them by which the Japanese Government seeks to atone for centuries of harsh domination and cruel repression. These efforts are mainly directed towards the protection of the Aino from their chief vice—an inordinate indulgence in deep draughts of *saké*, the intoxicating liquor, brewed from rice, which is the national strong drink of Japan. The luxuriant moustache and beard that cover the greater part of the Aino's face are a hindrance to his quaffing the flowing bowl to his heart's content, the bushy fringe of black hair that surrounds and covers his lips absorbing a considerable quantity of the precious liquid, so the ingenious native of Yezo has devised a short stick, smooth, sometimes curved, and usually lacquered red, with which, held horizontally, he lifts the overhanging curtain of hair from his mouth, and thus obtains the full enjoyment of the whole contents of the wine-cup.

One outward racial peculiarity, striking the observer at first sight, is common to the people of the three nations of the Far East—the coarse, almost always straight, generally intensely black hair which grows abundantly on their heads. In the very few cases in which the hair of a Turanian Oriental is, before age has bleached it, of any colour but black, great pains are taken to conceal the abnormity by the use of cosmetics.* Rare cases have been known of Japanese and of Chinese whose hair was of a reddish-brown, dark brickdust hue, a freak of nature they carefully disguised, red hair being associated in the Far Eastern mind with drunkenness. According to a legend of Chinese origin, popular in Japan, mythical beings, called by the Japanese *Shō-jō*, whose heads are covered with manes of scarlet hair, exist at the bottom of the sea, where they hold perpetual drunken carousal round a huge jar of *saké*. The red-haired *Shō-jō*, often represented in Japanese works of art, may be lured from their submarine haunts, so the legends tell, by jars of *saké* temptingly placed on the fore-shore, so that when

* Not all Japanese have absolutely black hair. Owing, probably, to a mixture of races in prehistoric times, many have hair of a very dark brown colour, softer and finer than the typical Turanian jet-black tresses. Women whose hair is of this deep brown hue darken it to the blackness of the raven's wing by the use of pomatum. In China, "Albinos" exist, with snow-white hair and pink eyes, but the cases are extremely rare.

they have partaken of the "free drink" until helplessly intoxicated, they may easily be captured with a view to securing their red hair and their blood as materials for the preparation of a brilliant scarlet dye. Thus does the practical, utilitarian spirit crop up in the most fantastic conceptions of the Far Eastern imagination.

In Japanese everyday life the *Shō-jō* serve a still more practical purpose—they are used as "awful examples" when parents are impressing on the minds of children the dangers that lurk in the *saké*-bottle. So typical of the craving for strong drink have the mythical scarlet-haired beings become, that a species of small fly, which appears to be very fond of *saké*, is called *Shō-jō*. Appert and Kinoshita, in their valuable and compact little handbook for collectors of Japanese art-objects, "*Ancien Japon*," published at Tōkio in 1888, shily hint—the suggestion is more likely to have emanated from the French author, a learned Professor in the Law College of Tōkio, than from his Japanese collaborator, the Chief Librarian of the Imperial University of Japan—that the myth of the red-haired topers may have originated with the first appearance of Anglo-Saxons on the China seas.

In the rare cases where the Far Eastern hair is not straight, but has a tendency to be wavy, as much trouble is taken to smooth the slight curl out of it as is devoted by Occidental ladies to obtaining just the opposite result. Hair with a wave, or a "kink," in it is regarded by the masses, in some parts of Japan, as connected with immoral ideas, a belief which does not prepossess them favourably towards the first curly-headed Occidental whom they meet.

If there be a Philosophy of Clothes, there is in the Far East, assuredly, a Philosophy of Male Hair-dressing. The costumes of the three typical men before us do not differ as widely as their modes of wearing their jet-black hair. Let us consider their apparel, and we will find that it is, in all three cases, becoming to their stature,

E

build, and facial type, and that it imparts a certain
stateliness to their bearing, a marked dignity to their
repose.

PARTING.

The dress of the Japanese civilian *Shi-zoku,* as worn out
of doors in all occupations which do not render the
adoption of European garments necessary or advisable, is
simple in cut, sombre in colour, neat to a degree, and in
excellent taste. The wide-sleeved silken gown, or *Kimono,*
of some quiet, dark colour, in very narrow vertical stripes
divided by black lines, showing at the breast, where the
left side is crossed over the right, the edge of an under-
garment of precisely similar cut, perhaps the edges of
two such under-gowns, the one worn next to the body,
the *ju-ban* (colloquially, *ji-ban*), usually of plain silk,
these edges of under-robes showing in a manner that re-
calls the superimposed waistcoats of a past generation in
Europe. Over the *kimono,* the wide *hakama,* commonly
translated by "trousers," but really a divided skirt, of
sober-coloured silk—probably of some bluish-grey tint with
narrow vertical black stripes, strikingly similar to the
"striped Angola trouserings" of the fashionable London
tailors. The *obi,* or girdle, of thick silk, four yards long
and two and three-quarter inches wide, is smoothly and
evenly wound about the waist. Over all, the *haori,* or
overcoat, of stiff, black corded silk, tied across the breast
by two silken cords slung in a graceful loop, the back of the
coat, just below the collar, and the sleeves bearing the
wearer's crest, his *mon,* beautifully embroidered in white
silk within a circle of about the size of a shilling.*

* The *haori,* "as now worn," reaches to below the knee Its silk lining,
often costly, is of a well-chosen colour, such as russet-brown or "old gold,"
with a beautiful woven pattern During the war against China, and immediately after it, linings decorated with representations of victories and
incidents of conspicuous gallantry were very popular in Tōkio.

The *mon* is sometimes worn in *five* places—those mentioned above and

These garments compose a costume which proclaims in its tasteful simplicity that it is the dress of a gentleman of refinement. And, indeed, the impression is confirmed by closer examination; it is borne out by every outward sign, from the crown of the hatless head to the small, well-shaped feet, still free from the painful deformities caused by the irrational foot-gear of Western civilisation, and encased in the most comfortable, hygienic covering imaginable, the soft, strong-soled socks, generally white, called *tabi*, which have a separate compartment for the big toe. This allows the big toe and the one next to it to have a firm grasp of the thick, padded loop, often covered with ribbed velvet, blue or grey, that is the only attachment to the foot of the straw sandal, the *zōri*, worn in dry weather and for walking on smooth ground, or of the *geta*, the wooden clog commonly used to keep the soles of the feet dry in the very damp climate on roads which are often rivers of slush. These pattens add a few inches to the small stature of the Japanese gentleman, just as the loose cut and wide sleeves, used as pockets, of his robes and- coat add breadth to his rather narrow shoulders. Had constant physical training in the naval or military service developed his muscles, and were he serving with the colours in any capacity, we would see him in uniform, Japanese officers being too proud of "the Emperor's coat" to be seen in public, in their own country, in "mufti"; but the *Shizoku* whose appearance we are considering is a civilian, whose actual military training (for every Japanese is, theoretically, at least, subject to the law of Universal Naval or Military Service) has not been long enough to counteract the evil results of generations of kneeling,

on each breast, but this, as well as the size of the crest, is subject to the fluctuations of fashion, more numerous in New Japan than at any period of the nation's history.

The costume here described is modified according to the season, as will be pointed out later on.

stooping ancestry. The normal Japanese position, equivalent
to our sitting, is a squatting on the heels, practised from
babyhood, which has the one advantage that it keeps
the feet warm in cold weather, but which forces the body
into an unhealthy attitude, and has resulted, in the course
of centuries, in producing the disproportionate figure of
the modern Japanese of the upper classes, the trunk too
long in comparison with the legs, the shoulders too
narrow and the chest too flat. ₁ Amongst the working
classes, whose labour entails much standing and walking,
the body is much more symmetrical, and the muscular
development, particularly in the loins and the lower
limbs, is often remarkable, especially in the case of
"coolies," *jin-riki-sha* drawers, and fishermen.

The Japanese gentleman has been described as hatless.
Would that this were always true, or that, at all events,
when he feels the necessity of a covering for his head,
he would wear one of the various shapes of shady, light,
and cool hats, of straw or of split and plaited bamboo,
used in summer by the labouring classes and wayfarers,
the kind most in favour amongst them being an inverted
bowl, or basin, with a light inner rim fitting round the
head, on the principle of the "sun-helmets" used by
Europeans in the tropics, a perfectly rational, hygienic
hat ! Unfortunately, his natural good taste seems to fail
him, unaccountably, at times, and he sees no incongruity
in wearing, with his graceful, dignified, silken costume,
any sort of Western head-gear, from the jaunty " Hom-
burg hat," of grey or brown felt, with a "complimentary
mourning" band, or of straw, with its cleft crown, or
the hard, low-crowned "bowler," to the straw hat of the
Occidental boating-man, and even—sad to relate !—to that
abomination of modern Britain—the shapeless cloth "stable-
cap," with its peak of the same material, or sometimes,
more hideous still, the double-peaked, ear-flapped, "fore-
and-aft" cap of sad-coloured cloth. If he be not always
hatless, he is certainly without gloves, so that we have an

opportunity of admiring his small, delicately-formed hands, with their slender, supple fingers—whose pliancy is cultivated, in childhood and youth, by the school-boy habit of twisting soft paper into tough string whilst poring over the lesson-book—fingers that can deftly handle the writing-brush or the eating-sticks, and that are kept soft and clean, with carefully-trimmed nails. Small and well-shaped hands and feet are characteristic of the Turanian races, but nowhere are they more noticeable than in Japan, where the roughest labour does not seem to obliterate the good shape of the extremities. It may seem a matter of small importance, but a moment's observation of the hands of the Occidental working-classes, and even, truth to tell, of many above them in the social scale, will give an idea of the æsthetic satisfaction to be derived from intercourse with a nation possessing beautiful hands and, high and lowly, keeping them perfectly clean.

The Japanese, as a nation, keep their bodies clean, not by way of devotional ablutions, nor from the hygienic reasons that drive the Englishman *of the upper and middle classes* into the invigorating, but hardly cleansing, matutinal cold "tub"; rich and poor alike, they boil themselves—for so it seems to the Occidental, unaccustomed to a bath at a temperature of about 110° Fahrenheit—once, *at least*, daily, merely for the personal satisfaction of being clean. All honour to them for it! Would that a similar spirit of cleanliness could be infused into the millions of Occidentals (not to speak of the semi-Oriental millions of Russia, "the Black People," as they are called from their abominable state of dirt) who are still to be counted amongst "the Great Unwashed!" It is not only in the lazy southern countries that we find this repulsive state of bodily filthiness amongst the bulk of the labouring masses. A walk through one of our English, or Scottish, manufacturing towns, or a Welsh village, a peep into an Irish cabin, a stroll down a back-street within a stone's throw of London's most fashionable thoroughfares, will reveal horrors of

personal uncleanlincss that sicken the heart. Go into the
thick of a British crowd on a hot day; the experiment
will not encourage repetition. In a Continental crowd
the effluvia would be still woise. In Japan, you may
mix freely with the throng in the crowded streets in
sultry weather and your olfactory sense will not be
offended. Poorly clad the people may be, in some cases
wearing a minimum of clothing, but patched and mended,
washed out into faded blue, or dusty from travel, as their
scanty clothes may be, they cover bodies that are
scrupulously clean.

The Japanese gentleman's clean, gloveless hand holds
a small and simple fan, of paper and bamboo; not one
of those garish articles the bad taste of Western purchasers
compels Japanese craftsmen to produce for export by hundreds of thousands annually. No Japanese would cool
himself, or shield his head from the sun's rays (a frequent
use of the fan), with one of the fans—too large, too bright,
the design badly printed from a worn-out block—that
Occidental ladies use without hesitation, and even exhibit,
as artistic decorations, on the walls of their rooms. The
Shi-zoku's ōgi, or folding-fan (not to be confounded with
the *uchi-wa*, the stiff, non-folding fan, or hand-screen) is
beautifully made of stout mulberry-tree paper, with a fine,
glossy, parchment-like surface, and of carefully - selected
split bamboo; it is light and very durable, and it closes
with a sharp click testifying to the accuracy with which
its faces are pasted on to the frame. Its decoration is
severely simple; usually a mere suggestion of clouds, in
pale gold and silver powdering on the colourless surface,
or a delicate little sketch in sepia—a scene from classic
literature, or an impression of romantic landscape, frequently
with the addition of a short poem, a *shi*, or ode in the
Chinese style, or an *uta*, purely Japanese, written with
consummate art by the brush of some renowned master
of caligraphy. When the fan is not carried in the hand,
it is stuck into the girdle, or into the bosom of the gown.

According to the season, the Japanese gentleman carries a paper parasol, an umbrella, or a walking-stick. The parasol is of purely Japanese design, now too well known to need description; the umbrella is, sad to tell, more frequently a local imitation of the most ungainly form of the cheap Occidental article than one of the light and graceful umbrellas of oiled paper and split bamboo still used by the masses. These purely Japanese umbrellas, that add a luminous touch of colour to many a village scene, the sun shining through their oiled paper surface as they rest before the houses, spread out to dry after a shower, are being gradually superseded by the imitation of the heavier, clumsy, but more durable, European pattern.* Japan is the gainer thereby, industrially and financially, her umbrellas made in the Western style, of silk, and, more generally, of cotton, being exported by hundreds of thousands to all parts of Asia, especially to China and to India, at such low, though remunerative, prices that they have virtually driven the British and the German article from the market. As for the Japanese paper parasol, it is exported to Europe and to America in very considerable quantities (although India is by far the largest buyer, China coming next). A Japanese writer on the Foreign Trade of his country tersely states that the demand in Western lands arises from the fact that in those parts "the parasol is used to adorn the front of stoves." How the Japanese sense of incongruity is tickled at the sight of the unexpected uses to which Occidentals put certain Far Eastern wares may be imagined if we reflect on the number of parasols, made in Japan, covering

---

* The Japanese umbrella is called *Kasa*, the same word being used to designate the Japanese hat, which resembles the native umbrella in shape The umbrella constructed on the Occidental principle is called *Kōmori-gasa*, "bat-umbrella," from the analogy of its structure to that of the bat's wing, which is said to have also served as the prototype of the *ōgi*, or folding-fan. The Japanese parasol is called *hi-gasa*, "sun-umbrella." It will be remarked that, by the operation of the Japanese etymological rule called *Nigori*, the *k* of *kasa* in the latter part of compound words softens into *g*.

the yawning gaps of British fire-places every summer, the innumerable *saké*-cups and handle-less tea-cups used as smokers' ash-trays, or as pin-trays on ladies' dressing-tables, the *tsuba*, or sword-guards, converted into *Menu*-stands, and the whisks of split bamboo, originally intended to make the powdered tea froth in the solemn and æsthetic rites of the ceremonial tea-drinking—the *cha-no-yu*, still practised by the devotees of art and of antiquities—sent by thousands to America and to British dependencies to be twirled in mixing the ingredients of the seductive "cocktail."

If the Japanese gentleman carry a walking-stick—a fashion increasingly prevalent—it will be of one of the numerous ornamental woods of the country, of rattan, or, more probably, of smooth, glossy bamboo, cunningly carved by one of those modest craftsmen whose work preserves to this day many of the best features of the glorious art of Old Japan. The same sober taste, the same delicate fancy, the feeling for appropriate decoration, the marvellous manual dexterity, are all manifested in every adjunct to the *Shi-zoku's* costume. The short pipe (*kiseru*), all of metal delicately chased and inlaid, or with bamboo stem and metal bowl and mouthpiece, that hangs on his right hip, in a case attached to a tobacco-pouch, is a dainty thing, its diminutive size pleading for moderation, for its bowl, scarcely larger than the cup of an acorn, holds only a tiny pellet of the golden-hued, or light brown, silky tobacco, cut to the fineness of human hair, and even much finer, and affords but three whiffs. The tobacco-pouch (*tabako-iré*), which may be of any suitable material, is a work of art, alike by reason of its simple shape, its fitness for its purpose, and its tasteful decoration.

As to the *netsuké*, the toggle that keeps pipe-case and pouch fastened to the girdle by means of the silken cord that runs through it, has it not conquered the whole artistic world? For from St. Petersburg to Sydney, and from San Francisco to Budapest, art-lovers bend admiringly over drawers and trays full of these exquisite little carvings, these "masterpieces in miniature," a collection of which forms an epitome of Japanese taste and patient skill, of the flora and fauna, the customs and the folk-lore, the poetry and the humour, the history and the superstitions of the Far East. Nowadays, the pipe and the pouch are often left at home; a case, equally artistic in design, filled with Japanese cigarettes, is carried instead, and the number of Japanese of the upper classes who do not, as they say, "drink tobacco" is increasing, some of their physicians having inveighed strongly against smoking.

The bulk of the nation, however, are still confirmed votaries of the small-bowled pipe, which is enjoyed by both sexes, and complaints are rife in the Japanese press that smoking is becoming increasingly prevalent amongst the boys attending the Elementary and the Secondary, or Middle, Schools. It is urged that the introduction of cheap cigarettes of native manufacture is responsible for this, as they render indulgence in the habit easier for the boys, and more difficult for the teachers to detect, avoiding the first cost, intrinsically small, but still considerable for the average Japanese boy to defray, of the pipe, its case, and the tobacco-pouch, such paraphernalia offering, besides, greater chances of detection and confiscation. Smoking, which has become such a thoroughly national habit, was introduced into Japan by the Portuguese about 1600. It was, at first, prohibited, under the most severe penalties, by the Government, but its attractions prevailed over the fear of punishment. People indulged in it by stealth, after the fashion of modern schoolboys, grave adults hiding under the arches of bridges to snatch the fearful delight of a whiff of the foreign herb, whose name, *tabako*, is one of the astonishingly few words of European origin adopted by the Japanese after more than fifty years of active intercourse with the Portuguese and the Spaniards in the sixteenth and seventeenth centuries, a period in which Christianity had spread into every part of the

Empire and numbered a million of converts. The fascination of tobacco ultimately proved too strong for the authorities to counteract; they withdrew the prohibition, cautiously and gradually, permitting, in 1651, smoking out-of-doors, and ultimately removing all restrictions.

In Old Japan, that is prior to the Great Change in 1868, the *Samurai* carried, hanging from his girdle, besides the pipe in its case and the tobacco-pouch, another product of native art-work which has been pronounced by some eminent experts to illustrate the combination of all the best qualities of Japanese art in their most complete expression. This was the *in-rō*, a nest of little compartments, elliptical in shape, fitting one on top of the other with the most accurate nicety, the whole set, with its lid, connected by a cord, or cords, and forming a small, more or less flattened, cylinder, slung from the girdle in the same manner as the pipe-case and pouch, the cord running through a carved *netsuké*, or toggle, which, once passed through the girdle, prevented the cord, and its appendages, from slipping out. The *in-rō* was, generally, of thin wood, lacquered and decorated; and it may be truly said that on no other article for personal use have the Japanese bestowed adornment with more loving care, with more exquisite taste, or with greater technical skill. Hence the value of the *in-rō* in the eyes of the art-collector all over the world. The dainty little compartments of this constant companion of the *Samurai* contained various medicines— an emetic, a styptic, the latter of great utility in days when every gentleman wore two swords, keen as razors, and an angry word was often followed by a sweeping cut —and it is, therefore, generally described as a "medicine-box." It was really, as its name implies, a "seal-box" as much as a medicine-case; for, besides specifics, and, sometimes, some perfume in solid form, it contained the. owner's seal, or *in*, and the vermilion colouring - matter for the impression, the seal in the Far East being really a stamp. Throughout the East, both Far and Near, the seal, or stamp, is of great importance, binding its owner legally, as a signature does in the West. Hence the necessity for carrying it constantly about the person.

The *Shi-zoku* of the present time has his seal always with him, engraved, as in days of yore, with his name in the simple, archaic Chinese ideograms used throughout the Far East for seals, for inscriptions on monuments, and for decorative purposes; and he also carries the vermilion colouring-matter, in a little, flat, round box, made, like the seal, generally of ivory, but they are no longer encased in an *in-rō*. They are kept in an oblong pocket-book, or *kami-iré*, if that may be called a "pocket-book" which is carried by a man who has no pockets, in our sense of the word. The capacious recesses of his wide sleeves and the bosom of his *kimono* serve the *Shi-zoku* as pockets, but the *kami-iré* is, usually, securely placed between the girdle and the gown, in front. It is a strong, serviceable article, of embossed leather, of strong silken brocade, or of one of those wonderful paper imitations of leather, or of crape, in which the Japanese excel. Whatever its material, its decoration is, to a certainty, appropriate and artistic, and its tiny metal clasp, probably, a thing of beauty.

This pocket-book contains not only the seal and colouring-matter—and, as its name, *kami-iré*, "paper-wallet," implies, a flattened roll of soft, smooth, thin, but strong paper—it also holds medicine, not, however, of the kind that was carried in the *in-rō* of days gone by. In the compartments of that dainty little work of art were to be found, besides the ordinary, and usually efficient, emetic and styptic, some of the choicest remedies of that fantastic pharmacopœia, borrowed, with its system of medicine, by Old Japan from Older China. To find parallels to the ingredients composing these marvellous remedies, still deemed infallible by millions of the modern Chinese and Koreans, we must go back to the gruesome recipes of mediæval Europe. Of the four hundred and forty-two

specifics enumerated in the Chinese pharmacopœia, many
are compounded from such extraordinary substances as the
dried skins of red-spotted lizards, human milk, stag's antlers,
the shavings of rhinoceros-horns (an ingredient of the
far-famed " Rhinoceros Pills," warranted to cure "tight-
ness of the chest, gnashing of the teeth, depression of
spirits," and other ailments too numerous to mention),
asbestos, and roasted and ground-up tortoise-shell.   The
ingredients of these loathsome drugs may induce a pitying
smile, but the advertisements which have, for centuries,
proclaimed, in bold Chinese ideograms, their universal
curative powers, bear a strange likeness to the familiar
announcements that inform us, from the pages of our
newspapers, the hoardings in our streets, and the sign-
boards in our fields, that " Cureall's Great Lung Pills are
the Best," and that one may practically defy disease
by using one box of Quack's Ointment.   The universal
medicine carried by the *Shi-zoku* of to-day is not mon-
strously compounded, but, as in the case of the old
specifics, practical omnipotence is claimed for it, and with
some show of reason.   It is, indeed, a sovereign remedy
to alleviate most troubles, consisting, as it does, of a
number of specimens of Japan's coinage, admirably struck
at the Imperial Mint at Ōsaka, and some notes of the
Bank of Japan.

I have said that the *Shi-zoku* has no pockets in his
garments, but, of late years, something very like one has
been introduced into the *obi*, or girdle.   By sewing up a
part of one of its folds, a safe receptacle is formed for the
watch, probably of Japanese manufacture, the chain of
which—of silver, of bronze, or of a combination of links of
the various alloys so skilfully blended and coloured by
the metal-workers of Japan—just shows an inch or two
of its length, with some small, cunningly-wrought pendant
attached, hanging over the upper edge of the *obi*.

Two other articles, the *Shi-zoku's* constant companions,
are essentially things of New Japan—the silken handker-

chief and the match-box. The handkerchief has almost entirely superseded, amongst the upper classes, the squares of soft, but tough, paper that have been in use in Japan, from time immemorial, for the purposes for which we carry a pocket-handkerchief. These squares of paper, folded into a flattened roll, were formerly carried in the wallet, already described, the name of which was, in those days, *hana-gami-bukuro,* " nose-paper-case," and paper is still carried in it, though no longer for use in blowing, or wiping, the nose. The masses still use "nose-paper," *hana-gami,* the squares that have done duty being folded up small and deposited in the sleeve, which is the real Japanese pocket, until, on reaching home, they are thrown into the receptacle for waste paper, akin to the British dust-bin, but with this advantage, that it is cleared of its contents *every morning* by the *Kami-kudzu-hiroi,* the Japanese counterpart of the Parisian *chiffonnier.*

This humble toiler, clad in patched garments of washed-out blue cotton, a kerchief of the same material bound over the lower part of the face, to keep the dust out of mouth and nostrils, does not carry a hook, like the French rag-picker, but a pair of bamboo sticks, used as tongs, with a dexterity the Japanese owe to their manipulation, at every meal, of the slender eating-sticks, the *hashi,* better known to us by their *Pidjin*-English name as " *Chop*-sticks." Throughout the Far East food is invariably conveyed to the mouth by means of these little sticks, similar to the longer of the crochet-hooks of the West in length and thickness, daintily held by the first two fingers and thumb of the right hand. Their constant use has made Chinese, Japanese and Koreans so expert that when they pick up a small article, too minute to be easily grasped with the fingers, or that they, for some reason or other, do not care to touch, they often seize it with a pair of sticks, where we would use tongs or pincers. Thus the Japanese artisan sometimes picks up the most minute parts of his work with two tiny sticks;

in the *hibachi*, the brazier over which the Japanese warm
their hands in winter (it warms little else), and at the
kitchen-stove, the *hi-bashi*, two slender iron rods, held in
the same way as "*Chop*-sticks," replace our poker and
tongs; the *tabako-bon*, or smoking-tray, one of the most
important pieces of furniture in the house, often has its
pair of metal *hashi*, wherewith the smoker may stir up the
embers in the little fire-bowl containing the glowing charcoal
to light his, or her, pipe.

The *Kami-kudzu-hiroi*, who picks up scraps of paper
and unconsidered trifles with his pair of bamboo sticks,
and throws them into his basket, is, generally, one of the
Eta, that class of mysterious origin, who were considered
as outcasts in Old Japan, earning their livelihood by
exercising callings that would have defiled any other
Japanese—occupations involving contact with dead bodies,
human or animal, or otherwise looked upon as degrading.
They were, and to a great extent still are, the undertakers, the grave-diggers, the executioners, the slaughterers,
and the tanners of Japan, the cobblers who mend the
geta, or clogs, and the gatherers of waste-paper and of
refuse of all kinds. They had no political rights; they,
and the miserable class of beggars, still lower in the social
scale, the *Hi-nin* (literally: "Not-human"), hardly had
a right to their lives, even if they succeeded, by their
industry, in amassing comparative wealth, as the *Eta*
sometimes, the *Hi-nin* rarely, did. The Great Change
brought many reforms in its train, but none more humane,
none that did greater honour to its promoters, than the
Edict issued by the Council of State on the twelfth of
October, 1871, eloquent in its simplicity, and commencing
with the words :—

"The designations of *Eta* and *Hi-nin* are abolished.
Those who bore them are to be added to the general
registers of the population, and their social position and
methods of gaining a livelihood are to be identical with
those of the rest of the people."

The Great Change was worth making, if only for this noble edict that made men of nearly a million of outcasts and placed them on a footing of legal equality with their compatriots. *Eta* and *Hi-nin* are mere names of the past. Those that bore them are now free men, and their sons have passed, and are passing, through the great national mill, that takes *Shi-zoku* and farmer, noble and craftsman, scholar and trader, the sons of the proud retainer of an ex-feudal lord and of the lowly *Eta*, of the wealthy *saké*-brewer and of the poor *Hi-nin*, and transforms them all into soldiers of the Imperial Army, marching under the same glorious flag.

So the *Eta* rubbish-picker may hold up his head now, save in the presence of dog-owners, amongst whom he has an evil reputation, for they accuse him of being a foul poisoner of many a sleek canine pet, done to death for the sake of his skin. The old *Eta* leather-dressing craft is still familiar to the "paper-picker"; dog-skins are used for making drum-heads and command a fair price. When no dogs are about to tempt him, the *Kami-kudzu-hiroi* is a harmless and useful toiler, clearing out the waste-paper-box with punctuality, and thus relieving the house of its daily accumulation of used paper-handkerchiefs. The idea of paper being used for cleansing the nose may, at first, be repugnant to us, but a walk through any street in Europe, or in America, much frequented by the proletariat, will soon lead us to wish that the masses of the West would imitate, in this respect, the people of Japan. Paper handkerchiefs are cheap, they save washing-bills, and, above all, they are far better than no hand-kerchiefs at all.

It is a far cry from the days of the prehistoric hero Prince Yamato-také to those of New Japan, yet through the intervening centuries his countrymen carried, and some of them, in the remote mountainous districts of the interior,

* The exact numbers, at the time of the issue of the Edict, were: 287,111 *Eta* and 695,689 *Hi-nin.*

still carry, the *hi-uchi-bukuro*, the "fire-strike-bag," containing the fire-kindling implements, similar to the one that we are told, in the legends of the dim past, was slung to the scabbard of the great warrior's magic sword. But flint and steel have had their day, and the modern Japanese carries a match-box filled with the products of one of the most flourishing industries of his country. He may use an elegant little match-box of chased and inlaid metal, or, if economically inclined, may carry a simple wooden box of Japanese "safety matches," not to be distinguished, at first sight, from the well-known boxes of Swedish "*tändstickor*," or of our own London-made matches. The manufacture of wooden matches of various kinds has progressed by leaps and bounds in New Japan, until they have become an important article of export, Tōkio, Ōsaka, and the Prefecture of Hiogo sending millions of gross of boxes to all parts of Asia, and even to Australia, in the course of the year, nearly the whole quantity being "safety matches." China and British India are the chief customers, and in those countries Japanese matches have virtually swept their Swedish and British rivals out of the market. This success has been achieved chiefly by the remarkable cheapness of the Japanese product, for the quality occasionally leaves much to be desired.

Japanese Consuls in China and in India have frequently reported loud complaints as to the inferior quality of a great part of the matches exported, complaints apparently justified, the irritation of some of the disappointed purchasers going so far as to cause them to class Japanese matches with those of the French Government Monopoly —the direst insult that can be offered to a match. The Japanese manufacturers of *tsuké-gi*, or "kindling-sticks," have taken the consular remonstrances to heart—for, unlike our British manufacturers, they study Consular Reports, and heed their warnings and suggestions—and a very notable improvement has taken place in the quality. Much as the boxes resemble those from Sweden, certain announcements on the labels are peculiarly Japanese; for instance, in the case of some of the brands most in favour in the country itself, the statement that "these matches are pure, and fit to be used for lighting the lamps of the gods." Thus are the scruples of those appeased who would otherwise hesitate to kindle the lamps before the household shrines, Buddhist or *Shin-tō*, sometimes both—the majority of the Japanese following the observances of one of the numerous Buddhist sects as well as those of the truly national ancestor-worship, the ancient *Shin-tō*—with a new-fangled invention, introduced from abroad, possibly involving the use of phosphorus, made from the bones of animals, and hence impure. For quite other, and more material, reasons do the Swedes assure the world, on millions of yellow labels, that their "safety matches" are made *"utan svafvel och fosfor."* *

I have described thus in detail the dress of the gentleman of New Japan, and its accessories, not only because of the opportunities of throwing side-lights on some manners and customs affected by the introduction of Western ideas—and on some of the new industries created, and the old ones affected, by the new conditions—but with the object of dispelling the prevalent misconception that the national costume is in danger of early extinction. There was a period in which it seemed doomed to give way before the dress of the West, as represented by hideous imported "slop-clothes" and native imitations thereof. From 1873 to 1887, especially in the last three years of that period, the adoption of European dress progressed rapidly amongst the upper classes. It had been made compulsory for officials, when on duty, in 1873, and had steadily gained ground amongst students, bankers, merchants, and others coming, more or less directly, under foreign influence. Officials and students returning from

---

* "Without sulphur or phosphorus."

F

abroad aroused the envy of their countrymen by appearing, on all occasions, in the latest productions of the fashionable tailors, hatters, and bootmakers, the best hosiers and glovers, of Bond Street and of the Rue Vivienne, of Unter den Linden and of Broadway, and their stay-at-home compatriots strove to imitate their apparel. The imitation was not always carried out with thoroughness, but, too often, piecemeal, separate articles of European attire being donned in conjunction with native clothing, with ludicrous results. A "chimney-pot" hat, its nap only too frequently brushed the wrong way, reared its ugly cylinder on the head of the wearer of silken *kimono* and *hakama*, a very short "covert-coat" of approved Melton Mowbray pattern was worn over an otherwise purely Japanese costume; even when all the garments were of European cloth and cut, some accessory was often sadly incongruous. Gentlemen might be seen attending an official garden-party in full evening dress, its effect marred by the trousers being tucked into high boots, and by an European bath-towel worn round the neck as a comforter. There is a dark and dreadful legend, I have been unable to trace to its source, of an elderly nobleman who attended an official reception on New Year's Day, the greatest festival of the Japanese year, in the evening dress of Europe, complete in every respect but one—and that an important one—the outfitter from whom he had ordered the ceremonial costume having, unfortunately, omitted to send home the trousers!

These eccentricities gradually diminished, native tailors began to produce excellent imitations of Western garments, the gentlemen of Tōkio were becoming accustomed to their proper use in accordance with European fashions, and the garb of Old Japan seemed doomed to disappear, after its relegation to the working class in the towns, and to the peasantry. The wave of German influence that swept over Japan from 1885 to 1887 carried the innovation to a still more dangerous point. The beautiful costume of the women of Japan, so absolutely becoming to its wearers

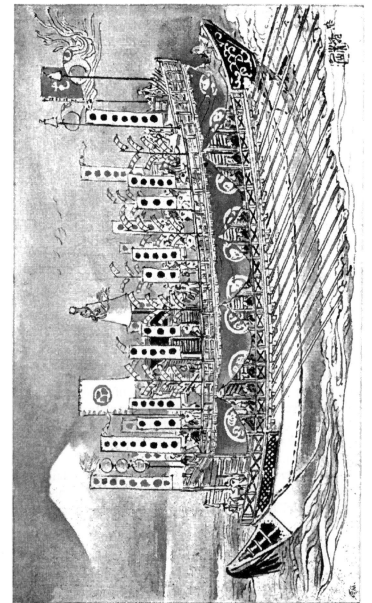

OLD JAPAN.

A Warship of the *Shōgun*, of the Period *Ka-yei* (A.D. 1848—1854).

Drawn by KUBOTA Beisen.

that one can hardly imagine them clad in any other way, was threatened, and, sad to relate, the ladies of the Court began to order dresses from — Paris.? No — the pen almost refuses to chronicle the appalling fact—*from Berlin !* In the nick of time, the reaction against a slavish imitation of Occidental customs unsuited to the country came to the rescue. In 1887, the national spirit, roused to indignation against the Western Powers by the failure of Count Inouyé's attempts to induce them to negotiate a Revision of the Treaties on the basis ardently desired by the Japanese, caused a sudden return to many of the old habits and customs that had fallen into abeyance. This reaction in minor matters, whilst not impeding the nation's progress in the adaptation of the essentials of modern civilisation, has since made itself increasingly conspicuous.

Its outward and visible sign is the resumption of their picturesque and becoming national dress by both men and women of the upper class. The uniforms, naval, military, and civil, are all of European pattern, so is the court dress of the nobility—more is the pity, for no statelier costume could be devised than that worn by the nobles of Old Japan—and, at most of the great court functions, the Empress, one of those gracious little *grandes dames* who look charming and dignified in any costume, appears in European dress, together with her ladies, some of whom, now accustomed to it, wear it with truly Parisian grace. Officials are clad in European costume during office-hours, but it may safely be said that, with the above exceptions, the Japanese of the upper class now wear their national dress at all times when the nature of their work, or recreation, does not render Western clothing much more suitable. As I have already stated, European headgear is frequently worn with Japanese clothes, usually with incongruous results. Occidental socks and boots, or shoes, overcoats, "Inverness" capes, waterproof coats and capes, comforters—all these are occasionally worn with native dress, and European woollen underclothing is coming into very general use,

owing to medical advice. Flannel shirts and woven "sing-
lets" are being more extensively used, year by year, even
by the working class, and cotton undershirts and drawers
are made in large quantities.

The dress I have attempted to describe is subject to
some modifications, according to the season. In winter, a
short under-jacket, or *dōgi*, of silk, or cotton, is worn; and,
in very cold weather, two wadded gowns, the nether one
called *shita-gi*, the upper one *uwa-gi*, keep the body
warm. In summer, the *kimono* is of thin material and of
lighter colour, the *ji-ban*, or shirt, shows a white edge at
the opening of the gown, and, indoors, or within the
precincts of his own garden, the *Shi-zoku* throws off the
summer *haori,* or overcoat, which is not necessarily black,
like the one worn in winter, the silken *hakama*, and even
the summer *kimono* of *ro*, or gauze-silk, and slips on a
yukata, a cotton bathgown, generally white with some
minute blue pattern—the perfection of a garment for
lounging in hot weather. The loin-cloth (*shita-obi*) of
bleached muslin is always worn next to the skin. Its
plebeian counterpart, the *fundoshi*, is the foundation of
the costume of every male Japanese who earns his rice,
or only his millet, by the sweat of his brow. When
working away from houses, and secure from observation
by the lynx-eyed policeman, he reduces his dress to its
simplest form—the loin-cloth, wondering greatly why the
powers that be should, at the instigation of the foreigners,
object to his thus baring his brawny limbs, his muscular
back and chest, just as untold generations of his ancestors
did unmolested.

The *Shi-zoku* has wisely reverted to his national dress,
but in one point of his appearance he belongs irrevocably
to New Japan. He wears his abundant hair cut in the
Occidental fashion, not always, sooth to say, in the most
approved Bond Street or Piccadilly style—too frequently,
an inverted pudding-basin would appear to have guided
the scissors in their course—but, uneven or sleek, his hair,

with its *parting* in the European fashion, is a sign of the
Great Change. One of the first acts of those who shaped
the policy of New Japan was to order all officials to
abandon the national mode of wearing the hair, the time-
honoured custom of shaving the centre of the front and
top of the head, leaving the backhair long, to be gathered
into a little cue, the *magé*, which was bound with a
string, wound round and round its base, and then bent
forward, lying well over the shaven poll, the ends neatly
cut and trimmed. A glance at any Japanese picture representing a scene of any period between the heroic
times and 1870, containing bare-headed male figures, will
show the *magé*, and will demonstrate its appropriateness
to the Japanese countenance, to which it imparts a look
of great intelligence, due to the high, shaven forehead, and
of peculiar dignity. But the *magé* was a troublesome
fashion, involving the frequent ministrations of the barber,
and the loss of much time that was required, under the
new dispensation, for the study of many difficult subjects,
such as chemistry, and political economy, and Parliamentary government. So the *magé* had to be cut off,
the smooth space on the head was suffered to grow a
crop of stubble, and the fraternity of barbers groaned inwardly, and learnt to cut the hair after the fashion of
the West.

The national way of dressing men's hair did not,
however, disappear suddenly, nor entirely. In the first
Japanese Parliament, which assembled in 1890, at least
three prominent members of the Lower House still wore
the little cue lying forward over the smooth, shaven space
on their conservative heads.

Now the *magé* has become rare. Some old men still
wear it, especially in country districts. With professional
wrestlers it is still *de rigueur ;* a large *magé*, about the
size and shape of a door-knocker, is as distinctive of the
fat *sumōtori*, the huge wrestler who towers over his compatriots like an obese giant, as is the *coleta*, the tiny

pigtail, curling slightly upward, the mark of the lissom bull-fighter, the graceful *torero*, of Seville. It gave the *Samurai's* feelings a sad wrench when he parted with his *magé*, the unmistakable badge of his nationality. His dress might be confounded, by the casual observer, with that of other Far Eastern nations, but the *magé* was purely Japanese. Hence, the man who abandoned it thereby proclaimed his adhesion to the new order of things, his receptiveness of the new ideas derived from intercourse with the foreigners whose mode of dressing the hair he was, from that time, to follow.

PIGTAIL.

How many years must elapse before the Chinese Mandarin makes up his mind to follow the example of the Japanese, and cut off the most striking outward sign of *his* nationality, the *pigtail?* On that day a new era will dawn for China, for the long plait, often lengthened by artificial additions, that hangs down between the shoulders of the Chinese—the black silk cord and tassel at the end (the cord is a *white* one if the wearer be in mourning), beating against his robe as he walks—is the symbol of the Chinese spirit as it now exists, a mass of contradictions, opposed in almost every particular to the ideals of our civilisation. Strangely enough, the wearing of this pigtail, inseparably associated in our minds with the natives of the Celestial Empire, is not a custom of Chinese origin. It is one of those puzzles that baffle the student of Chinese characteristics at every turn, that the most conservative race in the world, a people to whom anything " ancient " and " national " is equivalent to " sacred," should have adopted a fashion imposed upon them by a foreign conqueror, and made what was at first a badge of national humiliation into a respected mark of manhood.

When the Manchus put an end to the enfeebled Ming

dynasty and made themselves masters of China, establishing at Peking, in 1644, the alien Ts'ing dynasty that still
occupies the throne, they ordered the conquered people
to discontinue their mode of dressing their hair, which
they wore in various styles, according to occupation and
locality, but, as a rule, long and bunched up into a topknot. The Manchus compelled the vanquished to adopt
their own custom of shaving the head with the exception
of the back part, the long hair of which they plaited into
a tail. At first the humiliating innovation naturally met
with resolute opposition, many Chinese preferring death to
what they considered dishonour. The conquering Manchu,
finding that his attempts to impose on his new subjects,
at the point of the sword, his own national *coiffure* resulted
in innumerable risings and riots, adopted a different policy.
Acting on his knowledge of the national character, he
played on those feelings that are, even to this day, paramount in the Chinese: filial piety, and the desire to
"save one's face"—that is, to preserve the outward semblance of dignified respectability. The Manchu Emperor
decreed that none but loyal, law-abiding subjects might
shave the front part of the head and wear their back-hair
in a plait; all males convicted of crime were to forfeit
this distinction. Thenceforward conviction was followed,
and still is followed, by the loss of the cue and by an
unshaven pate, which thus became the mark of a criminal.
Moreover, sons mourning for a parent were ordered to
show their grief by leaving the head unshaven, and the
cue unbraided and unkempt, for the space of one hundred
days from the date of their bereavement, a custom still
rigidly observed.

The Emperor's astute move was crowned with complete
success. What had been a token of subjection to alien
rule became, and has remained for more than two
centuries and a half, a cherished badge of nationality,
apparently the most Chinese thing in China. In this
curious fact, and in the method by which it was brought

about, there is matter for deep reflection on the part of those who have in view the regeneration of China. If the millions of the Flowery Land could be induced to make an alien custom so entirely their own that its abolition at the present day would mean a revolution, surely there is some hope that native ideas may be brought under other, and more beneficial, foreign influences, provided the pressure from without be exercised in the same wise manner, by making use of the feelings that sway the Chinese mind. Thus, and thus only, can any *real* changes ever be effected in China, by constantly bearing in mind that *the Chinese are Chinese*—a fact lost sight of by the majority of those who propound schemes for the regeneration of the Celestial Empire.

Completely as the Chinese have, apparently, adopted the Manchu fashion of wearing the hair—and this and the official "button" on the hat are about the only things they have acquired from their conquerors, who, on the contrary, soon assimilated the civilisation of the more cultured vanquished—the opposition to the custom has, even yet, not entirely died out. Nothing ever dies out entirely in China. In the constantly recurring rebellions that shake the crazy structure of the decaying Empire, now at one point, then at another, the insurgents almost invariably allow the hair to grow all over their heads, as a sign of revolt against the Manchu usurpers. Whatever the real cause of the rising, unless it be an outbreak of some of China's many millions of Mohammedan subjects, it is almost invariably represented as a national "legitimist" revolution against Manchu rule, with the ultimate object of placing some mysterious descendant of the Ming dynasty on the throne that is his by right. Hence, the insurgents allow their hair to grow, as did their ancestors in the days of the Ming Emperors, and the Peking official proclamations thunder against the "Hairy Rebels." In many of the Secret Revolutionary Societies with which China is honeycombed, the conspirators conceal their pigtails under their caps when attending the meetings of their Lodge, the badge of subjection hanging peacefully down their backs when they go about their daily business as apparently contented, law-abiding loyalists. The turbans worn by the peasants of the southern provinces of Kwang-tung (called by Occidentals "Canton") and Fu-kien are said, by some, to have been originally devised to conceal the alien pig-tail, coiled round the head; but I consider it more likely that this head-dress (now worn by some of the regiments drilled on the European plan) owes its origin to a desire to shield the skull from the fierce rays of the sun. It seems to me to be akin to the blue cotton kerchief the Japanese craftsman, or labourer, winds so deftly round his head, tying it in front with extraordinary rapidity, when about to engage on any work likely to induce perspiration. It is also very similar to the small turban worn by the Malays and the Javanese, and to the still narrower head-cloth of the neighbours of the Southern Chinese—the Burmese and the Siamese.

In spite of the occasional evidences of patriotic opposition to the Manchu custom, the *pigtail* remains the distinctive outward and visible sign of Chinese manhood. At the age of thirteen or fourteen, the Chinese boy's head is shaved clean of the little tufts that have been allowed to grow on it, in separate circles, and have, in many cases, been braided separately * — but the tuft at the back is retained and plaited into what is to become the symbol of his having reached man's estate. The pigtail is treated with respect, almost with reverence, and carefully tended. It is the palladium of a man's honour and self-respect. To pull it is a dire insult; to cut it off a heinous crime, visited with severe punishment by law. So sensitive are the Chinese as to its safety, that from time to time —especially when there is trouble brewing, and more particularly when anti-foreign feeling is at fever-point—a

* In infancy, and sometimes even in boyhood, the head is shaved perfectly smooth all over.

"pigtail-panic" drives the populace almost crazy with
fear, gruesome stories flying about of respectable citizens
suddenly and mysteriously shorn of their silky plait.
Epidemics of the pigtail-cutting crime undoubtedly do
occur, as mysteriously and with as little apparent object
as the occasional prevalence in England of the maniacal
instinct which prompts the stabbing of women, in the
lower part of the back, with penknives or long pins.*
As usual, the anti-foreign agitators, invariably Graduates,
or "Literati," give the populace broad hints as to the
probability that the Missionaries are at the bottom of the
trouble. In Mediæval Europe, if there was a failure of
the crops, or an outbreak of the plague, the mob generally
burnt a Jew; in Modern China, in case of any calamity,
or any untoward event, such as the loss of a pigtail, they
stone a Missionary. There is little doubt that tail-cutting
outrages have sometimes been perpetrated by deep schemers,
with the prospect of raising a popular ferment, in view of
consequent anti-foreign outrages and the embarrassments
into which they lead the Government at Peking.

At times the panic reaches such a pitch that the
Mandarins feel constrained to allay it. This they do, in
their own peculiar way, by advising the lieges to remain
at home as much as possible, avoiding "strangers"
(whereby foreigners are, of course, meant, as the Occidental is generally considered to have the Evil Eye, his
glance having been known to burn off a well-grown pigtail at the roots—a fact, at least, a Chinese fact!). They
sometimes follow up this warning by prescribing pro-
phylactics against the loss of the cherished cue. According
to divers Metropolitan Police Notifications, issued in Peking
since 1875, cords of certain bright colours, braided with the
hair, medicines to be taken internally, and cabalistic characters written on bits of paper—some to be swallowed,
some to be burnt, others to be plaited into the cue, and
one to be affixed over the door of the house—are variously

* Almost any Superintendent of Police can supply instances.

prescribed as "Infallible Protectors against the Loss of Cues by cutting." To officials who issue such "Notifications" certain well-meaning Occidental enthusiasts attribute the desire and the capacity to regenerate the people who read and believe them !

The dress of the Chinese of the ruling class is too well known to need detailed description. With moral courage deserving our admiration and respect, he wears his national costume in our midst, braving the curiosity of gaping crowds and the ribald jests of the street-boys. At state ceremonials we see the Chinese Mandarin, representing his Emperor, or attached to an Imperial Legation, in all the glory of his full dress of office—the gorgeous satin robe of exquisite colour, marvellously embroidered, the black satin boots with thick, white-edged soles, and the official hat, with turned-up brim of dark satin, a tassel of thin, red silken cords falling over the crown, topped by the button indicating the wearer's official rank.*   If the

---

* Official rank is indicated by the cognisance embroidered, within a square, on the breast and the back of the robe, by the clasp of the silken girdle, worn in Court Dress, and by the button on the top of the official hat, as follows :—

RANK.	COGNISANCE.	CLASP.	BUTTON.
First (the highest)	*Civil :* Crane *Military .* Unicorn.	Jade set in rubies. Jade.	In Court Dress: Ruby, or other transparent red stone : at other times. Red Coral
Second.	*Civil ·* Golden Pheasant *Military .* Lion.	Gold set in rubies Chased gold	Red coral, chased.
Third	*Civil :* Peacock. *Military :* Leopard.	Chased gold	Sapphire, or other transparent blue stone.
Fourth,	*Civil* The *Yen*, a white migratory bird. *Military ·* Tiger.	Chased gold.	Blue opaque stone.
Fifth	*Civil ·* Silver Pheasant. *Military ·* Bear	Plain gold with a silver knob Plain gold.	Crystal, or glass
Sixth.	*Civil* Egret. *Military ·* Tiger-cat.	Tortoise-shell.	White opaque shell, or glass.

function take place in winter, we admire the costly furs lining the satin jacket worn over the robe. The whole costume, varied in summer by the wearing of robes of lighter silk and by a hat of straw, or of finely-plaited bamboo, of low conical shape, with the usual tassel and button, is remarkably stately, but it conveys, to Occidental minds, an impression of effeminacy. Seated, its wearer looks as grave and as imposing as a British Lord Justice on the bench. In motion, the effect he produces is pompous rather than dignified. The robes that fall about his legs, the long, wide sleeves that droop over his hands, impede his movements; his whole dress is unsuited to a man of action.

Throughout the length and breadth of the Chinese Empire, the official costume is the same, and its changes

Seventh.	*Civil* · Mandarin Duck.	Silver	Plain gold.
	Military · Tiger-cat.	Tortoise-shell	
Eighth.	*Civil* Quail.	Transparent horn	Chased gold.
Ninth	*Civil :* Jay	Black horn.	· Chased gold

It will be noticed that the *Civil* Cognisances represent harmless birds, whilst the *Military* ones depict wild beasts of various degrees of fierceness, according to Chinese "*un*natural history" Military Mandarins of the same nominal rank as civil officials never enjoy a tithe of the respect shown by the people to the latter In China the pen is, indeed, mightier than the sword.

By a "Chased" Button, of coral or of gold, a button is meant that has the "lucky" character *Sio* engraved on it in two places.

In the Chinese Navy the rank of the combatant officers was, at the time of the war with Japan, distinguished by the number and size of the dragons worked in gold on the sleeves

The hat-button denoting official rank is of Manchu origin. It was instituted, in an elementary form, by Ts'ung-tê, who ruled over the Manchus just before Shun-chih, who reigned in Manchuria from 1636 to 1644, when he became Emperor of China, the first of the Ts'ing dynasty, which still occupies the throne Shun-chih introduced the button into China.

The peacock's feather, with no "eye," or with one, two, or even three "eyes," projecting backwards from a small tube, sometimes of jade, inserted horizontally at the base of the gold setting of the hat-button, is not a badge of rank, but a mark of Imperial favour bestowed for meritorious service.

from summer to winter uniform, and *vice versâ*, take
place, irrespective of latitude and local climate, on the
same day, fixed by law and duly notified beforehand by
Imperial edict, much as in the German Army, whose
warriors must perforce shiver in white duck trousers if
the official "first day of spring" happens to be a bitterly
cold one. Residents in the principal capitals of the West
are by this time familiar, not only with Chinese official
costume, but with the dress of the private gentleman, as
worn by the members of the Legations when taking their
walks abroad. The flowing silken robe of rich colour,
with sleeves so long that they must be turned up to allow
free play to the hands, the deep cuff thus formed often
serving, in the West, as a pocket for the handkerchief (an
article unknown in China, and, unfortunately, without even
the paper substitute in use in Japan); the dark satin
jacket, closed by small loops of braid and little, round,
golden buttons; the trousers of light-coloured silk, tied
at the ankle; the satin shoes with their thick soles, carefully whitened at the edges; the small round, stiff cap of
black satin, with the "little round button at top"—these
are worn by the "Literati" and by the middle classes in
China to this day. In winter, the jacket is fur-lined, the
other garments are thickly wadded, and more warmth is
obtained by wearing additional clothes, till a gentleman of
Peking on a frosty day is covered with as many layers
as an onion. Summer or winter, the girdle worn under
the short, loose jacket (which sometimes has no sleeves)
and over the upper robe, has depending from it a silken
pouch with tassels of fringe, a case containing the ivory
eating-sticks,* and often another holding the tobacco-pipe,

---

* The Chinese carry their "*chop*-sticks" about their persons. The
Japanese keep theirs at home. In Japanese restaurants it is usual to
hand each customer a slender slip of wood, slit *almost* in two, lengthways,
the customer completing the separation into a pair of eating-sticks that
cannot possibly have been used before. This compares favourably with
the imperfectly cleaned forks of some Occidental eating-houses.

with a metal bowl, small, but approaching more nearly to ours than the tiny Japanese acorn-cup. As the Chinese enjoys his smoke, he is probably oblivious of the fact that the habit reached his ancestors, in the seventeenth century, in the North, through Korea, from Japan, where the herb had just been introduced by the Portuguese ; in the South, from Luzon, one of the Philippine Islands. The Chinese seem to have been in a receptive mood in the latter half of the seventeenth century ; their now cherished pigtails, their official hat-buttons, and their inveterate smoking habit, all alien customs, now so firmly established, date from that period.

A fan, similar to that used by the Japanese, is carried, in summer, by every Chinese. Here, again, the average Chinese is unaware that what he fondly looks upon as a truly national invention, dating from remote antiquity, was originally an importation from Japan. The *folding-*fan is, undoubtedly, a Japanese invention, due, according to tradition, to the widow of the young warrior Atsumori, slain by the hero KUMAGAI Naozane in the defeat of the Taira Clan by their rivals, the Minamoto, at Ichi-no-tani, near the present Kōbé, in A.D. 1184. The young widow became a Buddhist nun, and during her retirement at the temple of Miei-dō, at Kiōto, she cured the abbot of a fever, so it is said, by fanning him with a paper folding-fan, made by her in imitation of the structure of a bat's wing. This was the prototype of all the *ōgi* of Japan, and, therefore, of their imitations, the folding-fans of all other countries. The legend states that the fanning was accompanied by incantations, and leaves us to decide whether the abbot had to thank them or the fan for his recovery. The part played by the bat, as the model for the invention, was commemorated in the name of a fan used at the court of Old Japan, the *kōmori*, or "bat." To this day the priests of the Miei-dō temple are famous as fan-makers, and, throughout Japan, shops where fans are sold often hang out the name of that temple as a sign.

From Japan, through Korea, the half-way house of her ancient intercourse with China, the folding-fan reached the court of the third Ming Emperor, Ch'eng-tsu, who reigned from A.D. 1403 to 1425. It rapidly became popular, probably being looked upon as a Korean invention; as a Japanese one it would hardly have found favour, the Japanese having twice raided parts of the Chinese coasts during Ch'eng-tsu's reign. It was a slight return for Japan to make, this giving of a new, and more practical, kind of fan (the stiff, non-folding sort, evolved from the palmetto leaf, had come into China, probably from India, traditionally in 1106 B.C.; historically, they were in use under the T'ang Emperor Kau-tsung, A.D. 650 to 684,) in exchange for an entire system of civilisation, received from China, partly through Korea. In 1894 and 1895, Japan again gave China something, by the way of Korea, as usual—not a fan, this time, but a thrashing, destined to mark a turning-point in China's history.

Considered as a whole, the dress of the Chinese of the upper and middle classes is comfortable and fairly hygienic. It hangs loosely, tight clothing being considered by the Chinese to be highly indecent, as revealing the outlines of the figure. For those who can afford furs, or even sheepskin linings, or wadded garments, it secures a fair amount of comfort in winter, although its looseness and its wide-mouthed sleeves admit more cold air than is pleasant in the bitter weather experienced in the North, sometimes for months together. The Chinese dress is deficient in one respect that appears of great importance to Occidentals. In common with all the inhabitants of the Far East, the Chinese has no pockets. Whatever he wants to carry about his person must be attached to the girdle, thrust into the bosom of the robe (an unsafe receptacle), stuck into the fold of the turned-up sleeve, or the turned-up brim of a hat, put into his cap, or, if its size and shape will allow, tied up in the *tai-zu*, the tape, an inch wide, confining the trousers at the ankle.

(The fact of our wearing trousers open at the ankle, in winter, is a source of continual wonder to the Chinese, who inquire if we do not feel very cold about the legs in such irrational garments.) Some Chinese of the working class even use the ear as a purse, to contain, it is true, only a very small sum—just one "cash."

Of the body covered by the Mandarin's gorgeous raiment I would rather not write. The subject is an unsavoury one. If the Japanese be, and they undoubtedly are, the cleanest people on earth, the Chinese are certainly amongst the dirtiest. Their towns are indescribably filthy, the narrow streets reeking with offal and the stench of every abomination; their villages are nearly as bad; their houses—even their palaces—contain foul corners, grimy with ancient dust, and the state of their bodies makes a Chinese crowd malodorous to a degree. Public bath-houses exist for the benefit of the working class, who occasionally use them, but those high up in the social scale consider a perfunctory "lick" with a damp rag, and a wipe with a cotton towel about the size of a pocket-handkerchief, as complete matutinal ablutions. In the North, washing during the winter months, when frost and snow prevail, is looked upon as positively injurious to health, and the complexion of the natives becomes darker by degrees as the time for their "spring cleaning" approaches. Chinese in Occidental employ, however, soon learn to conform to our ideas of personal cleanliness, and the Mandarins and students who reside for some time in the West take to the use of soap and water quite readily, and become as clean as those with whom they come in contact. But in China filth and bad smells reign supreme, although there are, as in every country, some people who are distinguished by exceptional personal cleanliness and neatness. By the great majority clothes are worn long after they have become saturated with perspiration. The dear old lady who exclaimed, in her innocence: "Dear me! What dirty people the Chinese must be! Every time I see a telegram from Shanghai in the newspapers, it always ends with 'Grey shirtings unchanged'!"* was not very far from the truth, after all. In China prominent public men pay little, or no attention to personal cleanliness, even when they belong to the Navy, the service identified, in our minds, with a scrupulous cleanliness which is almost a religion. A friend of mine who had the honour once of sitting at an official banquet next to the late gallant Admiral Ting, one of the few great men modern China has produced, noticed, through the wide openings of the sleeves of the Admiral's gorgeous robe, that he was wearing an under-garment, once white, that was literally "grey" from being "unchanged!"

It is strange that this general lack of personal cleanliness should prevail amongst people who take such extreme care of their hair, as shown by the attention bestowed on the pigtail, on the moustache and chin-tuft, that appear late in life — when the Chinese of the class of the "Literati," or Graduates, invests in enormous spectacles (sometimes of plain glass) with frames of horn, to give himself a learned appearance—and who periodically cause their ears to be cleaned by the peripatetic barber. The chiropodist, too, exists in China, and is held to be of higher social status than the barber, because he sits whilst at work. Chinese hands and feet are generally small and shapely, but the hands of the people of position of both sexes are disfigured by the ridiculous length to which the nails are sometimes allowed to grow, as evidence that their owner does no manual labour, a length requiring the use of silver cases, worn like thimbles, to protect the tapering claws. The custom is, fortunately, much less prevalent within the last few years. It has its modified counterpart in Europe, where the officers of some armies, and some of those who ape them, notably in Germany

---

* A frequent item in Market Reports relating to Manchester goods.

G

and in Austria, allow the nail of the little finger of the left hand to grow to an inordinate length. This form of idiotcy is also, fortunately, tending to disappear.

TOPKNOT.

Now that I have described the appearance of the Japanese *Shi-zoku* and of the Chinese Mandarin, the Korean *Yang-ban* claims attention. Tall, stately, imperturbable, his handsome features, nearer to the "Caucasian" type than those of Japanese or Chinese, are calm and serene, as befits one of the aristocracy of *Cho-sön* (in the *written* language, *Tsio-sien;* in Chinese, *Chao-sien;* in Japanese, *Chō-sen,* or *Kōraï*) the Land of "the Morning Calm."* Truly an appellation bestowed by the Koreans on their country (officially since A.D. 1392) on the *lucus a non lucendo* principle, for it has been to the Far East, through many centuries, a battle-field for warring Empires, as the Low Countries were so often for the contending Powers of Europe ; when not occupied by foreign armies, or raided by Tartar hordes, its inhabitants seem to have kept up an interest in life by frequent rebellions. Within the last two centuries an era seemed to have dawned for Korea in which she might slumber peacefully and deserve her poetic name. The period of calm was not to last ; heroic French Missionaries, soon to be massacred, and daring American and German filibusters invaded her shores. The filibusters seemed to have acquired all the calmness appropriate to a country with such an appellation, for their simple purpose was to steal the coffins, reputed to be of pure gold, of several of Korea's kings. Their expedition, led by two men of genius—only such could have conceived the plan — named Oppert and Jenkins, sailed from Shanghai in 1867, reached the Korean coast, and, like another, more recent, Raid that Failed, found

---

* Literally, " Morning Freshness " or " Serenity "

that they had reckoned without their host, and returned crestfallen.*   After them came more Americans—those golden coffins were very exciting to the imagination of an enterprising race—and more massacres (when white people are killed, in any circumstances, by people of any other race, it is always a "Massacre"; when it is the white men who do the killing, it is called "Severe Losses of the Enemy," or "Great Slaughter of the Rebels"). The Koreans were, probably, encouraged in their prompt suppression of the second American attempt by the futile nature of the expedition, in 1866, of the French Admiral Roze, who, failing to receive satisfaction for the murders of French Missionaries, bombarded the forts of Kang-hoa, with meagre results, and sailed away.   In 1871, Admiral Rogers, of the United States Navy, appeared on the scene with an expedition specially organised for the purpose of avenging the burning of the American schooner *General Sherman*, with her crew, and of compelling the Hermit Kingdom to abandon its system of rigid exclusion of all Occidentals, for whatever purpose they might come.

The unlucky forts at Kang-hoa were again bombarded, the Korean troops, chiefly professional tiger-hunters from the interior, fought with unexpected determination against the American landing-party ; there were relatively heavy losses on both sides, and Rogers departed, as Roze had done, leaving Korea as much a sealed-up land as before, with her fear of foreign invasion intensified.   At last, in 1876, the Japanese, in consequence of an attack on some of the crew of their warship *Unyo-kan*, who had landed, again at Kang-hoa, sent an envoy, General Kuroda, backed up by a powerful display of naval force, and succeeded in

* A Roman Catholic priest was associated with the German Oppert and the American Jenkins in this enterprise, which was of the nature of a "syndicate venture"   The priest gave out that the object was to seize the Royal coffins, and to hold them until the King consented to open up the country and to tolerate Christianity   His partners were more direct; they drew up, it is said, a statement of the "Estimated Profits from Sale of Golden Coffins"

breaking the spell without recourse to arms. A treaty was concluded, and the Western Powers were not slow to follow suit. Here, as nineteen years later in China, Japan's action was the means of providing new markets for the trade of the West. In Korea, Japan opened the door wide, that had been only ajar to her traders, at the one port of Fusan, since 1443, and the Occident, represented by its Consuls and its merchants, its Missionaries and its adventurers, walked in. In China, Japan forced the half-open door back on its rusty hinges, opening a way, not only to fresh markets immediately available to the whole civilised world, but straight to the key of the position, admitting influences that are hurrying on the solution of the greatest problem now confronting our civilisation—the future of the Chinese nation. We have heard much talk of "the Open Door," but little of Japan's share in opening it wide and in keeping it open.

Since the treaty forced upon her by Japan in 1876, the history of Korea has been a succession of "alarums and excursions," of plots and counterplots, political assassinations and executions, rebellions, riots, and invasions. This truly "distressful country" has been the scene of the intrigues of the diplomatists of half-a-dozen states; she has been the prey of adventurers from all parts of the world. In turn she has been swayed by German "advisers," American military instructors and missionaries, Russian diplomatists and Japanese envoys. In 1897, Korea was the rope in a spirited "tug-of-war" between Russia and Japan, diversified, for a time, by a game of "pull devil, pull baker" between Russia and Britain, the whole tussle ending with "graceful concessions" by Russia to Britain and, for ulterior motives, to Japan.

Throughout all this turmoil, one class in Korea remained almost unshaken in its adherence to the line of conduct it had pursued for centuries. The *Yang-ban*, most indolent of Far Eastern aristocrats, is not to be hurried on the thorny path of reform by hectoring Japanese or per-

suasive Russian, by energetic German or smart American.
The younger generation are changing, slowly but surely;
the men still in the prime of early manhood were born
too long before the foreign influences came into play to
be more than superficially affected by them. The *Yang-
ban* whose appearance I shall attempt to describe clings
to his native costume, the quaintest in the quaint Far
East, in spite of the attempt made in 1897, under Japanese
influence, to induce him to don European, or semi-
European garb.

As he swings towards us with a ridiculously pompous
gait, the personification of supercilious swagger, his dress
presents a striking contrast to his deportment, his usual
walking costume (quite distinct from his official uniform)
being of almost Puritan simplicity—an impression heightened
by his hat, the distinctive headgear of his race, recalling,
by its shape, the hats of the days of Cromwell. The official
dress he wears at Court, or on any ceremonial occasion, is
copied, even to details, from that worn at the Court of
China in the heyday of the Ming dynasty, the last line of
purely Chinese Emperors, who reigned from A.D. 1368 to
1628. It consists of a long, loose robe of dark blue, or brown,
silk, replacing, at Japanese instigation, the gaudy robes, of
the same cut, of scarlet, bright blue, or yellow, worn by
all officials but the highest, and those of richly-figured
Chinese silks worn by the high dignitaries, prior to 1895.
On the breast and back are affixed shields, or panels, of
embroidery, displaying a cognisance indicating the wearer's
official rank—a tiger, for instance, or a crane, or stork (*not,*
as inadvertently stated by Lord Curzon of Kedleston, on
page 157 of the new and revised edition (1896) of his
Problems of the Far East, "a stalk"!). Over the robe a
clumsy-looking belt is worn, adorned with large plates, or
bosses, of gold, silver, jade, ivory, or horn, according to
the rank, the ungraceful effect of the belt, which is worn
high up, almost under the arms, being increased by the
fact that it is made to remain at a distance of several

inches from the body, in front, as if to allow room for the expansion of the official after an unusually hearty meal. Thick-soled boots, of cloth or satin, are worn, and a head-dress such as we see depicted on Chinese works of art representing scenes of the Ming period. This curious cap, a sort of mitre, is made of finely-cut and interlaced strips of bamboo, lacquered black, or of horsehair-cloth, and is subject to many modifications of shape, according to the wearer's rank. Its form varies from that of a small pile of flowerpots of graduated sizes, standing one within the other, to that of an ornate lamp-shade turned upside down; but the best way to obtain an idea of its more usual forms is to study the various moulds used by our pastry-cooks in the production of their sponge-cakes and their jellies. In the case of Ministers, and high officials generally, the cap is often adorned with four singular projections: two paddles, shaped like the petals of a flower, standing out on either side, above and behind the ears, and two shorter ones standing straight up. There is a tradition that these projections, all of the same material as the cap, and dating, likewise, from the Chinese Ming period, are meant to represent ears and wings. The extra pair of long ears are not intended as a reflection on the statesman's wisdom—the patience of the ass and his firmness of will, branded by us as obstinacy, rather commend the animal to the Oriental mind—they are meant to indicate his capacity to receive information and complaints, and to overhear plots. The wings are typical of the zeal and alacrity with which he flies to do his sovereign's bidding.

Our *Yang-ban* has laid aside, for the nonce, the antique dress just described, and appears in a costume hardly less ancient, that is more Occidental, in its general outline, than the clothing of the modern Chinese and Japanese. The key-note of his appearance is its spotless whiteness. His baggy breeches, drawn in at the ankle; his long smock, slit at the sides, very short-waisted (a black silken girdle-cord passing round it close under the

arms), the full skirts sticking out ridiculously from near
the armpits; his padded socks—all are white and all are
of cotton, which necessitates their being thickly wadded
in the severe winter. His hat and his clumsy cloth
shoes are the only things he wears, except his girdle,
that are not absolutely white.* The shoes are of black,
or dark blue, cloth; the hat, or *kat*, is black, of finely-split
and interlaced bamboo, or—in the case of cheap hats, such
as a *Yang-ban* would probably scorn to wear—of woven
horsehair. In either case the hat looks, to an Occidental,
as if it were made of black wire-gauze, such as is used
for meat-safes and fencing-masks. In shape the hat is
between a Puritan's and a Welshwoman's in those parts
of the Principality where the national head-dress still
survives. The crown is a truncated cone, the brim wide
and perfectly straight. What strikes one at first sight is
the insufficient diameter of the crown, much too small to
fit the head, so that the hat has to be lashed on by
broad black cords tied under the chin, often supplemented
by a string of amber and cornelian beads. This gives the
wearer the undignified appearance of a man who has
come away from a party with the only opera-hat left in
the cloak-room, someone else's and several sizes too small.
It has not even the sole redeeming feature of the absurd,
useless, unwarlike, "pat-of-butter" cap tied on (for it is
only the chin-strap which keeps it on) to the side of the
head of British soldiers of various arms; that has, at
least, a rakish appearance.

There is a reason for the peculiar construction of the
Yang-ban's hat, a work of art that may cost him over
twenty dollars; the ordinary man's hat, of the same
pattern but of cheap material, may cost three or four.
The *kat* is not intended as a covering for the head any
more than Mr. Thomas Atkins's "cap on three 'airs."
It is built up as a receptacle; an outer protection, for

---

* It is said that in former times the colour worn was pale blue.

another head-dress, a cap, the *mang - kun*, somewhat like the British joiner's paper working-cap, but without a crown, and made of the same material as the hat worn over it. The cap has a band which fits tightly round the head, and it contains, within its wire-gauze-like walls, the Korean's most cherished possession — his *topknot*. To him it is a constant reminder that, when the Manchu seized the throne of China, and held Korea in the hollow of his hand, he inflicted the *pigtail*, his, the conqueror's, own national custom, only on the Chinese, whereas the Koreans were allowed to retain the mode of wearing their hair they had adopted from the people of ancient China. The Korean boy wears his hair long, parted in the middle, and plaited into a long, thick cue, frequently augmented with artificial hair. This *coiffure*, never covered by any head-dress, gives the young Korean a strangely girlish look, with the "bread-and-butter Miss" expression of the average German *Backfisch*, whose hair is usually dressed in the same style as the Korean boy's. When the Korean youth is betrothed, as he is, generally, at a very early age, sometimes even at nine or ten years of age, his cue is unplaited, the hair is dragged away from the forehead, encircled by a fillet, and bunched up into a *topknot*, the *sang-tu*, the national symbol of manhood, to be protected, in later years, by the cap and hat that have already been described.* A bachelor of forty may not wear the coveted token of solid, married, or betrothed, respectability ; he must be content to wear the pigtail of boyhood.

The unbetrothed bachelor of forty, or, indeed, of any age over twenty, would not belong to the upper class, for all Korean parents in comfortable circumstances betroth their sons in boyhood, and marry them as early as possible, generally between the fourteenth and eighteenth

---

* The actual *mang-kun* is the fillet, continually worn, of which the cap and the hat are the adjuncts It is wound so tightly round the head that it makes an indelible mark on many Korean foreheads

years of their age, to brides almost invariably their seniors by at least three, and sometimes by as much as eight, years. The *Yang-ban* we are considering is, therefore, certainly a married man, entitled since his betrothal in boyhood to a topknot, and, since marriage, to the curious hat protecting it. (During the years of betrothal he wore a distinctive hat of straw.) The Korean, having attained the honour of a topknot, bestows the greatest care upon it, and is as anxious about its safety as is the Chinese about that of his pigtail. Epidemics of topknot-cutting occur in Korea, occasioning panics similar to those I have described as convulsing Chinese society from time to time.

In Korea, the hair-cutting crime is ascribed to a malevolent dragon, who dares to commit these outrages in the very precincts of the Sovereign's palace, attacking the topknots even of the Life Guards on sentry duty. In 1888, His Korean Majesty sent a gracious message to the *Chargé d'Affaires* of the United States, Colonel Chaillé-Long "Bey" (formerly of the Egyptian Army), requesting him not to be alarmed by any unusual noise that might proceed from the Palace Enclosure on the night following the delivery of the message. The noise, His Majesty explained, would arise from measures adopted, after consultation with the Court Astrologers assembled in Council, with a view to driving away a mischievous dragon, who had of late carried his misdeeds to the point of cutting off the topknots of the Guards on sentry-go at the very gates of the palace. It had been decreed, by Order in Council, that volleys of blank cartridge should be fired to scare the audacious monster, bullets being useless against an evil spirit, such as the dragon undoubtedly was, and noise being particularly obnoxious to all Far Eastern dragons. Is it not, as every Chinese and Korean knows, noise, and noise alone, but of an ear-splitting potency unknown in the West, that prevents the dragon from entirely swallowing the sun, or the moon, when an eclipse takes place?* In the case of the topknot-collecting dragon of Sóul, the discharges of musketry had the usual effect— and also that of keeping the gallant American warrior-diplomatist awake all night. The next morning His Majesty was graciously pleased to inform him *officially* that the dragon had been utterly routed and had disappeared.

The Korean's attention to his *sang-tu* is not confined to the hair composing it whilst actually growing on his head. He carefully preserves every stray hair that falls from it, or that is combed from it, throughout the year until the eve of the New Year. On that night, a particularly malevolent spirit roams abroad in the guise of a huge cat, and visits every Korean household, on the look-out for shoes. Alas! he is not animated by the kind intentions of our own genial Father Christmas. Far from him is the benevolent purpose of the German *Christkind-lein*, the French *Petit Noël*, or the American "Santa Klaus." His aim is solely to step into the shoes he may find—"dead men's shoes," indeed, for their owners will die, or, at least, meet with terrible mishap—offend a powerful *Yang-ban*, perhaps, and be sentenced, for some imaginary crime, to be cudgelled on the shins—during the coming year. It will be readily believed that on the last night of the year Korean children are as anxious to hide their shoes as little Occidentals are to leave theirs, and their stockings, about at the festive season. Paterfamilias sees to it that all shoes, those in use and cast-off ones, are gathered together and locked up in a box in the sleeping apartment, for he dreads the ghostly cat even more than do the little ones, superstitions in the Far-East appearing to gain a firmer hold of the people with their

* A similar superstition exists in Mohammedan countries. I remember seeing, at the time of the total lunar eclipse in February, 1888, a constable of the Metropolitan Police of Cairo, in complete European uniform (but for the red *tarbūsh* on his head), vigorously thumping his metal tobacco-box in a pious endeavour to scare away the wolf that threatened to swallow the moon

advancing years—except, of course, in the case of the
sceptical *New* Japanese. No shoes being left for the cat
to step into, the household would seem to be insured
against his evil influence for the year to come, but the
head of a Korean family is determined to neglect no precaution. He takes the family collection of stray hairs—
not only those from the topknots of the married, or
betrothed, males, but also those from the long plaits
wound round the heads of the married women, and from
the pigtails of the little boys and the young girls—carries
it out, in the evening twilight, into the street just before
his door, or the gate of his enclosure, and sets fire to it.
Then arises to the rapidly darkening sky a new odour,
and a vile one, to be added to the thousand stinks of a
Korean city. The spirit cat sniffs it from afar, his
olfactory sense revolts against it, he turns his ghostly tail
and departs—probably to the distant rugged peaks, the
mysterious haunts of the topknot-cutting dragon.

Since the war, undertaken nominally in his interest,
between Japan and China, the Korean has undergone
greater anxiety on account of his topknot than at any
previous period. It has been threatened by a foe more
daring than the dragon, more dangerous than the spirit
cat. The reforming Japanese, marching in their thousands to the Korean's unwilling regeneration, laying strong
hands on him to shake him out of his torpor of centuries,
were not to be scared with blank cartridge—they faced
bullets unflinchingly—and their noses, accustomed to the
well-manured fields of Japan, took scant notice of burning
hair. One of their first acts, on undertaking the heavy
task of Korean reform, was to cause the Government at
Sŏul—at that time a willing tool—to issue an edict abolish-
ing the topknot, and prescribing the "Occidental cut" in
its stead. Of all the unduly irritating decrees dictated,
along with many admirable, if often premature, measures
of reform, by the tactless zeal of Japanese "regenerators,"
during the first brief period of their sway at Sŏul, none

exasperated the conservative Koreans more than this edict.
It was made the pretext for savage rioting, enabling the
Koreans to give vent to their hereditary hatred of the
Japanese. The progressive minority, favouring Japan, cut
off their topknots, and became objects of scorn in the
eyes of all the other Koreans. The Japanese gradually
recognised their mistake in attaching too great importance
to a matter of detail. It was, they soon found, the
inside of Korean skulls that needed reforming far more
urgently than the topknots; the obnoxious "Hair-cutting
Ordinance" fell into abeyance and went the way of the
dragon and the spirit cat. In 1897, the topknot had
become entirely optional, and the more advanced thinkers,
the young men educated in Japan, or in Korea under
foreign guidance, wore their hair in the Western fashion,
whilst the great bulk of the nation retained the national
distinctive *coiffure*, or reverted to it in many cases where
it had been abandoned under Japanese compulsion. So
the topknot flourishes once more, and with it the Korean
hat.

The brim of the black hat varies in width from four
to nine inches; in former times it far exceeded these
dimensions. For several generations, and as late as 1816,
the *Yang-ban* wore hats of immense size, the crown, about
nine inches high, being surrounded by a brim of such
width that the whole head-dress had a diameter of *three
feet*. These huge hats have their rivals, as to size, at the
present time in the umbrella-shaped hat of plaited bamboo,
with six indentations on the edge of the brim, under
which the Korean mourner hides his grief, and the port-
able roofs of plaited straw carried on the heads of the
rustics and the drivers of the bulls that are used as beasts
of burden. There is a tradition, firmly believed by every
Korean, and probably true by reason of its very Korean
quaintness, relating that in olden times the nation was
compelled, by royal decree, to wear hats of the enormous
size of the mourners' "extinguisher" of to-day (about

A STREET IN SŎUL,

The Capital of Korea, in 1898.

Drawn by KUBOTA Beisen

three feet across), and of a similar shape, made of—
earthenware !

The reason for the selection of such an apparently un-
suitable material, and of such unwieldy dimensions, for the
hat the Koreans were, it is said, compelled to wear is
still, according to tradition, typical of the quaint shrewd-
ness with which the legendary lore of the Far East
invests many of the ancient rulers. It is a peculiar sort
of cunning, causing the eyes of Orientals to flash with a
sly, appreciative twinkle as they relate instances of it, but,
on examination in the cold light of Occidental common-
sense, it appears futile and unpractical. In the case of
these porcelain hats, called *tŏrip*, the ancient Korean king
is alleged to have introduced them in order to put a stop
to the continual riots and brawls that disturbed the country,
and to the numerous conspiracies that threatened his rule.
In those early days the Korean was, as he still is, a born
plotter and exceedingly fond of fighting—not, indeed, of
the strife with weapons on the battle-field, but of a good
rough-and-tumble contest with fists and feet, cudgels and
stone-throwing, such as the lower classes indulge in to
this day, in the first month of the year, ward against
ward in a city, village against village in the country. To
him it is as much a "divarsion" as to any "broth of a
bhoy" in the palmy days of Donnybrook Fair. This
sportive pugnacity is not the only point of resemblance
between the characteristics of Koreans and Milesians ; both
races combine charm of manner with a disinclination
for sustained effort in serious matters ; both are much
attracted by politics of a militant sort. The condition
of an earthenware hat, three feet in diameter, after a
lively scrimmage between rival factions, may be easily
imagined. Even that reproach to our civilisation, the
silk hat, would come better out of the fray.* Now,
a broken hat gives a disreputable appearance to its wearer

---

* It is extraordinary how the "reproach to our civilisation" continues
to flourish, in spite of the many attacks made upon it in the cause of

in any civilised community; in ancient Korea it entailed more serious consequences than mere loss ' of outward respectability. Its possession rendered the purchase of a new hat unnecessary, as it involved, when brought under official notice, the instant decapitation of the owner. Nor was this the only advantage of the hat as a preserver of the public peace; it became simply impossible for the dis-affected to put their heads together for the purpose of plotting treason when their skulls were surrounded by brittle brims a yard across. Shouted conspiracies succeed only on the operatic stage.

To judge by the immaculate whiteness of the *Yang-ban's* clothing, one would naturally suppose that he must be as observant of bodily cleanliness as the Japanese. Appearances are notoriously deceptive, and notably in this case. The Korean's clothes are, indeed, scrupulously clean. They are very frequently washed, and beaten with a heavy smooth stick, vigorously plied by the muscular women, until that degree of gloss is obtained that makes them look like white, faintly bluish, porcelain; in fact, they are sent to the wash so often, and taken to pieces (as in Japan) every time, that they are, as a rule, not sewn, but *pasted* together with starch. The loss of time, and the trouble, that would be involved in the unpicking and re-sewing are thus avoided. This agreeable cleanli-ness, common to the clothing of all Koreans not of the lowest class, does not, unfortunately, extend to their bodies. The *Yang-ban* keeps his slender hands (all Koreans have small, well-shaped hands and feet) perfectly clean and soft, but for his face "a lick and a wipe" are considered suf-ficient. The great bulk of the nation is dirty beyond description, not only because of the utter want of ablutions, save when fording a stream, but on account of various un-sanitary sins, both of omission and of commission, whereof

common-sense and of art Every writer who mentions it has a bitter word for it, but in vain I have just had my fling here at the hated monstrosity—and I shall wear one to Church next Sunday!

the absence of handkerchiefs of any sort is the least. So absolutely primitive are the Korean notions on the sewage question that it is often difficult to find a spot on the grassy banks of a high road, near a village, on which it is possible to sit down. Even the *Yang-ban*, cultured as he is, from the Korean point of view, dignified and exquisitely courteous, from ours, has some customs which are difficult to describe. For instance, when he goes into society, he is invariably accompanied by an attendant bearing a round brass pot, used occasionally as a receptacle for the ashes of tobacco, and as a spittoon, but the main purpose of which is simply that of the Occidental vessel usually kept in what Tottenham Court Road furniture-catalogues euphemistically call a "pedestal." This vase is as much part of his personal equipage as his long pipe, his constant companion.

The Koreans have been inveterate smokers ever since the Japanese, in the seventeenth century, passed on to them the habit they had just acquired from the Portuguese. Their home-grown tobacco is very mild in the manufactured state, but the poorer people use the coarse leaf merely dried in the sun and roughly broken up, producing smoke that should be a valuable defence against the spirit cat, as its odour is about as pungent as that of burning hair. The pipe has a bowl of brass, or, if its possessor be wealthy, of jade, the stem is straight, about three feet in length, and the mouthpiece of metal, or, in the costly pipes, of amber or of jade. The management of a pipe of such length, which rarely leaves the Korean's lips for more than a few moments, requires considerable skill—it renders rapid motion, or violent exercise, almost impossible. This is hardly a serious drawback in the eyes of a race usually averse to any unnecessary exertion, and having absolutely no notion of the value of time. When, for any reason, the Korean wants to have both his hands free, he thrusts his long pipe into the silken cord worn as a girdle, sometimes into a pipe-bag attached thereto, or he puts the pipe up his sleeve, or sticks it down the nape of his neck, between his inner and outer clothing. There is one occasion on which the Korean, if he be wise, certainly takes his pipe out of his mouth. That is, when an official of rank is coming along the street, perched high up on a towering saddle under which a little pony is almost concealed, an attendant supporting the great man's knee on either side—or borne aloft in a chair, with a leopard-skin thrown over the back of it. A motley rabble of lackeys and of so-called "soldiers," hangers-on who act as orderlies and constables, and run, fetch, and carry for the official, precedes, surrounds, and follows him. These men clear the way with much shouting and many sounding blows administered, right and left, with their long, flat wooden staves, not unlike a Harlequin's wand, but much thicker. Woe to the luckless wight who disregards their shouts of "Pipes out!" In an instant his pipe is taken from him, broken into pieces that are thrown away, and his head receives smart whacks from the lictor's fan. (Everybody in Korea carries a fan, at all seasons, on ceremonial occasions, and, in summer, all day long.) Under Japanese influence, the Korean Reform Government of 1895 discouraged the use of the long pipe as much as it did the topknot. It tried to abolish the three-foot stem as being conducive to idleness. For a time there was trouble in the land, as there always is amongst people whom someone is trying to "regenerate," but when the pendulum swung back towards a more Korean policy—to be followed by a term of paramount Russian influence, which in turn gave way, in 1898, to Japanese guidance, wiser and more gentle than that attempted after the war—the long pipes reappeared unmolested.

I have said that the Koreans, as a race, are dirty in their habits. Some idea of the want of bodily cleanliness amongst the majority of the people may be gained from the simple statement that the average Korean of the

middle and lower classes is completely washed at his birth
and at his death, and, perchance, once in between, probably
on his wedding-day.

There is, however, a ray of hope of reform in this
matter. It is evident that a new era is being heralded
for the grimy folk of Korea under the auspices of the
highest in the land. A memorial was presented to the
King of Korea by the High Officers of State, first in October,
1895, and then repeatedly in the course of the years
1896 and 1897, praying that His Majesty would deign to
set the seal on Korean independence by assuming the title
of Emperor. His Majesty, who is as modest as he is
charming in manner and kindly of heart, was rather coy
and did not show any unseemly haste in acceding to the
prayer of the memorialists. Indeed, I rather fancy it must
have been His Majesty himself who inspired the argument
brought forward by the small minority in the Cabinet,
who urged that "the strength of the nation secures the
independence of a state, not the title of the ruler." The
memorialists were, however, not to be denied. They "got
up" petitions, in a manner not unknown in the West,
from different classes of the population, most of whom
did not care a straw whether their ruler changed his title
or not. These remaining ineffective, in September, 1897,
they played their trump-card. For three successive days,
from the 1st to the 3rd of October, 1897, all the high
officials of the Government, led by the Prime Minister,
knelt in the courtyard of the palace, from two till six p.m.,
beseeching His Majesty to grant their petition, which
had already been laid eight times at the foot of the throne.
The strict regulations of the Court of Soul demanded that
it should be presented a ninth time. The kneeling statesmen, suffering by this time from "pins and needles" in
their legs, again brought their memorial, couched, as
before, in the classic style of ancient China—and His
Majesty yielded. The Court Astrologers fixed the seventeenth day of the ninth moon, otherwise the 12th of

H

October, 1897, as the most auspicious day for the imposing ceremonial of the assumption of the Imperial title, quite forgetting to mention that a steady downpour of rain would drench the brilliant throng of courtiers to the skin. Amidst the downpour, His Majesty Li-hsi, clad in Imperial yellow, instead of the royal scarlet hitherto worn by him, was proclaimed *Whang-Chei*, or Emperor, of *Dai-Han*, the new name bestowed on Korea—and nobody has since been "a penny the worse," or the better.

What can have been the high motive that, at last, decided His Majesty to yield to the entreaties of his Ministers? Can it have been the spectacle of the vast courtyard filled, for four long hours on three consecutive afternoons, with elderly statesmen, some presumably rheumatic, kneeling on the cold stones? No, it was undoubtedly—at least, so it must seem to the Occidental mind—His Majesty's intense admiration for the patriotic sacrifice implied in the last sentence of the memorial: "After fasting *and washing*, we unanimously beg your Majesty to grant us this petition."

CHAPTER III.

THE MEN OF NEW JAPAN.

I HAVE described, in the foregoing Chapter, the outward characteristics of the men who compose the bulk of the ruling classes in the Three Empires of the Far East; the object of the present Chapter is to give some account of the ideas that actuate them in their dealings with each other and with us of the West. I shall attempt to trace the working of the brains under the Parting, the Pigtail, and the Topknot; I shall endeavour to describe the spirit dwelling in the hearts that beat under the silken *kimono* of the *Shi-zoku*, the embroidered robe of the Mandarin, and the white cotton gown of the *Yang-ban*.

It may appear strange that I have not chosen any representative Far Eastern men from the ranks of the People, with a capital P, a factor we hear of so frequently, and know so little, in the West, and that is commonly supposed to wield such great power in the politics of the white races. In the Far East, the Masses do not, as yet, exercise any appreciable influence on the conduct of public affairs, although their *alleged* feelings, their opinions and prejudices, represented as ineradicable, are brought forward, whenever the occasion arises, by astute Oriental statesmen anxious to oppose a clinching *"non possumus"* to an Occidental Power's demand or advice. "It cannot be done. It is against the popular feeling. If we attempted it we would have a revolution, and then your commerce would suffer. Of course, *we* appreciate the

justice of your demands" (or, "the absolutely disinterested nature of your advice"), but *the People* are not
yet sufficiently enlightened ; *the People* would rise to a
man." How often have Western diplomatists had to
listen to such representations, and how often have they
swallowed them whole ! Were closer attention bestowed
in the West on Far Eastern affairs in ordinary times—
not, as is unfortunately the case, only when black clouds
gather on the Eastern horizon—it would be noticed how
frequently the alleged determination of *the People* to
resist, unto death, some proposed measure of Western
origin, melts into thin air as soon as it suits the Oriental
Government to enforce it, at some other time, as an
innovation of its own, to suit its own purposes. The
Chinese Mandarins have, by long practice, become experts
in the use of this stratagem of statecraft. To hear their
protestations one would think that no European politician
"playing to the gallery," no American Populist candidate
seeking the votes of the Many-headed, could be more
tenderly careful of the feelings of *the People*. As a
matter of fact, nowhere are those feelings so skilfully
manipulated, so easily controlled by the ruling class, as
in China, the country where a whisper from a Mandarin
can, and often does, fan the passions of the mob into
lurid flames and cause blood-curdling massacres.

In Japan, too, the People are well in hand, but, owing
to their superior enlightenment, and to the safeguards
guaranteed to them by constitutional government and by
the press (vigilant, though under restraint), they require
very careful handling. The ability to influence the masses
wisely is, fortunately for Japan, abundant amongst their
natural leaders, the gentry, or *Shi-zoku*, from whom the
bulk of the nation still derives its opinions in public
matters. In Korea, the poor, down-trodden, shiftless
masses are at the mercy of the *Yang-ban*, and "take
the time of day" from "the quality." In none of
the three Empires does "public opinion" originate

spontaneously from the mass of *the People.* But does it in the most self-governed Occidental countries ? Ask the vicar and the curate, the parish priest and the minister, the keeper of the "Nonconformist conscience" ; inquire of the labour leader, of the editor of a political journal, and, especially, of the experienced wire-puller at the headquarters of any political party.

If the Occidental popular mind is often made up in a way inscrutable to those not, to use an expressive vulgarism, "in the know," the workings of its counter-part in the Far East, and especially in China, are still more mysterious. Everything may be going on smoothly amidst perfect calm; all at once a mysterious Someone, unknown and never to be discovered, gives a sign—and millions are impelled to action, so deeply stirred that the movement bears all the appearances of proceeding entirely from a genuine popular impulse. Such inexplicable com-motions have subverted great Empires in the Far East, they have changed dynasties and embroiled nations in wars; at other times they have subsided as suddenly, as unaccountably, as they arose. The mysterious Someone has again made a signal, and everything has returned to its normal condition.* Multitudes have abandoned a

---

* These mysterious popular ferments are not confined to the Mongolian races. They exist in the Aryan and the Semitic East. Whole shelves are filled with histories of the Indian Mutiny, but the true story of its inception has yet to be written Even its repression has its mysteries. What became of Nana Sahib ? We have hanged Damodar Chapekar for the Poona murders of Jubilee Day, 1897, but what do we know of the conspiracy whose tool he was ? The Behar Mango-Tree-Smearing Mystery of 1894 is still unexplained, baffling our most astute " Politicals." The truth is not yet known, and probably never will be, as to the Great Diamond Case of 1891, when that gifted and mysterious person—I know him well—who deals in precious stones under the assumed name of "Mr Jacob," immortalised by Marion Crawford as " *Mr Isaacs*," defied the Nizam of Hyderabad, and the British *Ráj* to boot, and came off scot-free. What do we know of the hidden springs that actuate the onward movement of Bábism in Persia, or of those that made Mahdism a devastating power ? And who can clearly trace the extraordinary Revival of Islam, in the last quarter of the nineteenth century, to its source ?

movement, that seemed deeply rooted, as unanimously as they took it up. The Far East thinks and acts *by millions.*

Although the masses in Eastern Asia are so easily led by those to whom they look for guidance—in China this is facilitated by the purely democratic spirit of its institutions, those in power being, frequently, of very humble origin, and, consequently, understanding the People thoroughly—although the lower classes are docile and law-abiding to a remarkable degree, there is a point beyond which it is not safe to push them. In China, where the Mandarin is vested with such, apparently, tremendous power; in Japan, whose Government has stringent Press laws, and a perfect system of detective and repressive police at its disposal; in Korea, where the poor man is delivered into the hands of the aristocracy— in all three Empires there are limits, well-defined for those who know them, that the rulers dare not over-step. To ignore these bounds would at once transform the patient, toiling millions into fierce, irresistible multitudes, whole races in arms in a cataclysm that would sweep away the imprudent rulers and their work. And the rulers know it. The West, apparently, does not, to judge by what is daily written and spoken about the future of the Far East. Whenever the opportunity occurs in these pages, I shall strive to indicate these points of utmost strain to which the docility of Chinese, Japanese, or Koreans, can be subjected.

In dealing with the mental characteristics and natural dispositions of the predominant classes in Eastern Asia, I propose to consider the Japanese first, because it was the Empire of the Rising Sun that gave the Old Far East its death-blow. The New Far East is the Far East as Japan has made it by her adaptation of Occidental civilisation, and by the results of the policy towards her neighbours the new methods enabled her to pursue. This policy, although only partially successful, so far, and productive of some momentous consequences not foreseen by its originators, entitles Japan to be considered as the paramount Asiatic factor in the Far Eastern Question. Inactive—partly owing to wise, patient statesmanship, partly on account of difficult financial and economic circumstances—whilst the hubbub of the Occidental "scramble for China" raged most fiercely in her immediate vicinity, she wields, by her very reserve, tremendous potential influence. Quietly and steadily doubling her already formidable sea-power, unremittingly strengthening and improving her splendid army, she is daily increasing the value of her alliance to the nation fortunate enough to secure it. Without firing a shot, she obtained in Korea, early in 1898, what must appear, in the eyes of the East, a great victory over Russia, whatever its results may be in later years. And, above all, her position of prudent restraint has gained for her in China a moral victory greater, by far, than any material land-grabbing, or concession-snatching, success she might have achieved. Japan holds the key of the Far Eastern position. It is her ruling class we must study first if we wish to have a clue to the solution of the Far Eastern problem.

If we consider the various estimates of the Japanese character formed by the Occidentals who have enjoyed the best opportunities of studying it—from Saint Francis Xavier to Mr. Lafcadio Hearn, from Will Adams, "Pilot Maior," of Gillingham, Kent, to Professor Basil Hall Chamberlain, through a long series of observers, missionaries, merchants, diplomatists, sailors, men of science, poets, and travellers—we must be struck by the extraordinary diversity of their views. On the one hand, from good St. Francis Xavier's warm-hearted appreciation of the Japanese of the middle of the sixteenth century: "This nation is the delight of my soul," and honest Will Adams's encomium of those of fifty years later: "The people of this Iland of *Iapon* are good of nature, curteous aboue measure and valiant in warre; their iustice is seuerely executed without any partialitie. . . . They are

gouerned in great ciuilitie . . . not a lànd better gouerned
in the world by ciuil policie . . . ," confirmed nearly a
century afterwards by Engelbert Kaempfer, the observant
German surgeon, who wrote : " In the practice of virtue,
in purity of life, and outward devotion, they far out-do
the Christians . . ∴ ," down to the glowing poetic eulogies
from the pen of Sir Edwin Arnold, and the exquisite prose-
pictures of Lafcadio Hearn, in our day, praise has been
lavished on the Japanese by men whose judgment must
command our respect.

Unfortunately for the puzzled inquirer, an array of
other eminent men stands opposed to these laudators with
condemnation as severe as language can express.   We
may take for what they are worth the angry diatribes
written in the early 'sixties by men who were in constant
danger of their lives amongst a population on whom they
were forcing, *vi et armis*, their unwelcome presence, the
plaints of baffled diplomatists, tired out by Oriental pro-
crastination, designed to gain time, and overmatched by
Asiatic cunning ; we may dismiss the spiteful utterances,
frequent to this day, of disappointed would-be exploiters,
of sorrowing concession-hunters, and of irritated Occidentals,
chafing in their voluntary exile, who belong to the
numerous class to whom any Oriental is, morally, a
" nigger," when he is not a " damned nigger." To such
people, daily contact with a proud race, more intellectual,
more polished, more truly cultured than their own coarse
selves, becomes exasperating to a degree.   If we put
aside as untrustworthy the opinions of the ·classes just
enumerated, we cannot entirely disregard the deliberately
expressed views of some trained observers, of men of
science versed in psychology, of shrewd lawyers and level-
headed merchants, who find but little to praise in the
Japanese character, but much to blame, and to blame
strongly and *honestly*—not, as is· the case with some
travellers, merely for the sake of the supposed distinction to be obtained by differing from the majority

of judges, nor, like certain "smart" journalists, in order to raise a silly laugh by cheap and vulgar ridicule, or to start a "boom" by unexpected violent denunciation. Nor can we neglect to take into account the faint praise wherewith some eminent authorities, who have enjoyed exceptional opportunities, have condemned the Japanese in more or less guarded remarks, whose sub-acid flavour is perceptible through the very thin coating of sugar. And, lastly, what are we to think of the remarkable discrepancy between the opinions of our friend who has returned enraptured, after a stay of a month or two amongst "the most charming people in the most delightful country in the world," and who wants to revisit it soon (every traveller does), and those of that other friend of ours, come "home" for a holiday, who tells us savagely that Japan, the land where he earns his living by the sweat of his brow—a state of perspiration often induced by the various forms of violent bodily exercise that occupy a considerable portion of his bitter exile, football, for instance—is an overrated country, peopled by a race of arrogant pigmies, of debased morals and limited intellect ?

If we go deeper into all this conflicting evidence our confusion will grow worse confounded. We shall find the modern Japanese described as a gentle creature, so full of the milk of human kindness that he will pay for Buddhist prayers to be said for the soul of his dead dog, or cat, or ox, and cheerfully disburse thirty *Sen* for the decent burial, in the grounds of a temple, with a short service, of his lamented fourfooted friend, occasionally even a larger sum, so that poor doggie, or puss, may have a mortuary tablet, or *ihai*, to keep its memory green. We shall also find him held up to execration as a cruel savage, revelling in scenes of carnage, maddened by the smell of blood, perpetrating nameless atrocities on a vanquished, defenceless foe, and so callous to the sufferings of the brute creation that he eats fish *alive*, for choice, crimping it so deftly that the slices are held together only by the backbone, and fall asunder through the quivering induced by the addition of vinegar-sauce.* Horrible! Yes, just *a little* more horrible than the Occidental modes of skinning eels alive, of crimping cod, or of boiling lobsters and crabs in the full enjoyment of life and health. Go to Billingsgate Market, and hear the awful sound, a sort of hissing moan, when the great iron cage descends into the deep tank of boiling water with its freight of living crustacea!

We are told, at the same time, that the Japanese are of the sweetly simple, lovable disposition indicated by their extreme fondness for children and their unvarying kindness to them, extending even to the provision, in their pantheon, of a special divinity to watch over the little ones,† and of another, *Hotei,* a jolly, plump, smiling god, for them to romp with. On the other hand, we are warned to beware of the Japanese. They are, it is alleged, a danger to the white races, for their much-vaunted progress has been only in things material; their adaptation of our civilisation has merely laid a thin veneer over their native savageness. Hence our peril, we are told, and we are asked to consider the awful probability of a conflict some day with a determined race, hating us bitterly, turning against the West the weapons, the organisation and the training originally borrowed from it, but remaining at heart ruthless barbarians capable of the most fiendish atrocities. To those who thus warn us any argument seems futile. They at once meet it with two words: "Port Arthur." In their opinion, and, unfortunately, in that of a vast number of Occidentals, that closes the dis-

---

* The custom of crimping and eating alive the carp (*koi*) or the *tai,* the succulent sea-bream, is far less common than it was, although *raw* fish is still a favourite dish, sliced, as *sashimi,* or, under the name of *namasu,* with vinegar and cold stewed vegetables.

† The Buddhist divinity *Jizō* (in Sanskrit. *Kshitigarbha*), who typifies Compassion. Represented with the shaven head of a Buddhist priest, and a sweet expression of benevolence on his features, he holds in one hand

cussion. The cruel massacre by the victorious Japanese troops of a great part of the Chinese inhabitants of Port Arthur is, indeed, a blot on Japan's escutcheon, but before deciding to accept it as conclusive proof of the whole nation's incapacity for true civilisation we should remember the circumstances in which the dreadful deed was wrought. The massacre has been described *ad nauseam* in lurid columns of "expanded" telegrams, and of picturesquely gruesome "descriptive reporting," in the Western press; it has been brought before our eyes in sketches by special artists and in revolting photographs, the latter, it is to be feared, not always as truthful as sun-pictures are commonly supposed to be.* The more sensational of the English newspapers, knowing the insatiable appetite of their patrons for plenty of gore with their breakfasts, and those American periodicals that have since become notorious as "Yellow Journals," gloated over sickening details and emphasised them by "scare headlines." Nothing was neglected that could help to publish Japan's shame to the Western world. But how many of the journals that disseminated the detailed news of the massacre had the fairness to give *equal*

the mystic jewel, the *nio-i hōju*, that procures the fulfilment of all desires, In the other the *shaku-jō*, the staff with six clanking iron rings at the top, carried by mendicant priests. His smiling effigy is to be found all over Japan, more frequently than that of any other god He is the Helper of all who *travel*, of women pregnant and in *travail*, and, generally, of all creatures in *trouble*, but especially of children. The souls of dead children are exposed to the risk of cruel treatment when they reach the Japanese Styx, the River of the Three Roads (*San-dzu-no Kawa*). On its banks lurks the *Shōzuka-no Baba*, a hideous old hag who robs them of their clothes. Once across the Styx, further trials are in store for the children. On the banks of another river of Hades, the River of Souls (*Sai-no Kawara*), the poor little souls are condemned to the never-ending piling-up of pebbles, until kind *Jizō* comes to their rescue So, to lighten the labours of the little dead, all children, and many kind-hearted adults, when they pass a statue of *Jizō*, deposit a pebble at its base. It counts one to some tiny toiling spirit in the nether world. Some Missionaries, and some "enlightened" Japanese, look upon this act as a gross superstition, and one to be speedily abolished I do not envy their frame of mind

* My friend, Major H. Van der Weyde, M J S, the well-known expert in

publicity to the cause of the slaughter? Very few; some newspapers never mentioned the cause at all. Justice demands that the world should know that the lust of killing which possessed the Japanese on the day of the capture of Port Arthur was the fury of revenge. Every Japanese soldier who "ran *amok*" on that dire day was the avenger of his unfortunate comrades, captured, wounded and helpless, by the enemy during the attack on the great stronghold, and put to horrible, lingering death by fiendish tortures such as only the cruelty of Chinese minds can conceive. The best-disciplined troops of the phlegmatic Northern nations would have been maddened beyond control by the awful sights that met the eyes of the Japanese as they entered the captured town on that fateful 21st of November, 1894, after storming its defences, till then considered almost impregnable. I will not stain these pages by a description of the appalling evidences of Chinese barbarities that infuriated the Japanese, nor of the terrible reprisals that followed. Suffice it to say that the Japanese soldiers simply went mad for the space of some hours—mad with the lust for blood, the terrible craving to kill, and kill, and kill, without caring whom or how, that has, even in this century, possessed some of the most rigidly-trained European troops.

photography, who has had experience of battlefields during the American Civil War, made a careful examination of one of the most widely-circulated of these gruesome photographs, and unhesitatingly pronounced it to be a "faked" picture, cunningly "staged" with a view to sensational effect. The bodies of slaughtered Chinese had been so arranged, and some Japanese soldiers with fixed bayonets and drawn swords posed in such attitudes as to convey the impression that the photograph was an actual "snap-shot" taken during the massacre. The attention of certain London journals that were chiefly instrumental in disseminating circumstantial reports of the massacre, or in publishing photographs alleged to represent it, was called to the result of Major Van der Weyde's investigation, but in vain. An important newspaper, that had shown reluctance to publish details until the fullest inquiry had been made, was then approached, and pleaded, privately, that it could not take up the matter, as it would involve criticism of the methods employed by influential contemporaries—"a breach of journalistic etiquette"

We need not go back to the days of the Peninsular War for an instance of such "red fury" on the part of British troops, although the ghastly orgies that disgraced Wellington's heroes at Badajoz at once recur to us. In that case, there is no faintest trace of an excuse for the devilry that made the town just stormed—a town inhabited, moreover, by the very people whom the besiegers had come to rescue from a foreign foe—a prey to murder, rapine, and debauchery. The mad fit passed away, but not before the raving soldiery had killed several of their own officers who had tried to curb their frenzy. If evidence be needed that such terrible deeds — inspired, however, by revenge, a nobler feeling than the gross lust of pillage at Badajoz—have been committed by British soldiers within the memory of living men, we have but to ask anyone who saw and shuddered at the vengeance wreaked upon the mutineers at Delhi, and elsewhere, to the cry of "Remember Cawnpore!" And not on the mutinous Sepoys only, but on many others of their race. In such hours of revenge, but little discrimination is made between the innocent and the guilty. Not all the French villagers (women among them) who were shot by the Bavarians amidst the blazing ruins of Bazeilles on the fateful day of Sedan, had fired from their windows on the German troops. When the French Army of Order had fought its way from Versailles into rebellious Paris, a grimy face and dirty hands were accounted proof positive that a man was a *Communard;* dishevelled hair and poor clothing sufficed to convict a woman, old or young, of being a *Pétroleuse*—on such evidence they were added to the long files of the condemned, placed against the nearest wall, and shot, or bayoneted, by hundreds, in cold blood. When the soldiers of the Tsar, acting under orders from high quarters, destroyed a whole tribe of Turkomans, as a "salutary example," none were spared; the doomed tribe was annihilated, root and branch.

All these facts were forgotten in the storm of indignation raised by the news of the massacre at Port Arthur, and Japan's numerous enemies took care to improve the occasion. The impression produced on the Western mind was a lasting one, especially in Great Britain. When, in the winter of 1897–8, an alliance, or, at least, a co-operation for the defence of common interests in the Far East, seemed on the point of being arranged between Britain and Japan, a warning cry went up from thousands of well-meaning people, strenuously opposing the idea of an alliance with a "heathen nation" capable of barbarities such as those perpetrated by the Japanese at Port Arthur. From the sententious editor of a high-class weekly review to the indignant working man writing to a popular daily, the "Great Heart of the Nation" was stirred to excited protest. Cool reflection, and a closer investigation of the facts, brought the public gradually into a more judicious frame of mind, but the mischief done was almost irreparable; the "psychological moment" had gone by, a jarring note had been struck, and the opportunity was missed of concluding an understanding, based on national feeling in both countries, that would have altered, to the benefit of both, the whole course of events in the Far East. The harm done was all the greater because the feeling against Japan, arising entirely from the Port Arthur massacre, had reached circles not easily influenced by waves of popular sentiment. It is no secret that in august regions, the British equivalent of those described in the courtly language of Japan as "Above the Clouds," the indignation caused by the news of the massacre left lasting traces; and this is not to be wondered at when we think of the kind, sympathetic heart of the Lady of this Realm, shocked beyond expression by the tale of cruel deeds.

For much of this mischief the Japanese Government has only itself to blame. In the matter of the massacre it acted with a want of candour and of resolution that seems incomprehensible to anyone not thoroughly acquainted with the Japanese spirit. At first, semi-officially inspired versions were put into circulation, toning down the facts, as far as possible, and attributing the massacre to the Transport "Coolies" and military labourers who followed the Japanese army — rough, ignorant men, we were told, not properly subjected to military discipline (this was untrue, for the Japanese Provost-Marshal kept them, as a rule, in excellent order) and apt to use the dirks (*waki-zashi*) many of them carried, especially when under the influence of deep potations of *saké*. When the reports of war correspondents, and the sketches of special artists, who had been eye-witnesses of part, at least, of the massacre, made it impossible to conceal the truth, a Mr. Ariga—a clever Japanese lawyer, who was, with great foresight, attached as Legal Adviser to the Army Headquarters, in case of any incident arising that might involve a point of international law—was "turned on" to try and explain away the worst features of the affair. He was to reason with the foreign journalists and to endeavour to persuade them that it was not a "massacre" at all, but only the "perfectly legitimate" killing of Chinese soldiers, who had, as was their wont, thrown away in the hour of defeat the upper jacket and the hat, or the turban, by which the clothing of the Chinese "Brave" is distinguished from that of the civilian.* The facts that they were unarmed and unresisting, and, consequently, entitled to be treated as prisoners of war; that no notice had been given that quarter would be refused to them as a reprisal for their torture and murder of the Japanese wounded; and, lastly, that many of the victims were women and children—all these were airily brushed aside by the plausible Mr. Ariga; yet his efforts failed. Clever international lawyer

* This was the view embodied in the despatch addressed by the late Count Mutsu (then Minister for Foreign Affairs) to the Japanese Representatives abroad in December, 1894 It also alleged that such of the inhabitants as remained in Port Arthur after its investment were armed and fired on the Japanese

and plausible pleader he might be—and I have the pleasure
of knowing him as an amiable personification of that type,
so well-known in Germany and in Austria, the "Pacifica-
tory Court Councillor" (*Beschwichtigungs - Hofrat*)—his
case was too hopelessly bad.   Finding it impossible to
persist in denials, or in transparent excuses, the Japanese
Government appointed a Commission of Inquiry as a
sop to Occidental public opinion.   We know that Commission of Enquiry—it comes from Whitehall, from the
banks of the Seine, from Vienna, from Washington, from
any part of the world where there are inquisitive Members
of Parliament, pressmen who raise a "boom," or any
other inconvenient persons to be lulled into inactivity.
The Commission may have "inquired"; it has kept its
findings strictly secret, for it has not been heard of since
its appointment, and, probably, never will be.

A final and grave blunder, from the Occidental point
of view, was committed by the Japanese Government.
The best work on the war with China that has hitherto
appeared is, undoubtedly, *The China-Japan War*, by an
able writer who veils his identity under the pseudonym
of "Vladimir, lately of the **** Diplomatic Mission to
Corea."   This instructive book, published (with illustrations
and clear maps) in London (by Messrs. Sampson Low,
Marston and Company, Limited) in 1896, bears plain
indications of its having been, if not officially inspired by
the Japanese Government, at all events written by
someone in close touch with it.   Only in one particular—
the Port Arthur massacre—does this in any way detract
from its value as a trustworthy historical work, for, as
"Vladimir" writes in his introductory remarks headed
"To My Readers" : "My preference for Japanese sources
does not affect the impartiality of the narration—the
Japanese have been uniformly fair to their adversaries, far
more just than their own countrymen ; and it has always
been easier to find the truth in the histories of the victors
than in those of the vanquished.   The former have greater

self-possession, see events more clearly, and can afford to be impartial." Where the book seriously fails is in the omission of any mention of the massacre. An admirably clear and concise account of the capture of Port Arthur is given, even a description of the rejoicings with which the Japanese celebrated their victory, including the quotation of patriotic verses recited by General Nishi at the Officers' Banquet—but not a word about the massacre! Here the influence of Japanese officialdom is plainly evident. No, "Vladimir," that may be the way in which history is only too often written; it is not the way to write history!

What was the reason that prompted this strange apparent lack of wisdom on the part of a Government otherwise remarkably sagacious? What could have induced Ministers, at all other times so palpably anxious to make a favourable impression on the Western Powers, thus to flout the unanimous opinion of Christendom? The answer is: because one of those points had been reached, of which I have spoken earlier in this Chapter, one of those limits beyond which a Far Eastern Government fears to proceed. Here we have a striking illustration of the truth I have endeavoured to explain. A powerful Government was in the heyday of success, its policy seemingly justified by an uninterrupted succession of victories abroad, its every act ratified by a truly patriotic Parliament, transformed by the declaration of war against China, as if by magic, from a squabbling congress of petty politicians, split up into mutually hostile groups, into a grave assembly united in the face of a national crisis. The Government had, as every Japanese Cabinet has, all the power at its disposal that a Constitution, modelled on that of Prussia, can confer, yet it did not dare to take the right course for fear of the consequences. It knew the danger of any action on its part which would have seemed to cast a slur on the army, Japan's pride, that had just gained the great prize

I

of the whole campaign, Port Arthur, the fortress reputed impregnable throughout the Far East. Any reprimand addressed to the soldiers at the front would have been looked upon by the people in Japan as an insult to the whole nation ; moreover it would, of necessity, have included the officers who failed to restrain their men, and the chief who was immediately responsible for the storming of Port Arthur—Lieutenant-General Yamaji. Now, Lieutenant-General Yamaji, the grim and taciturn commander of the First Division of the Second Army Corps, the "One-eyed Dragon," as his soldiers called him*— he had lost an eye in his youth—was the darling of his troops. To censure *him*, the bravest of the brave, the warrior as modest and unassuming as he was daring, stern and resolute, the very incarnation of the Japanese knightly spirit—that was a task no Japanese Minister of War would care to undertake on the morrow of the "One-eyed Dragon's" great victory, or even at the close of an uniformly successful campaign. One, and one alone, could have administered a reprimand to those in fault without risk of causing dangerous discontent in the army and without fear of popular resentment—the Emperor's rebuke would have been unhesitatingly accepted as deserved, but there is little doubt that, had it been spoken, numerous cases would have occurred of both officers and men seeking death by their own swords as preferable to life under the stigma of Imperial displeasure at their conduct in war. Japanese Ministers, however, are far too prudent to make any but the most sparing use of the immense power latent in the person of the Sovereign,

* The Dragon is, in the Far East, symbolic of supernatural strength, intellect, and power The Japanese Press bestowed the same epithet— "One-eyed Dragon"—on another famous man who had only one eye— Gambetta ("*le Borgne de Cahors*"). The Japanese who studied European politics in his time were fascinated by the patriotism, the energy, the fiery eloquence, and especially the pluck of the great Tribune They cannot understand, and do not admire, our cold, flabby, vacillating, entirely unheroic, British "Statesmen" of the average type

which is only exercised in moments of the gravest national emergency. Imperial intervention being, in this case, out of the question, the Japanese Government had to choose between offending their own people and ignoring the public opinion of the West. They decided on the latter course, and the fact is worth noting, as a similar dilemma may present itself at some future time. The Japanese Minister who is able to solve it satisfactorily will be a great statesman indeed.

The detractors of Japan are ill-advised in dwelling too strongly on the unfortunate Port Arthur episode; as its consideration may lead those whom they seek to influence to make inquiry into the whole subject of the *general* behaviour of the victors during the war with China. The result of such an investigation must be a feeling of profound admiration for the Japanese. All who study impartially the history of the struggle in the Far East in the years 1894 and 1895 must recognise the existence of features in their national character that entitle them to a place not only amongst the nations we are agreed to call "civilised," but amongst the foremost races of the world, those that help to mould the destinies of mankind. Of their virility as a nation they gave conclusive proof from the very inception of the conflict, completely refuting the opinion, so often expressed by many who professed to know them well, that they were a race of clever children, with the engaging ways of children and their incapacity for serious thought, or earnest, persevering endeavour. Strangely enough, this erroneous estimate frequently emanated from observers of French nationality, the very ones that might, with some show of reason, be reproached with the neurotic hyper-sensitiveness, the fickleness and the levity that have earned for the latter-day French the epithet of "*enfants terribles* of Europe."

I do not propose to adduce evidence in proof of the manliness displayed by the Japanese during the war—and

war, be it remembered, is the touchstone of a nation's
virtues as well as of its defects—nor do I intend to
expatiate on their marvellous prowess in battle.   Those
who seek information on this subject will find a rich
fund of clearly arranged facts in *Heroic Japan*, by
F. Warrington Eastlake, Ph.D., and YAMADA Yoshi-aki,
LL.B., a most interesting collection of instances of Japanese
heroism, by land and sea, in the war with China,* every
case cited having been fully investigated by the painstaking
authors, even at the loss of much picturesque detail that
had accumulated round the facts, detail that had 'to be
stripped off in order to reduce to strict history what had
quickly become legendary.   In that fascinating book,
whose only defect is a looseness in the use of naval and
military terms, due to a want of technical knowledge, are
to be found plain tales from the battlefields, and from the
sea, that warm the cockles of the heart and set the blood
tingling.   These short narratives, most moving where the
authors have left them in the quaint, concise style of the
Orderly-room Report, or the Ship's Logbook, would require
the pen of Rudyard Kipling to do them full justice.   As it
is, many of them are now embodied in the songs that are
sung by every man, woman and child in Japan.   The record
of heroism includes not only "deeds of derring-do," accomplished against fearful odds, acts of the noblest self-
sacrifice, and instances of phenomenal endurance, but cases
of Spartan fortitude—often on the part of the women, the
children, and the old folks left at home—patriotic allo-
cutions full of inspired eloquence, and dying speeches that
ring out like the last notes of a bugle-call.   All this was
only what people who really knew the Japanese spirit had
expected, for on one point observers had all along agreed:
that the Japanese are brave to a fault, fearless, dashing,
and skilful in the use of arms.   What was not previously

---

* "Heroic Japan: A History of the War between China and Japan "
By F. Warrington Eastlake, Ph D , and Yamada Yoshi-aki, LL B., etc.
With many Illustrations and Maps   London, 1897.

known was their possession of the ability to keep cool in
the stress of battle that is requisite for the execution of
Western tactics, for the effective handling of the scientific
implements of modern artillery, and especially for warfare
conducted with the latest types of warships and of
torpedos.

The feature of the modern Japanese character, as
revealed in the war, to which I would call particular
attention is its humanity, shown by the *generally* admirable
conduct towards the vanquished (I have pointed to the
Port Arthur massacre as a sad *exception*) and by the
perfect arrangements for the care of the sick and wounded.
This humanity in war has not always distinguished the
Japanese. It is one of the best fruits of the new spirit
infused into the nation, at first only amongst the highly
educated, but gradually permeating all classes, ever since
the adaptation of Western civilisation commenced. In the
wild days of the strife between clans, the Japanese were
certainly not distinguished by any feelings of tenderness
for the vanquished, and it is no less certain that in our
days some of the older people wondered at the care that
was bestowed on the wounded Chinese, at the kind
treatment of the prisoners, and at the equitable administration of the enemy's territory occupied by the troops.
To such old Tories, untouched by the modern spirit, all
this seemed mere foolishness. "The Chinese dare to
oppose our Emperor's august will; they must be *killed*"—
such was their reasoning. But the great majority of the
nation acquiesced in the humane tendencies of the Government. This is amply proved by the readiness with
which the troops—flushed with victory, and sorely tried
by terrible hardships under the blazing sun of the Korean
summer, or, later, amidst the Arctic frost and snow of
Manchuria and of Northern China — obeyed the strict
orders of the Commander-in-Chief, enjoining them to
remember that they warred against the armies of China,
not against its unarmed inhabitants, whose lives and

property must be respected. And—except in the case
of Port Arthur—these orders were carried out to the
letter.

In every district occupied by the Japanese, a civil
administration was established almost before the last shots
of the engagement had ceased to echo, and the Chinese
population found themselves, for the first time in their
lives, in the enjoyment of absolute security of person and
of property, and of equal justice for all. The Civil Commissioners in charge of the occupied districts were chosen
from the Japanese Consular Service in China, and were,
consequently, thoroughly acquainted with the characteristics, the social and economic condition, and the language
of the people they were called upon to govern. They
held the scales of justice impartially, severely repressing
any pilfering, were it only of a fowl, or of a bag of
millet, on the part of the Japanese soldiers. (What would
our good friend Mr. Thomas Atkins say to this? The ghosts
of many chickens surreptitiously purloined, not only from
the enemy, but—as in South Africa—from friendly roosts
as well, arise in judgment against him.) Looting was
strictly forbidden, and all supplies obtained, even in the
smallest quantity, had to be paid for at current rates.
The same rule applied to the requisitioning of carts and
of beasts of burden, and to all services rendered by the
inhabitants, who were not slow in taking advantage of
the opportunity of earning money. Bringing ample
supplies to the markets that were established, they
greatly facilitated the work of the admirable Japanese Commissariat—the only commissariat—except the German, and
the excellent supply arrangements of the *Sirdar* Kitchener's
Sudan Field Force that captured Omdurman—which has
ever gone through a difficult campaign without provoking
curses, both loud and deep, from starving or ill-fed
soldiers. They worked, and worked well, as Transport
" Coolies," cheerfully carrying ammunition for the enemies
of their country. What did it matter? The war was

the affair of the Mandarins, not theirs. The Japanese treated them fairly and paid them honestly. "*A-Yaw!*" War was rather a good thing. Why, only last week a regiment of Chinese "Braves" had passed through the village—about two hundred men with rifles of a dozen different patterns, three or four hundred with spears, and bows and arrows, and one company of a hundred with German rifles, all alike, acting as the body-guard of the Military Mandarin in command. They stayed but one night near the village — they seemed anxious to lose no time on the march—but they left the place as bare as a Buddhist priest's shaven head; they killed the *Ti-pao*, the Village Constable, who had remon-strated with them, plundered his house and bore away his good-looking daughter. And when old YING Yu-lin, the Village Elder, complained to the Military Mandarin he got a hundred strokes with the thin bamboo for his pains, "for causing unnecessary disturbance," the Mandarin said.

Now a Japanese battalion was quartered in the village —it had followed close on the heels of the "Braves"— and it had brought a Civil Deputy-Commissioner with it, who held a Court daily, at which any complaints were promptly attended to and wrongs equitably redressed, and —marvellous to relate!—the only man who had been even threatened with corporal punishment was WANG Fung-sun, the village barber, who had, very naturally, provided himself with a few strings of brass "Cash" (silver was beyond his means) as a little *douceur* for the magistrate, when he came to the Court to sue Farmer TSO Ching-sing for payment of a debt. The soldiers, too, were quiet, well-behaved men, and their officers paid, cash down, for the supplies that were being gradually produced from sundry hiding-places. The able-bodied male inhabitants were all at remunerative work, conveying stores to the next Japanese camping-ground, under escort of a company, and the women were busy making thick wadded cotton mitts to protect the soldiers' hands from frost-bite, the Japanese Commissariat Officer supplying the pattern and paying a good price for the work. Truly, this war was rather a good thing! Small wonder, then, that all those in the village who could write affixed their signatures to the petition old Ying drew up on their behalf, and on that of the illiterate majority, at the close of this beneficent war, praying that "the Enemy" would be graciously pleased to remain, and continue a rule so mild and so just that the like had not been known in the land since the days of Yao and of Shun.* "*Vive notre ami l'ennemi !*" was the cry of the Chinese civilians, and a more justifiable one in their case than in that of those Parisians who greeted with it the Cossacks of Suvaroff after the great Napoleon's downfall. The Japanese Civil Commissioners had at their disposal a force of Imperial *Gendarmerie*, sent from Japan to act as Military Police with the armies in the field. These *Kem-pei*, as they are called, are a splendid body of men, armed with rifle, sword, and revolver, and perfectly drilled, doing constabulary duty on the high roads and by-ways, on lonely moors and rugged mountain-paths, throughout Japan, in the wilds of Formosa, and in the Japanese Settlements in Korea. They are selected from time-expired Non-Commissioned Officers and Privates of exemplary conduct, and are absolutely trustworthy.

I know of at least one case in which the services of the *Kem-pei* attached to a Civil Commissioner during the war were called into requisition against their fellow-countrymen. Some Chinese inhabitants of a captured town —Kin-chau, on the Liao-tung Peninsula—had complained to the Civil Commissioner that certain Japanese Transport "Coolies," armed with dirks, had "purchased" from them, for a few strings of "Cash," a number of valuable

---

* The Ideal (and probably mythical) Chinese Emperors Yao is *said* to have reigned in Shan-si (the cradle of the Chinese nation) from 2356 to 2255 B C, Shun from that year until 2205 B C.

robes of silk and satin, the infinitesimal price paid having been fixed by a very one-sided bargain, the "Coolies" ominously fingering their weapons, the Chinese speechless from fear. The *Kem-pei* were at once put on the track of the "purchasers," who were arrested in their camp the same day, haled before the Commissioner, forced to restore their "bargains" to the Chinese, and severely punished. The benefactions of the Japanese were not confined to the administration of such even-handed justice, to prompt and fair payment for stores requisitioned and for services rendered—payment, be it noted, in coin, not, as in the case of some European wars, in "Warrants" payable (ultimately by the vanquished nation) at the restoration of peace—and to the carrying out of wise sanitary mea-sures in the occupied districts. I have before me a photograph, a perfectly trustworthy "snap-shot," repre-senting a crowd of wretched-looking Chinese congregated in front of the building in which the Japanese Civil Com-missioner in charge of the town and district of Kin-chau, already mentioned, had established his Court. The Japanese Civil Flag, white with the red sun-disc, the *Hi-no maru*, in the centre,* floats over the gateway, guarded by two *Kem-pei* with fixed bayonets, and the crowd are waiting patiently, as only Orientals can wait. And what are they waiting for? They are the blind, the halt, the maimed, the lepers, and the aged paupers of Kin-chau waiting for their daily rations, served out to them from the Japanese Commissariat Stores by His Imperial Japanese Majesty's Civil Commissioner, who deems it right to feed the hungry and helpless, "enemies" though they be. O! You who harp upon that one massacre at Port Arthur, think of the Japanese Com-

---

* This is the flag that every Japanese merchant vessel flies. It is also the Diplomatic and Consular flag. On the Colours borne by the Army, and on the Ensign of the Imperial Navy, the sun-disc has rays (also red, and broadening towards their ends) radiating from it to the edges of the flag, a beautiful and distinctive one.

missioners feeding their poor "enemies" at Kin-chau, and at many other places—and acknowledge that there must be *some* humane feeling deep down in the Japanese heart!

It is easy to realise the consternation of the Chinese population of the Liao-tung Peninsula when, after experiencing the blessings of the just and honest rule of their conquerors, they were once more placed at the mercy of grasping, corrupt Mandarins. I can hardly hope to enlist much sympathy for these unfortunate people, who were permitted to have just one tantalising taste of good government and were then thrust back into the dark realm of oppression whence they had emerged for such a brief space. They are not picturesque, they do not send appeals to our press, and—above all—no political party in our midst has seen its way to utilising their woes as material for an agitation, but their case is, none the less, a hard one. Who deprived them of the new benefits they were beginning to appreciate so highly, who handed them back, bound hand and foot, to the corrupt barbarism of China? Three great Christian Powers: Russia, France, and—strange partner in this "Long Firm" —Germany.

I have used the term "Long Firm," and not without reason, for the annals of our Criminal Courts do not contain any more flagrant case of conspiracy to obtain valuable property by false pretences. The very nature of the arguments advanced by the three representatives of Christendom in "advising" the victorious Japanese to evacuate Port Arthur, and to retrocede the whole Liao-tung Peninsula to China, savours of the "confidence trick." The Russian Pecksniff, the German Chadband, and the French Tartuffe were only "advising" their "dear Friend" Japan for her own good; she could not be allowed to keep the territory she had won and paid for with the blood of her bravest sons, it would "endanger the Peace of the Far East," it would "perilously affect the Balance of Power in Eastern Asia," and—here the cat jumped out of the diplomatic bag, right under honest John Bull's dull eyes—"a Power holding Port Arthur would, inevitably, overawe Peking, and *have China at her mercy.*"*

The three Powers were, of course, careful to point out that their "friendly advice," given with their right hands on their sword-hilts, was uttered in the sacred cause of "Peace and Civilisation," a cause for which large tracts of Asia have been, at various times, given over to fire and sword. Japan, in presence of this significant admonition, looked round for helpful friends—and found none. Britain gave her good advice, an inexpensive commodity, wisely pointing out that Japan could not hope to resist, unaided, what was, virtually, the peremptory command of the three greatest military Powers. That was cold comfort, but it was all Britain had to offer. At all events, it was something that she was not cajoled into joining the Allies in their bullying policy, and Japan's gratitude for this small mercy is profound. As to the United States, they had, at that time, not yet discovered the importance of their interests in the Far East, and the Monroe Doctrine was still held to imply not only the non-interference of Europe in the affairs of the New World, but America's abstention from international politics in other continents. It had not yet come to mean America for the North Americans— and anything else they can get for them too. Italy's function as a factor in the Far Eastern Question had not yet been discovered, nor Belgium's, as the scramble for the Chinese spoils had not begun and the concession-hunter

---

* This last argument was advanced by Russia and her Allies early in the spring of 1895, yet only three years later British politicians were glibly explaining, in Mr. Toots's best vein, that the Russian occupation of Port Arthur was "really of no consequence," and continued to babble of "Open Doors," "Spheres of Influence," "the Yang-tsze Valley," and other mere catch-words, their minds still impervious to the fact that, as long as there is a Chinese Empire, the Power that can overawe its capital holds China in subjection to its will.

was biding his time. What was the conduct of the proud, sensitive Japanese nation, elated by its triumphs in the war, when suddenly ordered to give up the greatest prize it had secured at such cost? The statesmen who guided its policy—men of whom we had been repeatedly told that they were superficially clever, but unequal to the task of dealing with grave emergencies—resolved to bow to the inevitable. They made the people understand that there was no possible disgrace in giving way to such overwhelming forces, and the nation that had been so long misrepresented to us as incapable of exercising political common-sense, indeed as unable to grapple with any serious problem—that nation submitted with dignity to what was, undoubtedly, an act of injustice and, in the eyes of the Japanese, an almost irreparable blow to the attainment of their cherished object—the paramount position in the Far East.*

So Japan yielded, and the Chinese inhabitants of the Liao-tung Peninsula were handed over, in the name of Civilisation, to their former oppressors, who were not likely to be inclined to any particular leniency towards people who had fraternised with the enemy, and had petitioned him to remain in the country for good. These poor folk seemed destined to lead a sort of shuttlecock existence, for they had scarcely time to settle down to the old, miserable life once more, toiling desperately to amass what they had to struggle quite as desperately to keep safe from the claws of the Mandarins, when they were turned over to new masters, and again in the name of Civilisation. Germany, in order to suit certain exigencies of home politics, claimed her share of the international plunder rather prematurely, Russia had to follow suit, and seized Port Arthur. The "Peace of the Far East" could

---

* It is interesting to reflect on the probable behaviour of at least one of the three Allied Powers in a surrender similar to the one Japan was compelled to submit to. How the Boulevards would have rung with cries of " *Nous sommes trahis !* "

be kept much more easily when a police force of twelve
thousand Russian soldiers were snugly ensconced in the
great stronghold. As to the "Balance of Power," *that*
was all right—only a slight readjustment of the scales,
just the heavy swords of Russia and her Allies thrown
into the one from which the weight of British paramount
influence had been unceremoniously removed. And Japan?
Japan was told to be good, and to run away and play
with her nice new toy, Formosa, or romp about all by
herself in Korea, and not to trouble herself with what
the "grown-ups" were doing and, if she were *very* good
—well, she would see *what* she would see! But Civilisation got to work without delay in the new Russian
"Sphere of Influence."   She began, of course, by turning
the majority of the inhabitants out of Port Arthur—Civilisation generally does begin by turning somebody out of
house and home—she had a new three-tailed thong fitted
to her *Plet*, for she was a Russian Civilisation, and she
proceeded to "negociate" for the "purchase" of land
for the purposes of her railway. It is rumoured that some
of her bargains were rather of the nature of those concluded by the Transport "Coolies" who "bought" the
gorgeous robes at Kin-chau, and the poor Chinese of
Liao-tung sighed for the Japanese Civil Commissioner.

If the civilians of the districts temporarily occupied by
Japan had cause to be grateful to their conquerors, the
Chinese who fell into their hands as prisoners of war,
wounded or unscathed, and those who remained in Japan
during the conflict, had still greater reason to be thankful.
The latter remained practically unmolested, in person and
property, throughout the war, amply shielded by the
orders of the Japanese Government enjoining that these
numerous settlers should be respected, orders that were
scrupulously obeyed by the great bulk of the population.
The Government of the United States had offered to act
as their protector during the war, but the Japanese
Government had protested that it was fully able to shield

them from harm, and the result proved the truth of its assertion. The German residents who had to fly from France in 1870 were not so fortunate as the Chinese settlers in the ports of Japan during the war against their country, nor were the United States a perfectly safe country for Spaniards to inhabit during the height of the "spy fever" in the spring and summer of 1898.

The treatment by the Japanese of their unwounded Chinese prisoners was exceedingly humane. When the first batch of them reached Tōkio, the Prefect of Police of the Metropolis issued a proclamation reminding the inhabitants, and especially the younger generation, of the respect due to vanquished foes. Great crowds assembled to see the prisoners pass, but not an unseemly word was uttered. So comfortable were these Chinese "Braves" during their captivity that many of them were loth to return to China at the close of the war. In the depositions made before Her Britannic Majesty's Consul at Nagasaki, on 4th August, 1894, by Captain Galsworthy, of the British steamship *Kowshing* (the transport, chartered by the Chinese from the Indo-China Steam Navigation Company, sunk, with over a thousand Chinese troops on board, by the Japanese cruiser *Naniwa*, off Shopeiul Island, in the Korean Archipelago, on 25th July, 1894), and by his Chief-Officer, Mr. L. H. Tamplin, we have accurate and absolutely unimpeachable testimony to the treatment meted out to their prisoners by the Japanese. Both these British sailors concur in expressing their thanks for "every care and attention necessary for their comfort" received during their detention by the Japanese naval authorities. Lest it may be thought that they owed this considerate treatment to their nationality, or to their undefined status as "detained persons," not actually prisoners of war, I transcribe the following "P.S.," appended by Chief-Officer Tamplin to his account of the destruction of the *Kowshing* and of his detention :—

"I wish to add that the Chinese crew and officers of

the *Tsao-Kiang* were being treated with every care during
our stay at Sasebo, and the Danish gentleman, Mühlen-
steth (*sic*), had the same attention that we had. · The
Chinese and the Dane had all their personal property
with them."

The *Tsao-Kiang* was a Chinese despatch-boat, captured
on ·25th July, 1894, by the cruiser *Akitsushima*. Her
officers and crew, about sixty in all, were sent to Sasebo,
the Imperial naval station in the Island of Kyū-shū, in
the transport *Yayeyama*, together with Captain Galsworthy,
Mr. Tamplin, Lucas Evangelista (a native of Manila, a
Quartermaster of the *Kowshing*, who had been wounded
in the neck by a bullet from the rifle of an infuriated
Chinese, was picked up by a boat from the *Naniwa*
and "immediately treated by the medical staff on board"),
and a Danish electrician, named Mühlenstedt, who had
been taken prisoner at the capture of the *Tsao-Kiang*. A
few entries, taken at random from Chief-Officer Tamplin's
diary, will show that "detention" in the custody of
Japanese naval officers was not a very hard lot. Mr.
Tamplin writes : "We were very well treated" (on board
the *Naniwa*, whose boats had saved him and his captain
from drowning, and from the bullets of the Chinese
soldiers, maddened by despair when they felt the *Kowshing* sinking under them), "dry clothes and food being
given to us, and even the sailors bringing presents of
sweet biscuits and things for us to eat. . . . · The
officers and men of the *Naniwa* were continuous in their
efforts to give us all they could and to make things
pleasant for us as far as lay in their power. . . . Clothes
made on board were provided for us, and at noon" (on
the 26th July) "we were transferred to the *Yayeyama*,
the crew of· the *Naniwa* waving us farewell. On getting
on board the *Yayeyama*, Captain Hirayama received us
very kindly and told us to make ourselves at home. . . .
We were berthed in the captain's own cabin, and the
officers joined in making us welcome, inviting us to the

ward-room and offering us clothes and other necessaries."
On arrival at Sasebo, on 28th July, "we were introduced
to Lieutenant C. Tamari, Admiral's A.D.C., and taken with
him in his steam-launch to the jetty. We were then
conducted to the hospital, where a room was prepared
for us on the ground floor. Lieutenant Tamari gave us
to understand that anything that we could ask for should
be supplied. . . . Tailor and bootmaker were in attendance; soap, towels, and all toilet requisites were sent.
Beer and claret, cigars, etc., and anything that we fancied
would be sent for from Nagasaki. . . . Numbers of officers
visited us and expressed their sympathy .with us for the
loss of our comrades, and also for our unavoidable detention . . . 29th July: Continued round of visitors, bringing
flowers, eggs, and offers of various things . . . 30th July:
Passed in the same way, every attention being paid to
our comfort . . . 3rd August: Lieutenant Tamari called
with a letter from Rear-Admiral Y. Shibayama, giving us
our freedom, etc., to make arrangements for our departure.
We called, by invitation, on the Admiral in the afternoon,
and thanked him for the care and attention paid to us
by all. Many officers called in the evening to congratu-
late us. 4th August: The Government tender *Sasebo-
Maru* was placed at our disposal, and, with many fare-
wells, left with Lieutenant Tamari for Nagasaki, where we
arrived at 1.30 p.m., and were met by the Superintendent
of Water Police and the Superintendent of Police, tendering
their cards with offers of assistance."

Evidently, "detention" in the hands of the Japanese
naval authorities is not a bad way of spending a week or
so! I have devoted so much space to this subject because
it is in connection with the sinking of the *Kowshing* that
a very grave charge of inhumanity was brought, at the
time, against Captain (now Rear-Admiral) Tōgō, of the
Naniwa, and his officers and crew. As the character of
the whole Japanese Navy is at stake under such an
accusation, the circumstances require investigation. It has

been alleged that the Japanese, whilst doing their best to rescue the *Kowshing's* European officers and Manila Tagal Quartermasters, made absolutely no attempt to save any of the drowning Chinese, who perished by hundreds. It has been, further, maintained that the Japanese in the *Naniwa* continued to rake the *Kowshing's* decks and to pour a hail of bullets, from the machine-guns in their tops and from small-arms, on to the sea around the doomed ship whilst she was sinking. Under ordinary conditions of naval warfare, such conduct would have been barbarous, but in this case the Chinese themselves behaved in a manner that rendered the usages of war, as recognised amongst civilised nations, impossible of application. The Chinese soldiers, more than a thousand in number, panic-stricken and frantic, kept up a heavy rifle-fire from the ports and the deck, aiming not only at the *Naniwa's* boats, but at the *Kowshing's* European officers and *at their own comrades* who had jumped overboard, this insane firing continuing until the ship disappeared beneath the waves. By the rules of war, an enemy may lawfully be destroyed if he persist in resistance, and the *Naniwa* was justified in returning the fire as long as the Chinese continued to shoot. Had they ceased firing and surrendered, their lives would, undoubtedly, have been spared.

At the surrender of Wei-hai-wei, on 14th February, 1895, a large number of its gallant defenders, both naval and military—they deserved the epithet "gallant," for, placed between the Japanese and the deep sea, they had fought, for a time, like wild cats—fell into the hands of the victors. By Article II. of the Capitulation, the officers (213 Naval Officers and Cadets, and 40 Military Officers), and the very mixed body of "Foreign Naval and Military Advisers" in Chinese employ, were released on parole, and, by Article III., the 2,871 Warrant Officers, Petty Officers, Seamen, and Stokers, and the 2,000 rank and file of the Army, were disarmed, and were marched, under Japanese military escort, beyond the lines of the fortress,

J

taking their personal property with them, and were allowed to go free. This was a very wise course for the Japanese to pursue; the war being nearly at an end, it would have caused unnecessary trouble and expense to have taken the five thousand prisoners to Japan for the short time remaining before the conclusion of the Treaty of Peace, and the disbanded soldiers and sailors, dispersing to their homes, spread tales of their sufferings during the siege, and of Japanese prowess, that convinced the population of the futility of further resistance. In the letter intimating the surrender of the fleet and forts, addressed to Admiral Itō, on 12th February, 1895, by Admiral Ting —the last letter written by that gallant man, who committed suicide in his cabin, the same day, by swallowing a large dose of opium—the Chinese commander made the characteristic request that his men should be allowed a couple of days' time, before the Japanese took possession, "to exchange their uniforms for travelling garments." It must not be imagined that the Chinese warriors wanted to return to civil life clad in the local equivalent of "tourist suits;" their chief anxiety was to don anything that would conceal, until they reached their homes, the fact of their having served in the war. The Imperial uniform does not at any time command respect nor gain popularity for its wearers in China, and less than ever during a disastrous campaign.

To prove that humanity towards their prisoners was not confined to the officers and men of the Japanese Navy, I will cite an instance of merciful conduct which does honour to the kind heart of Field-Marshal Count Ōyama, the Commander-in-Chief of the Second Army Corps, operating in the Liao-tung Peninsula.* On the evening

---

* The military title of the Commanders-in-Chief of the Japanese Army Corps, and of the Chief of the General Staff at the Imperial Headquarters, is usually translated by "Field-Marshal," but it really corresponds to the British rank of "General," being the highest of the three classes into which General Officers are divided in the Japanese as in Occidental

of the 27th November, 1894, six days after the capture of Port Arthur, Marshal Ōyama was inspecting the lines in a heavy downpour that had soaked everything not under cover. Passing by a dismantled house, he noticed a group of Chinese prisoners standing, huddled together in shivering misery, under the eaves, the rain dripping from the roof on to their ill-clad bodies. Calling one of his *Aides-de-Camp*, the Field-Marshal said : "Those, too, are men. Their lives are more valuable than those of my horses. Take these men quickly to my stables, turn my horses out—they must take their chance in the rain—and see that the prisoners are warmly sheltered." The good Count's orders were immediately executed, much to the delight of the Chinese, who, when it had been explained to them to whom they were indebted, shed tears of gratitude, and were profuse in their thanks. And this humane action proceeded, be it remembered, from a commander some of whose soldiers had been ripped open as they lay wounded on the battlefield, stones and rubbish being poured into their disembowelled bodies, perhaps by the very men to whom he was extending his mercy ; at all events, by Chinese soldiery.

With the one exception of the outburst of avenging fury at Port Arthur, the Japanese, indeed, returned good for evil, throughout the war, in the matter of the treatment of the enemy's wounded. Their perfectly-equipped hospitals were often crowded with wounded Chinese, who received the same skilful attention, the same tender nursing, as the Japanese. The Chinese hospitals were not crowded with Japanese wounded, for the simple reason that there were no Chinese hospitals. To the Chinese, a wounded comrade appears merely an encumbrance, to be stripped of his arms, accoutrements and uniform, and left to die where he fell. "CHANG Ha-hsin is down. Who shot him ?" one "Brave" would ask another. "The

armies. (General, commanding an Army Corps ; Lieutenant-General, commanding a Division, and Major-General, commanding a Brigade)

Wo-jên" ("the Dwarfs," the contemptuous term employed by the Emperor of China in his proclamations during the war when referring to the Japanese). "*A-Yaw!* Very well, then let the *Wo-jên* look after him!" And look after him they did, picking him up from the blood-stained snow, bearing him carefully to their dressing-station, and then to their clean, airy field-hospital, where calm, skilful "Dwarf" surgeons operated, and then on to their great, roomy, tidy base-hospital, where gentle "Dwarf" nurses tended him with tiny, soft hands. Well might he think, as many Chinese did, that the Japanese bullet had killed him outright, for was this not Paradise? Surely those gentle women, with the low, sweet voices and the kind eyes, must be the angels who sprinkle the lotus with nectar in the Buddhist Heaven, tending the glorious buds, in each of which a tiny Baby-Buddha nestles? This must be the commencement of a new, and happier, existence— plenty of food, nothing to do, clean clothes and a bright, airy palace to live in! Thus the convalescent Chinese pondered, and he was, as a rule, quickly convalescent, for the wounds of all Far Eastern people heal with astonishing rapidity, owing to their living chiefly on a vegetarian diet— or, at all events, eating but little meat—and to their drinking, as a rule, only a moderate quantity of intoxicating liquor, and that not of a very injurious nature. It is the unfortunate fact of his being, in so many cases, too "beefy," and saturated with much poisonous alcoholic drink of the worst quality—often with a poison still more terrible permeating his system—that makes the British soldier die of wounds a Far Eastern would recover from within a month.

If the wounded Chinese was not absolutely beyond human help his cure was almost a matter of certainty, for of all the marvels Japan exhibited to an astonished world during the war the greatest was her Medical Service, afloat and ashore. Surgeon-Major-General Taylor, of the Royal Medical Corps, was sent, when a Surgeon-

Colonel, by the British Government to watch the working
of the Japanese Medical Service in the field, and was
attached to Headquarters at the seat of war. In a
lecture he delivered, soon after his return, before the
Military Society at Aldershot, he stated that "there was
only one word that would adequately describe the Medical
Services of the Japanese Navy and Army during the
war, and that word was—perfection. Not a life was lost,"
he added, "on the Japanese side that the Medical Service
could have saved."

The admirable arrangements for keeping the troops at
the front in good health, and for saving their lives and
alleviating their sufferings when sick or wounded, were
due not only to the perfect organisation of the Army
Medical Service, adapted from the German model, and of
the Naval Medical Department, originally formed and
trained under British inspiration, but also to the well-
directed efforts of the Red Cross Society of Japan. This
noble organisation, with a membership of over two hundred
thousand, with branches in every part of the Empire,
and an annual income of more than half a million *Yen*,
stands under the immediate and active patronage of the
Imperial Family, ever foremost in good works. During
the war it expended nearly four hundred thousand *Yen* on
its merciful work,* sending three hospital-parties, consisting
of surgeons, dressers, apothecaries, matrons, trained nurses,
accountants, clerks, porters, cooks, and even—grim detail
—"instrument sharpeners," to the seat of war, each party
being fully equipped with every requisite for the treatment of two hundred patients. Voluntary contributions
poured into the Society's treasury, and enabled it to
establish auxiliary hospitals and sanatoria for the convalescent in Japan, thus affording valuable aid to the
hard-worked staff of the regular Naval and Military Sani-

---

* The exact amount was 386,971 *Yen*, 40 *Sen*. The *Yen*, or Japanese
silver dollar, is divided into 100 *Sen*, or cents, of 10 *Rin* each. The average
value of the silver *Yen* throughout 1898 was 2 shillings.

tary Services. At these Red Cross Hospitals no fewer than 1,484 *Chinese* wounded were treated and discharged as cured. Besides the work appertaining more especially to the sphere of action of a Society for the Relief of the Sick and Wounded, the Red Cross Society (*Seki-jū-ji-sha*) constituted itself the organiser of the feelings of enthusiastic sympathy for those who were fighting for Japan that animated the whole population. It gave every detachment departing for the seat of war a warm "send off," and took a great part in arranging the jubilant receptions that awaited the warriors on their triumphal home-coming. Moreover, during the war, it undertook the free conveyance and delivery of the fifty thousand packages of gifts sent to the troops in the field, and of the six thousand seven hundred similar parcels forwarded to the men serving afloat—gifts of every imaginable article likely to add to the comfort of the gallant fellows, lovingly presented not only by relatives but by the general public, the idea of these "love-gifts," suggested by the *Liebesgaben* sent to the German troops in 1870–71, having taken firm root amongst all classes in Japan.

The Chinese, although completely ignorant of the Red Cross and of its sacred mission—China has not subscribed to the Geneva Convention, to which Japan adhered in 1886, and her "Braves" look upon its badge merely as a good mark to fire at, being distinctive and easy to hit— were not entirely without "love-gifts" of their own, if a decree published in the *Peking Gazette* was ever carried out. This Imperial Order was to the effect that Her Majesty the Empress Dowager, having heard of the terrible hardships undergone by the troops guarding the approaches to the August Capital from the contemptible and impudent "Dwarfs," whom they were about to chastise, felt moved by deep compassion, and had ordered the disbursement of a large sum from her Privy Purse for the purchase of a quantity of "yellow wine" (*hoang-chiu*)—a liquor made from the yellow, glutinous millet, and equal in alcoholic

NEW JAPAN.

Her Majesty the Empress presiding at a Meeting of the Council of the Ladies' Branch of the Red Cross Society of Japan Making Bandages for the Wounded (1895).

Drawn by Kubota Beisen.

strength to ordinary claret, and always drunk warm—
wherewith the "Braves" shivering on the icy hills of
the North-East, and round the walls of Peking, might
warm their numbed bodies and cheer their hearts. To
anyone who is acquainted with Chinese official methods
it seems highly probable that the poor "Braves" never
drank that *hoang-chiu*, indeed, that they never even
"looked upon it" when it was yellow or any other
colour, but that somebody or other about the Palace had
an appreciable increase of income at about that time, a
benefit likely to have been enjoyed, in a minor degree,
by several colleagues and subordinates, the rewards of
enterprise being as much sub-divided amongst Peking
Mandarins as amongst London "promoters" and their
friends.

Some of Japan's Occidental detractors have alleged
that the wonderful success of the Red Cross movement
in Japan, the flow of contributions from rich and poor—
often from the very poor—the large, admirably-managed
Permanent Central Hospital of the Society at Shibuya, a
suburb of Tōkio, the numerous Ambulance Classes for the
instruction of both sexes in "First Aid to the Injured,"
the devotion of the surgeons and nurses in the war, and
the zeal with which thousands of Japanese ladies, following the example set by the Empress, made lint and
bandages (six thousand bandages were made by her
Imperial Majesty, the Princesses, and the Ladies of the
Palace, and sent to the seat of war, through the Society,
in October, 1894)—that all this benevolent activity is
really foreign to the Japanese character, and partook, at
least during the conflict, of the nature of a fashionable
"craze," destined, besides, to look well in the eyes of
Occidentals. How unjust such an accusation is can be
readily proved by pointing to the grand work done by
the Red Cross Society in time of peace, both before the
war—in the relief, for instance, of the sufferers through
the eruption of the volcano Bandai San on 15th July,

1888 (when 461 lives were lost, and twenty-seven square miles devastated by boiling mud and ashes)—and after. In 1891, the Society already had experience of relief work on a large scale amongst the eighteen thousand and nine hundred people who were more or less severely wounded in the earthquake ot October 28th in the Provinces of Mino and of Owari, when more than seven thousand were killed outright. The populous towns of Gifu and Ōgaki were wrecked, and two smaller ones, Kasamatsu and Takegahana, were completely destroyed, great fires, originating, as is usually the case after an earthquake in Japan, amongst the ruins of the houses, raging amidst the heaps of wood and paper—the chief building materials of the country—and devouring what the shock had levelled with the ground. Altogether, nearly one hundred and thirty thousand houses were destroyed; great cast-iron piers supporting railway bridges were snapped like carrots; rails were left suspended in mid-air through the subsidence of embankments; in other places the railway was transformed into a "switchback" line; in others, again, the track was curiously bent into lateral serpentine undulations. Mountains slipped and fell into valleys, damming up rivers, and thus causing devastating floods, at a later period, to complete the havoc made by earthquake and fire. Every building left standing in the ravaged Provinces seemed tottering to ruin, except the grand old Castle of Nagoya, with the great dolphins of gold perched on either gable of its five-storied keep.* The solid masonry of the old

---

* These beautiful finials of the highest roof in the Castle of Nagoya are dolphins, nearly nine feet high, made of gold, in 1610, at the cost of the famous general, KATŌ Kiyomasa, who built the *tenshu*, or keep They are valued, according to that excellent work *Murray's Handbook for Travellers in Japan*, by Professor Basil Hall Chamberlain and W. B Mason, at 180,000 *Yen* One of the pair has been a great traveller and has experienced vicissitudes unusual in the quiet existence of a golden dolphin He had the honour of being sent by the Imperial Government all the way to Vienna, to form the central attraction in the Japanese Section of the International Exhibition of 1873, and the misfortune to suffer shipwreck on the homeward voyage, when the *Messageries Maritimes*

feudal castles, both at Nagoya (the fourth city of the Empire) and at Ōgaki (close to the centre of seismic disturbance) showed hardly any traces of the earthquake. Besides the castles, two things stood fast and firm in the devastated region—the wonderful, uncomplaining patience of the sufferers, and the merciful help of the Red Cross Society's Relief Corps. On receipt of the news of the disaster, the Empress immediately set the Society's organisation in motion. In an incredibly short space of time a completely-equipped Hospital Corps was sent to the scene of the catastrophe. It treated 4,600 sufferers, who had been injured seriously enough to necessitate their entering the Field Hospitals, and of this large number only *eleven* died of their wounds or burns. The Corps also distributed relief to the starving people and ministered to the immediate wants of the thousands of widows, of orphans, and of forlorn old folks.

I have mentioned the services rendered during the war in Korea, in Manchuria, in China, and in Formosa, by the sixteen hundred devoted workers equipped by the Red Cross Society, twenty-five of whom succumbed to disease and exposure in the Arctic cold of Manchuria and Northern China, or the steamy heat of the fever-stricken Formosan jungle. The Red Cross Formosan Hospital Corps, the last in the field, had but recently returned from that island when another, and a most urgent, call was made on the Society's zeal. On the evening of the 15th of June, 1896, the greatest natural catastrophe of recent -times in the Far East overwhelmed the North-Eastern coasts of Japan. The sea, impelled, probably, by a seismic convulsion on the bed of the Northern Pacific,

steamship *Nil* foundered. He was saved, with great difficulty, after a prolonged sojourn at the bottom of the China Sea, and reinstated in the exalted position he has so well occupied for nearly three centuries. It is rumoured that he occasionally irritates his companion across the roof— the other *Kinno shachihoko*—by loudly whistling rattling marches and dreamy waltzes learnt in the *Kaiserstadt*, or holding forth, at great length, on the manifold charms of the lively *Wiener Mädel* rose in a huge tidal wave, rushing inland, with awful speed, engulfing whole districts. Nearly *thirty thousand lives* were lost, and more than seven thousand people were injured, whilst many thousands were rendered home-less and deprived of all means of support. Here again the Red Cross Society was the means of saving thousands who would otherwise have perished miserably. Donations for the noble work of rescue poured in from all sides, and it does honour to the Japan Society that, immediately on receipt of the news of the appalling disaster, it commenced to raise a fund for the relief of the sufferers.* In the space of less than three weeks, the Society collected £3,895, and remitted that amount, by telegraph, by instal-ments (the first one, of a thousand pounds, on the morrow of the opening of the fund) to Japan, through the inter-mediary of the British Minister in Japan and the Japanese Minister in London. This prompt action on the part of Japan's friends in Great Britain, and the fact that the amount of their donation was almost three times as large as the total contributed from all the other countries of Europe, were much appreciated by the Japanese, who showed their gratitude in a very practical manner by subscribing liberally, according to their means, to the fund for the relief of the sufferers from the great famine in India in 1897.

How honestly, how impartially and practically, the funds for the relief of the sufferers from the tidal wave were administered, may be gathered from the testimony of many eye-witnesses, amongst others that of Monseigneur Berlioz, the Roman Catholic Bishop in Northern Japan, who wrote, at the time, to express his admiration of the promptness, the energy and the fairness with which the relief was distributed, and of the excellent, practical measures taken by the Japanese authorities immediately

* A public meeting, convened, at the Society's request, by the Lord Mayor of London, who presided, was held at the Mansion House, and the fund to be raised was placed under the control of the Society's Council as a Committee.

after the cataclysm. I will cite two instances of the spirit in which the relief was received by the sufferers. In one village, near Kamaishi, money was given to the few survivors of the Fishermen's Guild, to enable them to purchase a boat, nets and tackle. A month later, they returned about a third of the sum to the Relief Commissioner, stating that they had procured what they required at smaller cost than they anticipated. At a hamlet in the same district some miserably poor folk, the survivors of an industrious population who earned a precarious livelihood by cultivating small patches amongst the rugged mountains near the sea, and by fishing, were visited by the Relief Corps of the Red Cross Society. Of one large family the sole survivor was found to be an old woman ninety years of age ; of another, a baby two months old. Houses and boats had all been swept away, in a moment, with nine-tenths of the inhabitants. The Relief Corps at once commenced a liberal distribution of food, clothing, and money for the purchase of farming implements, boats and nets. The Headman of the little village, acting as spokesman for the rest, requested that the relief tendered to them be reduced in quantity, "as the people in the next village were in a worse plight, and needed help more than they did." Honorary Secretaries of Occidental relief funds, and Almoners of charities, please note—and compare !

I shall now relate a few instances of the behaviour of the Japanese Medical Staff during the warfare at sea, because a modern naval action, with its accumulation of horrors, is calculated to test to the utmost the efficiency and the devotion to duty of those whose work is carried on under the greatest difficulties and earns the smallest meed of glory. Moreover, the three episodes of the great sea-fight off the Yalu that I have selected out of many throw a vivid light on typical features of the Japanese character. So I shall tell the plain, unvarnished tale of three MEN, and how they bore themselves in the fierce battle.

The first of the three is Inspector of Hospitals and Fleets KAWAMURA Hōshū, M.D., the Principal Medical Officer of Vice-Admiral Itō's squadron.   When, at three minutes past noon on the seventeenth of September, 1894, the Japanese naval ensign was hoisted at the main on the flagship *Matsushima*, as the signal to engage, every officer and man stood at his post clad in the "rig of the day," not, however, as might have been expected, in the oldest clothing compatible with the requirements of the Dress Regulations, but in his "Number One" garments, hastily donned in accordance with the knightly tradition of Old Japan, that a warrior should face death in his best apparel.* As the squadron steamed towards the enemy's centre, reserving its fire, in spite of the provocative cannonade directed against it, until well within three thousand yards' range, Inspector Kawamura and his staff stood to their quarters at the operating tables in the cockpit.

At 2.30 p.m., the *Matsushima* being hotly engaged with Admiral Ting's flagship, the great battleship *Ting-yuen*—"made," and very well made, "in Germany," and ultimately torpedoed by the Japanese at Wei-hai-wei—wounded men began to be carried below, and the Medical Staff were soon busy. Whilst they were at their work, a shell from one of the heavy guns of the ironclad *Chen-yuen*—that had come to the assistance of her sister-ship, the *Ting-yuen*, now on fire, and stood by her bravely—entered the *Matsushima* at the bow, and burst, shattering a gun and making havoc on the lower deck, involving in the ruin the surgery where the doctors were operating. The deck was burst open beneath their feet, and Dr. Kawamura was thrown with tremendous force against the deck above. Falling amongst the wreck of the surgery, he lay stunned for a while. On regaining consciousness, trembling violently from the shock, he crawled through

* In our own Royal Navy it used to be the custom for men ordered to abandon a ship, sinking or on fire, to put on their "No. 1 rig," if time permitted, so as to save their most valuable clothes.

the *débris* and was picked up by a Bluejacket, who tried to carry him to a comparatively safe place. The man had not taken his burden many yards when the Inspector, now fully conscious, asked him if he were "not a Seaman-Gunner?" On receiving an affirmative reply, he took the astonished Bluejacket severely to task. "What are you doing away from your station at the gun? Put me down instantly and go back to your post!" he ordered sternly. The man pleaded that he had no station to go to, now that the gun he served had been destroyed by the enemy's shell. "Then your place is at another gun, to fill up some casualty," rejoined the imperturbable Doctor, adding, with the politeness that never leaves a Japanese, be he bleeding from a dozen wounds: "I thank you for your well-meant exertions, but I order you, as your officer, to put me down! There are men properly told off to bear the wounded—the Bandsmen, for instance." The Bluejacket urged that the gallant musicians had fallen in as volunteer gunners, to replace men killed or wounded (and right well they performed their unwonted duty). "Never mind," said the Inspector, "there are the Stewards and the Writers left to attend to the wounded. No fighting man may do so unless specially ordered.* Put me down!" The man reluctantly obeyed, and went off at the double to help at a gun. The Doctor, sitting on the deck, tried to remove his shoes, which were full of blood, his legs and feet being severely wounded by the explosion. The pain caused by the attempt made him lose consciousness a second time. A Sick-Bay Attendant, who had escaped uninjured, now came up, took off the Inspector's shoes and socks, and bore him to the Captain's cabin, which

---

* In the Japanese Army, as well as in the Navy, the modern German rule is strictly followed in this respect. It puts a stop to what has been called "Victoria Cross hunting," and ensures the presence of every combatant where he is most needed—in the fighting line "Been to take a wounded comrade to the rear, sir!" is not accepted as an excuse for absence from the front

had promptly been transformed into a surgery after the wreck of the original cockpit. Regaining consciousness, the Doctor called for a bucket of sea-water. A bucket was let down over the side into the .sea, lashed into foam by the hail of shot and shell, and brought up. Kawamura plunged his feet into it to stop the flow of blood, bandaged them temporarily, and resumed his work of directing the labours of the remaining surgeons and their assistants. I think I am justified in asking the printer to describe him as a MAN, in capital letters.

The next naval medical officer of whom I shall write is my friend Surgeon USUI Hiroshi, of the Imperial Japanese Navy, a member of the Japan Society of London, who was, when an Assistant-Surgeon, the medical officer in charge on board the *Akagi*, a gunboat of 615 tons, with a speed of only twelve knots—the smallest and slowest of Admiral Itō's ships—an armament of one 24-centimetre Krupp gun, one 12-centimetre gun, also from the great works at Essen, and two machine-guns, and a complement of one hundred and twenty-six officers and men—heroes every one of them.

The naval annals of Britain are full of instances ot desperate gallantry against fearful odds, but none more worthy of admiration than the running fight kept up, against overwhelming superiority of numbers, of speed, and of armament, by this plucky little gunboat of Japan's young navy, on the memorable day off the mouth ot the Yalu. The *Akagi*, owing to her slowness, greatly hampered the movements of Vice-Admiral Itō's squadron, and—although every effort was made to afford her and the other slow ships, the *Hiyei* and *Fusō*, and the armed ex-merchantman, *Saikyo-Maru*, all possible protection—she had repeatedly to face the fire of several ot the large Chinese vessels, who singled her out as a presumably easy prey. They had reckoned without their host, for the brave man who commanded her—Commander SAKAMOTO Hachiroda—knew but one way of defence : the best way,

that consists in taking the offensive, and, when they
bore down upon him, he blazed away furiously at the
great Chinese battleships and cruisers, directing his fire, of
course, only to the parts where they were vulnerable.
This gallant officer, who honoured me with his friendship,
was not only brave and skilful, he had great technical
knowledge of his profession, gained, partly, during the
years he had spent in the Russian Navy and, afterwards, as Naval *Attaché* to the Japanese Legation at
St. Petersburg. He was an excellent Russian scholar, and
I well remember how, whilst sharing his countrymen's
not unnatural distrust of Russia's intentions in the Far
East, he used to speak with affectionate and grateful
admiration of his old shipmates in the Tsar's Navy, and
of the charming people who had captivated him, as they
do all strangers who sojourn on the banks of the Neva.
Alas! This brilliant officer, who seemed destined to
render such great services to Japan, was not to see the
close of the battle in which the service he adorned won
undying fame. Early in the action, he had swept the
bridge of the Chinese ironclad *Lai-yuen* with his starboard
guns, killing or wounding all those upon it, and held his
own against the furious onslaught of the enemy's left
wing, delivered at 800 yards. The hail of Chinese shot
and shell was, fortunately, badly directed, or the *Akagi*
must have been destroyed at this stage, but presently the
enemy got the range, and one of his shells burst just over
her, killing Midshipman HASHIGUCHI Kojirō and wounding Lieutenant SASAKI Kōshō, who was immediately
attended to by the Surgeon, Dr. Usui.

The next missile that burst on the *Akagi*, at 1.20, p.m.,
did dire execution. It killed brave Commander Sakamoto
at his post and two Seamen-Gunners at one of the machine
guns, whilst two others were borne below to the Surgeon,
who from this moment was uninterruptedly at work, aided
only by one Hospital Attendant, for the rest of the
engagement. The death of the Commander supplied a

crucial test of the quality that weighs more in the scale of victory than heavy armour or great guns—coolness under fire. Without a moment's hesitation, Lieutenant SATŌ Tetsutarō, the Navigating Officer, took the Commander's place on the bridge, and assumed the command which devolved upon him as the senior surviving officer. As he was calmly directing the little ship's stout fight, a shell, bursting in the engine-room, killed four stokers, wounded a fifth, and cut through a steam-pipe, whilst another shell, almost simultaneously, struck the upper deck, exploded, and killed three Seamen-Gunners.

The *Akagi's* plight was now a desperate one. Clouds of scalding steam from the broken pipe filled the engine-room, and the supply of ammunition to the fore part of the ship was cut off. The Assistant Engineer, ISOBÉ Ichijirō, rushed back into the hissing steam, followed by Petty Officer IWANO Namisuké. Together, they managed to open a port, which allowed egress to some of the scalding vapour, and the Engineer, putting a blanket over his head, approached the broken pipe and succeeded in fastening the blanket over the fracture, thus enabling Chief Engineer Hirabé and his staff to execute temporary repairs so satisfactorily that the vessel's speed was not lowered to any appreciable extent. Shot after shot was, meanwhile, telling on her decks. The wounded had to be removed to the ward-room, and when that became unsafe—splinters flying through it and killing a man as he lay waiting for his turn to have his wounds dressed—the captain's cabin was transformed into a surgery, the dining-table being used as an operating-table. Presently, the Hospital Attendant was wounded, and Dr. Usui had to perform all the operations thereafter without the use of anæsthetics, having no trained man to administer them whilst he plied the knife or the probe. Not a sound escaped the lips of any of his patients, save one, mortally wounded, who gasped: "Has the *Ting-yuen* been sunk yet?" He was told that the Chinese flagship was badly

damaged and on fire. " We have her at last ! " he cried—
and died with a look of exultation.

I have seen a water-colour drawing, by an officer who
was present, representing the upper deck of the gunboat
at this stage of the fight—shambles is the only word to
describe that deck, strewn with bodies and reeking with
blood. Changing her course repeatedly, the plucky ship
fought on valiantly. A shell carried away her mast, from
which the ensign and signals were flying. Instantly, three
Petty Officers, IWANO Namisuké, the same who had rushed
with the Engineer through the escaping steam, UYEDA
Jūtarō, and IKEMOTO Nobuchika, rigged up, on the
remaining stump, the mast of one of the ship's boats as a
jury-mast, from which the flags soon fluttered once more.
At 2.15, a shell again struck the bridge, wounding Lieutenant Satō. Handing over the command of the ship to
Lieutenant MATSUOKA Shūzo, the only remaining combatant officer able to stand, he went below to have his
wound hastily dressed by the Surgeon. As soon as this
was done, he returned to the bridge and resumed command
of the ship. Had Lieutenant Matsuoka been killed, or
disabled, during his brief command, and had Satō's injury
been so serious as to incapacitate him from returning to
duty, the command of the ship would have devolved,
according to the hierarchy of the Japanese Navy, upon
the only available commissioned officer—Assistant-Surgeon
Usui—the Engineer Officers could not be spared from the
engine-room—the world would have been treated to the
novel spectacle of a doctor fighting a ship, and, from what
I know of Dr. Usui, I feel sure he would have quitted
himself as manfully on the bridge as he did in the cockpit.

By this time, the number of men fit for duty had been
terribly reduced. One of the machine-guns was served
by the Signalman, and, during Lieutenant Satō's absence
in the surgery and Lieutenant Matsuoka's command in his
stead, the duties of Gunnery Officer, or Officer of Quarters,
were ably performed by a Leading Seaman-Gunner. At

K

2.20, the *Akagi's* most obstinate adversary, the ironclad *Lai-yuen*, closed to 300 yards. With a desperate effort, the crew of the gunboat's stern-gun poured a rapid fire on the *Lai-yuen*, and succeeded, with a well-aimed shell that struck her deck aft, in setting the great Chinese warship a-blaze. The other Chinese ships went to their consort's assistance, and the gallant little *Akagi*, justly proud of her share in the day's great deeds, drew off to safe quarters to complete the repairs to her steam-pipe, and to give the crew a well-earned rest, and rejoined the flagship at the close of the engagement. Assistant-Surgeon Usui was the only man on board for whom there was no rest on that day, nor for many days to come. The *Akagi* had lost two officers and nine men killed, and had two officers and twelve men wounded, most of them severely ; a total of twenty-five casualties out of a complement of one hundred and twenty-six. The Doctor was promoted to Surgeon, received the decoration "For Valour,"* and was asked what special favour he would desire from the Imperial Government. His answer was: "To be sent to London, for a couple of years' study at St. Thomas's Hospital." His desire was fulfilled. Another MAN, I trow !

One more true tale of the great sea-fight, and I shall have done with scenes of bloodshed. In the thick of the fight, the *Hiyei* was penetrated by a Chinese shell, which exploded in the ward-room, transformed into a hospital, where the medical staff, assisted by the Paymaster and his Clerks, were ministering to the numerous wounded. Staff-Surgeon Miyaké (the ship's principal medical officer), Paymaster Ishizaka, and several of the wounded lying in the ward-room were killed, and the whole medical staff killed or wounded. The place was filled with the burning, acrid fumes of the high explosive ; heartrending groans arose from the confused mass of wreckage. Suddenly, a

---

* The Japanese equivalent of the Victoria Cross—the *Kin-shi*, or " Golden Hawk."

figure started up from a dark corner and staggered to its feet. Could *that* be a man? The face was mangled and distorted beyond recognition, the hair and eyebrows burnt off, but the husky voice was still audible that addressed the men who had rushed down from the upper deck to render assistance. And the voice said: "I am First-Class Hospital Attendant MIYASHITA Sukejirō, and sorely wounded. My poor body is now useless, but my mind is still clear. I can tell you, who are unskilled in surgery, what to do, and how to dress the wounds of these others. The antiseptics are over there, in that locker. There is not much of them left, even if the explosion has not destroyed them. Please use them sparingly." And, scarcely able to stand, he began to direct them how to attend to the horribly mangled men who lay on the deck all round. Lieutenant-Commander SAKAMOTO Toshi-atsu, filled with admiration at the Petty Officer's devotion, addressed him thus: "Your words and bearing prove you to be a truly gallant man, and a loyal subject of our Emperor. Should this day be your last, I shall see to it that your noble devotion be known all over Japan." Miyashita, almost blinded by the explosion, replied, attempting to salute: "Are you Commander Sakamoto? You see how that shell has served me. Well, I am quite willing to die, if die I must; but what vexes me is that my hands and feet are now useless, so that I cannot do my duty whilst there is life in me." With clenched teeth and panting breath, suffering tortures, he still tried to find instruments, bandages and drugs for the improvised hospital ward to which the survivors were being removed, but the Lieutenant-Commander ordered him to consider himself off duty, and insisted on his lying down. He was landed at Sasebo several days after, with the other wounded who could be moved, and it is pleasing to know that he recovered at the Naval Hospital there so completely that he was able to return to duty. Truly, again, a MAN!

I have related the tale of the steadfastness of three

Japanese men; it is only right that I should state that
the records of the war-time teem with instances of heroism
on the part of Japanese women. Their brave hearts and
staunch patriotism did not lead them to deeds of valour
in actual fighting—although many volunteered for the
army and were sorely grieved at their services being
refused—but to serve their beloved country in the many
ways open to their sex. Of their services as nurses in
the field, and in hospitals at home, I have already
spoken, also of their activity in making bandages, and
charpie, but these occupations were, of course, only
possible for a minority of the women of Japan. One
way of serving the national cause was within the reach
of all of them, and all, without exception, adopted it—
they encouraged their relatives leaving for the front, many
worked hard and uncomplainingly to keep the little home
together whilst the husband was away fighting; they sent
comforts of all kinds, lovingly prepared, to the warriors in
the field or at sea, and if the dread news came that a
loved one would never return, they bore their sorrow
with noble resignation. There were many like that grand
old dame, whose husband and eldest son were killed in
action, whilst her only other son died of sickness in a
field-hospital, and who, when the first two bereavements
were announced to her, shed not a tear. But when the
news of her second son's death was broken to her, as gently
as might be, by an officer home from the seat of war,
she wept, because, she said, she had no other sons to
send out to die for the Emperor and for Japan.

In all the good works done by the women of Japan
during those months of national stress their natural leader,
the Empress, gave a noble example. It was this gracious
lady, as kind-hearted and gentle as she is graceful and
accomplished, who took the lead in every movement for
the mitigation of the horrors of war. She it was who
gladdened the wounded and the sick by her periodical
visits to the hospitals, where not only her own country-

men but enemies, too, were being tenderly nursed, and it was her womanly heart that prompted the humane action of the Japanese authorities, who, when articulated artificial limbs, made, and beautifully made, in Japan, were given to those of the Emperor's soldiers and sailors who had been maimed in the war, included in the distribution those Chinese prisoners who had undergone amputation in Japanese hospitals. If that be not practical Christianity, it seems to me a very good working imitation.

Finally, to give an insight into the feelings of chivalry that can move the Japanese even in these prosaic days, and at a time when they might well have been exasperated by the unexpectedly protracted resistance of their foes, I shall give some account of Vice-Admiral Itō's relations with Vice-Admiral Ting, and of his conduct on being informed of his gallant adversary's death.

The relations between the opponent leaders will be best understood, and the character of the great Japanese Admiral most clearly revealed, by the perusal of the letter he sent to Admiral Ting on the 25th of January, 1895, five days before the commencement of the actual attack on Wei-hai-wei. This document is of such importance as to warrant its reproduction unabridged. These are the words of Itō Sukéhirō, Vice-Admiral, and Commander-in-Chief of the Imperial Japanese squadron off Wei-hai-wei :—

"I have the honour to address this letter to your Excellency. The vicissitudes of the times have made us enemies. It is a misfortune. Yet it is our countries that are at war. There need be no hostility between individuals. The friendship that formerly existed between you and me is as warm as ever to-day. Let it not be supposed that in writing this letter I am actuated by any idle purpose of urging you to surrender. The actors in great affairs often err; the onlookers see the truth. Instead of calmly deliberating what course of procedure on his own part is best for his country, best for himself, a man sometimes allows himself to be swayed by the task in which he is actually engaged, and takes a mistaken view; is it not then the duty of his friends to advise him and to turn his thoughts into the right channel? I address myself to you from motives of genuine friendship, and I pray you to appreciate them.

What is the origin of the repeated disasters that have befallen the Chinese arms? There is, I think, little difficulty in discovering the true reason if one look for it calmly and intelligently. Your discernment has, doubtless, shown you the cause. It is not the fault of one man that has brought China into the position she now occupies; the blame rests with the errors of the Government that has long administered her affairs. She selects her servants by competitive examination, and literary attainments are the test. Thus it results that her officials, the repositories of administrative power, are all literates, and that literature is honoured above everything. Her practice in this respect is as uniform to-day as it was a thousand years ago. It is not necessarily a defective system, nor does it necessarily produce a bad Government. But a country can never preserve its independence in practice by such means. For you know well what troubles Japan had to encounter thirty years ago, what perils she had to surmount. She owes her preservation and her integrity to-day wholly to the fact that she then broke away from the old and attached herself to the new. In the case of your country also, that must be the cardinal course at present; if you adopt it, I venture to say that you are safe; if you reject it, you cannot escape destruction.

"In a contest with Japan, it has long been fated that you should witness results such as are now before you. Can it be the duty of faithful subjects of the Empire, men really solicitous for its welfare, to swim idly with the tide now sweeping over the country by the decree of an ancient fate, making no effort to stem it? A country with a history running back thousands of years, and territories stretching tens of thousands of miles, the oldest Empire in the world, can it be an easy task to accomplish for such a country a work of restoration, placing its foundation on a permanently solid basis? A single pillar cannot prevent the fall of a great edifice. Is there any latitude for choice between the impossible and the disadvantageous? To hand over squadrons to the foe, to surrender a whole army to an enemy, these are mere bagatelles compared with the fate of a nation. By whatever reputation a Japanese warrior may possess in the eyes of the world, I vow that I believe your wisest course is to come to Japan and wait there until the fortunes of your country are again in the ascendant, and until the time arrives when your services will be again needed. Hear these words of your true friend. Need I remind you that the annals of history contain many names of men who have removed a stain from their names and lived to perform great deeds? MacMahon, of France, having surrendered and passed over into the enemy's country, came back after a time and assisted in reforming the French administration, the French not only forgetting his disgrace but even elevating him to the post of President. Similarly, Osman

Pasha, after losing the fortifications at Plevna, and being himself captured, came home to Turkey, where he rose to be Minister of War, and acquired a high reputation in connection with his military reforms. If you come to Japan, I can assure of the good treatment you will receive, and of the Emperor's favour. Not only has His Majesty pardoned subjects of his own who had raised the standard of rebellion, but he has rewarded their talents by elevating them to positions of high trust, as in the case of Admiral Enomoto, now a member of the Cabinet, and of OTORI Keisuké, a Councillor of State. There are many such instances. In the case of men of note who are not His Majesty's subjects, his magnanimous treatment of them would certainly be even more marked. The great question that you have now to determine is whether you will throw in your lot with a country that you see falling to ruin, and be involved in a result inevitable under unchanged administrative circumstances, or whether you will preserve the strength that remains to you and evolve another plan hereafter. It has generally been the habit of warriors of your country to use haughty and rough language in addressing their foes, but I address this letter to you from motives of pure friendship, and I entreat you to credit my sincerity. If happily, reading these words, you accept my counsel, I shall, with your permission, address some further remarks to you on the subject of giving practical effect to the idea.

(Signed) " ITŌ Sukéhirō,

" Vice-Admiral, Commander-in-Chief of His Imperial

" Japanese Majesty's Squadron."

It has been hinted by some that the phraseology of this remarkable document is not the gallant Admiral's own ; indeed, some think they can recognise the style of a clever civil official who was attached to the Headquarters of the Second Army Corps. But whether Admiral Itō be responsible for the style, or only for the ideas so forcibly expressed, the letter was signed by him, and its contents are known to represent his views. There is a savour of heroic days in this appeal addressed, on the eve of a desperate struggle, by Japan's foremost naval commander, but recently the victor in the greatest sea-fight of our time, to his erstwhile friend and present adversary, the vanquished in that battle—Admiral TING Ju-chang, a sailor almost as able as himself, and equally brave. Had China possessed a dozen leaders of his stamp, men imbued with the courage and the high sense of duty displayed by Ting, by one or two of his officers, and by General Tso Pao-kwei,* the war would have been protracted, and her defeat—inevitable in the face of Japan's superior organisation—would, at least, have been an honourable one. But the handful of capable, brave men on the Chinese side— not all of them Celestials, as the doughty Major Constantine von Hanneken's name shows—were powerless in the midst of the general corruption and dense ignorance of those above, around, and subordinate to them. They were bound, besides, with endless coils of yellow tape, still more constricting and paralysing than our own red variety. At every turn they were hampered by the civil authorities in a manner only worse in degree than the conduct of the criminal idiots for whom victories were won, in spite of them, by Nelson, whose great heart they nearly broke, almost driving him out of the service. A narrative of Admiral Ting's constant struggle against official stupidity, malignity, and corruption on shore, would read like an account of Nelson's perpetual conflict with those British Mandarins who pared down his requisitions, ignored his proposals, and often thwarted his plans. That Admiral Ting achieved as much as he did—little as it practically amounted to—in opposing Japan's victorious forces for

---

* General Tso Pao-kwei was killed in the great battle at Phyŏng-yang, or Ping-yang, in Korea, on 15th September, 1894. He commanded the *Feng* Brigade. Wounded early in the fight, he tore up his clothes to bind up his wound, and continued directing his troops, nor did a second wound dismay him. A third bullet killed the brave general, whose death threw his brigade into confusion, and thus facilitated the capture by the Japanese of the "Peony Hill" (*Mok-tan-San*), a commanding position, and the scene of the defeat of the Japanese by the Chinese and Koreans in 1592. The interval of three hundred and two years had not effaced from Japanese minds the humiliation of that defeat, suffered by their famous Christian General, KONISHI Yukinaga, many of whose warriors were also Christians, converts of the Portuguese missionaries. Every Japanese soldier storming the fortified "Peony Hill" felt that he was avenging the defeat of three centuries ago. Centuries appear mere years in the long annals of the Far East, reaching back into the mythical period: the Japanese take a keen interest in the past history of their nation, and they "remembered Peony Hill."

nearly a fortnight before his inevitable surrender, is matter for wonder when the obstacles he had to face are considered.

His whole career gave proof of the man's indomitable energy and ability. Acquiring his naval training late in life—he was originally a cavalry officer—he made himself so proficient that Captain Lang, R N., the British Naval Adviser whom the jealousy and bad faith of arrogant Mandarins had driven to resign his position in disgust, stated, at the beginning of the war, his confidence in the Chinese Admiral's capacity was so profound that "he would be ready to follow him anywhere." But the atmosphere of corruption and arrogant imbecility in which Ting had to work would have overcome a greater man. Thwarted by the civil authorities, who are supreme in China, even in naval and military matters—a situation not without analogies in the history of some Occidental countries—feebly supported by some of his own captains, actually deserted by others, and without any intelligent co-operation from the land forces, he undertook the hopeless task of defending Wei-hai-wei, one of the "Gateposts of Peking"—the other one, Port Arthur, was already in the hands of the Japanese. From the outset, he encountered ill-will and ignorant obstinacy on the part of the military commanders holding the great fortifications that German scientific skill had created and armed, at Wei-hai-wei as at Port Arthur, at the cost of a huge expenditure of Chinese money. The General commanding the troops refused his offer to land Seamen-Gunners from the four thousand good sailors who still manned his fleet, the remnant that had escaped from the defeat off the Yalu, and some vessels that had not yet been engaged. Ting proposed that these well-trained gunners should serve the great guns mounted in the shore-batteries and forts. Had his proposal been accepted, the Japanese troops would not have captured the works on the eastern side of the harbour without great loss, and, more important still, when the forts had ultimately to be abandoned

before the irresistible rush of the Japanese storming
parties, the sailors would certainly have destroyed the
guns, or rendered them useless. The Chinese military
artillerists neglected this precaution in the hurry of their
evacuation—their chief thought, at that moment, was to
put as much ground as possible between themselves and
the Japanese, who placed the uninjured cannon and their
ammunition in charge of the Naval Brigade attached to
the attacking columns. The smart Seamen-Gunners soon
turned the captured ordnance on the Chinese fleet, drove
it into the western part of the harbour, and kept it there,
nestling close to the protecting guns of the great fort on
Liu-kung Island, throughout the siege. Admiral Ting
prevented a repetition of this in the case of the Western
Forts, when he saw they were doomed to be captured,
and apprehended the peril .his fleet, and the sheltering
island-fortress, would be in were the guns on these
works to be turned against him at the comparatively
short range their position would ensure. Knowing how
useless it was to place any reliance in the soldiers
garrisoning the forts, he landed, on the 1st of February, with a body of volunteers from his fleet and
destroyed the guns, to the intense disappointment of
the Japanese, who entered the forts on the next day,
the "Braves" having fled to Chifu. I mention these
incidents of the memorable siege because they indicate
the absolute necessity for strong fortifications, heavily
armed and *properly manned*, on the *land-side* of Britain's
new naval base, if a fleet is to ride safely at anchor in
the harbour.

On the 25th of January, 1895, the captain of a British
man-of-war delivered to Admiral Ting the letter in which
his old friend, now his adversary, urged him to surrender.
To this communication he made no reply until the 12th
of February. Then, but not till then, the stout heart,
weary and sore with disappointment and disgust, gave way
to the pleading of the frenzied inhabitants of Liu-kung

Island, and Ting—his best ships, including his flagship, the great ironclad *Ting-yuen*, destroyed by the enemy's torpedos or shells, his torpedo flotilla captured whilst attempting to escape, the forts—all save Liu-kung—in ruins, or in the hands of the Japanese, and his decimated men, running short of ammunition, worn out by a succession of terrible nights spent in efforts to repel the magnificently daring attacks of the Japanese torpedo-boats—saw no alternative to surrender. A telegram from Li Hung-chang had informed him, on the night of the 11th, that no help could be offered him, so, on the morning of the 12th of February, he sent Captain Chang, of the *Kuang-ping*, in the *Chen-pei* flying a flag of truce, to Admiral Itō, with the following letter :—

"I received the letter of suggestions addressed to me, by the Officer in Command of ————" (here follow characters which may mean "Sasebo," the Japanese naval station in Kyū-shū, and would, in that case, be an error, or they may be an attempt to reproduce phonetically—always a difficult task with Chinese ideograms—the name of the British warship that brought Itō's letter, probably H.M.S. *Severn*) "but did not reply because our countries were at war. Now, however, having fought resolutely, having had my ships sunk and my men decimated, I am minded to give up the contest, and to ask for a cessation of hostilities, in order to save the lives of my people. I will surrender to Japan the ships of war now in Wei-hai-wei harbour, together with the Liu-kung Island forts and the armament, provided that my request be complied with, namely, that the lives of all persons connected with the navy and army, both Chinese and foreigners, be spared, and that they be allowed to return to their homes. If this be acceded to, the Commander-in-Chief of the British Squadron will become guarantor.* I submit this proposal, and shall be glad to have a speedy reply.

(Signed) "Ting Ju-chang,
Ti-tuh (Vice-Admiral) of the *Pei-yang* (Northern Squadron).
" Eighteenth Day of the First Month of the Twenty-second
"Year of *Kwang-hsü*" (12th February, 1895). †
"To His Excellency Itō,
" Commander-in-Chief of the Japanese Squadron."

* *I.e.* The British Admiral would see that the terms of the Capitulation were strictly fulfilled.
† The Period of the Reign of the present Emperor of China, who

To this letter the Japanese commander immediately replied, as follows :—

"I have received your letter and noted its contents. I am prepared to take over to-morrow the ships, forts, and all the other material of war in your possession. With regard to the hour and other particulars, I shall be glad to consult with you when I receive a definite reply to this communication. When the transfer of everything has been concluded, I shall detail one of our warships to escort all the persons indicated in your despatch to a place convenient to both parties, but I desire to offer an expression. of opinion on one point. As I had the honour to advise in my recent communication" (his letter, delivered on 25th January, urging a surrender), "I venture to think that, for the sake of your own security and in the future interests of your country, it would be best that you should come to Japan and remain there until this war is over. If you decide to adopt that course I offer you the strongest assurance that you shall be treated with every consideration and shall receive the fullest protection. But, if you prefer to return to your own country, your wishes shall be respected. With reference to the suggestion that the British Naval Commander-in-Chief should act as guarantor of this arrangement, I think such a precaution wholly unnecessary. I place implicit reliance on your assurances as an officer. I trust that I shall receive a reply to this letter by ten o'clock to-morrow morning.

(Signed) "Itō Sukéhirō,

"Commander-in-Chief of the Squadron; on board

"H.I.J.M.S. *Matsushima*,

"12th February, 1895.

"To His Excellency Ting Ju-chang,

    "Commander-in-Chief of the *Pei-yang* Squadron."

succeeded to the throne in 1875, at the age of four. The name means : "Brilliant Succession." In the chronology of the Far Eastern nations, "Reign-Periods" answer the purpose of the Christian Era with us, or the *Hejra* of the Moslem world. In order to fix a date, it is, therefore, necessary to know when each Period commenced, no easy matter in Japan, where they did not always coincide with the actual Reigns, being sometimes changed to celebrate an auspicious event A simplification was introduced in Japan in 1872, when it was decreed that thenceforward each Reign should have but one *Nen-gō*, or "Year-Period." The present Chinese Reign-Period, *Kwang-hsü*, began in 1875; the Japanese, which bears the title *Mei-ji*, "Enlightened Rule," commenced on 1st January, 1868. The Gregorian Calendar was introduced, by decree, in Japan on 1st January, 1873. To make chronological matters still more confused, in 1872 a new era was proposed in Japan, by which all years should be reckoned, viz, from 660 B C, the supposed year of the accession of Jimmu Tennō, the first Emperor of Japan, according to tradition. Some Japanese adopt

There are three noteworthy points about this letter, which breathes Itō's manly spirit in every line. Firstly, the Japanese admiral was under no obligation to consent to the condition, proposed by Ting, that the Chinese officers and men should be allowed to proceed to their homes, and their Occidental advisers and instructors suffered to depart scot-free. The granting of this concession was purely a wise act of mercy on Itō's part, as, further resistance being useless, the Chinese had no course open to them but to surrender, becoming, *ipso facto*, prisoners of war; the Occidental mercenaries, not being subjects of the belligerent state, might be treated as pirates, and strung up to the yard-arm, or handed over to their respective Governments to be dealt with for breach of the Proclamations of Neutrality.* Secondly, it is interesting to note Admiral Itō's evident anxiety to induce his great adversary to come to Japan. This desire arose, not only from the natural wish to intern, at some place on Japanese soil, for the sake of prestige, the greatest and ablest of the country's foes—all the Chinese officers taken prisoners so far having been mere nonentities—but also from a sincere regard for his safety. The Japanese knew that the Chinese Government would surely behead their only truly great man if they got him into their power, as they had decapitated Captain Fong, one of their best naval officers, for alleged cowardice, although he had bravely fought his ship, the *Tsi-yuen*, against greatly superior forces, off the Island of Phung, near the western coast of Korea, early on the 25th July, 1894. Fong had earned the admiration of his Japanese opponents, and of his German Chief Engineer, Herr Hoffmann, and the praise of his chief,

this method, by which A.D. 1898 (31st year of *Mei-ji*) becomes 2558 A J, that is, the two thousand five hundred and fifty-eighth year since the foundation of the present Imperial Dynasty, the only one that has ever reigned in Japan.

* When the French invaded Madagascar, in 1895, they made it widely known that they would shoot any Englishman, fighting on the Malagasy side, whom they might capture.

Admiral Ting, who tried to save him, but in vain ; the literary Mandarins at Peking wanted a scapegoat, and this brave officer had to die. Probably he could not raise sufficient funds to bribe his judges into postponing the execution of the sentence for a year, as in the case of the runaway generals from Port Arthur, nominally, to give the culprits time to reflect on the enormity of their offence ; really, it is said, to enable them to purchase the lives of wretched bankrupts, willing to sell their heads to save their families from ruin and starvation.*

There was another, and a very potent, reason for the efforts repeatedly made to induce Admiral Ting to come to Japan. The Japanese hoped that the gallant old sea-dog, brought under their influence, would, on his return to China after the war, with his life guaranteed by a special clause in the Treaty of Peace, become, as he un-doubtedly would have, a powerful factor in the regenera-tion of his country. And, lastly, it is noteworthy that the Japanese commander assures his foe that his word "as an officer" is sufficient guarantee for him. This is a thoroughly Japanese idea, and Ting was, probably, the only Chinese leader of note who could understand it. To Li Hung-chang it would seem mere foolishness. With the letter, Admiral Itō sent his old friend some presents of wines and spirits and tinned delicacies, knowing that Ting's larder and cellar must need replenishing after the long bombardment. The liquors sent were champagne, claret, and whiskey—whether the latter was Irish or Scotch, I know not ; I cannot, therefore, add to the fame of either country—and it is a fact pointing to the dif-ficulties which surround historical research, even into recent events, that the brands of wines selected by Admiral

* Cases of the execution of substitutes have occurred repeatedly in China, although they are by no means common. They give satisfaction all round The condemned is, of course, satisfied ; so is the substitute, who preserves his family, sacred to every Chinese, from want ; so are the family, and so is the executioner, who is "squared" to overlook the fact that he has beheaded the wrong man.

Itō have not been ascertained.   For once, the great art of advertising has been baffled.

On the next day, at 8.30, in the morning, Captain Chang returned to the Japanese flagship, this time in the gunboat *Chen-chung*, flying the Chinese ensign at half-mast, with another letter from Admiral Ting—and the three cases of gifts.   The letter, the last the great Chinese sailor ever wrote, was to this effect :—

" Your answer, just received, gives me much satisfaction on account of the lives of my men.*   I have also to express gratitude for the things you have sent me, but as the state of war existing between our countries makes it difficult for me to receive them, I beg to return them herewith, though I thank you for the thought. Your letter states that the arms, forts, and ships should be handed over to-morrow, but that leaves us a very brief interval at our disposal. Some time is needed for the naval and military folk to exchange their uniforms for travelling garments,† and it would be difficult to conform with the date named by you. I, therefore, beg that you will extend the period and enter the harbour from the 22nd day of this month, according to the Chinese calendar (16th of February), appointing a day for taking over the Liu-kung Island forts, the armament, and the ships now remaining. I pledge my good faith in the matter.

(Signed) " TING Ju-chang,
" 18th Day of the First Month (12th February, 1895)."
" To His Excellency Itō,
    "Commander-in-Chief, etc.
    Returned with the above, three packages of articles." §

How pathetic those words : " the ships now remaining" !   One can imagine the sturdy old fighter's heart breaking as he signed away the remnant of his once mighty fleet.   As soon as he had signed the letter to the

---

* This care for his subordinates, so different from the callous desertion of their men in defeat usual with the Chinese generals, was a grand feature of Ting's character.

† I have explained this quaint request in an earlier part of this Chapter, when dealing with the manner in which the Japanese carried out the liberation of the Chinese who surrendered at Wei-hai-wei.

§ Ting was undoubtedly wise in returning Itō's gifts. Had he accepted them, the Chinese would have said that he sold Wei-hai-wei for a case of champagne, and by this time it would be a historical "fact."   Men have been branded as traitors in Occidental countries on evidence almost as slender.

Japanese Admiral, Ting sent a telegram to Lɪ Hung-chang, retired to his cabin, and deliberately poisoned himself by swallowing a large dose of opium. His example was followed by the General commanding the troops, and by the chief naval and military Staff Officers. They well knew that their lives were forfeit if they returned to their homes, and that the probability was that, according to the terrible punishment for high treason in the Chinese Code, their whole families, from the hoary grandfather to the babe in arms, would be exterminated.

The news of Ting's death by his own hand was brought to Itō by the Chinese officer who carried his late Admiral's last letter and returned the gifts. The Japanese Admiral was deeply moved. His grief was bitter, for he and Ting had been friends, and his admiration for the brave Chinese sailor's character and ability was profound. And now, note how the warriors of Japan gave expression to their respect for their gallant foe who was no more. The noble tale is best told in the simple language of the naval documents. The following is an extract from the terms of the Capitulation of Wei-hai-wei :—

"Article X.—In order to pay due respect to the memory of Admiral Ting, who died in the discharge of his duty to his country, Admiral Itō will decline to receive the Chinese warship *Kwang-tsi*, but will leave her at the free disposal of *Tao-tai* Nɪu Chang-ping" (the Chinese Civil Governor of Liu-kung Island), "who will carry away in her the remains of the Admiral and of the other officers who died with him; these steps to be taken between noon on the 16th and noon on the 23rd of February. The ship will be inspected by Japanese Naval Officers on the morning of the 15th."

(By Article V. of the Capitulation, it had been provided that the Chinese officers, and the foreigners in Chinese pay, would be allowed to leave Wei-hai-wei, on parole, in the *Kwang-tsi*, thus forming, as it were, a bodyguard to their valiant leader's remains. By Article VI., they were to be permitted to carry away their personal effects, but not their arms.)

The next episode of the narrative is supplied by a signal:—

General Signal made by the Japanese Flagship *Matsushima* at 10.40, a.m , on 13th February, 1895.

"Vice-Admiral Ting, the enemy's Commander-in-Chief, committed suicide yesterday, after surrendering his ships, the forts on Liu-kung Island, and the armaments, garrison and crews. Great honour and respect must be shown to the spirit of our late gallant foe, who manfully did his duty to his country. His remains will be conveyed to a Chinese port in the prize *Kwang-tsi*, that the Commander-in-Chief will return to the Chinese for the purpose. Ships' bands are to play only funeral marches, or dirges, until the *Kwang-tsi* shall have passed out of the lines. Vice-Admiral's honours are to be paid to the remains by all ships as the *Kwang-tsi* passes them. This order is to be communicated to all ships' companies Torpedo-boats will keep a bright look-out round the fleet to-night. Watchfulness must not be relaxed."

The last two sentences are characteristic. The Japanese knew by bitter experience that a Chinese officer's undertaking was not necessarily to be trusted, and now the one Chinese leader whose word was his bond was dead. The *Kwang-tsi* did not report for inspection, as arranged, until early on 16th February, having been prevented from leaving her moorings by very rough weather. The inspecting officers found in her three torpedos, four guns of small calibre, and thirty rifles. The torpedos and rifles were taken out of her, but the guns and blank charges were left, so that she might fire a salute when her Admiral's body was brought on board. Her officers and crew were allowed to remain in charge of the ship. Before she left on her mournful voyage, the officers of the Japanese fleet, and many from the troops on shore, visited her to pay their last tribute of respect to the fallen foe. Slowly they passed before the coffin, each one solemnly and reverently saluting the remains of the enemy who had fought so stoutly for his country. The Chinese officers and civil authorities and the foreigners who witnessed the impressive scene were deeply moved. As one of the foreign officers in Chinese pay expressed it : "You would have thought the Japanese were mourning for their own Admiral." The Chinese gun-vessel, having taken on board the coffins of the other

L

officers who had died by their own hand, as a grim staff to sail with the Admiral on his last voyage, embarked the Chinese officers and foreign instructors liberated on parole, and steamed for Chi-fu. As she passed through the long lines of the Japanese squadron, flying at half-mast the Dragon Flag that Ting had served so faithfully to the end, every Japanese ship dipped her victorious ensign, minute-guns were fired, and the "Admiral's Salute" rang out from Japanese bugles in honour of the gallant enemy who would fight no more.

And these things that I have truly related were done by the men of whom we have been solemnly told that they are "after all, a nation of heathens, barbarians at heart, with whom civilised Christian Britain cannot, must not, enter into an alliance"!

"Is Chivalry dead?" The question was discussed not many years ago in many columns of a great London daily—of course in the "Silly Season," when the public freely rushes into amateur and unpaid journalism. The "Constant Reader," the "Voice from Clapham," "Paterfamilias," "An Englishwoman," "Fairplay," the "Mother of Six," and our old friend "*Audi alteram partem,*" were all on the warpath, but the discussion was inconclusive. If admiration for the thing implies its existence in our midst, then I can vouch for it that chivalry yet lives amongst us. I have told the true tale of Admiral Ting's death, and of Japanese chivalry, on scores of platforms, to many thousands of men and women, and boys and girls, high and lowly, throughout the British Isles, from Aberdeen to Cork, from Liverpool to Dover, and every time, after I had narrated the touching story, there was a moment of deep silence, and then—such a rousing British cheer as gladdens one's soul, for it shows that the great, warm heart of the People is in the right place after all.*

* At Newcastle-on-Tyne, after I had told the story at a crowded meeting of the Tyneside Geographical Society, in March, 1896, a sturdy

The success of the Japanese in their struggle against China was so complete, that it will afford a truer test of their national character if we consider their behaviour in a region where their progress has been less triumphal, and the obstacles in their way so great that they have had to strain every nerve to overcome them. In their splendid new possession, the beautiful and fertile island of Formosa, ceded to them, along with the Pescadores, or Ho-Ko Islands, by China as one of the conditions of the Treaty of Peace of Shimonoseki, in 1895—the Japanese have had to contend against both man and nature. Not only were the Chinese whom they had to defeat members of the redoubtable "Black Flag" bands, half soldiers, half banditti, who inflicted such heavy losses on the French in Tong-king—men of a far different stamp from the "Braves" they had routed on the mainland—but they had to chastise into obedience, and later to conciliate, the numerous Chinese population, men of Southern Chinese stock, excitable and pugnacious, and the still larger number of the *Pi-po-hoan*, those aborigines who had adopted the civilisation of their Chinese conquerors. As to the wild aborigines in the mountains of the interior, the Japanese, as a rule, are on very good terms with them, as anybody who has killed one of the hated Chinese is looked upon by the Formosan savage as a man and a brother. Moreover, the fairness and humanity with which the Japanese treated these hill-men, after chastising where punishment was due, in the expedition of 1874, undertaken to avenge the murder of shipwrecked mariners, produced a lasting impression. Nevertheless, the neighbourhood of their haunts is not a desirable location, as they are inveterate head-hunters, with a taste for human

Novocastrian, with a "burr" like a drum, went up to a Japanese who had been amongst the audience, scrunched his delicate hand in the brawny Northumbrian fist, and said. "Ah! but you are *men*, you are. God bless you!" But the cheers of the Etonians, and of the boys at our other great public schools, they were worth hearing! Admiral Itō's ears must have tingled far away on Far Eastern seas brains dissolved in rice-spirit,* and are, occasionally, not very particular as to the nationality of the person from whose body they obtain a head to add to their collection. The hard struggle the Japanese have had before establishing some degree of order in Formosa was carried on in a tropical climate, its enervating, steamy heat more dangerous to the most hardened soldiers than the intense cold—averaging 25° Fahrenheit, on one occasion the thermometer marked 30° *below freezing-point !*—they had borne so well in Manchuria, and the icy winds of Wei-hai-wei, where the crackling of the crust of ice on the waters of the Bay used to betray the movements of the torpedo-boats in their daring night attacks. Much of the country through which the Army of Occupation in Formosa had to march, often fighting every yard of the way with active, unseen foes, is about as difficult for military movements as Madagascar; high, steep, unexplored mountains, clothed with almost impenetrable jungle, that also fills the deep, narrow gorges and the precipitous ravines.

In such circumstances, the establishment of Japanese civil administration in Formosa was attended by so many obstacles, some of them due to inexperience in the difficult art of governing alien subject populations, that Japan's friends began to doubt if order would ever be evolved from such chaos. Governors followed one another with bewildering rapidity, and the policy adopted towards the inhabitants changed with each Governor, now erring by excessive leniency, construed by the Chinese, as usual, into weakness, anon by extreme harshness, goading the people into fury. "Carpet-baggers" from Japan swooped down on the fair island, eager for lucrative official posts, and terrible tales of shocking tyranny, cruelty, and extortion were industriously circulated by the enemies of Japan, some

---

* This gruesome beverage is drunk for the purpose of acquiring the strength and valour of the deceased. With the same object, Southern Chinese will buy from the executioner small pieces of the fried liver of a notoriously brave criminal, and eat them. Whether the Formosan hill-men be cannibals in the ordinary sense of the term is still a moot point.

Europeans in Formosa spreading blood-curdling reports on
the merest hearsay evidence.   Towards the middle of 1896,
the Japanese Government, alarmed at the state of the
Island, seriously devoted its attention, now free from other,
and weightier, preoccupations, to the matter.   With what
success its efforts towards reorganisation have been attended,
what the Japanese can do, when they devote themselves to
the task in earnest, with a possession apparently so intract-
able, we may learn from some "Notes of the Work during
1897 of the Formosa Mission of the Presbyterian Church
of England," contributed to *The Chinese Recorder* by my
valued friend, the Reverend W. Campbell, F.R.G.S., M.J.S.,
of Tai-nan-fu, on the south-western coast of Formosa, a
pioneer of the Gospel amongst the islanders of various
races, as broad-minded as he is devoted.   I fancy I can
see his honest Scottish face—tanned by many years of
exposure to the Formosan sun, during long wanderings
over the coast plains, or in the mountains amongst the
Head-hunters, with whom he is on terms of intimacy—
lighting up with joy as he penned sentences like the
following :—

"As already remarked, our Local, or Congregational, Schools form
another department of work in which decided advance has been
made during the past year.   The Japanese themselves have also
been giving much attention to education in Formosa, having established up till date no fewer than seventeen high-class schools
throughout the Island, at which Chinese youths are being taught the
Japanese language and other subjects.   It may be that the stir
thus caused—for the pupils attending those seventeen schools receive
a monthly salary from Government funds—has had an influence on
our native brethren, but the fact remains that we have very seldom
witnessed a better sustained effort made by them to give their
children a good education."

These "native brethren" are mostly people in humble
life, and would, I dare say, be stigmatised as "pore bloomin'
savages" by the "civilised" parents of corresponding social
status in our midst, who look upon the School Board as
an invention of the Evil One, and its Inspector—the "Kid-

Copper" they call him, with lurid adjectives—as their deadly foe. Mr. Campbell further states :—

"Under this head it may not be out of place to state that, on request being made to the proper" (Japánese) "officials, three pupils of our Blind School were admitted to the Government Institution" (for the blind) "at Tōkio; and that, in order to secure funds for their four or five years' residence, a charity concert was held there" (at Tōkio) "which turned out to be a great success; what gave it widespread favourable notice being an order from the Imperial Palace to send one hundred first-class admission tickets. The three boys—who are also members of the Church in Tai-nan-fu, entered on their duties at the beginning of the winter session, and there can be little doubt that four years' training at such a high-class, well-equipped institution will solve the question of their being able to earn a living for themselves. Many of the Japanese blind make good wages at *massage*, a method of treatment often prescribed by their own medical men; but, were our three pupils to acquire nothing more than facility in speaking the language of their adopted country, immediate use could be made of their services in any of the public offices in Formosa"

Government Institution for the Blind—Charity Concert, under Imperial patronage, to provide scholarships for three boys, of Chinese race and a foreign faith—great financial success, and, I presume, an artistic one, too, probably owing to Miss TANOSHII Yūkiko's delicate rendering of an air for voice and *samisen*, or the masterly execution of an *intermezzo* by MEKURA Mōjin, the celebrated blind *koto* player !*

---

* The blind in Japan are, as a rule, either musicians or shampooers *Massage*, or shampooing of the body for therapeutic purposes, which has but recently come into such high favour in the West, has been practised in Japan for centuries, playing as important a part in native medicine as acupuncture, or the moxa (this term, one of the few Japanese derivations in English, is a corruption of the Japanese *mogusa*, contracted from *moyé-kusa*, "burning-herb," because of the mugwort, a species of *Artemisia*, burnt on the body as a cautery) By a very ancient and wise custom, the practice of the art of *Massage* and, to a great extent, the *professional* playing on the *Koto*, or Japanese harp (in appearance more like the dulcimer, the *Czimbalom* of the Hungarian Gypsies, and the Tyrolese *Zither*, it being laid flat on the floor to be played upon, as those instruments are laid upon a table,) are reserved for the blind of both sexes, thus providing them with a livelihood The blind *Amma San*, as the shampooer is called, is a familiar figure, as he taps his way through the streets with his staff, and his plaintive chaunt " *Amma, kami-shimo go-hiyaku Mon!*" (" Massage, above and below, for five hundred *Mon !*"

One hundred stalls taken by the Imperial Family and the Court. They do these things well in Japan!

The Rev. W. Campbell closes his "Notes" with the following words, well worthy of attention, as he is known as an authority on all things Formosan, and an impartial judge of the conduct of the island's new masters. His summing-up shows him to be absolutely free from prejudice, able to discern high motives in a race who do not follow his creed.

"In conclusion, a few words may be added on changes which have taken place since Formosa came under control of the Japanese. Those beneficial changes have been neither few in number nor easy of accomplishment, considering the obstacles which had to be over-come on taking possession of the Island. There was a large popu-lation of strange speech, who increased the difficulty of the position by setting up a mushroom Republic, and inciting each other to withstand the victorious march of those who were then within striking distance of Peking. The plain truth upon this subject is that any brief perusal of Consular Reports and the *Peking Gazette* since 1864 places it beyond doubt that, owing to a turbulent spirit and the prevalence of bad opium-smoking habits—now being vigorously curbed by the" (Japanese) "authorities—Formosa has all along been a difficult Island to govern."

I venture to interrupt my quotation of Mr. Campbell's remarks in order to explain that the "Mushroom Republic,' set up by the "Black Flag" Leader, Liu Yung-fu, lasted just ten days, its second, and last, President, the aforesaid Liu, ultimately escaping to China disguised as a woman, with a baby in his arms. It is almost certain that the idea of establishing a Formosan "Republic" was the suggestion of some Occidental, for neither Liu nor his predecessor, Tang,

---

500 *Mon*=5 *Sen*, or Cents, *i.e.* 2¼ pence,) and the peculiar notes of his whistle, are typical sounds in every Japanese town. In spite of his moderate charges for his very soothing ministrations, the *Amma San* does fairly well, so well, sometimes, that he accumulates capital, which he lends—for a consider-ation. The blind *Koto* players are well paid. The instrument has a very pleasing, harp-like sound. It requires years of study to master it thoroughly, and the blind players teach the amateurs, who are chiefly ladies. The *Samisen* mentioned in the paragraph to which this Note refers, is a three-stringed banjo, played by women, with a *plectrum*, called *bachi*. It was introduced into Japan, probably from Manila, early in the eighteenth century.

the last Governor appointed from Peking—upon whom Liu
had thrust, at the sword's point, the evanescent honour
of being the first President—had any clear conception of
what the word implied. Tang's honours were so uneasily
borne, that Liu had him continually watched, yet he
managed to escape on board a steamship in the harbour
of Tamsui, at two o'clock in the morning of the fifth of
June, 1895, having induced his vigilant body-guard to look
the other way, the inducement coming from the Presidential
purse to the extent of fifteen thousand dollars. He had,
probably, "squeezed" many in his time ; his turn had come
to undergo the process.* Mr. Campbell speaks of the
opposition encountered in Formosa by the Japanese "who
were then within striking distance of Peking." The comparative ease with which the victorious Japanese army could
have reached and captured the Sacred Capital of China, after
its "Gate-posts," Port Arthur and Wei-hai-wei, had fallen
into their hands, has not been sufficiently recognised by
Occidentals. Powerful indeed must the reasons have been,
that induced the Japanese to forbear crowning their succession of victories, by land and sea, with the most ardently-
desired and logical consummation—the triumphal entry into
the Imperial City. Various causes have been alleged for the
sudden termination of the war at the very time when every
serious obstacle had, apparently, been cleared from Japan's
path, but the true motive remains a mystery. The *Peking
Gazette,* mentioned by Mr. Campbell as containing numerous
reports of Formosan lawlessness, is, of course, the Official
Gazette of China, the oldest periodical in the world.†

* Far Eastern "Republics" are short-lived. The one established, with
unofficial French encouragement, in Yezo, the great Northern Island of
Japan, on 27th January, 1869, came to an end in July of the same year.
Its originator was Admiral Yenomoto (or Enomoto), mentioned in Admiral
Itō's letter advising Ting to surrender

† The *Peking Gazette* may be described as the Official Gazette of China,
as the documents it publishes (daily Court News, Imperial Decrees,
Rescripts, and Memorials to the Throne), are all authentic, and are
supplied to the Editor by the Imperial Government, but the publication
is a private enterprise

The strict suppression of opium-smoking enforced by Formosa's new rulers, who have a horror of the insidious drug—a measure Mr. Campbell considers a powerful factor in the pacification of the island—induces bitter comparison, when it is remembered that Britain forced her opium upon protesting China at the cost of fierce war. This is how Mr. Campbell sums up the results of Japanese activity in Formosa in the face of the difficulties he has described :—

" As one, therefore, who wishes to see it " (the Island) " prospering in every good sense of the word, and in view of what the Japanese have done for its welfare within the past eighteen months, I cannot here withhold an expression of gratitude for their arrival. The officials with whom we are privileged to come in contact are courteous and always ready to make every reasonable concession; while it is simply marvellous what they have been able to accomplish in the way of surveying, census-taking and road-making; in setting up civil, police and military establishments; in opening postal and telegraph offices, and in the appointment of a regular service of steamers round the Island and to the Pescadores. Their efforts in the matter of education I have already referred to "

Mark the good Missionary's final words ; they condense into a few lines the secret of the success of New Japan :—

" Probably no Eastern nation has come in for a larger share of European flattery, lecturing, and mean, ungenerous criticism than the Japanese, but they manage to quietly hold on their way, well knowing that they have a lofty purpose in view. May God enable them abundantly to realise it! Long live the Emperor!"

In the preceding pages of this Chapter, I have endeavoured to show how those who guide the destinies of New Japan strove to attain their "lofty purpose" during the struggle with their huge adversary; I have cited some examples of the tools they have at hand for its accomplishment—the valour, the devotion, the chivalry of the people. It may be objected that these qualities would, naturally, come very much to the fore at a period of intense patriotic enthusiasm, and that a time of stress and storm is not a fitting opportunity for the study of a nation's conduct in ordinary circumstances. I cannot fall in entirely with this view, for history teaches us that it is in times of national

emergency the worst as well as the best points of a
people's character are most plainly manifested.   Yet, it is
right that an answer should be given to the question :
"How does this warlike nation behave in piping times of
peace ? "   The unhesitating reply must be: "Admirably
well ! "   The men who "rushed" the forts with irresistible
fury, who manned torpedo-boats in night attacks within
the enemy's harbour—work so daring that it would
have warmed the cockles of Nelson's heart and set the
blood tingling in Cochrane's veins—these very men are,
at home, units in the most peaceful, the most cheerful,
the most law-abiding, the kindliest population in the
world.   Patiently and industriously toiling for a pittance
that suffices to provide them not only with the necessaries
of life, but with enjoyments unknown to the nations of
rougher fibre—pleasures simple in themselves, but æsthe-
tically complete—the great mass of the Japanese nation
go through life with a smile on their lips, a courteous
word on their tongues, and in their hearts that kindness
towards their fellow-creatures, that tender love for children,
and that absence of selfishness that amply compensate for
their "impersonality of mind," their "inability to grasp
abstract ideas," and similar sad shortcomings of which they
have been convicted by learned investigators.

Why, then, if the Japanese possess such admirable
qualities, should their character have often been so merci-
lessly criticised by people whose reputation, learning, and
opportunity for close study entitle their opinions to our
respect ?   Chiefly because the critics were, perhaps unconsciously, irritated by the fulsome stream of undiscriminating
praise poured out on the Japanese by indiscreet friends—
some true, others false—whose lavish flattery has done
more harm to the nation than their bitterest foes have
ever inflicted.   A reaction was bound to set in against
the exaggerated praise uttered by those who choose, either
from excessive enthusiasm, or from motives of personal
interest,   to   give   a   one-sided   view   of   Japanese   life,

ignoring anything that might cast a shadow over the glowing picture. If you want to become aware of a man's defects, even the smallest, you have only to let people know that he is, in your opinion, very near perfection. It is the same with nations; we were never told of the heinous sins, the general moral turpitude and intellectual limitations of the Japanese until a score, or more, of writers had depicted them as almost angelic beings. No, the Japanese are not angels; they are just human beings, with the in-born passions and instincts, and the restraints, some inherited, some acquired, that go to make up that strange compound of apparent contradictions common to human nature the world over. Consequently, although "impersonality," that is, a very general conformity to certain national characteristics, may be a distinctive feature of the Far Eastern mind, it is unsafe to generalise about the Japanese, for of no race of human beings—not even of the Chinese, whose habit of thought crystallised centuries ago —can a picture be drawn that will be a faithful presentment of every individual. Exceptions may be rare amongst the people of Eastern Asia, gregarious by instinct, and enthralled, to our individualistic minds, by rules of conduct and modes of thought, adopted ages ago, and not easily cast off, that give an identical direction to the ideas of millions, but the exceptions must be taken into account if we would judge clearly. Taking note of the exceptions, it is absolutely safe to pronounce the Japanese of to-day *a good nation.*

But as I have said, they are not angels, far from it. There are Japanese murderers, Japanese thieves of various kinds—burglars who force bolts and bars, and enter, in spite of the heavy wooden shutters, the *amado*, in the night-time, house-breakers (to break into a Japanese house in the day-time a fist has only to be put through a paper screen, the *shōji,**) pickpockets (or rather "cut-sleeves," for the sleeve is

* A Japanese house consists, practically, of four wooden corner-posts, standing in stone sockets resting *on* the ground, and supporting a heavy roof—tiled, thatched, or shingled. The floor is a platform, covered with thick mats, the

the Japanese pocket,) forgers, swindlers,—the new civilisation has opened up channels previously undreamt of for their unholy enterprise—and political bravos, the *Soshi*, a curse of New Japan. There are Japanese impostors—sometimes of the religious variety, collectors for bogus missions— quacks, begging-letter writers, and fraudulent company promoters—in fact, almost every kind of evil-doer known in the West is to be found in New Japan. (The wicked plumber has not yet made his appearance.) But the number of these criminals is far from alarming. *Taken as a whole*, the people are wonderfully law-abiding, honest, docile, respectful to those in authority over them and to the aged, loving to their children, dutiful and affectionate in their conjugal relations, according to their ideas of the relative position of the sexes, devoted and subject to their parents to a degree hardly to be imagined by Occidentals, kind and helpful to all. Their good humour is proverbial, their intelligence universally recognised ; their artistic feeling has no parallel amongst modern nations in its absolute spontaneity, its true taste, and its general diffusion amongst the masses. Their patriotism, their loyalty, and their heroic valour are patent to the whole world by their manifestations in the war with China. Yet, I must repeat the warning, they are but men and women, with the foibles and frailties we are all heirs to ; we must not let our discovery of the fact bias our judgment, however disappointing it may be to find that there is no perfect nation.

Unfortunately for the reputation of the Japanese, it is to the most serious, the most critical amongst those who have studied their character, that its defects have been most frequently revealed. It is the Occidental who has had occasion to deal with the Japanese in the serious business of life who is, as a rule, their least clement

space between the corner-posts may be left open in summer, or it may be wholly, or partly, shut in by the *shōji* (sliding screens of semi-transparent paper) ; at night it is closed by heavy wooden sliding-panels, the *amado*.

critic, for reasons I shall endeavour to explain later. The traveller, on pleasure bent, the artist revelling in the charm of the scenery and in the glories of the art of Japan, the people of leisure, seeking a Lotos Land, all these return from Japan fired with enthusiasm for the lovely country, and all aglow with sympathy for the good, courteous, merry people who have made their sojourn amongst them a time of delight. Who has travelled far from the " Treaty Ports "—which are in their morals much like ports all over the world—into *the real* Japan without bringing away golden memories, to last a life-time, of innumerable little acts of kindness and consideration experienced at the hands of the people, mostly from those of the poorer class that, in Anglo-Saxon countries, look upon a stranger with dislike, and upon courtesy as a loss of dignified independence ? The helpful people who so busily assisted to mend his broken-down *jin-riki-sha;* the total strangers who performed those many little acts of cere-monious courtesy, evidently sincere and entirely disin-terested; the good landlady of the little inn at the village in the mountains, who was so genuinely distressed when he came in, wet to the skin, from a long walk in the rain—it *can* rain in Japan and it *does*, about every other day, except in the dry autumn—and nursed him, as if he were her own son, when he had that dreadful cold in consequence; the sturdy *Kuruma-ya* who dragged him in his baby-carriage, at a swinging trot, for miles, in all weathers, at a charge of about threepence a mile, and who doubled himself up in lowest obeisance on receipt of a gratuity a British cab-man would hardly acknowledge with a " thank-you "—all these linger in the traveller's recollection, mellowed by the golden haze of the past tense, as dear, familiar friends.

As he surveys the cherished odds and ends that bring back every scene of his delightful journey so vividly to his mind—his bill for the *hatago* (supper, bed and breakfast; lights, fire, bath and attendance included) at the *yadoya*, the inn, clean as a new pin, at the end of the village, situated

just where the most beautiful view of the valley, the lake, or
the bay is to be obtained—a bill half a yard long, amounting to less than three shillings; the *annai-jō*, or letter of
recommendation, on decorated paper, with which mine host
passed him on to the next inn-keeper on the road, the little
paper wrappers in which the *ko-yōji*, the slender wooden
tooth-picks, were handed to him; the fan with a view of the
hostelry, and the little blue cotton towel, with a flight
of white birds across it, that were presented to him, with
all the solemnity of an investiture at court, when he
departed, after bestowing largesse (the customary *chadai*,
nominally for the tea consumed, which never figures in the
bill, being *à discrétion*,) to the tune of eighteen-pence, or
even two shillings, if he remembered that every foreigner is
supposed to be a millionaire on his travels; all these—letter,
wrappers, fan and towel—each one a dainty little work
of art applied to the humblest purposes, transport him back
to the fair land.

How well he remembers, too, the departure from
the *yadoya*, the landlord and landlady wishing him a
pleasant journey with parental solicitude, the row of plump
little waitresses, in their charming costume, bowing, all
together, and smiling, as only Japanese girls can smile, and
twittering: "*Mata irashai!*" ("Please come again!")—and
the young schoolmaster, who had been fetched in, the
night before, "because he could speak English"—local belief
being scarcely borne out by his perspiring, gallant struggles
(resulting in: "I am very grad wercome honourabre foreign
guest. You from Rondon come? Misteru Herbert Spencer
book I dirigently study. It is very important!")—and
the dignified policeman, saluting stiffly, the same who lent
the table and chair, typical of advanced administrative reform, from the Police Station for the greater comfort of the
I-jin San ("Mr. Foreigner,") unused to squat on his heels
and to eat off a table the height of an ordinary footstool;
the children, too, those absolutely delightful little people,
in raiment bright as humming-bird's plumage, bowing as

ceremoniously as any of their elders! The whole episode is lived over again, and memories dearer still haunt the traveller's mind. He cannot forget, nor does he wish to, the winsome ways of sweet O Kiku San, prettiest of *Gei-sha* (every traveller's particular *Gei-sha* is always the prettiest in all Japan), the little fairy with the roguish eyes and the baby hands, who dressed with such exquisite taste, and taught him, amidst peals of silvery laughter, to play *kitsuné-ken*, and other games of forfeits; the smile of Komurasaki San, the inn-keeper's charming daughter, is a tender reminiscence, and every day of his journey is marked in his memory with the face of some demure little damsel who waited on him at an inn—kneeling near him, ready to pour out the *saké*, or to fill the rice-bowl, and teaching his great, clumsy, Occidental fingers to manipulate the slender "eating-sticks." And all these fascinating recollections blend together in the remembrance of that melodious word—perchance the last one he heard as he left the Enchanting Isles, maybe from the lips of a regretful *musumé*—wherewith the Japanese so well express "the sweet sorrow of parting": "*Sayōnara!*"

Small matter for wonder if memories such as these drive out of the traveller's mind all resentment against the "curio"-dealer, who sold him forged antiquities, the artful guide and interpreter, who took his "squeeze" from every purchase, the drunken wharf-labourer who reeled against him at Yokohama (*saké* having been the cause, his intoxication would, at all events, be evanescent), the ruffian of the same class, sober but truculent (contaminated by intercourse with the scum of all nations), who was rude to him on the *hatoba*, the wharf, at Kōbé. These petty annoyances are forgotten, as indeed they may well be, for they were almost unperceived in the whirl of surprises, each more delightful than the last, and the joy of feeling one's self surrounded by kind, courteous, gentle people, who have verily solved the great problem— how to be happy though poor.

Two other problems have been solved by the people of Japan; they have discovered, ages ago, how to be deferential without loss of dignity, and how to frame the soft answer that turneth away wrath. In the art of living amongst their fellow-men, that *savoir vivre* which is the most difficult art of all, they are past-masters. In courtesy of speech and demeanour, the humblest Japanese could give points to many in the well-dressed, well-groomed mob that calls itself "Society" in Occidental countries. Note the demeanour of a Japanese crowd— and the streets of the populous cities are usually crowded; at the time of a festival they swarm with people. Observe the low bows and polite apologies exchanged by people, of the poorest class, who have inadvertently come into collision, the readiness with which a way is made for the bearer of a burden—and think of the husky "'Oo are you a-shovin' of?" so frequent in our holiday multitudes. Walk through the clean, soft, yielding Japanese crowd, perfectly sweet to the nostrils, with just a faint odour of *ja-kō*, the musky perfume wherewith the boxes are scented in which they keep their best clothes; you will pass along, without the slightest difficulty, merely by the exercise of a little patience. Think of the state of your ribs and your toes were you to elbow your way ("to elbow your way"—a Japanese would not understand the phrase!) through the crowd thronging the streets of London City to witness the poor pageant of the Lord Mayor's Show. Remember how one is hustled in a Berlin crowd, pushed unceremoniously off a New York side-walk, jostled in a Boulevard throng, the latter, however, somewhat restrained by the fear of *une affaire d'honneur* if apology be not quickly tendered. Strange code of "honour," that demands blood to wipe out an injury to a corn! Amongst the thousands pouring through the main streets of a Japanese city on the day of a *matsuri*, a popular festival, you may, occasionally, see a man too festive from unwise potations of *saké*—you will never see an intoxicated woman; nor will you hear any voice raised in anger above the level of the rippling, laughing chatter of the merry crowd. Wherever you may be amongst Japanese, you will never be shocked by the disgusting blasphemy and obscenity that assail the ears in almost every Occidental land, but especially, alas! in English-speaking countries. The fact is, the Japanese cannot swear, even if he had a mind to; his language will not allow itself to be thus defiled—it contains absolutely no "swear-words." This limitation has its inconveniences; when a Japanese takes to playing golf he is obliged to learn English.

From what I have stated, it may be gathered that the Japanese are a nation delightful to live with under ordinary conditions of every-day intercourse between friends, acquaintances, or even strangers. The moment the Occidental's relations with them point to his having a material object in view, presumably for his own benefit, their character undergoes, in most instances, an unwelcome change. The man who lands in Japan with the intention of making a fortune, or of carving out a career at the expense of the natives, has bitter disappointments in store. The competition is daily growing keener and more embittered, not only amongst the resident Occidentals, especially between the old settlers and the new-comers, but between them and the Japanese, who, day by day, become capable of producing for themselves many articles they were formerly obliged to import, and of dispensing, in nearly all directions, with the help of Occidental brains. Keen competition does not tend to soften hearts, nor to promote the cultivation of courtly manners, and there are other influences at work to make the impatient Occidental merchant, who sees his rate of profit dwindling, the disappointed contract-seeker, and the Foreign Adviser nearing the end of his engagement, take a gloomy view of the character of the Japanese. The very people whose simple dignity and cheerful humour, whose unfailing kindness and exquisite courtesy, would fill him with

M

admiration in any other circumstances, become simply exasperating when the eager Occidental lets it be understood—and the quick-witted Japanese perceive his motive long before he thinks fit to reveal it—that he is aiming at personal benefit of some sort. Nor is it necessary, to produce this disagreeable transformation, that the foreigner's motive be purely selfish. Even if the success of the business, of the scheme of reform, or of the new development of any kind, that he is proposing must inevitably bring increased prosperity to certain Japanese, or benefit the whole nation, the mere fact that a foreigner would participate immediately in the profits, or even only in the honour and the glory of the results, is sufficient to arouse the hostility, open or latent, of the majority of Japanese. The best men in the country's service, the wisest of Japan's statesmen, the most enlightened of her writers and thinkers, the foremost amongst her financiers, her manufacturers and merchants, do not share this feeling of shortsighted exclusiveness. They deplore it, and are working manfully to eradicate it, but they have a hard task before them. The feeling is one that Britons and Americans, accustomed to extend a warm welcome to enterprise that will benefit them, no matter whence it comes, or of what nationality their partners in the undertaking may be, cannot understand. Their marvellous prosperity has advanced, by "leaps and bounds," by means of that very broadness of view, the introduction of which into Japan is now the chief aim of her really great statesmen.

The spirit of exclusiveness they are battling against, to which I shall refer more in detail in a future Chapter dealing with economic matters, is not confined, as one might expect, to the trading community. It obtains, unfortunately, to a regrettable extent amongst the less enlightened officials and politicians, who have a large following amongst the *Shi-zoku* and, consequently, amongst those still lower in the social scale. The display of this feeling, the utterance, in the Press, in Parliament, and on the platform, of the cry:

"Japan for the Japanese, and for nobody else!" are sure means of gaining cheap popularity, of a kind not unknown nearer home. How many absolute nonentities have climbed into prominence in French politics to the accompaniment of frantic shouts of "*l'étranger, voilà l'ennemi!*" Thus also in Japan, *l'étranger* fares badly with his proposals, unless he have the rare good fortune to lay them before one of the really enlightened leaders, and the latter happen to be in power, and strong enough to contend with the national prejudice, the popular fear of being "exploited," as was often the case in the early days of New Japan, by the foreigner.

This fear is all the more notable, in that the Japanese have a very good idea of how to "exploit" others. They are the most expert "brain-pickers" in the world. Strangely enough, they are ever ready to accuse others of the practice. It is a common subject of complaint with them that in many "translations" from the Japanese, and in numerous, more or less scientific, books on Japan by Occidental authors, the services of the "Native Assistant," who has contributed so materially, in most cases essentially, to the work, are curtly acknowledged in a brief mention in the Preface. They seem oblivious of the fact that they adopt a precisely similar course in many excellent publications written by Japanese in foreign languages, but revised and "prepared for press" by "Foreign Assistants." Some Japanese are remarkable linguists—although the Chinese are their superiors in this respect—and some of Japan's statesmen and diplomatists write and speak European languages, especially English, German, and French, with perfect accuracy and fluency, but more than one able public address, delivered by a less gifted Japanese in a foreign tongue, has owed its absolutely correct periods, its elegant diction, at which the audience marvelled greatly, to the polishing process undertaken by an anonymous foreign reviser. It is thus a fair game of "give and take," and there is not much harm in the practice after all.

The feeling of exclusiveness in matters of material benefit, and even of purely sentimental *kudos*, shelters itself, of course, like so many other unworthy or unwise motives, under that ill-used word " Patriotism." The Japanese, who are happy in the possession of the *real* patriotism, in its purest and highest forms, should have no need to indulge in displays of spurious varieties. The true cause underlying the exclusive spirit I am describing is a deep-rooted *mistrust* of the foreigner and of his aims, a feeling of suspicion born of centuries of strictest seclusion from the outer world, consequent on a bitter experience, in the seventeenth century, of the intrigues of foreigners whose internecine strife wrecked the noble work of their immediate predecessors, the men who had raised the edifice of Christian Japan. From the expulsion of the Portuguese and Spanish to the advent of Commodore Perry, the Dutch and Russians were, with the exception of a few British who laboured under the disadvantage of prejudice fostered by their commercial rivals, the only white men from whose behaviour the Japanese could form any estimate of the character of the peoples of the Christian world, and the examples were not calculated to excite their admiration or their respect. The few glimpses they had of the Muscovites were not encouraging, and seem to have strengthened their determination to seal up their country more closely than ever. As to the Dutch, we may easily imagine what a proud, chivalrous, military nation like the Japanese, amongst whom trade of any kind was, until 1871, an occupation no gentleman could stoop to—in fact, classed below agriculture and all crafts—thought of the money-grubbing Hollanders, who submitted willingly to gross indignities for the privilege of trading at Nagasaki.

And with the opening of Japan to the trade of the world came, in the 'fifties and the 'sixties, it should be remembered, not only reputable merchants, diplomatists, naval and military men, physicians and missionaries, but, in their train, a motley crew of adventurers, flotsam and jetsam of

the Pacific Coast and the China Seas, rowdies from the gold-
diggings of California and of Australia, "Beach-combers"
from the South Sea Islands, naval deserters, unfrocked
priests, an epitome of Occidental vices and follies let loose
to prey upon an unprepared nation just awakening from
its torpor of two centuries. It makes one blush to think of
the barefaced swindles that were perpetrated to the detriment of the Japanese in those days, of the brutality of the
San Francisco "Hoodlums," and the Australian "Larrikins"
towards Japanese women and defenceless "coolies," and
. the vulgar arrogance of British cads of the type that strolls
about amongst the kneeling worshippers in a foreign cathedral, talking loudly the while, and goes to the opera in
Paris in a bicycling suit. And the outrages and the
arrogance brought bloody reprisals, not always on their
perpetrators, for, in such cases, the innocent usually suffer
for the guilty. In one notorious instance, at least, under-
bred arrogance met with prompt and terrible punishment.

When it is considered what an impression must have
been made on the Japanese mind by the first foreigners
with whom they were brought into close contact in
modern times — and, unfortunately, nations are prone to
accept the worst specimen of a foreign race as typical of
the whole—on what a stock of traditional hatred and
contempt the new hostility was grafted, and how fuel
was added to the flame by the merciless indemnities
exacted, with fire and sword, by the foreign Powers
for the outrages committed on their subjects, who had
often provoked them; when we add to all this the
manifest injustice displayed, for many years, by the
same Powers in their dealings with Japan, and now—
the wound is still raw—the iniquity of the Russo-Franco-
German intervention in 1895, and the Russian grabbing of
Port Arthur in 1898, it seems nothing short of marvellous
that the Japanese are as friendly to foreigners as we
find them.

Time heals all, and in the course of a few years—

things proceed rapidly in New Japan—the mistrust at
present inspired by the Occidental will disappear, especially
in the case of the peoples against whom Japan has no
grudge, but rather a debt of gratitude. The people of
Britain stand foremost amongst these; Japan will never
forget it was Britain that first consented to treat her on
an equal footing. Until that happy time comes, the
Occidental must apply himself, if he would succeed in
Japan, to establishing a feeling of mutual confidence that
will dispel the national habit of suspicion. For it is a
national habit, and applies, although to a less degree, to
the relations of the Japanese amongst themselves. This
ingrained suspiciousness is, without doubt, the result of
two centuries and a half of a Government which relied,
as that of the Tokugawa *Shōgun* undoubtedly did, for
its efficiency on an elaborate system of spying. The
Shōgun at Yedo spied on his Councillors, the Councillors
on the officials, the officials on the people, and the
people on one another. The feudal Lords, the *Daimiyō*,
themselves spied upon by the *Shōgun's* Government
(whose spies swarmed also about the Imperial Court at
Kiōto), spied upon their *Karō*, or Councillors, when the
Lords were not, as was often the case, mere puppets in
the hands of their *Karō*; in every Clan the spying system
was but a replica of that organised at Yedo, and the Clans,
jealous, always intriguing, frequently hostile, spied upon
one another. This system has left two legacies to New
Japan, one good, the other bad: the most efficient detective
police in the world, and the unfortunate habit of exaggerated
mistrust. The curious thing about this suspiciousness is that
the Japanese affect not to be aware of its existence. Ask
a Japanese: "Why are your people so mistrustful, so
suspicious?" He will reply: "We are not suspicious at
all." And, as he says it, his eyes are boring through you,
to try and discover the hidden, and presumably interested,
motive that prompted your query.

With other charges that are most frequently brought

against the character of the modern Japanese I propose
to deal, as opportunity offers, in subsequent Chapters
treating of subjects in connection with which the alleged
vices, or defects, may most fittingly be considered. For
instance, the allegation of commercial dishonesty will,
naturally, be most conveniently investigated in the course
of the Chapter on " The Almighty Dollar ; " that of lack of
chastity will be examined in the Chapter on "The Women
of the New Far East." Impartially looked into, some of
the charges brought against the people of New Japan
cannot be sustained, others admit of extenuation, almost
all will have to be retracted within a generation.

Taking them all in all, the people of New Japan have
no great vices ; they have no glaring defects that cannot
be removed, as they probably will be before many years
elapse. For the nation, thoroughly in earnest, is eager
to fit itself for the great part it is destined to play in the
Far East—and in the world at large. Truly, again to use
the words of the good Missionary in Formosa : " They
have a lofty purpose in view. May God enable them
abundantly to realise it ! "

CHAPTER IV.

THE MEN OF OLD CHINA.

OLD—that is the epithet which comes inevitably to the mind as the most distinctive one to apply to the huge Empire of China. Although the momentous events that mark the closing years of the nineteenth century have transformed Eastern Asia into the New Far East, China, paradoxical as it may seem, still remains Old China. Japan has been reborn within the last thirty years of the century; Korea, an epitome, till late in the 'seventies, of the China of three hundred years ago, has been rudely shaken out of her long sleep, turned inside out and upside down, and tumbled into a confused heap, out of which something totally unlike her former self will be gradually and painfully evolved. China alone remains unchanged, unreformed, Old China to the backbone.

"What?" I fancy I can hear the Reader exclaim, "has China shown no signs of progress since her crushing defeat by the allied British and French, in 1860, humbled her pride? Has she not, in many ways, indicated that the great lesson of her complete collapse before the arms of little Japan is beginning to bear fruit?" The answer must be a negative one. To begin with, China's defeat by the two allied Powers—would that their alliance could be re-established for the good of humanity!—was never looked upon by the Chinese as a "crushing" one. Those Chinese who, at any time, bestow a thought on the subject, as very few of them do, argue, with truly

Oriental logic, that the allies *cannot* have been victorious,
else they would have established their rule at Peking. It
must have been, they say, fear of the punishment that
would overtake them, for their criminal insolence, when
the Son of Heaven had completed his preparations to
that end, that caused the Foreign Devils to retire from
the gates of the Imperial City. The same reasoning
satisfies the average Chinese, living away from the coast,
who know anything about the war with Japan—by no
means a majority of the nation—that the presumptuous
"Dwarfs" retired from the sacred soil of China just in
time to avoid the annihilation that was inevitable once
the Imperial Power had really begun to exert itself.
Otherwise, they maintain, would the Japanese have
refrained from marching into Peking? Would they not
be ruling there now? They are not there; consequently
they must have been smitten with awe by the mere
rumours of the tremendous preparations that were being
made to chastise their impertinence, the thousands of new
bows and arrows that were in process of manufacture, the
assembling of hordes of "Braves" under the walls of
the capital, and so forth. In short, the vast majority of
China's teeming millions know nothing of the collapse,
in two campaigns within thirty-five years, of the defensive
forces of the Empire, and the minority who witnessed it
on either occasion attributed their country's defeat to any
causes but the real ones, ascribing it to reasons involving
no national humiliation whatever, no condemnation of the
obsolete principles of government and the crass ignorance
that brought their power into the dust. The most striking
"object lessons" ever given to a great Empire were thus
wasted on the bulk of the population of China.

But, it may be objected, what of the tangible proofs of
China's awakening of which so much has been heard?
What of the desire, evident for years past, to profit by
the latest discoveries of Western science, at all events
for purposes of national defence? Surely, China *had* a

fleet of ironclads; she *had* regiments armed with modern weapons and drilled by Occidental Instructors; she has some still.　What of the telegraph lines extending throughout her immense territory?　What of the railways, some in operation, some being constructed, and a great many more projected?　Why, to judge by the newspaper reports, the whole vast Empire will soon be covered with a network of trunk lines and branch lines!　In every Club smoking-room the talk is all of the line from Something-king to Somewhere-fu, and who is going to get the concession for it; and in the library the maps of China are becoming frayed at the edges, cut at the folds, and are scored all over by the toothpicks of experts, tracing the course of the iron roads so soon to exist.　Are there not Colleges in China, where students are carefully trained in all the Western sciences?　Have not scores, perhaps hundreds, of intelligent young men been educated in America, and some in Europe, at the cost of the Chinese Government?　Think of the impetus that must have been given to the advancement of China by the journey of her greatest statesman.　Surely the thoughts of Li Hung-chang, brought face to face, on that memorable tour, with Occidental civilisation in its most striking manifestations, must be bearing fruit?　We know that he possesses the ability to profit by the knowledge thus acquired, for—long before he left China—he had conceived the idea of providing his country with defensive forces of the most modern type, selecting, with rare strategical insight, the two points where the approaches to Peking from the sea could best be commanded, and causing German and French skill to convert them, at immense cost, into fortresses deemed practically impregnable till they fell before the fierce onslaught of the Japanese.

Then, is it to be assumed, even for a moment, that long years of devoted missionary labours, embracing scholastic and medical efforts, have not leavened the masses of China with the germs of a new, and higher,

civilisation ?   Consider, too, the object lesson the Chinese
have had before their eyes, for so many years, in the
well-ordered Foreign Settlements at Shanghai, and in
the thriving British Colony of Hongkong.   See the unmistakable evidences of the fitness of the Chinese for
intelligent activity in every branch of commercial enterprise to be found in the flourishing condition of the
Chinese trading under the British flag in the Straits
Settlements.   Look at the type of high official that is
sent abroad to represent the Empire at foreign Courts.
"Only the other night," the Objector will tell me, "I
heard His Excellency the Chinese Minister at the Court
of St. James's, Sir Lo Fêng-lu, make a speech at a
public dinner—one of the best and wittiest after-dinner
orations I have ever heard. and in excellent, idiomatic
English.   In the course of it His. Excellency casually
quoted Shakespeare, Milton, and Tennyson, and mentioned, just by the way, that he had translated Blackstone
into Chinese.   I sat next to one of the Secretaries of the
Imperial Legation ; such a pleasant companion, in lovely
blue silk, who chatted away, in perfect English, on the
folly of the Anti-Vaccination Movement, and on the
Incidence of Local Taxation in the United Kingdom.
If that is not a sign of New China, what is ?"

Thus speaks the Objector, and I answer him once
more, deliberately, that the enormous, inert Empire
between Russia in Asia and British India is still the Old
China of yore.

I shall take the Objector's points *seriatim*.   China *had*
a fleet of powerful ironclad battleships, and cruisers and
torpedo-boats—I shall not enumerate their quaint names,
for nearly all those that are not at the bottom of the sea,
beyond hope of salvage, now bear Japanese names—but
to what do the masses in China attribute the loss of their
fine ships ?   To the "fact," amongst other equally cogent
reasons, that *their eyes having been poked out* by their
malevolent German and British constructors, the poor ships

were unable to avoid the enemy's shells and torpedos! The hawse-holes of the steel monsters could not possibly serve to guide them in the sea-fights. Now, if they had possessed a pair of well-painted eyes at the bows, like every decent junk, the result would surely have been victory for the Dragon Flag. Lest it should be thought that opinions of this kind are held only by the common herd, it ought to be known that. the Mandarin charged with the inquiry into a railway accident near Tien-tsin, in 1898—China possessed at the time but three hundred and twenty miles of railways in operation, but they had already attained to the dignity of an accident—expressed his belief that the disaster was caused by the absence of eyes, which ought to have been painted on the engine. As to China's "foreign-drilled" troops, I shall have occasion to refer to them in a subsequent Chapter dealing with naval and military matters, but suffice it to say now that most Chinese are agreed that the Occidental weapons and training adopted for a part—and a small part only—of their motley army are totally unsuited to the idiosyncrasies of the Chinese warrior, hampering his agility and thwarting his native valour. They look upon the introduction of foreign drill and the attempt at foreign discipline in the armies of certain Viceroys—not all the Viceroys have called in the aid of Occidental military science, and there is, practically, no organised Imperial army, in our sense of the word, for service throughout the Empire—much as our wooden-headed old Admirals of former days looked upon the introduction of "tea-kettles," as they called steamships, into the Navy, as their successors regarded, and bitterly opposed, armoured vessels and, quite recently, breech-loading ordnance; much as the peppery veterans in our Service Club windows—and, it is to be feared, not a few younger than they and still in command—condemn our "short service" system, our magazine rifles, our scientific officers, and every other innovation, tending, in their opinion, to "send the Service

to the dogs, sir!" The great fault the average Chinese
finds with the "new-fangled" Occidental arms of precision is their shortness. Your true Chinese likes a weapon
with a good long handle—a trident, or a crescent-pronged
spear, for choice—about ten feet long; it keeps the enemy
so much further off.

During the war between China and Japan, I was conversing one day with a highly-educated young Chinese
official, of high rank for his age, who had a perfect command of English. I was expressing the hope, in which
I felt sure one so thoroughly imbued, as I thought, with
Occidental ideas, would concur, that China would profit
by the terrible lesson she was receiving. To my astonishment, he replied that he had apprehended some such
disaster, for, he said: "Our people should not be expected
to fight with European weapons, and according to methods
foreign to their national spirit. I believe we would defeat
the Japanese, were our men to oppose them with the
arms we have always found suitable, and according to
our ancient rules of warfare, that enabled us in the past
to subdue so many nations ·of the East." Bows and
arrows, matchlocks, "stink-pots," tridents, and shields with
ugly faces painted on them to terrify the enemy—these
used—and bows and tridents were used—against Mélinite
shells, smokeless powder, quick-firing ordnance, range-
finders, the Murata rifle, the bayonet, revolvers, and
machine-guns! Poor China!

As a matter of fact, the modern destructive engines
are not at all beyond the comprehension of carefully-
trained Chinese. They can, when properly led, use them
with deadly effect, as was proved by the stout defence of
Wei-hai-wei under the gallant Admiral Ting, and the
heavy losses inflicted on the Japanese on several occasions
during the attack; but the result showed that courage,
endurance, and skill in the use of perfect arms, even
under gallant and experienced leadership, cannot enable
the Chinese to prevail, on land or sea, against the same

conditions *plus* perfect organisation, military spirit, and scientific tactics. The fact is worth remembering by those who talk so glibly of a Chinese army, under British officers, holding in check and presumably defeating, if necessary, the legions of the Tsar.

The telegraph and the telephone are now firmly established in China. She possesses thousands of miles of telegraph lines, transmitting messages *in Chinese*. Why these italics? Because the invention of a system by which Chinese can be telegraphed is a masterpiece of ingenuity.* The difficulties seemed insuperable. How could the Morse alphabet of dots and dashes reproduce a language that has no alphabet at all, but possesses, instead, a beautifully elaborated system of characters, evolved from ancient hieroglyphics — attributed, in their primitive form, by the Chinese to Fuh-hi, their great, and mythical, ruler of the early period of 2800 B.C., or thereabout, and by Occidental learners to a much more ancient celebrity with hoofs and horns—characters that represent ideas, not sounds? It stands to reason that an ideographic system of writing must contain as many characters as there are ideas, or conceptions, concrete or abstract, that may have to be communicated—in fact, words—so that the unfortunate telegraphists were confronted by the evidently hopeless task of inventing combinations of dots and dashes equivalent to the three thousand, or so, of characters a Chinese must be able to distinguish before he can be said to be able to read fairly well. There is, probably, no man living, nor ever was, with a knowledge of *all* the characters of the Chinese language, nearly *forty-four thousand* in number, although

---

* Due to the clever brain of Professor Schellerup, Professor of Astronomy in the University of Copenhagen, the seat of the Great Northern Telegraph Company's headquarters, who devoted his leisure hours to the framing of his lucid scheme, which was perfected and tabulated for practical use, in 1871, by an equally clever Frenchman, Monsieur S. A. Viguier, then Divisional Inspector at Shanghai in that admirable service, the Imperial Chinese Maritime Customs.

some extremely learned Graduates may have enjoyed that reputation.

A way out of the telegraphic difficulty suggests itself at once to the Occidental mind. Why not telegraph Chinese with the Morse signals corresponding to the Roman letters forming the representation, according to some definite phonetic system, of *the sound* of the words? This cannot be done, because, in the first place, the Chinese language being monosyllabic, every sound has numerous significations, to be distinguished only by the context, or, in some cases, by the particular intonation—level, rising, falling, guttural, or acute—given to the syllable; and, secondly, because the vernacular varies so greatly in the different provinces that a man from the coast of Fu-kien is totally unable to converse with a fellow-countryman from Shan-si, and even with a native of a province nearer to his own, unless both happen to know the "Mandarin," or official, language, which implies high educational attainments; even then their pronunciation would differ considerably. So entirely different are the provincial dialects —some of them attain to the dignity of separate languages —that I have heard a man from Canton and a native of Tien-tsin conversing in *Pidjin*-English, the only possible medium of communication between them, as, being men of the artisan class, they did not speak "Mandarin," and were acquainted with only a few of the most usual characters, quite insufficient for their purpose. Had they possessed a fair knowledge of writing, they could, of course, have communicated freely on paper, just as *educated* Chinese, Japanese, and Koreans can, as they all use the Chinese ideograms, although not always with *exactly* the same meaning, and placing the parts of speech in a different order in the sentence, according to the syntax of their entirely different languages. This entails a considerable amount of trouble, the Chinese, for instance, having to look for the verb at the *end* of a Japanese sentence, much as we have to wade through half a page of German before we find the *geworden sem soll,* the *gehabt haben durfte,* or other gruesome verbal combination, that tells us what it is all about. In spite of this difficulty, the educated people· of the three Far Eastern Empires can, and do,·communicate with one another in writing, and read one another's books, provided they be printed in the Chinese character. During the war, the Japanese soldiers could always make the Chinese population understand their requirements by tracing· the more commonly-known characters in the snow, or in sand, with the point of the bayonet. When that novel Japanese writing instrument traced the word "run" in the air, the Chinese "Braves" understood it, in most cases, without a moment's hesitation.

It is impossible to over-estimate the enormous advantage over all Occidental nations that this possession of a common written language—not to speak of a classical literature familiar to both—gives the Japanese in all their dealings with their neighbours, the Chinese and Koreans. Devoutly as it might be desired that they should abandon their present, diabolically complicated, system of writing—or, rather, systems, for they have three, with variations—that causes the youth of Japan to spend, in its acquisition, long years which would suffice for learning three Occidental tongues, and replace it by the Roman character, used phonetically, as·advocated by the *Roma-ji-Kwai,* or Roman Character Society, of Tōkio, there appears no prospect of such a reform for many years to come. Japan is not likely to give up the powerful lever she possesses for working on the Chinese mind when the day will come for her to resume her task, interrupted, for the nonce, but nowise abandoned, of leading her tottering Celestial "Elder Brother" along the path of reform she herself has so fearlessly followed.

In the meantime, their common *written* language is of incalculable advantage to the people of Eastern Asia in their international mercantile transactions. A Chinese

Graduate once said to me : "What is the use of this *Volapük* there is so much talk about ?" (He had met with an enthusiastic European student of that short-lived "Universal Language.") "Why don't you Western people all learn to write Chinese ? If you all knew a certain sign, two strokes" (all that remains of an archaic hieroglyphic drawing of a man, just his striding legs,) "as the character for 'man,' you might pronounce it 'man,' *homme, Mann, uomo, hombre, homem, ember, muzh, barbatu,* according to your nationality, it would convey the same idea to all the minds that had learnt it. Believe me," he concluded, "Chinese is the only true Universal Written Language."

One example will suffice to show the appalling difficulties inherent to the problem of adapting the Morse code to the intoned monosyllables of Chinese, and inseparable even from ordinary speech. *Pao*, as we would spell it—the Chinese "write" it by painting—with the writing-brush and what we call "Indian" ink because it is not made in India, rubbed, with water, on a smooth stone—a little diagram, something like a gridiron attached to a bird-cage—*Pao* means, pronounced with the level intonation, "treasure." A slight inflection of the voice, which we can only render, quite arbitrarily, by an accent, or an apostrophe, makes it sound *Pa'o*, written with quite another little picture, and signifying "faggot, bundle of sticks." Thus, when a Chinese happens to be suffering from a violent cold in his head, the wife of his bosom cannot make out if he is calling her his "treasure" or his "bundle of sticks."

The problem of telegraphing in the Chinese language has, however, been solved by a code of numerals corresponding to nearly seven thousand carefully-selected ideograms in every-day use. For instance, the ideogram for "Cash" (*Ch'ien*), the word that most frequently occurs to the Chinese mind, is expressed, in the Code now in use, by the numerals 6030. In telegraphing, the

N

operator merely sends the code signal along the wire. It is translated at the receiving office at the other end into the ideogram for "Cash." Of course, if the cardinal number 6030 is to be conveyed, the signals used would be the three combinations of numerals fixed by the Code to represent the words "six," "thousand," and "thirty."

It may be thought that proper names would not readily lend themselves to transmission by this system— some of our English ones, Higginbotham or Satterthwaite, for instance, certainly would not—but in China there are only one hundred surnames, said to have been originally bestowed on the people by the great Fuh-hi, nearly three thousand years B.C. It is characteristic of the thoroughly Chinese spirit of this ruler, real or mythical, that his avowed object in giving his subjects family names, or rather "Clan names," was to facilitate their registration for purposes of taxation. The Chinese to this day refer to themselves as "the Hundred Names," as we would say: "the People," "the Nation." And from this limited stock every foreigner who holds communication with Chinese must select a name by which they are to call him; always of course, a monosyllable, as like as possible to the radical sound of his own surname. Thus Morrison becomes "Ma," Thompson is rendered "Tan," White becomes "Wei," Manson, "Man," Bale, "Pê."

In Japan, the difficulty was much more easily overcome when the admirably-managed, cheap telegraph system that now extends all over the Island Empire was commenced in 1871. Amongst the bewildering variety of modes of writing possessed by the Japanese, the *Kana* is phonetic. Of the two kinds of *Kana*, the *Kata-kana* and *Hiragana*, the latter, consisting of a syllabary, was framed by the celebrated Japanese Buddhist Saint Kōbō Daishi (Abbot of Tōji in Kiōtō in A.D. 810, and called Kūkai during his lifetime). It is composed of forty-seven syllables, each expressed by a cursive form of a Chinese ideogram. Unfortunately, the *Hiragana*—hardly ever used for whole books, except books

for children, "Penny Novelettes" for women, and religious
or moral tracts for the lower orders, seldom, nowadays,
for letters, but always for the affixes denoting the cases
of nouns and the moods and tenses of verbs—has become,
in the course of nearly eleven centuries, very complicated,
owing to the numerous abbreviated forms in which its
forty-seven signs may be written.

The Saint would hardly recognise his own syllabary—
the Japanese A B C, which, being a Japanese, he drew up
poetically, in a stanza beginning: *"Iro ha"* *—if he saw
it in some of its present forms. His soul would revolt
at them, for he was the most marvellous penman, or,
rather, "brush-man," that ever lived. He could write,
it is said, with five brushes at once; one in each hand,
one grasped by the toes of each foot, and the fifth held
in his mouth. But, universal genius though he was, he
cannot be said to have been entirely original in his conception of the *Hiragana* Syllabary, for, nearly half a
century before his time, the great scholar and statesman
Shimomichi-no Mabi, (or Kibo-no Makabi,) commonly
known as Kibi Dai-jin (died A.D. 776), invented, according
to tradition, a much simpler system, the *Kata-kana*, or
"Side-Characters," consisting of the forty-seven syllables
expressed by very easily-written signs which are only
sides, or parts, detached from Chinese ideograms. It is a
beautifully simple system, there being only one form of
each of the forty-seven characters, with two kinds of
modifying marks for some; unfortunately, the Japanese,
although they all know it, use it only for terminal affixes
and particles, and for the attempt—chiefly far from successful—to render the phonetic value of foreign proper
nouns, and other foreign words. The impossibility of
doing this successfully becomes apparent when it is
stated that there is no *true* L-sound in Japanese, and,

* *I, Ro, Ha*, being the first three syllables in Kōbō Daishi's metrical
table, are used, like our A B C, to indicate the whole syllabary. A Japanese
child "learns its *Iro ha*" as ours "learn their A B C."

consequently, no sign to represent such a sound, just as there is no *true* R-sound in Chinese. Curiously enough, the Japanese attempt to pronounce our L results in an R-sound; they say "Rondon" for London, whereas the Chinese, in trying to articulate a foreign word containing an R, pronounce it as an L, and inform you quite calmly that their staple food consists of "*L*ice." * A Japanese would remark, conversely, that "*R*ice are very unp*r*easant insects."

The Koreans are as exasperating to the Occidental student as the Japanese in their adherence to the Chinese ideograms, instead of using generally the much simpler phonetic character, called *Ön-mun*, they possess. Introduced by Royal Edict in A.D. 1447, it consists of only twenty-five *letters*, representing, not syllables, but eleven vowels and fourteen consonants, constituting, therefore, a real phonetic *alphabet*, and, moreover, a highly logical and scientific one, with characteristic bases for each group of letters, according to the sounds—labials, dentals, palatals, gutturals, and laryngeals. This remarkable alphabet, the letters of which are easy to form, and pleasing to the eye, is so beautifully simple that the wrong-headed Koreans treat it with supreme contempt. It is considered so ridiculously easy that no attempt is made to teach it. Every Korean boy and girl is expected to learn it by his, or her, own slight exertions. The numerous schoolmasters, often *Yang-ban*, for tuition is the only occupation an impoverished Korean aristocrat can turn to for a living, reserve their energies for teaching the abnormally difficult Chinese ideographic writing. So the beautiful alphabet is looked upon as common and vulgar; the Korean gentry, although they all know it, use it only when writing what women (who use it habitually) and the uneducated classes are to read. Hence its use, mixed with the Chinese ideograms of common occurrence, in Proclamations to the people.

* In the language of Peking there is a sound, exasperatingly difficult for Occidentals to imitate, which is somewhat like "*rij.*"

Chinese ideograms, Japanese *Hiragana* and *Kata-kana*, and Korean alphabetic characters, are all written, with the same kind of brush, ink, and stone as implements, in vertical columns from top to bottom, beginning at the right hand top corner of the paper, so that a book in any Far Eastern characters begins where our books end—not the only Far Eastern custom that appears topsy-turvy to our eyes. From the phonetic nature of the Japanese *Kana* and the Korean alphabet it may be inferred that the introduction of telegraphy into those countries did not encounter the linguistic obstacles that were, ultimately, so ingeniously surmounted in the case of China. And now China has telegraphs, and actually works them herself, with pig-tailed operators—all of the male sex, whereas in Japan dear, demure, little *musumé* are, almost exclusively, employed in the Telephone Exchanges.

China's adoption of telegraphy was, like all her moves in the direction of progress, the result not so much of a desire to confer benefits on the population, nor even to enrich the national exchequer, as of the compulsion of necessity. When, in 1879, the Chinese Special Envoy, CHUNG How, instead of inducing the Russians to evacuate the Chinese Territory of Ili, in the extreme North-West—where the Tsar's troops had occupied Kuldja during the commotion caused by the establishment of Yakub Beg's Kingdom of Kashgaria—had signed the humiliating Treaty of Livadia, the Regents at Peking had become thoroughly alarmed at the want of means of rapid communication that had placed the interests of China at the mercy of an incompetent, some say a venal, Envoy, placed beyond their control. Had they been aware of the course of the "negotiations" by which CHUNG How was bullied, or cajoled, or "persuaded" in the manner so well understood by both parties to the Treaty, into a surrender that bore all the appearances of a betrayal, they would have broken off the *pourparlers* and at once recalled their faithless, or inefficient, representative.

But there was no telegraph station nearer to Peking than Shanghai, where the enterprising Great Northern Telegraph Company, a powerful international corporation—principally Danish and Russian—had surreptitiously landed the shore end of their coast cable from Hongkong in the silent watches of a dark night in 1871. Had the Mandarins noticed the operation, the usual opposition would have been encountered by the Company—permission had not been sought, as it would not have been granted without years of wearisome negotiations and, probably, more than one hard "squeeze"; once the cable was in full working order, and wealthy Chinese merchants had been coaxed into using it, the authorities accepted the accomplished fact, as they generally do.

When, at last, the Regents at Peking realised the dangers they had incurred by the delay in communicating with CHUNG How, they resolved to follow the advice of their famous Viceroy, the late General Tso Tsung-tang, a really great Chinese, one of the same stamp as Admiral Ting, and to adopt the mysterious invention of the Outer Barbarians that would enable them to "talk over the wires" with their Envoys in distant lands, to receive instantaneous reports from all parts of the huge Empire, and to flash orders to the great army in the far North-West, the host that had, under Tso's leadership, annihilated the Mohammedan Kingdom which Yakub Beg had set up in Kashgaria. CHUNG How returned to China in January, 1880, not without grave misgivings, for he must have begun to reflect that his signing away to Russia an important tract of Ili, with all the strategically valuable passes in the Tien Shan mountains, the great trading city of Yarkand, and an "indemnity" of five million roubles thrown in, was not likely to strike the Regents as a piece of brilliant diplomacy. It did not; the Regents repudiated him and his precious Treaty, degraded him, and resolved to purify their Diplomatic Service by decapitating him. CHUNG How was, however, reprieved and set free, an act of clemency that was attributed, by Occidentals, to the intercession of the Foreign Ministers in Peking. It is quite possible that it was due to different causes, never to be known in the West, and, perchance, not entirely unconnected with some process of disgorging ill-gotten gains. Another famous Chinese statesman, the late Marquis Tsêng, went to St. Petersburg and negotiated a fresh Treaty, ratified in August, 1881, that was almost as great a surprise to the world as CHUNG HOW's, but in the opposite direction— it actually afforded the unusual spectacle of Russia giving up something she had "acquired"! By its terms, Russia returned nearly the whole of the Territory of Ili, including Kuldja, to China, retaining only a strip on the western frontier of the territory, and receiving from the Peking Government an "indemnity" of nine millions of roubles "in full satisfaction of all claims." Twice within seventeen years, in Kuldja, in 1881, and in Korea, in 1898, Russia, has, in her admirable wisdom, given up what she had gripped in her hand of iron—retiring both times for inscrutable reasons, but, we may be sure, always to her ultimate benefit. There is an appropriate French idiom: *Reculer pour mieux sauter.*

The fear of war with Russia, that had seemed imminent, passed away, but the resolve to introduce telegraphy, which the peril had induced, remained, and the land lines were commenced in 1881, after the public mind had been calmed by the assurance, on the part of several renowned "Literati," that telegraphy was really only a revival, in a highly-developed form, of an invention originating, like all others, in the early days of Ancient China, when two famous sages had held converse at a distance along a stretched string. Now the lines extend unto the utmost parts of the Empire, from north to south and from east to west. A sign of real progress, truly, but slightly diminished in its significance when we consider what sort of Government Messages occasionally flash along the wires

"On His Imperial Majesty's Service." That very modern giant, Electricity, must wince .when he is bidden to convey a message from the Governor of a Province to Peking, reporting that he has had a whole street pulled down because a case of parricide had occurred in one of the houses and, as every Chinese knows, there must have been gross remissness on the part of the neighbours, who cannot have exerted their influence to preserve a high moral tone in the locality. The Governor asks, too, whether—considering the heinous nature of the crime, the worst one possible—he shall have the city wall pulled down at one corner, and a round bastion substituted for a square one at the East Gate. How the wires must quiver when they bear the intelligence from the Capital that a famous Chinese Mohammedan rebel chieftain, who had long defied the Imperial authority in the wilds of Kan-su, has paid the penalty of his high treason—considered in China as parricide, revolt being construed into an attempt on the life of the Emperor, who is the Father of his People, and, like all Chinese fathers, "He who *must* be obeyed"—and transmit, in curt sentences, an account of his undergoing the extreme punishment appointed by the law, the *ling-chi*, or slow death *by slicing*, after the extermination by the executioner's sword, in his presence, of his whole family, including his grandfather, eighty years of age, his mother, his wife, and his five children, the youngest ten months old ! * Or, perhaps, the message that speeds along is from His Excellency the Governor-General of the Two Kwang, reporting a drought, and asking that chastisement be meted out to him by the Board of Punishments, as the drought was inflicting serious damage on the Provinces for which he was responsible. Thus did Li Hung-chang, when

---

* In cases of forgery of important official documents (such as a Memorial to the Throne, as on 9th February, 1896) the punishment of the innocent members of the culprit's family is tempered by clemency (!). The lives of the sons under sixteen are spared, but they are turned into eunuchs, and the daughters are sold into slavery, generally to brothels

reporting to the Throne, in the summer of 1888, on the overflow of the Yung-ting River, that had caused fearful damage in the Province of Chih-li, under his government, propose that his subordinates — who appear to have manfully done their best to stem the flood and to succour the inhabitants, even at the risk of their own lives—should be reduced in rank all round, and that his own name .should be submitted to the Board of Punishments for the pronouncement of such sentence as might be thought commensurate with his "crime." According to Chinese ideas, any disaster, however unavoidable, is held to be a mark of the unworthiness of those in power —not, as in mediæval, and, in some circles, still in modern Europe, as a "judgment" on a sinful community. The Emperor himself, in numerous Proclamations, assumes his share of the responsibility for national disasters, attributing them to his own manifold shortcomings, imploring the forgiveness of outraged Heaven, whose wrath has been plainly manifested by flood, famine, or rebellion, and promising to reform his conduct. The same notion prevails in Korea, where the monarch, autocrat though he be, makes public and abject confession of his unworthiness whenever more than usually acute troubles arise in that distressful country. Even in New Japan, the belief in the intimate relation of the sovereign's personal worth to the national prosperity, or misfortune, lingers in men's minds, and, as this, originally Chinese, conception cuts both ways, the masses attribute the glorious success of the nation's enterprises, in peace and war, to the resplendent virtues of their Emperor.

The official messages conveyed along the wires in China are sometimes of a more cheering nature than those of which I have given specimens. For instance, the telegraph may be used to communicate the Imperial Edict, just sealed with the Vermilion Seal, ordering certain local authorities to erect a Memorial Arch in honour of the spirit of the late Widow Chung, distinguished by her good deeds,

and especially by the example of filial piety she gave, some
years ago, by cutting a slice off her thigh, and cooking it,
that it might be eaten by her mother-in-law, for whom
this diet had been prescribed by an eminent physician, as
a probable cure, provided the patient were kept in ignorance of its nature, for an obstinate disease. Or the
Governor of An-hui may "wire" to Peking, as he did
in the spring of 1889, the gleeful intelligence that of the
competitors at the examination for literary degrees—the
only path to official rank and civil employment—held in
his Province, thirty-five were over eighty years old, and
eighteen over ninety. A life-time of being "ploughed"
could not daunt these indomitable old boys, whose
essays were reported to be "perfectly accurate in diction,
and the hand-writing firm and distinct." It is satisfactory
to know that those who could prove that sixty years—
the *real* "Cycle of Cathay"—had elapsed since they took
their Bachelor's Degree, and that they had been "plucked"
at the three last examinations for the higher step, were
entitled, should they fail in this fourth attempt, to claim
an Honorary Degree. There used to be a doggerel verse
current at an English University, which proclaimed the
fact that :—

> "There was a man at —— Hall,
> Who knew next to nothing at all.
> He was forty-three
> When he took his degree;
> Which was young for —— Hall."

Had he studied in An-hui, he might have "chummed"
with an Undergraduate of sixty-four—a mere Freshman.

On the third of January, 1896, at early morn — for
Majesty transacts its business betimes at Peking, confer-
ring with the Cabinet Ministers at 4, and even at 3, A.M.—a
package labelled "Respectful Memorials from CH'EN Pao-
chen, Governor of Hu-nan," was opened in the "Pink Forbidden Precincts." Within an hour—some things are done
quickly in China—a message was on its way, partly by tele-

graph, partly by courier, to the Governor, informing him
that "on the package being opened, the usual Memorial
asking after the Imperial healths of Their Majesties the
Emperor, the Empress Dowager, and Empress, was absent,
which is a grave dereliction of etiquette," and that, "in
punishment thereof," he would be "handed to the Board
of Civil Appointments for the determination of an appropriate penalty." One wonders what the Board would
consider ."appropriate" to "make the punishment fit the
crime," as Mr. W. S. Gilbert puts it. Perhaps "Something humorous and lingering, with boiling oil in it"?

Lest it be thought that these instances of the very
Chinese nature of official acts in what is still Old China
might be looked upon as fanciful distortions of fact, I may
state that every one of them is to be found, amidst
hundreds of others of a similar character, recorded in the
cold, dry, official style of the *Peking Gazette*, that epitome
of all "things Chinese," the official journal of the Empire,
and the oldest periodical on earth. It has appeared daily
since the middle of the fourteenth century (although not
always under its present title, as Peking did not become
the Capital until the Emperor Ch'eng-tsu, of the Ming
dynasty, established his court there in A.D. 1421,) so that
the earlier back numbers are scarce. An excellent English
translation of this unique newspaper is now issued annually by the Shanghai *North China Herald*, as a reprint
of the abstracts from the *Gazette* that have appeared in
its columns during the year. Those who want to know
Chinese life in all its intricate detail, to study the extraordinary medley of contradictions that constitutes the
character of the Chinese, and to marvel at the nature of
the Government, so nearly perfect in theory, so defective
in practice, that has, with all its faults, managed to
control three or four hundred millions of people for a
period longer by far than that covered by any other rule
in the history of the world—should read the translation
of the *Peking Gazette*.

They should study these unique annals, however, by the light of some of the excellent books that have been written, in popular style, by men who have devoted their lives to the investigation of the Mystery of China. Of the more recent works of this kind, Professor R. K. Douglas's *Society in China* contains, for its size, an immense amount of information; *Chinese Characteristics*, by the Reverend Arthur H. Smith, twenty-two years a Missionary of the American Board in China, *The Chinese, their Present and Future : Medical, Political, and Social*, by Robert Coltman, Jr., M.D., formerly a Medical Missionary in Northern China, and *The Real Chinaman*, by Chester Holcombe, for many years Interpreter, Secretary of Legation, and Acting Minister of the United States at Peking—these are all veritable treasuries of Chinese lore. The works by Smith, Coltman, and Holcombe are so admirably written, sparkling with humour, and full of good—and true—stories, that they may be thoroughly enjoyed even by those who took no particular interest in China before their perusal. It will be strange if they do not become thus interested after reading these fascinating books. When their appetite is once whetted, they will relish the fare set before them in *Stories of Everyday Life in Modern China*, "told by Chinese and done into English by" T. Watters, late H.B.M. Consul at Foochow (or, according to the new, and more scientific, orthography: Fu-chau,) in *A Corner of Cathay*, "studies from life among the Chinese," by Adele M. Fielde, an American lady who resided for fifteen years in China, chiefly at Swatow (or Swa-tau), in the south-eastern corner of the Empire ; and in *A String of Chinese Peach-Stones*, by W. Arthur Cornaby, who has strung together a large number of vivid sketches of life and character in Central China, presented in the form of a story.

Thus the enquirer into the truth about China may equip himself for his study of the *Peking Gazette*, and become able to weigh judiciously the views as to the great Chinese Problem propounded by many eminent writers—notably in *China Present and Past*, a collection of valuable essays by R. S. Gundry, in Lord Curzon of Kedleston's brilliant *Problems of the Far East*, in the pregnant chapters of Colquhoun's *China in Transformation*, in Valentine Chirol's amplification in book form, under the title of *The Far Eastern Question*, of his admirable letters to the *Times*, and in the breezy pages of *Pioneering in Formosa*, by W. A. Pickering, C.M.G. But no views as to the future of China can be appreciated at their proper value, no personal opinion can be rightly formed, unless it be constantly borne in mind that *the Chinese are Chinese*, not Occidentals, and that, consequently, our own standards must be discarded in measuring their capacity for national reform and regeneration. How very unlike ourselves the Chinese are in their modes of thought, how widely divergent from us in their way of considering almost every subject, can, I think, be shown most clearly by continuing to cite instances of recent occurrence which go to prove that China is *Old* China still.

The public mind in Occidental countries seems to have become imbued with the idea that China is yearning for railways. No such feeling has entered into the Chinese heart. It never yearns for any innovation from abroad. There can be no doubt, however, that the attitude of the official class towards the introduction of railways throughout the Empire has undergone a very marked change since 1887, when a Memorial proposing the construction of an "experimental railway" from Ta-ku to Tien-tsin was presented to the Empress Regent by the Board of *Admiralty* (!) and led to the issue by Her Majesty of an Imperial Edict formally sanctioning the scheme. Sullen opposition and active interference have been replaced by lively interest, and the great Mandarins lend willing ears to the persistent representations of energetic would-be *concessionaires*, whose pockets bulge with plans and estimates for lines from anywhere to everywhere within the borders of the Flowery Land.

What is the cause of this welcome change of front? Have the ruling classes become penetrated by the conviction that the iron road will, as many Occidentals maintain, prove to be China's salvation? Are they, at last, alive to the incalculable benefits to accrue to Chinese commerce, to the development of the country's immense resources, and especially of its almost untouched mineral wealth, by the general introduction of railways? Are they now convinced of the prosperity it would bring to millions of the people? In the case of a few enlightened officials the change of opinion has, undoubtedly, been brought about by considerations of this nature, for, be it remembered, there are Mandarins who are as capable of appreciating the benefits of Western civilisation as are the men of New Japan, but the number of such is lamentably small and increasing but slowly. The great majority of those officials who give their countenance to railway projects do so either honestly, from a desire to see their country provided with the greatest facilities for rapid transport, not of produce, or minerals—questions of economic development do not, as a rule, engross their attention—nor of passengers—in their opinion the existing facilities for travel are sufficient—but of troops and material of war for the prompt repression of the ever-recurring insurrections and for the purpose, cherished secretly in their hearts, of some day driving the hated "Foreign Devils" from the sacred soil of China; or they have been converted to their present frame of mind by a reason potent beyond all others with the average Mandarin; they have discovered railway enterprise to be a lucrative opportunity of "Squeeze-*Pidjin*." Even if the line be never constructed, the eager concession-hunter will have been well "squeezed," an operation that affords not only profit, but the delightful consciousness that the lucre is being extracted from the pockets of the despised foreigner. Should the

construction be really undertaken, the opportunities for
further extortion, from natives as well as foreigners, are
unbounded. In the transfer of the necessary land, the
supply of materials obtained locally, and of labour, the
official "squeeze" can be applied in ways too numerous
to mention. Every contract and sub-contract will leave
a substantial percentage on the Mandarin's palm, and, far
from allaying its normal itching, will only increase the
craving for a repeated application. Once the railway is in
operation, new "squeezes" will be invented with astonishing rapidity. From the plate-layer to the General Manager,
every servant, or official, of the line will have to pay
tribute to the Mandarin, either directly or, more probably,
through the numerous "suckers" of the Chinese official
octopus—the *Yamên* "Runners" and others of the
motley crew of parasites that cluster round every man
in authority in the "Middle Empire." It has been truly
said that the British Empire is "Entirely Supported by
Voluntary Contributions." The Empire of China may, with
equal justice, be said to derive its financial means of
existence from a system of illegal "commissions." The
normal taxation is so light that it cannot possibly satisfy
the calls of the Treasury, the revenue from the Maritime
Customs, the only honestly-administered source of income,
is hypothecated to the foreign creditors of the State, and
the amounts forwarded to Peking by the Viceroys and
Governors-General to fill up the permanent deficit, as well
as the sums requisite for the administration of the Eighteen
Provinces and the Territories, must needs be produced by
other means.

What those means may be is left to the discretion of
the wretchedly underpaid officials—a Viceroy, governing
territories as large as, and far more populous than, France,
receives, as yearly salary and "Anti-extortion Allowance,"
not more than six thousand pounds sterling—and the
result may be easily imagined. The British race, with that
admirable common-sense that still distinguishes it in private

matters, although it seems, unfortunately, to have occasionally deserted it in affairs of State, long ago recognised the
great truth that to pay a man well is the surest way to
keep him honest. . China is oblivious of this great principle.
So is Korea, and even in Japan, whose administration is, in
many respects, a model worthy of imitation, the salaries,
especially in the judicial branch, might be raised with
great advantage to the efficiency of the public service.
In China, the Mandarin robs unblushingly right and
left, because, unless he have considerable private means,
he is obliged to ; and the necessity for theft increases as the lower grades of officials and hangers-on
are reached, who are dependent on their "pickings" for
a living. "We must live," plead the peccant petty
Mandarin, his Clerk, the "Precedent-Searcher" who hangs
about round the *Yamên,* and assists litigants with his
knowledge of ancient cases (he is the Chinese substitute
for our Solicitor, and leaves "the daughter of the horse-
leech" far behind in unsatisfied greed), the Constable, and
the hundred and one rapacious underlings who form a
disreputable body-guard to the thief on a grand scale
who sits enthroned in the *Yamên.* "We must live," is the
cry of all of them. One feels tempted to reply, as the
French judge did to the thief's similar plea : "*Je n'en vois
pas la nécessité.*"

Truly, the lowest depths of official corruption and
extortion appear to have been reached in China, although
there are, as there must always be, some bright exceptions
to prove the rule—a few officials as honest and as zealous
as any in the world. But the majority are dishonest, inefficient and cruelly extortionate, the only limit to their
exactions being the twofold fear of having to share too
palpable booty with a superior whose cupidity might be
attracted by its magnitude, and of pushing the people to
the verge of insurrection, a sacred right even the marvellously patient Chinese resort to when too harshly oppressed.
And the occurrence of riots, or of the more passive resistance

frequently adopted, in the shape of a general strike on the part of the aggrieved shopkeepers, or craftsmen, leads to notice being taken at Peking and to an enquiry being ordered. The enquiry is duly held, with all the show of absolute impartiality peculiar to the theoretically perfect form of paternal government. Fathoms of "Yellow Tape" are unwound, yards and yards of thin paper are covered with ideograms, and, nine times out of ten, the offending Mandarin is reported to the Throne as being guilty. His punishment depends greatly upon the degree of safety with which the Government may disregard popular feeling in that particular district. If it may safely be appeased by merely transferring the guilty Mandarin to another locality, that is all the punishment that will be officially meted out to him, with a warning as to his future conduct. This he generally receives with a genuinely contrite mien, as he thinks of the large sum he has had to part with to the powers that be in order to secure the lenient sentence.

If, on the contrary, the district be a turbulent one, and likely to give serious trouble—one, for instance, with a large proportion of Chinese Mohammedans, sturdy and independent, in its population; or, if the district be situated in Southern China, one with a large number of those hulking, ill-conditioned, rough fellows, with pigtails thick as stout ropes coiled round their villainous heads, who live from hand to mouth by odd jobs and questionable expedients, and, when they emigrate to the Straits Settlements, become the *Samseng*, the loafers and bullies who are the terror of Singapore,—then the high authorities will make the Mandarin suffer severely for his misdeeds. In such cases, even his ill-gotten wealth may be powerless to save him from degradation and dismissal, for his superiors are determined in their purpose to make a severe example of an official who robs so clumsily and so greedily as to provoke what the *Pidjin*-English tongue aptly describes as "too muchee *bobbery*." *

* *Bobbery*, trouble, commotion, disorder, row, fuss.

O

That is the first principle of Chinese administrative science: No "*bobbery.*" The Province that has no history is the happy land; the Viceroy who is but seldom heard of is *persona gratissima* within the "Pink Forbidden City." The chief aim of that greatest of all Chinese, KONG Fu-sze, whom Occidentals have Latinised into "Confucius," appears to have been the regulation of public and private life in all their phases, so that the existence of every human being, as a duly-subordinated link in an endless chain of mutual responsibility, might run smoothly without any "*bobbery.*" Not a very high ideal, perhaps, and savouring more of a set of "Rules and Regulations" than of the moral and social code to be expected from one of the world's greatest leaders of thought, but these rules, such as they are, some of them trite, some admirable, all of them severely practical in purpose, have served to keep hundreds of millions of men together as a nation, with a highly-developed civilisation of a peculiar sort, for the space of two thousand and four hundred years, keep them together to this day, and will continue to do so for generations to come. Whatever flag may wave over Peking, the Chinese will continue to be governed by the rules of life laid down by Confucius, but having their origin in racial characteristics that existed ages before his birth in 551 B.C.

Confucius himself plainly intimated that his guiding principles were not original. He called himself a "Transmitter" and claimed no more than the glory of being the wise man *par excellence*, sapient with the accumulated wisdom of past generations, and striving to reconstitute, by the help of his study of ancient records, the state of idyllic happiness that is said to have prevailed in the days of Yao and of Shun, monarchs of the mythical, or semi-mythical, period, some two thousand three hundred years B.C. He taught that man, originally good, could, by strict adherence to the ancient rules of conduct he professed to revive, attain to the perfection, and consequent happiness, of the people of that Golden Age. There is no doubt that the Sage, himself a typical Chinese, knew his country-men thoroughly, and framed for them a rule of life he knew to be suited to their racial peculiarities. Hence the extraordinary sway his teaching has exercised since his death, in 479 B.C., over the minds of the Chinese. Surely the memory of no man, not even of Mohammed, is venerated by so many millions at the present time, and this veneration of Confucius had existed for a thousand years when Mohammed preached Islam. The secret of the vitality of the Confucian system of social order—it is more a Police Code than a Philosophy; it is certainly not a Religion—lies in the fact, pointed out above, of its being thoroughly Chinese and based on the traditions of remote antiquity. Very Chinese and very old—these are recommendations that outweigh all others in the Chinese mind.

I have stated that Confucianism is not a Religion. Of the two creeds that overlap each other in China, the people following the practices of either, or both, as the occasion prompts them—Taoism was based by Lao-tze, a contemporary of Confucius, but his senior, on the Brah-minical Philosophy of India—but has degenerated into a confused farrago of addled metaphysics and of grotesque magic rites; Buddhism, which was a real *Religion* when it was established in China, coming from India, in the first century after Christ, has also degenerated. In contact with the matter-of-fact Chinese mind, it has lost the element of faith, and has sunk from its original purity, its noble simplicity, its sweet spirit of universal love and charity, so nearly akin to the original precepts of Chris-tianity, to its present degraded condition, stifled by elaborate ritual, overgrown with gross superstitions, de-based by the low moral tone of the majority of its priesthood. Neither Taoism nor Buddhism could flourish in their pristine purity in China, because neither was founded on Chinese lines. That extraordinary racial

vitality, that changeless spirit of firm adherence to
national peculiarities, that marvellous imperviousness to
outer influences, that have enabled the Chinese to assimi-
late, one after another, the alien nations that conquered
them, as they assimilated their present Manchu rulers till
no outward trace of their origin is left, also enabled them
to modify the religious systems imported from abroad.
Buddhism attempted to convert the Chinese, and the
Chinese converted Buddhism. If Christianity ever obtains
a firm hold in China, it will be by adapting itself to the
Chinese mind, at present antagonistic. This truth was
recognised, in the late seventeenth and early eighteenth
centuries, by those wonderful Jesuit Missionaries who
gained the favour of the great Emperor K'ang-hi; it is
acknowledged to-day by the most enlightened Missionaries
of all denominations who know China. Once Christianity
has taken firm root amongst the "Hundred Names," a
native pastorate will become a necessity. The foreign
teachers will have to go, and then we may expect strange
developments. It is quite certain that Christianity in its
Occidental form will never commend itself to the bulk
of the Chinese race. A Chinese form, evolved by the
Chinese themselves from the broad principles inculcated
by the foreign Missionaries, may prove the salvation of
China. At all events, whatever may be the form of
religion adopted by a reformed China—if there be ever
a reformed China seeking for any religion at all—it will
be a Chinese form on Chinese lines. In the meantime,
Confucianism holds sway as the moral system that checks
the vices of the average Chinese and encourages them to
virtue.

The teachings of Confucius, the works of his commen-
tators, the ancient classics imbued with his spirit, the
much more ancient classics that inspired him, these still
constitute the educational equipment of the Chinese
Graduate. Efforts have been made, indeed, to introduce
Occidental sciences, notably mathematics, as optional

subjects in the great Competitive Examinations, but hitherto with scant success. There are Colleges, it is true, few and far between, at which the students are put through a complete Occidental curriculum under foreign teachers; at Peking, steps were even being taken, early in 1898, to found a University on the Occidental plan, and the diplomatic representatives of foreign states, including Italy and the Netherlands, immediately claimed Professorships for their compatriots, thus keeping up the tradition that every one of the slight indications of a progressive movement on the part of China is to be the signal for an undignified game of grab by the Western countries—each one for itself, and the *Tsung-li Yamên* take the hindmost—with the result, usually, that the contemplated step forward is never taken, China being unable to satisfy all the contending nations, and afraid to offend some by favouring others.

Small as are the beginnings of Occidental education in China, they have already borne good fruit, thanks to the zeal of the foreign teachers, and to the marvellous perseverance, the natural abilities, and the extraordinary memory of the students (there are many Chinese scholars who can recite a bulky classic by heart). But the point that demands attention is that, in establishing a University, Colleges, and special Schools for the Navy and the Army, and so forth, the Imperial Government, and the various Viceroys who have established these institutions independently, without any plan of co-ordination, have not in view the general raising of a standard of useful knowledge throughout the Empire. Their purpose—and it applies also to their sending students to Europe and to America—is merely to ensure a supply of technically trained officers for their modern navy and the "foreign-drilled" portion of their land forces, linguists for employment as interpreters and translators in the *Tsung-li Yamên's* continual negotiations with foreign Powers, engineers for their arsenals, and Secretaries and *Attachés* for their diplomatic service. The men who fill the highest offices of the State, and direct its policy, have not enjoyed the benefits of an Occidental education. The great Lɪ Hung-chang himself, in spite of what he learned on his long journey, would be quite unable to pass the Sixth Standard of a Board School, even were the examination conducted in Chinese.

It is too readily assumed in the West that the aged Chinese statesman's "grand tour" of the principal capitals must needs have convinced him of the superlative excellence of our civilisation. He had long ago recognised the great importance to his country of a reform, on Occidental scientific principles, of her defensive forces; he even contemplated taking the offensive against Japan as soon as the navy and the army he had created could be trained by the foreign Instructors in his pay to a degree of efficiency ensuring, in his opinion, a certainty of success. I have already referred, in the First Chapter, to his schemes to this end. Lɪ Hung-chang had also resolved, long before his journey, on calling in the aid or steam and electricity for the development of the resources of the Provinces under his rule, more especially of those portions constituting his own private estates. He had introduced Occidental expert assistance and modern scientific appliances with this end in view, and to these far-seeing measures he owes, no doubt, to a great extent, the very flourishing state of his exchequer, his private fortune being estimated at various immense sums, expressed in millions of pounds sterling. He had likewise established Colleges where young men might be trained in Western knowledge so as to become efficient assistants to carry out his plans. Even the medical science of the Occident found in him a generous patron, for he understood the importance of skilful physicians and well-ordered hospitals in preserving the lives and the health of the people who were helping him to make his Provinces prosperous, and himself enormously wealthy.

But as for a recognition of the principles under-

lying the strength and prosperity of the West, that
was, probably, as far from his mind on his return to his
Yamên at Tien-tsin as when he left China to represent
the Son of Heaven at the Coronation Ceremonies at
Moscow. Need we wonder if the impression he brought
back was not very flattering to our estimation of the
moral results of our vaunted civilisation? At every capital he visited, he found elaborate preparations to impress
him with the paramount importance of that particular
country. The German Emperor, with that instinct for
stage-management and effect that aroused the envy of the
late Sir Augustus Harris, received him seated on his
throne, with stern, impassive mien, a sword laid across
his knees—a truly impressive type of Imperial Majesty,
armed and omnipotent. Li understood it all; it was so
like Peking and the Dragon Throne in the Pink Forbidden Precincts. But it was when he came into contact
with the representatives of our great industries, of our
commerce and finance, that the narrow eyes began to
twinkle. Those who had the best opportunities of watch-
ing him closely during his visit to the manufacturing and
commercial centres must have been struck not only by
his pleasing geniality of manner, so unlike the pomposity
usual in the Mandarin, but by the instructive expression
of his face as he listened to the many addresses of welcome, the numerous toasts in his honour, all duly translated for his benefit by his skilful interpreters. I stood
by his side at his reception by the President and Council
of the London Chamber of Commerce in the magnificent
Hall of the Fishmongers' Company, and I scrutinised
his striking features intently as he listened to the translation of the various speeches addressed to him. I shall
never forget the contemptuous expression that came over
his face, the slight movement of the shoulders of the
towering figure, and, above all, the amused, cynical twinkle
in the almond eyes behind the great spectacles, as he
heard the assurances of " the warm sympathy with his

ancient country, "the profound respect" for himself or those who lavished fulsome praise on an Empire they considered rotten, and on a man whose chief importance in their eyes lay in his presumed willingness to give away large contracts. Then he was "the enlightened statesman who was guiding his great country's destiny towards a splendid future," but he knew full well that, once he had departed, and with him the hope of contracts and concessions, he would be "the rapacious old intriguer who hoodwinked Europe and America." What a dance he led those effusive old gentlemen, in resplendent white waistcoats and with hats of superlative glossiness, who swarmed round him from morning till night, explaining the hundred and one inventions, every one of which was sufficient in itself to regenerate the whole of China. He listened and smiled, and the "free samples" of heavy castings for steam-engines, of bayonets, bicycles, and torpedos, of sewing-machines and patent harness-paste, of steel rails and lawn-mowers, and all the other indispensable adjuncts to the regeneration of a great nation, accumulated at his door, and were shipped to Tien-tsin, together with reams of railway projects and financial schemes, and hundredweights of "improving literature." But the tall old man continued to smile, and smile, and bowed himself out of the country, and fierce envy filled the heart of every would-be regenerator, because he knew someone else must have got that contract, for he had not. Then the regenerators compared notes and they found that not one of them had got any contract at all, no—not even those who had caused champagne to flow like water and had wasted their substance on flags and triumphal arches, decked with paper roses, in grimy manufacturing towns. And they waxed wroth, so that a battalion of them would easily have stormed the great Island Fort at Wei-hai-wei, had not the Japanese long previously hoisted their flag on it.

Those who believe that China is ripe for reform often

allege that the strenuous efforts of devoted Missionaries
of various denominations, working for years amongst the
people in every part of the Empire, must have prepared
the way for the proximate regeneration of the Chinese
race on a Christian basis.   Here I approach delicate
ground, for those who best know China are divided in
their opinion on the whole subject of Missionary efforts
in Far Cathay. I shall at once please many, I feel sure,
by declaring my firm belief that the Missionaries, both
Roman Catholics and Protestants of all denominations,
have done a vast amount of good in the Far East, and
especially in China, the greatest share being, undoubtedly,
due to those who have adopted educational or medical
work—particularly the latter—as their sphere of action.
But I must be strictly impartial, and I am compelled to
add that the sum total of the results achieved is but a
drop in the Chinese ocean. Insignificant as these results
are, compared with the enormous population, they have
been obtained only at the cost of many precious lives,
and of an amount of devotion and energy, and an expenditure of money, that ought, if properly directed, to
have achieved a far greater measure of success.

The prime cause is to be found in the lamentable
rivalry existing between the three great branches of Christianity, Roman Catholic, Greek Orthodox, and Protestant,
and between the denominations, too numerous to mention,
into which Protestantism is split up. Hence a frittering
of resources, an overlapping of spheres of activity, and—
worse still—a pernicious effect on the minds of those
whose conversion is to be attempted. Those who do not
scoff at the sorry spectacle of the dissensions between
the Missionaries of the different denominations, each
recommending his own way as the only safe road to
Salvation—dissensions fortunately now less violent than
in the past—are bewildered by the multiplicity of spiritual
guides. On several occasions, when I have asked some
highly-educated Oriental, trained in Western knowledge

and, apparently, in every respect capable of seeing eye to eye with Occidentals, why he did not embrace Christianity, he has answered : " *What sort of* Christianity ?" And there has been an ironical tone in the apparently innocent words.

Even with the disadvantage of scattered and disunited forces, Christianity might have made greater headway in the Far East had not its modern preachers begun their labours at the wrong end. In China, governed by an omnipotent literary bureaucracy, absolutely uninfluenced by any spiritual movement among the masses, the Missionaries have, in the nineteenth century, devoted their attention almost exclusively to the lower social strata. A few of the more enlightened ones—notably the Reverend Dr. W. A. P. Martin, the American President of the Imperial *Tung-Wên* College at Peking, the Reverend Dr. A. Williamson, and the Reverend Gilbert Reid, M.A., an American of Scottish descent—long since recognised the fallacy of this method, and advocated an entirely opposite course. The late Sir Thomas Wade, for many years Her Britannic Majesty's representative in China, strongly supported the view that any important change in the attitude of the Chinese towards Christianity must proceed from the upper classes. The history of the successful introduction of alien creeds into Far Eastern countries teaches the same lesson. When Buddhism entered into China, from India, for the second time, in A.D. 61—on the first occasion, in 219 B.C, its Missionaries were unsuccessful—when it was first introduced, in A.D. 552, from China, through Korea, into Japan, it made its first appearance at court, not amongst the people. It was by Special Ambassadors whom the Emperor Ming-ti, of the Later Han Dynasty, had sent abroad to make enquiry into the existence and powers of the mighty spirit *"Fo"*—as the Buddha is called in Chinese—that the Indian religion was brought to China, where it spread with amazing rapidity under the powerful patronage of the Sovereign. The Indian priests, who had accompanied the Ambassadors on their return to China, had a hard struggle against the scepticism of the Literati —Confucianists to a man, then as now—but the Emperor had adopted the new faith, and that was enough; the bulk of the people followed suit. Similarly, in Japan, the first tangible evidences of Buddhism—a golden image of Buddha and some scrolls of the sacred writings—came to the Emperor Kimmei as presents from the King of Kakusai, one of the states into which Korea was divided. The Ambassador who brought these gifts spoke so eloquently in favour of the new religion that the Emperor was inclined to adopt it, but the majority of his Councillors were opposed to it, fearing that the truly national gods, the *Kami* of the *Shin-tō* cult, would object to the foreign intruder, however highly recommended. The Prime Minister, SOGA-NO Inamé, alone favoured the adoption of the new creed by the Emperor, who, in his perplexity, took a course not unusual with those who receive an embarrassing present—he passed on the golden image to someone else, in this case to the Prime Minister, who was ordered to make a trial of the new god. SOGA-NO Inamé accordingly made his country house into a temple for the Golden Buddha. This seemed to displease the *Shin-tō* deities, who felt that the moment had come to discredit their alien rival, the Buddha who was enshrined, so to say, "on approbation," and they caused a pestilent fever to devastate the land. The conservative majority in the Council at once pointed to the golden image as the prime cause of the epidemic. It was promptly hurled into the sea by the command of the indignant Emperor, and its temple was razed to the ground, which seems rather hard on the Prime Minister, whose country house it was. The new faith was not going to allow itself to be so easily disposed of, and it sent such a succession of calamities to punish Japan for its inhospitable treatment that the *Shin-tō* gods' pestilence seemed but a minor temporary inconvenience in comparison. Straightway the

Emperor repented ; a new temple was erected, the golden Buddha was miraculously recovered from the sea (not, however, by a diver, like the golden dolphin of Nagoya Castle, mentioned in the last Chapter,) and the country was at rest.* The Emperor Kimmei's successors favoured the new religion ; the great nobles followed the Imperial example, and—as always in the East—the masses moved with a common impulse in the wake of their rulers.

Buddhism, the faith that counts the vast majority of Far Eastern people amongst its adherents—in Korea alone has it lost ground within the last five centuries, being there little more than a shadow of its former glory—was thus introduced into both China and Japan under Imperial patronage. It permeated the whole social fabric from *above;* there seems but little hope of any religion spreading through the nations of the Far East from below. The first European Missionaries who landed on the shores of China and of Japan, the fearless pioneers from Portugal and, later, from Spain, seem to have judged the situation aright from the very first. They wasted no time, but proceeded straight to the fountain-head of local authority —in Japan the court of the feudal Prince, in China, the *Yamên* of the most important Mandarin—and ingratiated themselves with the highest in the land. The Jesuits— Frenchmen and others of various European nationalities— established themselves in the Palace at Peking, erecting their church within its pink ramparts, and became the trusted high officials and intimate friends of at least three of China's greatest Manchu Emperors. In China, as in Japan, Christianity, introduced under such high auspices, flourished, for a time, to a remarkable degree, numbering its churches by hundreds, and its adherents by hundreds

---

* The miraculous image is preserved to this day in the great Temple of Tennōji at Ōsaka. Sad to relate, it has been found to consist only of gilded copper. Like most relics, it has a rival, a group of three figures of real gold in the Temple of Zenkōji, at Nagano, also claiming to be the original present of the Korean King to the Emperor Kimmei.

of thousands. But for the internecine quarrels of the various religious orders, the intrigues carried on against one another by the different Roman Catholic nationalities, and against all of them by the Dutch—nominally staunch Protestants in those days, but, in the East, really serving the great god Mammon alone—and, above all, the misguided interference of a meddlesome Papal Legate, the whole of the Far East might now be Christian. The mission of that Papal Legate, sent to settle a controversy between the learned and practical Jesuits and the perfervid, narrow-minded Dominicans, was fatal to the churches in China. It convinced the great and enlightened Emperor K'ang-hi, who had issued, in 1692, an Edict of Tolerance that was one of the noblest to which a Chinese ruler had ever affixed the Vermilion Seal, that behind the wonderful men from the West—who devoted their blameless lives to the service of their God, and their extraordinary talents and profound knowledge to the service of the Emperor, without any thought of personal profit—there was a mysterious *foreign* Power actively controlling the millions of all races who entered the fold of the Church. From that moment, Christianity lost its footing at the Court of Peking as it had lost it in Japan, and the terrible persecutions began which succeeded, after long years of heroic resistance on the part of the European pastors and their native flock, in almost obliterating the traces of the glorious work achieved by a band of men as steadfast, as brave, wise and accomplished as ever sallied forth, with their lives in their hands, to do battle for the Cross.

Untaught by these lessons of history, the modern Missionaries devote themselves, almost invariably, to the conversion of the lower classes. To appreciate the futility of this proceeding, we have only to imagine Britain governed absolutely by an administration composed of Newdigate Prizemen, men who have graduated high in Classical Honours, and Senior Wranglers. What would we think of the wisdom of Buddhists who, wishing to convert

the whole of the British Empire to their faith, commenced
operations with a mission to the costermongers in Golden
Lane and Newport Market, and to the inmates of the
Salvation Army's "Shelters"?   That is, broadly indicated,
the position of Missionary enterprise in the Far East.
The reason for it is not unconnected with the fact of the
greater ease with which the poorer classes may be brought
within the fold.   Christianity, the religion of consolation
and sympathy, appeals directly to the suffering poor,
with its comforting promise of a better hereafter for those
whose bitter lot in this world is almost beyond human
endurance.   The poor in China lead lives of such unremit-
ting bitter toil, working from dawn till long after dusk,
and barely escaping from starvation, that it is surprising
more of them do not flock to hear the Glad Tidings, as
the negroes used to in the days of slavery in America.
As it is, the majority of the converts are people in humble
life, their number increasing rather suspiciously in the
times of the ever-recurrent famines, when the Missionaries
work hard in the distribution of relief.   Unfortunately
for the progress of Christianity in China, the very fact that
it is there, more than anywhere else, the religion of the
lowly and the oppressed, attracts to the Chapel a crowd
of wastrels and social wrecks, who—requiring, as they do,
the consolations of the faith more urgently than their
prosperous brethren—yet do great harm to the Missionary
cause.   If dishonest, and they are often sad impostors,
making a trade of their conversion,* they bring discredit

---

* I knew a Chinese from Canton who tramped all over England, in
Chinese dress, and fared sumptuously and gratuitously merely by sitting by
the roadside near the gates of Vicarages and Rectories, poring over a copy
of the Gospels in Chinese.   The following colloquy invariably ensued:—
Vicar, or *Rector:* "What are you reading?"   *A-Hu:* Belong Bible Book.
My catchee inside Blitish-Foleign Bible House, London-side.   Belong
Numba-One first-*chop* Book, allosame some part velly hard makee believe!"
The good Cleric at once undertook to remove the obstacles obscuring A-Hu's
comprehension of difficult points of dogma, a process necessitating restoration of the wayfarer's exhausted frame, and extending in some cases over a
fortnight.   I would be afraid to say how often A-Hu had been "converted,"

on the Missionaries and make them ridiculous in the eyes of the Chinese ; if honest, their sad plight, and the low social status to which they have fallen, make their better situated countrymen hesitate to join the same congregation.　The Chinese authorities are continually complaining that every Mission-house becomes a veritable Alsatia for all the vagrom men and shiftless fellows of the neighbourhood.　This complaint is exaggerated, no doubt, but there is a substratum of truth.　In short, Christianity in China is not "fashionable"; it is not even considered "respectable," and that is a grave drawback to its success with a nation that prizes respectability—"face," as it calls it—above all things.　I will not dwell on the actual mischief wrought by the excessive zeal, or the narrowness of mind, of some few Missionaries; by the imperfect linguistic knowledge of others, leading to absurd and irreverent expressions used, by the misplacing of an intonation, where solemn words were intended ; by the insufficient acquaintance of novices with Chinese manners, customs and thought; and, lastly, by the dictatorial interference of Missionary Societies and Boards at home totally ignorant of Chinese conditions.　These faults have caused the loss of many lives ; they have brought "the inevitable gun-boat" into play, and have caused millions of Chinese to look upon Christianity, and Western civilisation, with scorn and loathing.

What, then, is the course to be pursued in order to introduce the religion of Peace and Good-will into China so that it shall reach *all* classes and be permanent in its effects ?　To this end we must send out men as devoted, as fearless, as energetic, as those who now labour in China, but, if possible, still more highly trained for their duties, and, above all, entirely free from bigotry.　Let us have no men amongst them capable of recording, as the Reverend George Leslie MacKay, D.D., a Canadian Scot,

but he certainly had a capacity for raising knotty points equalled only by Bishop Colenso's Zulu, or the late David Friedrich Strauss

has done in his interesting book *From Far Formosa :
the Island, its People, and Missions,* that in *Pe-po-hoan*
villages, on the Kap-tsu-lan Plain, he "more than once"
dried his rain-soaked clothes "before fires made of idol-
atrous paper, idols and *ancestral tablets.*" Let such carefully-selected men as I have indicated go out to live
blameless, charitable, helpful lives amongst the Chinese
people, carefully observing, in their behaviour, every rule
of native propriety and etiquette. Let them, besides the
mute, but telling, example of their good, pure lives, afford
the Chinese *gratuitous* instruction; to the upper classes
let them teach European languages, and the Occidental
sciences, to the middle and lower classes the rudiments of
practical Western knowledge, such as are imparted in
our elementary schools. Let them minister to the ailments of all, and inculcate sanitary reforms. Especially
let them lecture, with magic-lantern views, about distant
parts of the Chinese Empire—the ignorance of the natives
in this respect is profound; the majority, although often
calling their country "the Eighteen Provinces," are unable
to name more than three or four—and about foreign
lands. Let them teach the farmer and the craftsman
the use of tools more efficient than their rudimentary
appliances, unchanged for many centuries. Let them teach
the Chinese how to make their labour more productive
and *more remunerative;* in the country where every
third word one hears is *Chi'en* ("Cash,") that consideration will carry great weight. Let them lead the Chinese
to think of the great Outer World, at present a blank
to them, and tell them under what conditions its inhabitants live. To do all this they must, of course, become,
as other Missionaries do, proficient in the language. But,
above all, let them never utter a word about *Religion*
unless they be asked; let them never allow a word to
escape them deriding the creeds of the Chinese, the cult
of their Sage, Confucius, the system of their family life—
far more sacred to them than any religious tenets—nor

the worship of their ancestors. The two last—the family system and the ancestral cult—form the keystone of the Chinese social fabric. Who shakes them, makes China totter to her very foundations; who shatters them, brings down the whole edifice of four thousand years and buries three hundred millions of human beings under its ruins.

But, it will be objected, how will the labours of these purely "Secular" Missionaries effect the spiritual regeneration of the Chinese race? When the Chinese begin to realise the advantages of Occidental civilisation in its material aspects, their sharp minds will soon begin to enquire into the conditions of government under which this civilisation has reached its actual development, and they will strive for a purer administration and more even-handed justice in their own Empire. These once obtained, they will further enquire into the moral system that governs life in civilised nations, the spirit that animates their social institutions—and the phenomena we have witnessed in Japan will be repeated in China. Ever since the Great Change in 1868, the Japanese have been adapting to their requirements, with miraculous energy and skill, the best fruits of the material civilisation of the Occident. To its animating spirit, Christianity, they have remained, practically, impervious. For thirty years of feverish activity, they have answered the Missionaries' urgent plea in these words : "We are too busy just now to think about religion. We have so many, and such difficult, things to learn ; all about steam, electricity, and chemistry; all about medicine and surgery, and mining, and railways, and ship-building, and finance; all about constitutional law, and parliamentary government, and political economy. All that it took you several centuries to build up, we have to learn, and adapt to our wants and our means, in thirty short years. When we have acquired all these things, and we know how to use them, *then* we will think of religion. We are now in the

P

position of starving men, hungering for the bread of science, thirsting for the water of practical knowledge. When we have eaten and drunk our fill, *then* we will willingly investigate this religion you recommend to us."

And now that the Japanese have satisfied the cravings of their hunger for science, now that they have slaked their thirst for practical knowledge, their wisest minds are beginning to enquire into less earthly matters. Week after week, month after month, they discuss, in the reviews and magazines that abound in New Japan, the question of the adoption of Christianity by their countrymen, gravely weighing the arguments for and against it ; and they discuss the subject calmly, with a sobriety of expression too often wanting in the religious polemics of the Occident. For the present, the question remains undecided, but signs are not wanting that, before another generation has grown to maturity, a large proportion of the Japanese race will profess Christianity. I fancy I hear the Reader's query, uttered with an anticipatory flutter of hope, as to what particular form of Christianity the Japanese will adopt. *Not yours*, dear Reader, whatever sect, or denomination, you may belong to. That is quite certain. The Japanese will never enter the fold of a religion whose Pontiff is enthroned in Rome—they shed torrents of Japanese blood, in the seventeenth century, to assert that fact. Bishop Nikolaï, admirable Missionary though he be, will never —in spite of his grand Byzantine Cathedral, dominating Tōkio from the height of the bluff of Surugadai—never induce the majority of the Japanese to adopt a creed whose Supreme Head on Earth is the Tsar, and whose Prophet is Gospodin Pobedonostzeff, Procurator of the Holy Synod. Nor will the Japanese enter into union with, or affiliation to, a Church whose Chief Primate's See is at Canterbury ; nor will they join, *en masse*, any of the denominations of which the caustic Frenchman said we had a hundred, as against but one fish-sauce. No, the Japanese will not import their religion ready made. They did so, it is true, in the case of Buddhism, in the sixth century, but they soon managed to add native features to the imported creed, to twist it and turn it to suit their national idiosyncrasies, till it bore but slight resemblance to its former self. Even in the state in which Buddhism reached them from Korea, its Indian founders would not have recognised their beautiful faith, for it had passed through five centuries of Cathay, and that extraordinary Chinese race had left its indelible impress upon it, as upon so many other systems and civilisations that had come into contact with it, only to be recast in a Chinese mould.

The Japanese will, in time, profess Christianity, but it will be Christianity of a Japanese pattern. The same series of phenomena will culminate, in China, in a similar result. The Chinese, too, will first acquire and adapt the material civilisation of the West, and will then, at their leisure, enquire into the spirit that animates the Occident. A topsy-turvy mode of proceeding? Perhaps so, but we must bear in mind that, in the Far East, the roof is built *before* the house it is to cover.

It must always be remembered, in considering the future of China, that, although they grumble at times as heartily as any Britons at the hardships they endure and at the delinquencies of the administration, its people are, on the whole, satisfied with their lot. There is in them none of that general, savage, sullen discontent that filled the masses in France in the last years of the eighteenth century, and found vent in the "red fool fury of the Seine," in 1793; nor are the occasional outbreaks of the normally law-abiding, placid Celestials directed against the form of government under which they suffer, but against some particular official, or gang of officials, whose extortion and injustice have gone beyond the limits, wide as they are, of Chinese endurance. Petitions and Memorials innumerable have been sent up to the Dragon Throne, and the Son of Heaven has ordered strict enquiry. But the inculpated officials have set in motion some of the intricate wheels within wheels that revolve in the Forbidden Precincts, and the extortion and cruelty continue unchecked. At last the people, after trying the silent protest of a strike, rise in open revolt, drive the offenders from their offices, and, sometimes, put them to death with torments so cruel that they equal some of the acts that caused the rebellion. As related by Professor Douglas in his *Society in China*, in a revolt that took place in the Shanghai district, in 1852, the mob invaded the *Yamên* of an unjust and extortionate Mandarin, and, having captured him, did not kill him, but merely *bit off his ears*, every man in the crowd "having a bite," so as to divide the responsibility equally amongst them all, and to prevent the indictment of any particular rioter. If the rising threaten to become serious, overwhelming forces are ultimately sent to suppress it in the slow, but sure, way the Chinese authorities have of discouraging rebellion. The chastisement of the ringleaders and their families is simply appalling in its calculated ferocity, but, once order is restored, and "peace" reigns over smoking ruins strewn with corpses, a comparatively mild and just official is, usually, placed in authority over the district. In most cases, this wise appointment is made before the rising attains to grave dimensions. If so, the easily-governed people soon subside into their every-day life of patient toil, and love the just magistrate, literally "like old boots," for, on his being, eventually, transferred to another district, they beg for a pair of his cast-off official boots and hang them up, with a suitable inscription, in the archway of the gate through which he left the town. But, stubbornly rebellious or easily pacified, the people ascribe the defects in the administration to the misdeeds of individual officials, not to the rotten system that allows abuses to prevail. The system is old, very old, and Chinese, very Chinese, hence it must, in their opinion, be a good and wise system, infinitely superior, in principle, to anything devised by the brains of foreign upstarts.

The Occidental may exhaust his argumentative powers in the attempt to persuade the Chinese to reproduce, in the native quarters of Shanghai, some semblance of the admirable sanitary precautions, the municipal order and cleanliness, the innumerable evidences of Occidental ideas of security and comfort, that characterise the Foreign Settlements in that city—the Chinese, who has these advantages daily before his eyes, remains unmoved. To every suggestion of reform he opposes the absolute *non possumus:* "No belong China-fashion !" This "China-fashion" holds the nation enthralled, from the Emperor to the "coolie." Even when the enlightened, travelled Chinese —diplomatist, naval or military officer trained abroad, technical student, barrister-at-law of an English Inn of Court, graduate of an Occidental University, or wealthy merchant—returns to Far Cathay he has not been a day on his native soil before he is made to conform, humbly and reverently, to the ways he has learned to regard as antiquated and absurd. He may *think* so, to his heart's content, but—unless he be a mighty personage indeed— woe to him if he venture to express such subversive opinions, or to translate them into acts. The very fact of his residence abroad makes him an object of suspicion on his return, and relegates him, if an official, to minor posts, where his knowledge may be utilised without the fear of his gaining dangerous power. If he belong to the humbler ranks of the population, if he be a small trader, an artisan, a seaman, or a labourer, returned, with a small capital earned, by incessant industry, under a foreign flag, he resumes the native mode of living without an effort, just as if he had not helped to build railways, or to clean steam-engines, as if he had never travelled in a railway train, nor in an electric tramcar— the contrivance he has so aptly described as: "No pushee, no pullee ; go like Hellee !" A sponge passes over his memory of all these things as he steps once more on the soil of the Middle Kingdom. Great is "China-fashion," and to it every Chinese must bow! And he bows to it, as a rule, willingly, for is it not the good old fashion that has been kept up for untold generations in his family, the fashion of his forefathers ?

There we have, in two words, the essence of Chinese life, the guiding lines of Chinese patriarchal government, the foundations of Chinese society—*Family* and *Ancestors.* The former term really includes the latter, for, throughout the Far East, the ancestors form part and parcel of the actual family, just as if they were still living. Not only the poor, but the dead are always with the living in the lands of Eastern Asia. In fact, the idea of a parent being *dead*, in our sense of the word, does not occur to the Far Eastern mind. He, or she, has "passed away," has "become a Buddha" (the very words "dead," "death," "to die," are avoided in speaking of the deceased,) but the spirit remains with the children, to watch over them and note their actions. The spirits of the ancestors attach themselves to the tablets, bearing their posthumous names, that are placed on the family altars, or that hang, in the case of the wealthy, in what are really "ancestral halls." They see and hear all that goes on amongst their descendants, whose rule of conduct through life is summed up in the ideas: to do nothing that would displease the ancestral spirits, to do everything likely to afford them satisfaction. To bring shame upon the family, that is, not only among its living members, but upon all their predecessors from the beginning of human existence, is the one thing every Far Eastern child is taught must be avoided through life; to add to their glory is the one thing to be striven for. Thus, a Chinese who has deserved well of the State has no livelier satisfaction than when he reads in the *Peking Gazette* that His Imperial Majesty has been graciously pleased to

reward his services by the bestowal of an honorific title
on his grandfather, who passed away thirty years ago, or,
perchance, on an ancestor much more remote. In every
act of his life, the Chinese, the average Japanese, or the
Korean, has ever present to his mind the thought of his
forefathers. He lives surrounded, as it were, by a crowd
of ghostly relatives, eagerly scanning his every action.
With the Japanese, racial instincts cause the feeling to
predominate that prompts them to add fresh lustre to the
ancestral roll of honour by valiant deeds in war, or by
acquiring civic fame in times of peace. With the Chinese,
entirely lacking in martial ardour, and with poorly developed
public spirit, the whole duty of man towards his ancestors has gradually narrowed down, in the vast majority of
cases, to a slavish adherence to the ways that commended
themselves to his forefathers, and an intense dread of
offending them by any departure therefrom. They are
here still, to his mind's eye, all around him, and he dare
not ignore them if he would. The population of China
is roughly estimated, on the best data available—the
Government Census returns are not to be implicitly
trusted — at about three hundred and fifty millions.
This is misleading. There are *milliards* of Chinese,
for we must count with the living all their ever-present
dead.

What is the prospect in view for the regeneration of
the seething mass of pig-tailed humanity ? How is the still
small voice, crying for reform, to reach ears that will not
hear ? What chance have the handful of really enlightened,
patriotic Chinese against the hordes of their narrow-minded
compatriots, backed by the ghostly influence of the milliards
of Chinese of past ages ? Are the present three hundred
and fifty millions—for the most part good people, industrious beyond comparison, thrifty to a superlative degree,
of unequalled patience, and wonderfully cheerful, dutiful
in their domestic relations, peaceful, intelligent, fond of
learning—-to continue to live in their actual condition,

to the vast majority of them a strenuous daily struggle to
keep body and soul together ?   Are they, the heirs to the
most ancient civilisation in the world, to remain a prey
to rapacity and revolting cruelty, because their civilisation, through its very antiquity, is mortifying in a living
death ?

Surely, the present condition of China cannot endure
much   longer.   Something *must* happen   to   save   the
wonderful nation from its doom.   That something will
come either as a violent shock from the outside, or, it is
to be hoped, as the result of more humane influences
working by the power of reason.   If salvation come to
China by the violent means, it will be the work of some
Power that, knowing the Chinese thoroughly, will break
down their stiff-necked pride as it has never been humiliated
in modern times.   The invaders, whoever they may be,
will capture the Emperor within the Forbidden Precincts,
and will let his people see him led, a prisoner, in their
triumphal march through the streets of Peking.   They
will remain at Peking and will rule, gradually, over the
whole land, either directly, or, more probably, through a
Puppet-Emperor, either a Manchu, or a descendant of the
Mings for choice.   And they will rule with a rod of iron,
humbling Chinese pride at every turn, trampling ruthlessly
on every vestige of the old system, replacing it by the
new ; educating, drilling, surveying, mining, making China
a rich country and the Chinese real men, for the first
time these many years.   But much blood will be spilt
in the process, for the vampires who are draining China's
life-blood will not willingly abandon their prey, and, being
Mandarins, they will know how to raise the people in
fierce, if futile, insurrections.   But the end would be
Peace, and the Chinese would be saved in spite of themselves.

The task I have foreshadowed may seem one beyond
the strength of any single Power.   Yet one nation, admirably equipped for the gigantic work, dreams of undertaking

it, and the dreams of Russia have a tendency, unpleasant for some States, to become accomplished facts.

What is the alternative course for the fulfilment of China's regeneration? It lies in the conversion of a number of her most capable and honest dignitaries to ideas of reform. Let these men, few in number as they may be, but realise the absolute necessity for a radical change in the system which threatens to ruin their magnificent heritage, and be assured of sound guidance and strong support, by force of arms, if necessary, in their efforts, and they will undertake, and carry out, the salvation of China by the Chinese. They will repeat in the Middle Kingdom the process that has created New Japan, not with the same miraculous rapidity, nor, perhaps, with the same artistic finish; the Chinese lack many of the qualities that enabled the Japanese to effect their marvellous transformation, but they have compensating characteristics of sterling worth for the task at hand. What nation is so pre-eminently fitted to influence the Chinese towards reform, to assist them to regenerate their country, to guide them by the light of her own experience, as the Japanese? Cognate in race, they understand the Chinese nature far better than any Occidental can hope to do. Able to communicate with the Chinese by means of a common written language, versed in a common classical literature, imbued with similar philosophical ideas, the Japanese are in a position to educate the Chinese into reform in a quarter of the time any Occidental Power, or combination of Powers, would require for the same purpose. Signs are not wanting that the Japanese are willing, and ready, to undertake the beneficent task, but it is hardly to be expected that they should do so without support of the strongest kind from a Power, or Powers, guaranteeing them, and their pupils, from interference by the armed forces, or the scheming diplomacy, of the nation that would see its prey escaping from its clutches. Britain and America would profit most by a *peaceful* regeneration of China through Japanese influence. To them would fall the duty of supporting the reformers with their whole might. Let the English-speaking peoples realise the facts, and we may live to see the greatest work of reform ever undertaken—the Men of New Japan regenerating the people of Old China.

CHAPTER V.

THE WOMEN OF THE NEW FAR EAST.

IT may safely be assumed that a glance at the heading of
this Chapter will evolve, in the minds of nine out of ten
of those who read it, a picture of a charming little person
with elaborately-dressed black hair, her slender form clothed
in a sheath of delicately-tinted silk, and her waist encircled
by a broad, stiff sash, also of silk, of a contrasting, but
harmonious, colour, tied at the back in a huge bow.
When an average Occidental thinks of the Far Eastern
woman, it is the woman of Japan that appears to the
mental vision, her sisters of China and of Korea being, to
Western minds, vaguely-known entities, dim, shadowy
forms, filling no frames in the mind's picture-gallery of
national female types. The Japanese woman, on the contrary, seems a familiar friend, so frequently has the Western
mind come in contact with her in the literature of fact, and
in that of fiction; so often has the eye dwelt on her coun-
terfeit presentment. Tiny as she is, she looms larger in
the Occidental conception of Eastern Asia than the
Japanese male. And there are strong reasons for this
preponderance of the Eternal Feminine in our thoughts
about Japan. The traveller just returned from that delect-
able land expatiates in glowing terms of praise on the
lovely landscapes whereon he has feasted his eyes, on the
stately trees and the exquisite flowers, the marvels of
ancient temples, the treasures of delicate art, the soft,
winning manners of the people, their quaint customs, the

marvellous results of their energy and their intelligence, and on the ridiculously small sums for which he, the specially-favoured one, has acquired masterpieces of their taste and skill.

He pauses, at last, and you interject, enquiringly: "And the women?" "Ah! the women . . . " and, if the traveller was enthusiastic before, he now becomes absolutely ecstatic. Surely, those must be charmers indeed who could thus bewitch the stolid Anglo-Saxon! It is quite certain that the daughters of no other land he has visited in his wide travels have ever claimed such a large share of his attention. He has acquired a fund of interesting information, varied and peculiar, about the manners and customs of Japanese women; he even displays a perfectly surprising acquaintance with the details of their costume, although, in matters of the Occidental feminine wardrobe, he may be incapable, and pardonably so, of distinguishing a hat from a bonnet, and either from a *toque*, and cannot tell a *dolman* from a jacket. O Hana San, it seems, taught him how to use the eating-sticks, O Kiku San, the bright-eyed *Gei-sha*, instructed him in many quaint games of forfeits, O Yuki San danced before him, O Také San, another pretty *Gei-sha*, sang to him, accompanying herself on the *samisen*, the three-stringed banjo, struck deftly with a *bachi*, or "plectrum," and O Kin San made for him a variety of astonishing little figures of birds and beasts, and men, and flowers, all made out of flimsy paper with a twist or two of her exquisite little taper fingers. He has got the little paper toys now; he will show them to you, and also his collection of portraits. He has brought home excellent photographs of all these "august Misses" whose names he has just so glibly recited. Here is demure little "august Miss Blossom," the dear little waitress, his instructress in the art of eating with "*chop*-sticks"; here "august Miss Chrysanthemum," the *Gei-sha* with the lustrous eyes, looking, in the photograph, as dignified and sedate as if *ken*, and other rollicking

games of forfeits, were frivolities far beneath her notice.
Here is a picture of "Her Augustness Miss Snow,"
"taken," instantaneously, in the very act of dancing.
Here is, actually, her little dancing-fan, red, with bright
flowers painted on it, and the point of junction of the
ribs weighted with lead, so that she may the more easily
balance it and poise it in the posturing which constitutes
her dance—a precious treasure this, a *souvenir* of a fairy-
like entertainment at the *Kōyō-kwan,* the Maple Club, in
the beautifully-wooded Park of Shiba, at Tōkio, the Club
at which the "smart set" of Japanese society entertain
those Occidentals whom they would · honour. Now he
will show you the portrait, signed by her, of that other
Gei-sha, "august Miss Bamboo," sitting on her little
heels, playing the *samisen,* just as she sat when she sang
to him, and the photograph of skilful little "august Miss
Gold," the artistic manipulator of bits of paper.

And—well, that picture was taken out of the drawer
with the others, but was evidently not intended for
exhibition, as it is hastily pushed back under a pile of
others—"such a heap of them, you know, could go on
showing them to you till to-morrow morning"—but not
before you have caught a furtive glimpse of a *jin-riki-sha*
"made for two," and drawn by two sturdy runners—the
"man-power carriage" to seat two, *ni-nin-nori-no kuruma,*
and drawn by a "pair," *ni-nim-biki,* is the exception—
and, on the seat of the baby-carriage, your travelled
friend himself, looking absurdly overgrown, but radiant,
and by his side, a perfectly delicious little "august Miss
Somebody," like an exquisitely-finished doll, with beautifully smooth hair in artistic convolutions, and a light-
coloured summer *kimono,* with an *obi* a foot wide round
her little body, a dainty paper parasol in one baby-hand,
and a small fan in the other. Happy traveller ! · Why
conceal this pictorial record of cordial relations established
with the nation predestined to be Britain's ally in the
Far East ? Well, our traveller happens to be a· Vice-

President of a Young Men's Mutual Improvement Society in his district, and Honorary Secretary of the local Association for the Enforcement of Compulsory Virtue, and some people are so apt to misunderstand.

You have listened to the traveller's talk, you have admired the photographs in his collection, and you feel that you are in the presence of an authority who has added much to your knowledge regarding the women of Japan. Not that it required much extension, you think, for the Occident in general rather prides itself on the amount of information it possesses on the subject. It has read, over and over again, and accepted as a true representation of *the whole* womankind of Japan, the beautiful word-pictures in "Pierre Loti'"s *Madame Chrysanthème;* it has also read, with delight, the poetic prose of Sir Edwin Arnold, likewise his graceful verse, and wondered how much to ascribe to the poet's inspired enthusiasm, how much to the traveller's keen gift of observation.

And now Sir Edwin has solved the doubt by giving the best possible proof that his pæans in honour of Japanese women were sincere; Lady Arnold, the first daughter of *Dai-Nippon* to bear the British Dame's prefix of "Lady," is a living example of the qualities, the grace and the charm the poet has sung. If ever a poet's marriage was blest by a sense of fitness, it was when Miss "Jewel" (Tama) Kurokawa — "the august Miss Jewel," how prettily the Japanese name their daughters! — became Lady Arnold. The Occident in general has read little, or nothing, about the women of Japan beyond what is contained in the works of "Loti" and of Arnold, and in the bright pages devoted to them in Henry Norman's *The Real Japan*—a book which is a marvel of keen and rapid observation, picturesque description, and unprejudiced opinion, with hardly any inaccuracies to make it fall short of perfection, when it is considered that it is the outcome of a short sojourn amongst the Japanese. The author's trained journalistic eyes and ears made excellent use of that brief period, and his "Studies of Contemporary Japanese Manners, Morals, Administration, and Politics" well deserve the title under which they appeared, for they represent *The Real Japan* as the "Travelling Commissioner" of the *Pall Mall Gazette* saw it. Those Occidentals who take a special interest in Japanese matters have, of course, read what that Past Master in Japan-lore, Professor Basil Hall Chamberlain, has written, under the heading "Woman," in his terse, crisp "Notes" on all *Things Japanese*, forming a handy encyclopædia for the enquirer, at times rather caustic in its appreciations, for, if the learned author has "set naught down in malice," neither has he "aught extenuated." I need hardly refer to *The Mikado's Empire*, by the Reverend W. E. Griffis, to Professor Morse's *Japanese Homes*, nor to A. B. Mitford's delightful *Tales of Old Japan;* they are classics, as indispensable to those who would understand Japan aright as is Professor William Anderson's monumental work, *The Pictorial Arts of Japan*, to the collector, or the student, of Japanese art. In all of these works passages are to be found—in Mitford's, for instance, many pages—throwing much light on the position of women in old Japan and the Japan of the transition-period in the years following closely on the Great Change, but they cannot, owing to the dates of their publication, give us any account of the Japanese woman as the end of the nineteenth century finds her, after the influence of Occidental ideas has been at work for thirty years.

Two men, an Occidental and a Japanese, have striven to enlighten the English-reading world on the subject of the Japanese woman of the 'nineties, the Occidental by showing us the inner workings of her heart and mind; the Japanese by depicting the conditions of family life amongst his compatriots. No two men could have been found better fitted for their task, for there is certainly no Occidental who has so thoroughly explored the

recesses of the mysterious Japanese heart as that sympathetic " artist in words " Lafcadio Hearn, Lecturer
on English Literature in the Imperial University of Japan
—every line of his numerous writings should be read,
and read attentively, by those who would know what
the Japanese think and how the Japanese feel—and no
Japanese has ever given us a more lucid account of
" The Family Relations in Japan ", than my friend GOH
Daigoro,* in his valuable Paper under that title, published in Vol. II. of the *Transactions and Proceedings of
the Japan Society, London.* Another Japanese, Dr. HATA
Riotaro, Secretary of the Imperial Japanese Legation
in Vienna, has enabled those who read German to
obtain an insight into the views of Japanese men on
the much-debated question of the position of women,
not only in his own country, but throughout the world,
by publishing, in Vienna, in 1896, *Gedanken eines Ja-
paners über die Frauen, insbesondere die Japanischen,*
a translation, by himself, amplified and annotated, of
his book " On the Women of Japan," written in his
own language, that appeared in Tōkio, in 1890. But
absolutely *the best* book on the subject is due, as is
only natural, to a woman's pen. A clever American
lady, Miss Alice Mabel Bacon, making good use of unusual opportunities, has given us, in her *Japanese Girls
and Women,* not only a delightful book, but a true
picture of the Japanese female character, and a store-
house of information about the life of the daughters
of Japan of all classes. Could I be certain that *Japanese
Girls and Women* was a work easily obtainable by all
those who read these pages, the remainder of this Chapter would consist of the one line :—Read Miss Bacon's
book !

As it is, the Occidental public has, undoubtedly,

* Late Japanese Consul at Bombay, and, in 1892-4, Chancellor of the
Imperial Japanese Consulate in London, and Hon. Secretary of the Japan
Society.

derived the most lasting impression regarding the fair
sex in Japan from "Pierre Loti' "s *Madame Chrysanthème,*
and more is the pity! The fascinating pages of Commander Julien Viaud's work—to give the French Acade-
mician his right name—do, indeed, represent, with that
picturesque local colouring of which he is a master, a
phase of Japanese female life—*but only one phase.* The
book should bear on its title-page a warning somewhat in
these words :—"This is the story of a French Naval
Officer's *liaison* with a Japanese girl of the lower class
and of easy virtue. It must not be taken as purporting
to describe, in any way, the *average* Japanese woman,
high-born or in humble life." Of the *average* woman
of Japan, the brilliant French writer had no experience,
engrossed as he was, during his stay at Nagasaki, in his
close study of the fascinating little butterfly whom he
has painted so deftly that she has been accepted by
many thousands of Occidentals as a type of *all* Japanese
woman-kind. Fair, but frail, charming and graceful,
but empty-headed, affectionate, but fickle, caressing, but
mercenary, pretty, unchaste little O Kiku San—"the
august Miss," not *Madame,* "Chrysanthemum"—has, un-
wittingly, done grievous harm, throughout the world, to
the fair fame of her countrywomen. How could she
know, poor little feather-brain, that the French Naval
Officer was making a dispassionate study of her little
ways, and as much of her little heart as he, the man
from a different world, could understand, with the deliberate intention to put down his observations in cold
black on white, with the daily regularity of a ship's log,
in order that many thousands of the *Guwai-jin,* the Foreign
People, should read them, and say "how charming, but,
then, how sad"! That is, without doubt, the feeling
with which most readers have laid down "Loti'"s famous
book, an impression of subtle charm and a deep pity
for a nation whose women can be at once so sweet and
so frail. But those who read attentively will have noticed

Q

that the author disclaims, in at least one passage, any knowledge of Japanese *ladies.* He speaks of meeting two of them, a mother and her daughter, at a photographer's in the outskirts of Nagasaki, where they had just been "taken" amidst the incongruous *Louis Quinze* furniture of the "studio," much the same all over the world, from Nagasaki to the Old Kent Road. He acknowledges their "incontestable distinction," and notes that they look poor little Chrysanthemum "up and down" with evident contempt, although, as he is careful to state, her dress was every bit as "*comme il faut*" as their own. And he adds that they exercised a strange fascination over him, these "ladies of quality," with their long, narrow, oval faces—the aristocratic type of Japan—and that he could not take his eyes off them. They captivated him, he writes, "as things unseen before and incomprehensible." Truly "incomprehensible" to one who knew only O Kiku San — the cousin of *jin-riki-sha* runner No. 415, cabman and cab-horse in one—and her companions; "incomprehensible," indeed to one who could so recklessly brand a whole nation with the cruel and untrue taunt that the word "*honnêteté*," not in its primary signification of "honesty," but in the sense of "modesty," "virtue," "has no meaning in Japan"!

One wishes that "Pierre Loti" had enjoyed the privilege of the acquaintance of a Japanese *lady*, or, at least, of one of the vast multitude of Japanese women and girls of the middle and working classes who are as "*honnêtes*" as the great majority of his own charming countrywomen. What a picture his masterly hand would have drawn for us, not—as in his book—of the *grisette* of Japan, but of the good, virtuous, gentle being whose admirable sense of duty makes her the best of daughters, the most tender of mothers, an exemplary wife, a loving sister—in one word, the *average* woman of Japan! And as the celebrated French author erred, so do seven out of ten of the Occidental travellers, and even sojourners, in Japan. Coming into close contact chiefly with such Japanese women as are condemned by their poverty, or by the penury, or the greed, of unscrupulous parents, to stray from the path of virtue, *as strictly defined* amongst decent people in the Far East as in the West, these Occidentals assume that the "morality" of the woman tempted by their money is the morality of all Japan. With as much justice might a Japanese returning from abroad publish a narrative of his experiences on a midnight walk along some of our London thoroughfares, say from Piccadilly Circus along Regent Street, of an evening spent at the Casino de Paris, or the Folies-Bergère, or of a night devoted to going the rounds of the hells of the wicked city of Chicago, and inform his compatriots that, as they might infer from his descriptions, "virtue had no meaning" amongst the women of the Occident. It is greatly to the credit of Japanese travellers that, whilst many of them have had but few opportunities, if any, of becoming acquainted with Occidental ladies, whilst they have had before their eyes glaring evidence of the terrible depravity common in all our great cities, not one of them has written a book containing sweeping assertions as to the absolute lack of virtue amongst the women of the white race. Their common-sense taught them not to generalise from isolated instances, or from one particular class, a truism that seems to be entirely overlooked by the Occidental detractors of Japanese female virtue.

There have been, however, a few amusing instances of Japanese travellers, with insufficient preliminary knowledge, drawing hasty conclusions from the manners and customs of one particular class, or locality, although it has never led them into such mischievous allegations of national immorality as those I have been discussing. One of these instances may be quoted from my Paper on "Some Difficulties encountered by beginners in the study of the Japanese Spoken Language," read before the Japan

Society on 12th June, 1895, and published in Vol. III. of its *Transactions and Proceedings*. In order to impress on the beginner the importance of avoiding the, fatally easy, picking-up of "Yokohama *Pidjin*-Japanese" words and idioms, so distressing to the ears of the educated Japanese, to whom the corruption of their beautiful mother-tongue appears a sacrilege, and who resent it accordingly, I stated an analogous hypothetical case. Although it might have seemed far-fetched, and even farcical, I ventured to submit it, not at all for the purpose of raising a smile, but well knowing the value of an exaggerated example in fixing a rule in the student's mind. Let us suppose, I said, that a Japanese seaman has recently returned to Nagasaki from a voyage to London, which metropolis he has explored on both sides of the East India Dock Road and as far westwards as Cable Street, St. George's-in-the-East, perhaps even as far as the Minories. What would be the feelings of an English gentleman hearing this hardy mariner explain to his friends that English is a remarkably simple language, very easy to pick up, consisting chiefly of a forcible, though apparently meaningless, adjective? Imagine him adding: "There are a few difficulties in English, to be sure, such as the double negative, in one case even a treble one — 'there ain't no nothink.' A policeman is spoken of behind his back as 'the bloomin' copper' and to his face as 'Mr. Orficer.' Male and female of the superior classes are addressed as 'Guv'nor' and 'Lydy,' respectively; the greeting among friends is 'Wot che'r?' or 'Cheerō!'—the intimation of assent is 'Yus,' of dissent it is 'Gar'n.' Surprise is expressed by 'Strike me pink!' —and, if tinged with disgust, by 'Blimy!'"

This may seem ridiculous, *outré*, but it is not a whit worse than what is perpetrated daily by scores of highly respectable foreigners in Japan, who fondly imagine they are talking correct Japanese. The words and idioms I have put into the mouth of the supposititious mariner

give a very fair sample of the sort of English picked
up in and around the Docks, in 1877-8, by a sturdy
Satsuma sailor of my acquaintance, and used by him in
blissful ignorance of its quality. He was mate of the
S.S. *Niigata Maru*, the first vessel flying the Japanese
flag that entered the Port of London, a merchant steamship owned by the *Mitsu Bishi* Company, now the great
and prosperous *Nippon Yū-sen Kuwai-sha*, the " Japanese
Mail Steamship Company." The worthy Mate's acquaintance with London was confined, practically, within the
boundaries I have indicated, but this did not prevent
him from sending to a leading Tōkio newspaper, the
Nichi Nichi Shim-bun ("Daily News,") a series of most
interesting letters on "Life in London," in one of which
he commented rather severely on the want of refinement of the "ladies of the metropolis," who "commonly eat fruit as they walk along the streets, and
frequently take their meals of shell-fish, fried fish,
stewed eels, or potatoes, at perambulating food-stalls in
the open air."

Many of the statements made by superficial Occidental observers with regard to the women of Japan
rest on researches as limited in their scope as those of
the Mate of the *Niigata Maru* amongst the "lydies" of
Ratcliffe Highway. There is considerable excuse to be
made for the error into which the investigators from both
hemispheres have fallen. The Japanese sailor ascribed
the free-and-easy demeanour, the raucous voices, the
anything but refined appearance of those whom he took
for representative English ladies entirely to racial
differences. Had they been Japanese women, even of
the lowest class, he would have been inexpressibly
shocked by their conduct and their general coarseness.
But they were English, and, the canons of good manners
and of good taste being so widely divergent in England
and in Japan, for all he knew to the contrary, Sal
from Tiger Bay and Poll of Limehouse might be behaving

in accordance with the highest social "good form" of the West.

Conversely, how can the average Occidental Globe-trotter, especially the Briton, be expected to believe that the gentle little woman, with hands like those of a duchess and a low, sweet voice, with exquisite manners and a quaint, solemn kind of dignity in her courteous obeisances, a curious refinement in the graceful motions of her hands and arms, and delicate, quiet taste displayed in every item of her admirably becoming costume, is, socially, on a par with brazen 'Liza of the New Cut, in her tawdry finery, her ill-made clothing of startling aniline hues, her monstrous hat bedecked with hired ostrich plumes—poor 'Liza with her coarse, red hands and her hoarse voice, her manners of the gutter and her wit of the gin-palace bar? Small blame attaches to him if he really believes the little charmer to belong to, at least, the middle class of Japan, and, consequently, accepts her moral standard as that of a vast number of her countrywomen belonging to what would be called, in the West, "respectable" families. Reasoning from this erroneous premise, he assumes that those Japanese women and girls whom he sees working for their living, and, presumably, originally of lower social rank than the particular "Madame Chrysanthème" he has been study-ing, must be equally frail. Has it not been repeated to him, *ad nauseam*, that these people have no concep-tion of virtue, or of modesty? So he frequently treats the maids at the inn, the charming human humming-birds who wait upon him at the tea-house, and the *Gei-sha* summoned to entertain him, with a cavalier familiarity that would infallibly lead to his summary expulsion from any well-regulated hotel or public-house, or other place of public entertainment, at home, did he dare to show such want of respect to a chamber-maid, or to one of the haughty fair ones serving at a bar. He means no harm, in nine cases out of ten; he has been told that "Japanese girls don't mind what you say to them, and as to the tea-house girls, well, they're no better than they should be!"

And he has been totally misinformed, for there are tea-houses *and* tea-houses. The ordinary *Chaya* is a well-conducted, orderly, bright, clean establishment, generally in a picturesque situation, where light refreshment may be obtained at very small cost, where the weary traveller may rest, where friends may meet and converse—it is the Japanese counterpart of the French *café*, the German *Bierhalle*, and the Viennese *Kaffeehaus*, not of the British public-house, nor the American "saloon." But there are tea-houses less respectably conducted, frequented by shady characters for questionable purposes, just as there are certain *cafés* in Paris to which no Frenchman would take his wife, but which the travelling Briton, in the innocence of his heart, sometimes patronises with Mrs. Briton and their daughters. The Japanese inhabitants know perfectly well which tea-houses in the town are respectably conducted, and which are not. In the former, the attendants are good, hard-working, girls — smiling sweetly at the customers, certainly, but that is second nature in the land of smiles and bows—ready to greet any little pleasantry with silvery laughter, for is it not the "Honourable Guest" who has been pleased to crack the "August Joke"? But they are good little women, as capable of guarding their virtue as any in the world, and it saddens one to think how often they endure, from a feeling of consideration for the foreigner "who does not know any better," they pityingly think, cavalier treatment they would not submit to from a Japanese. In the other sort of tea-houses it is otherwise. The attendants look for no respect, and they get none.

I have devoted so much space to a defence of the character of Japanese women, and especially of the classes with which the traveller is most frequently brought into contact, because I know, by experience, how wide-spread

is the Occidental belief in their lack of chastity. There
are unchaste people, male and female, in Japan—about
as many as in any Occidental country. That is the truth
of the matter.

What is the social position, then, of the Japanese
woman ? Truth compels me to state that it is not commensurate with her good qualities. And lest it should be
thought that I am inclined to take too favourable a view
of those qualities, and of the position to which they entitle
her, I may as well state, at once, that I am rather well
qualified to judge impartially in the matter, as I am, of
all the laymen who have written about the Japanese
woman, one of the few—perhaps the only one—whose
opinion is not in danger of being warped by sentimental
considerations.   My memory holds no tender reminis-
cences of sweet dalliance with any fair "august Miss
Plum" (O Ume San) or "august Miss Spring - time,"
(O Haru San) with O Kiku San, or O Hana San, with
"Little Miss Violet" (Ko - murasaki San *) or "august
Miss Harp" (O Koto San). Unknown to me are the
pangs of parting from a dear little figure, in a soft
grey *kimono* and a mauve *obi*, standing, disconsolate and
tearful, on the fast receding shore. But of one kind
of Japanese woman I am, perchance, entitled to speak
with an amount of personal acquaintance not easily to
be acquired by Occidentals, for it has been my great good
fortune to enjoy the friendship of several Japanese *ladies*,
who have honoured me with an insight into their pure and
elevated minds. It is to these true-hearted women, of a
class with which the Globe-trotter hardly ever, and the
average foreign resident but seldom, becomes acquainted,
the *dames de qualité* so "incomprehensible" to the brilliant
French impressionist, that I owe what knowledge I possess
of that honour to humanity—the real Lady of Japan. In

---

* Literally: "Little Miss Purple"

many hours of conversation on the topic of the position assigned to themselves, and to their sisters in the lower social ranks, by law and by custom in Japan, by close observation of their conduct towards their husbands and their children, I have formed my estimate of the worth of the educated, high-bred Japanese woman, and it is a high one. Gifted with every domestic virtue, absorbed in the manifold duties devolving upon her according to the Far Eastern social constitution—too much absorbed in those duties to realise the Western ideal of a woman moving in Society—the Japanese woman of our day, her mind enlightened by the excellent education a wise Government has placed within her reach, has attained an intellectual level undreamt of in the days of her mother's youth. Fortunately for Japan, the new light that has entered into her mind has not caused her to abandon the solid principles of duty, filial, conjugal and maternal, handed down to her through generations of patient, obedient, helpful wives and loving, devoted mothers. And, as I have already stated, she does not occupy, as yet, the position in the social fabric to which her worth entitles her. The average Japanese man seems not to be aware of his good fortune and, whilst kind, even loving, to his womankind, stoutly denies them a place on an equal plane with himself.

Let it not be thought, even for a moment, that the Japanese woman is made unhappy by the superiority arrogated to himself by the Japanese man. She is, as a rule, quite content with her place in the social system, and, though deeply grateful for the improvement in her legal status effected by the new Civil Code, promulgated in 1890, it is very doubtful if she would, for a long time to come, have agitated for the limited rights it has pleased the men of New Japan to confer upon . her. To the "advanced" section of British womankind, and to the great body of the women of America, their Japanese sisters must appear poor, spiritless creatures, content to occupy an inferior position through life. Whether that position is *really* as lowly as it appears is a moot point. In the meantime, let our female champions of "advanced" views take heart of grace—the women of New Japan are moving forward, slowly but surely, towards emancipation, not exactly, however, in the direction so dear to the aforesaid champions—not towards the attainment of political rights. The progressive, emancipatory tendency is manifested rather in smaller, social matters. Thus, at a dinner-party in purely Japanese style given, in Tōkio, by an ex-Cabinet Minister, the host's wife helped her husband to entertain the guests, the married men were accompanied by their wives, and there was actually a Japanese spinster present of the ripe age of twenty-six— a rarity in a country where people marry early. It should be noted that the entertainment was in *Japanese* style, so that the invitation of husbands *and* wives and of the independent spinster was a startling innovation. According to the custom of Old Japan, the host would have invited his male friends to a "Stag Party," the female element indispensable for the gaiety of the feast being supplied by *Gei-sha*, or "Accomplishment-mongers," hired professional entertainers; the hostess would not have appeared, but would have invited her female friends —not necessarily the wives of her husband's guests—on another occasion. Had the ex-Cabinet Minister's entertainment been one of those excellent dinners *à l'Européenne* he and his wife know so well how to give, the function would have differed in no respect from a dinner in Grosvenor Square, save for the physiognomy of the hosts, the guests—excepting the sprinkling of Occidentals sure to be present—and of the servants, and the Japanese dress worn by some of, unfortunately not by all, the ladies present. From *hors d'œuvre* to savouries, the repast, the table decorations and the service would have been indistinguishable from those arranged under the superintendence of an experienced Occidental hostess. But the dinner was

in Japanese style, and there was, thus, no necessity for
the introduction of such thoroughly Western and subversive customs as were implied by the presence of both
sexes at the same board, or, rather, assemblage of boards,
for, at a Japanese meal, each person has a separate little
table, but a few inches high, and on it a tray, laden with
dainty bowls and saucers of Lilliputian dimensions, so as
to give the impression that a number of adults have
relapsed into childhood and are having rare fun at a
dolls' dinner-party. The mixed assembly at the ex-
Cabinet Minister's dinner proved most successful, and led
to imitation by bold social reformers in various quarters.
The influence of the novel conditions under which the
"pioneer" mixed dinner was given made itself felt at
once. A Japanese friend of mine returned from the feast
in a highly perturbed state of mind. Stood Japan where
it did? Was Fuji's sublime peak still in existence? Well
might he ask himself these questions. His experiences at
the dinner-party had, indeed, been startling. To begin
with, he had been introduced by the hostess to the aforesaid spinster—a charming lady, certainly, pretty and clad
in *kimono* and *obi* of artistically-assorted colours—but the
idea of being solemnly marched up to a lady, to be
formally presented to her as she rose from her seat,
namely, her own heels, tucked under her on the floor,
and then to be requested to "take her in to dinner"!
To a Japanese mind the idea was most incongruous. Had
the lady been attired in European dress, well and good—
no Japanese would have thought of behaving towards her
in any but the most correct manner prescribed by Occidental etiquette, but to treat her so deferentially when
clothed in the costume of Old Japan—that went against
the grain. This strange difference in the treatment of
women according to the clothing they adopt is very
marked in the relations between husband and wife. The
same Japanese who, without compunction, strides along
the street, or enters a room, with his wife meekly trotting

behind him, at times lets her stand whilst he remains seated, and allows her to kneel before him, bending her pretty forehead to the mats, in humble salutation when he leaves home, or returns to it—all this when they are both in native garb—gives her his arm when walking, follows her into a house, or an apartment, and will not sit whilst she stands, when both have donned Occidental clothes.

To return to my friend's experiences at the innovating function : he was placed next to the unattached lady. Their trays full of dolls' dinner-service ware—a fresh tray for each course—were set down close to each other, and, from the preliminary *hors d'œuvre*, the *suimono*, or soup, served in lacquered bowls, and the various relishes, washed down with *saké* in tiny cups, through the other two courses, each consisting of several dishes, to the final rice, conversation flowed freely between him and his fair neighbour. So freely, on her part, as fairly to bewilder him, for she spoke, and spoke well, on the current topics of the day, giving her opinion frankly, especially on matters of art ; she was a professional artist, a painter, and was executing a commission for some panels, painted on silk, for the drawing-room of the host's "European-style" house (like many wealthy Japanese he had a house built and furnished—generally in very bad taste—after the Occidental fashion, communicating with a beautiful Japanese dwelling *un*furnished in the purest style of Japanese domestic decoration). My friend was shocked, he could not help confessing that he had enjoyed the evening immensely, but the lady's want of restraint had jarred upon his nerves. Just fancy, a woman who gave her opinion unasked, who contravened all rules of decorum by starting subjects of conversation ! She had evidently forgotten the wise maxims the Japanese apply to women as we try to apply them, with but scant success, to children in the nursery, that "they should be seen, not heard," and that "they should speak when they are spoken to."

When the heaven-born progenitors of the Japanese race, Izanagi and Izanami, first stood on the Floating Bridge of Heaven, and had created the Islands of Japan out of the coagulated foam dripping from the *tama-boko*, the "Jewel-Spear" of Heaven, wherewith they had stirred up the primeval ocean of Chaos, spreading beneath them "like floating oil," they set up the spear as a Central Pillar, and they walked round it separately, the Male, Izanagi, turning by the left, the Female, Izanami, by the right. When they met, the Female spoke first, exclaiming: "How delightful! I have met with a lovely youth!" Truly, this Japanese Eve was intensely human; her *cri du cœur* rings fresh and true across the ages that separate the Night of the Gods from our days. But her outburst displeased her Adam, who said: "I am a man, and by right I should have spoken first. How is it that, on the contrary, thou, a woman, shouldst have been the first to speak? This was unlucky. Let us go round again." And they went round again. When they met, this time, the Male spoke first, saying: "How delightful! I have met a lovely maiden"! Now that the proper natural relations of the sexes, according to the ideas of Old Japan, had been restored, the courtship of Izanagi and Izanami ran its smooth course. Those who would know more of the delightfully *naïve* story of the Creation, and of the highly interesting exploits of the "August Deities" of the *Shin-tō* religion, should read one of the scholarly translations, erudite but very readable, of the most ancient Japanese works extant: the *Kojiki*, or "Record of Ancient Matters," completed in A.D. 712, translated by Professor B. H. Chamberlain, and published in the Supplement to Vol. X. of the *Transactions of the Asiatic Society of Japan*, and the *Nihon-gi*, or "Chronicles of Japan," completed in A.D. 720, rendered into English by W. G. Aston, C.M.G., and issued, in two volumes, as Supplement I.

to the *Transactions and Proceedings of the Japan Society.* The *Nihon-gi* has also been translated into German, with the painstaking thoroughness characteristic of his nationality, by Professor Dr. Karl Florenz, of the Imperial University of Tōkio.

The origin of the *Shin-tō* Myth of the Creation is shrouded in the mist of prehistoric ages, but Izanagi's re-proof to Izanami remains the terse expression of Japanese male opinion on the subject of the Eternal Feminine. My Japanese friend who took his "advanced" countrywoman in to dinner had enjoyed all the advantages of modern Japanese education on the Occidental plan ; to him Izanagi and Izanami were shadowy figures, to be regarded with purely antiquarian interest, yet the idea embodied in their first conversation was so deeply rooted in his mind that it took him a long time to overcome the feeling of pained surprise with which he listened to remarks, clever and to the point though they were, offered spontaneously by a Japanese lady in her national dress. The culminating shock was given to his sense of propriety when the fair painter handed him her card, drawn from the beautiful "pocket-book" of brocade worn in her *obi,* and expressed the pleasure it would give her if he would call, some afternoon, and discuss her pictures over a cup of tea ! And this extreme type of the New Woman of Japan represents a class that is grow-ing—very slowly, it is true, but still growing—of women who are determined to treat men on an equal footing. It is quite certain that they will meet with resolute opposi-tion. It is not that the men of New Japan have any rooted objection to the intellectual advancement of their womankind ; on the contrary, every effort in that direction enjoys the patronage of the ladies of the Imperial Family, and especially of the Empress—who spends a great deal of her time in visiting and inspecting educational institu-tions for girls and for the training of female teachers—and the active support of the Government. I have had many earnest talks on the subject with several of the men who direct the thoughts of New Japan, and I found them all agreed as to the necessity of educational facilities of the highest order for the rising generation of Japanese women, facilities already far in advance of anything within the reach of the female population of many European countries. One and all, the leaders of Japan are in favour of an extension of the admirable system of female education—a combination of adaptations from the best features of the systems in vogue in the State Schools of Germany, Scandinavia, the Netherlands, Switzerland, and the United States of America—now firmly established in the Island Empire. It is when we begin to inquire into the reasons for this enthusiasm for female education that we perceive the vast difference between the Japanese point of view and our own.

The majority of Japanese men desire to see their womankind well educated for reasons hardly to be distinguished from that given by the St. James's Street " Johnnie," who averred that " education of the lower orders is a rippin' good thing, don't you know; at least, teachin' them to read, so that when you come home in the small hours you can pin a paper on your bedroom door tellin' your man not to call you till nine thirty." The educated woman will be the better able to perform her duties as a daughter-in-law—the first consideration—as a wife, as a mother and a daughter; therefore let her be educated. That is the Japanese reasoning. To be helpful is the one object the Japanese woman is taught to strive for; helpful to her husband's parents, to her husband, to her children, just as she has, in girlhood, been helpful to her own parents. And nobly do the women of Japan realise what is expected of them, often under most adverse conditions. The mother-in-law, so often and, in many cases, so unjustly, made the butt of cheap satire in the Occident, is a veritable terror in the Far East, but on the other side of the family. In Eastern Asia it is not the wife's mother who watches over her child's domestic happiness with a jealous vigilance popularly supposed to entail domiciliary visits hardly to be endured by the terrorised husband, but *the husband's mother* who insists on being obeyed by her daughter-in-law, and on seeing that her beloved son is made thoroughly comfortable by the wife he has brought home, in most cases, to live under the paternal roof. So exacting is the old lady, at times, so exasperating does her continual "nagging" become, especially when enforced, as it sometimes is amongst the lower classes, by blows with her metal tobacco-pipe, that wives have been known to seek release in death. Even in those households where the same dwelling does not shelter two or three generations, and the parents of husband and wife are only occasional guests, the wife is obliged to show the utmost deference to her husband's parents, and to all his relatives older than himself. One might expect that a long continuance of such subjection to the will of others, together with the heavy burden of domestic duties, and the engrossing care for, and training of, the children, would have crushed all spirit out of the Japanese woman and reduced her to a mere household drudge. Such is by no means the case.

The gentle, low-voiced, soft-mannered, little woman—apparently existing only for the purpose of doing the bidding of her husband and of his parents, of keeping his house and his clothes in good order, and last, but certainly not least, of rearing a family—gives proof, when occasion arises, of the possession of an iron will. When honour and duty are at stake, the meek little lady becomes a heroine, towering, head and shoulders, above the ordinary run of womankind. The heart that flutters beneath the soft *kimono* is as stout in the hour of national emergency, or of imminent peril to personal honour, as that of any *Samurai* of old. The tiny, soft hands are as ready to-day to bear arms in defence of Japan's sacred soil, or to grasp the dagger that will bring death as the means of escape from dishonour, as they were in the days of Old

Japan, when every lady was trained in the art of fencing with the halberd, in order to defend the women's apartments, the last stronghold of the castle overrun by the enemy. During the war with China, women volunteered in large numbers for service in the field, and were much mortified at the refusal they met with from the authorities. Unable to take an active part in the warfare, they did wonders in the more appropriate work of nursing the sick and the wounded, and, in innumerable instances, both in the hospitals and at home, gave convincing proofs of fearless devotion, of stoical resignation and of ardent patriotism. The latter virtues were made especially manifest in the manner of their receiving the tidings of the death in the field, or at sea, of husband, or son, and in the way in which the bereavement was borne.

And, in many cases, the bereavement meant the loss of the bread-winner, and threw the task of supporting herself and her little ones on the widow, or compelled aged parents to return to work. All was borne without a murmur; the beloved ones had fallen fighting for their country, with the cry *"Hei-ka ban-zai!"* ("Long live His Majesty!" literally: "Ten thousand years to His Majesty!") on their lips. They died for Japan and in the moment of victory; a Japanese woman would rather her dear ones perished thus than quietly passing away on a bed of sickness.* The records of the conduct of "the folks at home" during the war teem with instances of patriotic devotion on the part of women. A typical case is that of the grand old lady, bereft of all her male relatives, husband, brother, and sons, all killed, or carried away by sickness, at the seat of war, who received the successive tidings with stoical calm, until the sad news

---

* Or, more correctly, "on a mat and quilt of sickness," for there are no beds in Japanese houses. The idea of resting on an elevated sleeping-place is terrifying to the un-Europeanised Japanese mind. Several of my Japanese friends have told me that, on first attempting to sleep in an Occidental bed, their rest was much disturbed by the necessity of having repeatedly to climb on to the bedstead after rolling off it on to the floor.

R

reached her of the death of her younger son, the last of
the family to fall in defence of his country. Then the
old mother burst into tears, exclaiming : "I weep at last,
but do not misunderstand the cause of my tears! I
weep because I have no one left whom I can send out
to die for our country, and because, were I to marry
again, I am too old to give the Emperor more warriors to
fight his battles."

It does not need the stimulus of war to prompt
Japanese women to deeds of self-sacrifice. In May, 1891,
a young servant-girl journeyed by train from Kanagawa
to Kiōto for the express purpose of offering her innocent
life in sacrifice as a vicarious atonement for the disgrace
to the national honour resulting from the murderous
attack, at Otsu, on the Tsarévich Nikolai Alexandrovich,
who has since succeeded to the Throne of All the Russias,
by the fanatically demented Policeman TSUDA Sanzó.
Yuko, "Valiant," that was her personal name—her family
name was HATAKEYAMA—was in full possession of her
senses when she cut her slender throat on the threshold
of the Government Buildings at Kiōto. Her touching farewell letter to her brother proves it ; so does the document in which she informed the authorities of the old
Imperial City of the motives for her deliberate suicide.
She had read in the newspapers that His Imperial Majesty
was grieving sorely because of the foul attempt on the
life of the nation's honoured guest, and she trusted that
the voluntary sacrifice of her own pure young life would
expiate the crime, remove the blot from the national
scutcheon, and lift the burden of sorrow from the Emperor's heart.

Calmly and quietly she proceeded to carry out her
plan, entering every little item of her modest expenditure,
to the very last moment, in her note-book—the most
pitiful "Cash Account" imaginable—down to the purchase of a newspaper and to the trifling fee paid to a
kami-yui, a female hairdresser, for putting a keen edge

on the little razor with which she ended her life. She entered, too, the amount of money remaining in her purse, five *Yen* and a few *Sen*, sufficient, she hoped, for her funeral expenses; and, with the purse, the account-book, and the two explanatory letters she had written, placed in her bosom, she tied her long under-girdle of silk tightly round her clothing, just above her knees, for she was the daughter of an impoverished *Samurai*, and knew that a Japanese of good breeding, like a citizen of Ancient Rome, must fall decently in death. To us Occidentals the story of the poor girl's self-immolation seems unspeakably pitiful, but the men of New Japan relate it with a strange light gleaming in their eyes, and they say: "She was a true Japanese woman; in her heart burned the flame of the genuine *Yamato Damashi-i*, the undying Spirit of Old Japan."

The men of Japan frequently speak of a girl of equal social rank as "a good, dutiful girl, one who would make a good wife and a good mother," seldom as "a sweet girl"—sweetness "goes without saying" in the land of gentle, amiable women—never of a "jolly girl." The jollity is left to those girls who have to live by it, the tea-house waitresses and, especially, the "Accomplishment-mongers"—the *Gei-sha*, who are the Professional Flirts of Japan. Amateur flirting does not exist in Japanese social life. The accomplishments that ensure a woman's social success in the Occident are relegated, in the Far East, to those who are paid to entertain the men; theirs are the wit and the power of repartee, the interesting small talk on the topics of the day, the amusing little affectations,—in short, all the delightful frivolities that go to make up the every-day conversation of the "charming woman" of the West, but that are considered beneath the dignity of the Japanese lady, absorbed in the serious business of female life.

I fancy I hear my fair Readers exclaim: "Not the least little bit of innocent flirtation! What a stupid

country to live in!" Certainly, the absence of that
freedom in the relations of young people of different sex,
which is usual with the English-speaking nations, deprives
the young Japanese of much harmless pleasure, but it is
not, as might be thought, a hindrance to marriage, for,
in Japan, everybody's betrothal is arranged through the
intermediary of the *Nakōdo*, or "Go-between," who ne-
gotiates with the parents on both sides. Perhaps the loss
entailed on the community by the restriction of flirting
to professionals may be counter-balanced by the gain
accruing from greater security of female morals. The
average Occidental may well be startled by the mere
suggestion that the virtue of women may be efficiently
protected—more efficiently, perchance, than in the West—
by the institutions and customs of a nation he has been
taught to look upon as lacking morality. I venture to
maintain that such is really the case. Japanese girls of
the lower, and the lower middle, classes spend a considerable part of their leisure hours in a manner, apparently, identical with that in vogue in the corresponding
classes in Great Britain and in America. They array
themselves in their best clothes, not, it is true, in cheap
finery, imitating the dress of the class above them, as
their Western sisters do, but in neat, clean attire, tasteful
and becoming; then they "take their walks abroad," just
as in Occidental countries, generally in couples, hand in
hand, or in joyous groups, merrily chatting, and whispering
to one another those mysterious confidences, common to
girlhood all the world over, that lead to fits of uncon-
trollable giggling, and, occasionally, to peals of silvery
laughter. They have even been known to let the glances
of their bright eyes rest, for a moment, on the passing
stranger of the opposite sex, and even to smile at him,
especially if he be an *I-jin San*, a "Mr. Foreigner," for
he is, in all respects, such an abnormal creature that a
little lapse from strict decorum is pardonable when he is
the cause of it.

So far, the Japanese girl's behaviour may be said to be indistinguishable from that of the English-speaking Occidental girl of the same social standing—the lower, and lower middle, classes—but it differs in this respect that she does not walk out in the company of her brother's male friends, nor does she become acquainted with young men on the slightest, perfunctory introduction, nor, as is sometimes the case in the West, on no introduction at all. She does not "walk out," nor "keep company" with anyone, as her English-speaking sister in Western climes frequently does with a young man of whose antecedents and moral character she knows little, or nothing.

Herein lies, I maintain, the superiority of the Japanese social system. I am, of course, fully aware that I am treading on dangerous ground, as it is an Article of Belief amongst Britons and Americans that there is no harm in this free intercourse between young men and girls of the classes that work for their living themselves, or whose parents are in that position. "I can trust my boys and girls to behave themselves in any circumstances," proudly avers the British Paterfamilias; "Our girls are smart, you bet, and can take care of themselves all the time," is the boast of the American father.

The truth is that the fathers being too busily engaged in the accumulation of pounds sterling, or dollars, their wives too much engrossed in domestic duties and social pleasures, and their sons too deeply interested in business and in sport, to be able to devote much attention to the doings of the girls of the family, it is found generally convenient to indulge in a feeling of absolute security without enquiring very closely into its justification, and assurances such as those I have quoted are repeated until they come to be implicitly believed. As a matter of fact, the wide latitude given to young people in English-speaking countries is, in the majority of cases, harmless; but in a very considerable

minority, on the other hand, it leads indubitably to evils
from which Japan is remarkably free.*

Happily as the Japanese ·people are situated in this
respect, they are not entirely spared those *drames pas-
sionnels* so frequent in the West. Passion works havoc
in every race. Cases of conjugal infidelity occur amongst
the Japanese, as in every nation, and every girl is not
content to await the good offices of the *Nakōdo*, the
"Go-between," and her parents' subsequent bidding, before
uniting herself to a man. Instances are not rare—and
supply material for innumerable novels and plays, and
for sensational paragraphs in the newspapers—of young
people plighting their troth spontaneously, and resolving to
die together when they despair of obtaining the parental
consent to their union. These double suicides through
love, called *jō-shi*, or *shin-ju*, sometimes terminate a
clandestine *liaison* that has been, or is in danger of being,
discovered; much more frequently they are pure "Bridals
of Death," sealing for eternity the hitherto platonic affection of two young hearts—the victims are often mere boys
and girls—despairing of the fulfilment, in this world, of
their yearning.

In such a case the lovers will plight their troth to
each other, sometimes, "for three, or more, successive
existences"—using, curiously enough, an idea borrowed
from the Buddhist belief in the transmigration of souls
in connection with suicide, an act strongly condemned by
Buddhism—sometimes "for ever and ever." They then,.

---

* So much one may say, without writing one's self down a sour old
curmudgeon, wishing to curtail the pleasant liberty enjoyed by girls and
young men in British communities and in America. No, I am not sour,
Reader, nor a curmudgeon, I am not even old, and my attitude towards
youth is that of "Edward Lear's"

> ' . . . . . Old Derry-Down-Derry,
> Who loved to see little folks merry,

and of Béranger's immortal optimist:—

> "*Et gai! C'est la philosophie
> Du gros Roger Bontemps.*"

in many instances, partake together of a little feast and die, by their own hands, clasped in a last—often in a first—embrace. They invariably leave a written statement of their motives. Occasionally, they commit suicide separately, and in places distant from each other, but, as a rule, they die clasped in each other's arms, by dagger, or poison, or, more frequently, by casting themselves, tightly bound together with the girl's under-girdle, into a river.

The introduction of railways has added an additional method of consummating the Nuptials of Death, and the Tōkio express, thundering along the line, has sent more than one couple of unfortunate lovers to seek blissful reunion "for ever and ever" in the *Mei-do*, the World Hereafter. Should, by any chance, one of the lovers be saved from death by the intervention of others, the survivor is bound, in honour, to commit suicide at the earliest opportunity, so as to rejoin the beloved twin-soul. A girl, thus saved, who long survived her lover's suicide would be despised by her companions as a craven; a man neglecting his obligation to abide by his plighted troth, and remaining in this world as the survivor of an attempted *jō-shi*, would be hounded out of the society of his comrades as a base coward and a perjurer.

On the whole, it may safely be asserted that the state of morality amongst the women of the lower and the middle classes of Japan compares very favourably with the conditions obtaining in the Occident. As to the highest classes, a few, very rare, exceptions apart, their women are virtuous and set a worthy example of good works and of personal dignity to their less fortunately situated sisters. Their life is spent in a calmer atmosphere than that of the overheated, overstrung conditions of Western social life. Free from the rush of excitement, the mad race after pleasure, constantly sought, but seldom found, that whirls along the "Society Women" of the Occident, they are, as yet, untainted by the neurotic craving for "smartness" that saps the foundations of family life in those Western social circles whose actions are most prominently before the public.

It must not be assumed that Fashion has no power over the female mind in Japan, but its tyranny is less capricious than in the West, and its decrees take a longer time to permeate through the social strata. In Japan, one does not see the costumes of the highest classes repeated, in cheap and tawdry imitations—within a few weeks of their introduction by fashion's decree—on the persons of serving-maids and factory-girls out for a holiday. *All* Japanese women dress well when wearing their native costume, because their clothes are simple, clean, artistic in colouring, neatly arranged, and becoming, not only to the wearer's face and figure, but to her station in life. The British housemaid enjoying wages to the amount of eighteen pounds *per annum*, the shopgirl, or the barmaid, in receipt of a munificent salary of seven shillings and six-pence a week, with board and lodging, or, possibly, a pound a week if living at her own expense, the "Chorus-lady," earning from twenty-five shillings to a maximum of two pounds a week, sally forth in their leisure hours attired in clothes and trinkets that would, were they really what they pretend to be, imply the outlay of at least half a year's income on their purchase. In Japan, on the contrary, in matters of feminine apparel "things *are* what they seem," and this genuineness extends to the person of the wearer—except in the matter of the complexion, often artificially modified with the help of powder, and of paint, and sometimes, in the case of professional entertainers, even of gilding, applied to the centre of the lips.

But the "make up" is so palpable, the powder is so thickly strewn, the little patch of red on the lips so brilliant and sharply outlined, that there is no attempt at deceit. As to the figure, it is truth itself; "improvers" of various kinds are mysteries unknown in the Japanese female dress, the small cushion sometimes worn at the back, under the waist, being intended solely to support the great bow of the wide sash, the *obi*. The clothes and ornaments worn by Japanese women being really composed of the materials indicated by their appearance, and these being, frequently, of a costly nature, a woman's complete costume sometimes represents a sum entirely out of proportion to the means of her husband or her parents. This arises not from extravagance, but from the fact that she is wearing heirlooms, for the beautiful wear-resisting products of the silk-looms of Old Japan are handed down from mother to daughter, the changes of fashion being so slight that they can easily be followed by minor alterations that do not injure the fabric, nor require the ornament, such as a particular kind of hair-pin, to be discarded. The Japanese lady prides herself on the simplicity of her raiment and on the unobtrusive colour and pattern of its materials.

The women who devote the greatest amount of time and attention to their personal adornment, which forms no inconsiderable part of their stock-in-trade, the *Gei-sha*—the professional entertainers, singing-girls, and trained flirts—are equally careful that their dress should be in the quietest taste, but they are easily to be distinguished from the ladies of the land, just because the simplicity of the *Gei-sha's* costume is too apparently a studied effect. The quiet colours and simple adornment of her dress are too evidently the result of much fore-thought and of a determination to be *très-chic*. That fascinating little person, the *Gei-sha*, has insinuated herself into such world-wide notoriety, she has conquered such a prominent position in every one of the most popular works on Japan, that I shall devote no more space to her and to her artfully artless little ways. With her well-developed commercial instinct, for she is a business-like little charmer, she might cause to be noted the number of sticks of incense that burn down to their

sockets, one after another, in the small square marked
with her name on the "time-board" kept at the *Gei-sha-
ya*, or Agency, that lets her out for hire, whilst I am
writing about her, and the next mail from Japan might
bring me a bill a yard long, claiming many *Yen* for "the
space of fourteen and a half sticks of incense of the time
and services of the august Miss Lotus (*O Hasu San*)"
or "the august Miss Snow (*O Yuki San*)." It is, however, necessary that I should devote a few lines to the
Gei-sha to clear their character from an imputation that
has been sown broadcast. The general impression with
regard to them prevailing amongst Occidentals is that they
are, *without exception*, as frail as they are charming. This
is an erroneous view, for, although the circumstances in
which they exercise their calling expose them to great
temptations, to which they frequently succumb, there is
absolutely nothing in the nature of their vocation rendering laxity of morals inevitable. There is no more reason
for a *Gei-sha* to be immoral than there is for an Occidental public entertainer — actress or concert-singer — to
abandon the straight path of virtue.

In one phase, and a most important one, of the great
question of woman's place in the social fabric the men
of Japan have progressed far in an honest attempt to deal
with an evil, as old as the human race, that has baffled
social reformers throughout the West. The Japanese have
succeeded, for many generations, in stripping vice of its
most dangerous, repulsive, and degrading attributes, without thereby increasing its prevalence. The "Social Evil,"
to use a cant term, exists in Japan under the vigilant care
and strict control of the State, wisely exercised in a manner
that safeguards the health of the whole community and the
virtue of chaste women, whilst raising their fallen sisters
to a level of comparative decency that saves them from
utterly hopeless moral and physical degradation, and gives
them a chance of returning, some day, once again to a
virtuous life.

The existence of the unfortunate inmates of the *Yoshi-wara* at Tōkio, and of the similar quarters of provincial cities, is sad enough, in any case, but especially in the frequent one of a girl who has sold herself, for a term of years, into the worst kind of slavery so as to obtain, by the purchase money, sufficient funds to save her father from bankruptcy. Yet, sad as is their lot, the *Jo-ro* are in an infinitely better position than the Sad Sisterhood in the West, whom the Occidental, with cruel irony, calls *" Gay* Women," for the Japanese fallen women have prospects, however faint, of social redemption, and are, indeed, often fit for it, as—with the exception of a few who have become contaminated by association with the scum of all nations at the Treaty Ports—they are sober, clean in their persons and their speech, and retain, in spite of their immoral mode of life, a certain courtesy and refinement of manner, a gentleness of disposition, that enable them, if fortunate, to re-enter the ranks of their respectable sisters without bearing too glaringly the brand of their Past.

In Old Japan, a curious sort of hieratic glamour used always to surround the most popular *Oiran Sama* —"the Lady Prostitute," the respectful designation indicates the feelings of the people—and it still lingers in the minds of the masses, a remarkable survival, perhaps, of the intimate connection existing in past ages, in almost all parts of the world, between women of easy virtue and the celebration of religious rites. It would be difficult to trace the connection between the *Nautch*-girls still attached to Hindu temples, the Priestesses of Venus (and of other cults) in classical antiquity, and the extraordinary respect shown in Old Japan to the *Oiran Sama ;* especially as the *Mi-ko,* "the Darlings of the Gods"—the young priestesses, clad in long, white robes over crimson silk *hakama* (divided skirts) who perform sacred dances in some *Shin-tō* temples—are virgins ; though, in the latter years of the Empire, Rome had her Vestals at the same time as she had those Priestesses whose ministrations in the temples of various imported Eastern deities necessitated their being the very opposite.

~ Those travellers who have been witnesses of the strange ceremony known as *Hachi-mon-ji-ni aruki,* the "Figure-of-Eight-Walking," at one of the three seasons when the flowers are changed in the gardens of the Tōkio *Yoshiwara,* have been impressed by the apparent solemnity of the weird scene. The favoured *Oiran Sama,* selected to "view the blossoms" as representatives of the whole frail sisterhood, gorgeously attired, powdered and painted until their faces look like masks, their heads ornamented with a profusion of enormously long hair-pins, their *obi* of costly brocade tied *in front* in a huge bow,* are mounted on *geta,* or wooden clogs, a foot high, and walk with slow and

* The sash-bow tied *in front,* and *more than three* hair-pins (*kan-zashi*) are badges of their calling imposed on the prostitutes of Japan, formerly by old sumptuary laws, and to this day by custom. This is a fact to be noted by Occidental ladies, so that they may avoid the awkward mistakes frequently made by them when appearing at Fancy Dress Balls in Japanese costume, mistakes that provoke much sly merriment on the part of spectators who know Japan. It had happened to me more than once to be interrogated by some charming European lady, looking perfectly bewitching in a beautiful *kimono*—usually, however, crossed *right over left,* and, therefore, in the manner of grave-clothes, every *live* Japanese wearing the clothing crossed *left side over right*—and a gorgeous *obi,* and her pretty head encircled by *a dozen hair-pins* and ornaments —"My dress is *quite* correct, is it not?" What could I say? I own that I took refuge in ambiguity worthy of the Delphic Oracle, answering: "Certainly, *quite* correct, but so much depends upon what particular type of Japanese you intend to represent."—"Ah! I *knew* I was correct. I copied all the details of the head-dress from a *lovely* Japanese fan" I had thought as much. The Japanese *uchi-wa,* or non-folding fan, of the cheap kind so common in the Occident—some grocers "give them away with a pound of tea"—is often decorated with a highly-coloured print, a fancy portrait of some famous beauty of the *Yoshi-wara,* the purely conventional face surrounded by a halo of hair-pins. These portrait-fans, and the cheap, brilliant colour-prints (*nishiki-yé,* "brocade pictures,") representing famous *Oiran Sama,* are gradually being displaced in popular favour by photographs, the Frail Sisterhood in Japan being as much alive to the utility of photographic advertisement as their Occidental congeners, with this difference, that in the Far East—where scant attire or even nudity is considered quite permissible when it is necessary or convenient, *but only then*—the portraits offered publicly for sale are those of decently-clad females.

measured steps, through the admiring and respectful crowd. The height of the clogs compels them to proceed very deliberately, at the rate of about one step a minute, placing one foot before the other in such a way that the print of the clogs forms the Chinese character, in use throughout the Far East, for "Eight" (Λ), in Japanese : *hachi.*

The wonderfully-apparelled *Oiran,* moving like an automaton on her high, black pattens, her hands supported by an attendant on either side, her whitened face absolutely impassive, gazes straight before her, with the abstracted mien befitting a priestess of a once universal cult. There is no direct evidence that the weird procession in which she is taking part had a religious origin, but the probabilities all point that way, when we bear in mind the extent to which phallic worship prevailed in Japan until 1868, and the traces of it that still linger in remote districts.

I have stated that vice is not increased by its regulation by the State in Japan, nor is it thereby palliated in the eyes of the self-respecting section of the community. In Old Japan, the *Samurai* who visited the *Yoshi-wara* concealed his features beneath a broad, pudding-basin-shaped hat, or a cloth tied over his face. To this day, no respectable Japanese would like to be seen passing through its gates, unless in the company of a foreigner, to whom he is showing the sights of the Metropolis. Whatever we may think, individually, of the whole system, with its strict police control and regular medical inspection, in one respect we must acknowledge its complete efficiency : it succeeds in confining vice to one particular district, where only those who deliberately seek it come in contact with it, and it leaves the rest of the streets of the great city clean and pure. Kanda is the most "rowdy" *Ku,* or Ward, of Tôkio, the "Quartier Latin" of the Japanese capital, the home of students and the location of clandestine drinking-shops and tea-houses of shady reputation. Its inhabitants are the typical *Yedo-ko*—literally, the *Enfants de Yedo*—in fact, just as the true-born Cockney, in the strictest acceptation of the word, must have first seen the light of day in a locality within sound of Bow Bells, the *Parisien de Paris* within ear-shot of the rumbling of the Boulevards, and the *"echter Weana,"* under the shadow of the *Stefanskirche*, so must the genuine "Son of Tōkio" be able to boast that: *"Kanda-no jō-sui-de ubu-yu-wo tsukatta"* — "He was washed at birth in hot water from the upper waters of Kanda." A Japanese lady might walk through the streets of Kanda at any hour of the night without seeing anything that could possibly offend the most sensitive feelings of propriety. A man may stroll along *Ginza*, the Regent Street of Tōkio, at midnight without being once accosted. For aught he could see, or hear, in nocturnal rambles through the city, such a thing as vice might be absolutely unknown in Tōkio. Compare this with the state of London streets between eleven o'clock at night and the small hours of the morning! "They order these things better in"—Japan!

Since 1880, a great and beneficial change has taken place in a most important, probably *the* most important, feature of the conjugal life of Japanese women of the higher, and of the upper middle, classes—the institution of Concubinage, deprived, for the first time, of all legal sanction by the Penal Code promulgated in that year. In the years since the publication of that Code concubinage has steadily fallen into disfavour. It was always confined, in Japan, in China and in Korea, to the wealthy classes, as, naturally, only the man who could afford to keep another woman besides his wife would avail himself of the privilege conferred by immemorial custom. Throughout the Far East, concubinage had its origin in the desire for male issue. Should the wife—and there has always been, except in a very few cases amongst the highest classes, in ancient times, *only one legal wife*—fail to present her husband with a son, he took, if his means allowed it, a concubine, in the hope of securing the continuance of the family in the male line. Numerous instances are on record of wives, unable to bear male offspring, actually requesting their husbands to take a concubine, for the sake of perpetuating the family name without having recourse to adoption, the course followed by those son-less men too poor to keep up a plural domestic establishment, or too fond of a wife to divorce her on a flimsy pretext and marry another. Whatever is here stated on the subject of concubinage and of divorce must be taken to apply in the present tense to China and Korea, but already in the past tense as regards a large proportion of the population of Japan. The Japanese law of 1880 forbade the recognition in the *Ko-seki*, or Family Register, of the son of a *Mekaké*, or *Shō*, a concubine, as the heir, failing male issue by the wife, and the *raison d'être* of the whole system thus fell to the ground.

But other causes than the desire of a son and heir had, in the course of centuries, operated in favour of the custom. The ineradicable polygamous instinct common, in varying degrees, to men of all periods, suggested the addition of concubines, beyond the requirements of family continuance, to the household capable of supporting them. Hence, concubinage dies hard in Japan, the polygamous instinct being unaffected by the law depriving the custom of its logical excuse, but it is dying for all that. The *Mekaké* was always a kind of upper servant rather than a consort: she waited on the wife, in cases where they lived under the same roof—only wealthy households had a separate establishment, a *shō-taku*, for the concubine—she addressed her respectfully as *Oku Sama*, "Madam," whilst she herself was called only by her personal name, even by her own son, should she be fortunate enough to have borne the heir, whereas he would call the legal wife his "Mother." To her son, the *Mekaké* would stand in the position occupied in many Occidental households by a

faithful, valued nurse, who "brought up the young Master";
towards his father's wife, although united to her by no
ties of blood, he would observe the severe subjection of
Far Eastern filial piety. Now, the concubine has no legal
status in the family; Japanese women, inspired by the
new thoughts instilled with the modern education, are not
slow to realise the fact, and it may safely be assumed that
the lapse of another generation will mark the virtual
extinction of the *Shō*, or *Mekaké*.

There are not wanting keen Japanese observers of
social conditions who are in considerable doubt as to the
ultimate benefit to accrue to the nation from the dis-
establishment of the system of concubinage. They shake
their heads ominously and express the fear, based on their
observation of Occidental life, that the disappearance of
the *Mekaké* as a recognised institution may lead to evils
of another kind. The husband, they say, may seek
variety in his sexual relations in other, and less open, and
therefore more pernicious, ways; he may lead a double
life, squandering his means on a clandestine establishment
with a mistress, perhaps raising an illegitimate family, and
thus creating a class, happily hitherto almost unknown in
Japan, of those unfortunate innocent beings who suffer so
cruelly in the West for the transgression of their parents;
he may frequent the *Yoshi-wara*, or he may cast lustful
eyes on his neighbour's wife or daughter. These are
grave forebodings, and those who utter them point to the
wrecked lives, so common in the Occident, in confirmation
of their apprehensions, for it is a peculiarity of the Far
Eastern observers of our social conditions that they are
not deluded by the conventional fictions we find so comforting, but probe deep into our national sores. At the
same time, they are, as a rule, just and acknowledge that
the family life of the majority of Occidentals is worthy
of imitation, but they absolutely reject the gratifying assumption, to which the West clings, that this majority
is an overwhelmingly large one. They know, by the

results of keen, unprejudiced observation how large the
minority is, and they hesitate before recommending, the
adoption, *en bloc*, of a social system that allows, in their
opinion, of the existence of so much unhappiness, so
much undeserved suffering, so much hypocritical deceit.
"The *Mekaké*," they say, "was, under the old dispensation, a respectable woman, her children had equal rights
with their fellow-creatures; if we abolish concubinage
entirely, we lower her to the position of a clandestine
mistress, and her children will be condemned to the hard
lot of bastardy. Moreover, the husband, who, hitherto,
saw no wrong in his conduct, will, in future, visit his
mistress by stealth, become a moral coward, and practise
deceit towards his wife, who, for her part, will be tortured
by pangs of jealousy, suspicion, and hatred she never
knew before." To these warnings the ardent social reformers of Japan reply that husbands must learn to conform strictly to monogamy, the purest and best form of
matrimony, and the objectors return to the charge with
the assertion that continence is not given to every man,
that marriages are often unhappy from physical causes
entirely beyond control, and, finally, that counsels of perfection do not enter into the range of practical social
reform. So the battle of the opinions rages in the Far
East, but, I repeat, concubinage is doomed in Japan, and
so is the ancient, unjust system of divorce, strictly Chinese
in spirit, whereby the husband can dismiss the wife, at
least in theory, almost as readily as he can get rid of a
hired servant.

Here again, the reformers meet with opposition. The
objectors are ready to concede that the wife should be
allowed to free herself from a bad husband—a right
hitherto practically denied to her—but they are against
any restriction of the present wide facilities for divorce,
urging that no good can come of compelling people to
remain fettered together who should be united solely by
bonds of mutual esteem, of trust and affection.

S

Slowly, very slowly, but surely, the Japanese woman is approaching emancipation from the many disabilities incidental to her inferior position. Her sisters in China and in Korea have, as yet, no such bright prospect before them. In both those Empires, the women of the working classes lead a life very similar, in its conjugal aspects, to that of the married female toilers in the West, with, probably, the balance of happiness slightly in favour of the Far East, for, although cases of wife-beating are not unknown, by any means, in China, the working man of Eastern Asia is, almost invariably, sober and, nearly always, a kind husband and father. The working woman of China, the patient, hardy, thrifty toiler, in baggy blue cotton clothes, and the sturdy, hard-featured, strong, white-clothed worker of Korea—it is almost unnecessary to state that the woman is meant, for the Korean man seldom works really assiduously—are estimable types of woman-kind. Industrious, independent, excellent wives and mothers, they live on a footing of companionship with their husbands, just as the women of the Japanese labour-ing classes do, and their active lives, free from the trammels imposed on their social superiors by rigid customs of hoary antiquity, approach very nearly to the Occidental ideal of conjugal happiness in humble circumstances. It is the women of the higher classes, in China and in Korea, who are reduced to the condition of mere automata, serving merely to propagate the family and to minister to the pleasures of their husbands. Poor dressed-up dolls, gaudily apparelled, painted and powdered, they spend soulless lives in the seclusion of the women's apart-ments, surrounded by the concubines with whom they share their husbands' affection, and by a swarm of slave-girls who are also at the disposal of the Lords and Masters. I have written the words "soulless lives"; on second thoughts, I must qualify them, for no woman's life can be considered spiritless that is illumined by maternal joys, and, in most cases, the gladsome laughter

of children sheds its sunshine into the monotonous gloom
of the Chinese, or Korean, lady's married life. And they
fully appreciate the blessing, for there are no more con-
scientious mothers, and none more tender, than these
women of the Far East.

As a rule, the ladies of China and of Korea take little,
or no interest in intellectual pursuits, their education
having been of a severely practical character, limited to
fitting them for the ordinary duties of domestic life and
of motherhood. But there are brilliant exceptions, in the
upper middle class as well as in higher circles. Some
women, generally the favourite daughters of Literati, have
received an advanced education and shine in poetry, in
elegant prose composition, and in the arts. Moreover,
however low the general average of female intellect may
be in China and Korea, owing to the severe repression
to which the women are subjected, there are among
them strong, masterful characters, and shrewd brains, as
in the case of the two women who have played such an
important part in the history of their respective countries
in the 'nineties—the Empress-Dowager of China, and the
late Queen of Korea, who was foully murdered in her own
Palace by a band of Korean and Japanese conspirators.
It seems passing strange that two women should have
exercised, of late years, such preponderating influence on
the destinies of nations that relegate their womankind to
such a low position in the social scheme. Close enquiry
into the domestic life of Far Eastern peoples reveals,
however, the fact that this position of subjection is often
more apparent than real. Hen-pecked husbands are not
uncommon in Eastern Asia, although their condition of
abject servitude is often concealed from outsiders by a
strict observance of the conventionalities of conjugal life.
The woman who shows her husband all the prescribed
marks of respect in the presence of strangers will, sometimes, when he is at her mercy in the privacy of her
apartments, let loose the torrent of invective that comes

readily to Chinese, or Korean, lips, and the unfortunate man will hide his diminished head. Many a stern Mandarin, who sits in his tribunal, as awe-inspiring as Rhadamanthus, and grimly throws out of a bowl, on to the floor of the Court, the little slips of bamboo, each of which is a voucher for five strokes, to be well and duly laid on the unfortunate prisoner, lying on his face on the ground before him, by the executioner armed with the thick, or the thin, bamboo—many a hectoring, dogmatic Graduate, trembles at home in the presence of a little, sharp-tongued woman—wife or concubine. The law of the land permitting the husband to divorce his wife for, amongst other reasons, "a scolding tongue," it is strong testimony to the patience of the .hen-pecked men that they do not, as a rule, avail themselves of the privilege.

The mind of the average Chinese woman is cramped and confined within the narrow limits of the national prejudices and superstitions, just as her feet, small by nature, are tortured into stumps rendering walking, unaided, a very difficult matter. If she be of Tartar race, she escapes this cruel and absurd custom; even if of Chinese blood, but of the working class—a peasant, or a boatwoman, for instance—her feet are allowed to retain their natural size and shape. One of the most hopeful signs of impending reform in China is the formation, in 1897, of a purely Chinese "Society for the Abolition of the Feet-Compressing Custom" amongst the inhabitants of the southern Province of Kwang-tung ("Canton"). The chief obstacle in the Society's path is the fact that the compressed feet are looked .upon as a mark of "gentility." Like the long finger-nails of the Mandarin, they imply: "See how 'genteel' I am; *I* have never needed to do any work!" And when women once get it into their heads that a certain custom, or fashion, is "the correct thing," it needs a *very* powerful Society, energetically conducted, to alter their opinion, especially if, as in this case, the fashion has won the approval of poets, who have composed well-known stanzas on the "Golden Lilies," the tiny, compressed feet, on which the lady-love sways to and fro "like the graceful willow."

Cramped at both ends, mentally, as to her brain, physically, as to her feet, the Chinese lady cannot be expected to have much knowledge of the world, and is, naturally, deficient in the conversational powers that require such knowledge. If her husband wants to sharpen his wits by conversation with a brilliant female talker, he must needs seek one of the sprightly inmates—sprightly, from a Chinese point of view—of the "Flower Boats," or of similar establishments on shore. The wife can talk to him, shrewdly enough, about matters of the nursery, and of domestic economy in general. On other subjects she has no conversation. Her Korean sister is in the same case; although her feet are not deformed, she makes but little use of them, being secluded within the boundaries of her house and garden. One may travel from one end of Korea to the other without ever seeing a native lady. One may encounter, in the streets of Söul, women of the middle class, out "shopping," or going to visit friends, but one gets but a vague idea of their figures, and the merest glimpse of their features; as a rule, only a peep at two bright dark eyes. The voluminous white skirt, standing out stiffly from the body, which bears to it the proportion of the clapper to a bell, begins at a waist that is placed high up under the arm-pits; it covers baggy white trousers reaching to the ankles, as many as *three pairs* being sometimes worn. The head and shoulders are concealed under a sleeved gown, generally of a bright, deep green, which is not used for its natural purpose, but only as a hood and cape, much in the same way as the London carman's boy throws his jacket over his head in a sudden down-pour of rain. The folds of this gown are held together in front of the face, leaving only the eyes exposed, the sleeves hanging down on either side. The traveller does not have much time to examine this curious costume, for, the moment its wearer sees him, she bolts into the first house the door of which stands open, to seek the sanctuary every Korean dwelling offers to a woman *in danger* of meeting a man. For the casual meeting of persons of opposite sexes is looked upon as a grave peril amongst the higher and middle classes in Korea, and to obviate it, as far as possible, and, at the same time, to give the women an opportunity for exercise, a strict curfew regulation enjoins—or enjoined, for ancient laws are repealed and re-enacted with astonishing rapidity in New Korea—that no male do venture out of doors between the hours of 8 P.M. and sunrise, except on official business, or to summon aid to a sick person's bedside, so that the ladies may roam abroad without hesitation. Woe betide the luckless Korean man who infringed this regulation; if he fell into the clutches of a police patrol he would be soundly flogged for his audacity.

The working women of Korea are not restricted to the hours of night for their walks abroad, nor need they conceal their faces, prematurely seamed and hardened by constant drudgery, under the gown worn as a hood. They move about freely at all times, clad in loose white trousers and full white skirt, with an apology for a jacket, an exiguous garment, also of white cotton, that covers the shoulders, but reaches only to the upper part of the bosom, leaving the greater portion of the breasts exposed. There is another class of Korean women who enjoy a great amount of freedom in their movements—the *Ki-saing* (pronounced, nasally, *Ki-sêng*), or dancing-girls, who are the counterpart of the *Gei-sha* of Japan, but less reputable, as their calling is, almost invariably, supplemented by prostitution. It is in their society the Korean men seek the intellectual relaxation they cannot find in the company of their worthy, but humdrum, wives. Throughout the Far East, the men are often driven to the perilous company of professional entertainers—dangerous because their fascinations often prove irresistible — owing to the "goody-goody" dulness of their homes. It is the story of classical antiquity all over again. The ladies of Athens, and the Roman matrons, were most estimable women, without doubt, exemplary wives and mothers, but their conversation was limited to home topics—the price of provisions, probably, or baby's new tooth, or the misdeeds of the household slaves—and they must have been singularly uninteresting companions. So their husbands sought solace, often for the mind only, in the brilliant society of the *Hetaira*, who shone as much by their wit, and often by their learning, as by their beauty.

The education of women in New Japan is fitting them more and more to brighten home life intellectually, as well as with the light of their domestic virtues, and there is little room for doubt that, in the course of the coming generation, the wives will be able to compete successfully with the *Gei-sha* in the art of interesting and amusing their husbands. Many of them already do so. In China, the great majority of the women are still benighted, but a beginning has already been made, although on a very small scale, towards providing some of them with education in the Occidental sense of the word. In Korea, American and British Missionary efforts have already had some effect in the same direction. A whole generation, at least, must pass away before any appreciable results can leaven the whole womankind of China and of Korea with a higher conception of the part reserved for it in the social fabric. *Then* the Women of the New Far East will become more learned, more self-reliant, more capable of holding their own in the wide world; more obedient daughters, more dutiful wives, and more devoted mothers they cannot possibly be.

CHAPTER VI.

THE ALMIGHTY DOLLAR.

THE. interest in the Far East, now so keenly felt by Occidentals, is based, to a great extent, on the magnitude of the industrial, commercial and financial questions involved. Not only have huge sums accumulated, in the past, in trade with Eastern Asia, not only is the vast importance of its commerce with the West constantly increasing, but very weighty economic questions, affecting all countries, await solution in those parts of the world.

This may seem a sordid cause to which to attribute the interest of the West in the affairs of the Far East, but it is, nevertheless, the principal factor at work, especially in the great industrial and commercial nations, with which the *"argumentum ad pockctum"* increases daily in force. Millions of Occidentals look to the New Far East as the Land of Promise whence golden streams are to flow into the coffers of Europe, of America and Australia, in exchange for products that are becoming a glut in the markets of those continents, and for the output of industries that must find new outlets if they are to live. The general impression seems to be that Occidental commerce has in Eastern Asia a magnificent field, the surface of which has hitherto barely been scratched, that those Lands of the Dawn abound in resources beyond the wildest dreams of the most sanguine imagination— that of the promoter of companies, or of the mining expert, for instance—and that the "teeming millions" of the yellow races are eagerly awaiting the day that will place the commodities "made in the Occident" within their reach.

This impression requires to be considered, if we would make sure of its accuracy, by the light of a knowledge of the local conditions and, especially, of the character of the peoples in question, rather than by the light of statistics alone. Fellows of the Royal Statistical Society, and others who expect serried columns of bewildering figures in small print, are hereby warned off. I do not intend to quote statistical returns, because those who hanker after them can find them, duly tabulated, in the excellent, interesting, often even amusing, Reports on Trade of Her Britannic Majesty's Diplomatic and Consular Representatives—issued by the Foreign Office at very moderate prices, and to be obtained through any bookseller—and in the minutely detailed Returns published, in English, by various Departments of the Japanese Government, and by the Imperial Maritime Customs of China. In the case of Japan, a valuable *Résumé Statistique de l'Empire du Japon* is also issued annually. I refrain from giving tables of carefully marshalled figures for another reason also, and a weighty one : the rapidity with which such statistics pass out of date in the Far East, the region of commercial and industrial surprises, and especially in Japan, where trade and manufactures have acquired a habit of advancing, not by the slow stages to which we are accustomed in the West, but by amazing "leaps and bounds." Returns out of date are worse than no statistics at all, as they are apt to be totally misleading, so I prefer to convey such information as I have to give in general terms, and to confine myself, as far as possible, to the consideration of broad principles and ethnographical facts, —that will be as true five, ten or twenty years hence as they are now—of such racial characteristics as are likely to undergo change, and of local conditions that will probably be altered, pointing out the direction in which the transformation will, most likely, be effected. I venture to think such a course will be more profitable than long rows of noughts, and many decimals, or than accurate statement, to a *Catty,** of the fish-glue, or of the dried mussels, exported from Ning-po in 1896, or, to a *Yen's* value, of the kerosene landed at Kōbé in the first quarter of '1898. One more word of warning to the Reader: vitally important as the Silver Question is to Far Eastern commerce, intimately as that great problem is bound up with the question of the currency in China, I shall not enter into any consideration of Bi-metallism, for or against, —"that way madness lies." Indeed, it would be premature to hazard an opinion on the subject at a time when data are still lacking to prove who were right, those who applauded Japan's adoption of the Gold Standard, in 1897, or the pessimists who predicted national ruin as the ultimate result of the bold step.

This matter of the Japanese Gold Standard offers an excellent opportunity of pointing out the tendency, amongst Occidentals in general, to attach the greatest importance to Far Eastern questions which are, no doubt, of vast magnitude, but really secondary in comparison to others receiving far less attention. The financial and commercial world is greatly excited over the probability of the Japanese being able, in the future, to pay their debts in gold, or the eventuality of their being compelled to return to payment in silver, but the great question lies far deeper than this. It is, really, not a question so much of the medium of payment, nor even of the ability of the Japanese to pay in any medium, but of their *willingness* to pay at all. In short, the *honesty* of the Japanese is the great point on which the mind of the Occident should be fully satisfied before any further consideration of the prospects of extended commerce with them can be profitably entered into. And their honesty

* 1⅓ Pound Avoirdupois, or o 60453 Kilogramme.

in matters of commerce is not a foregone conclusion; it has been questioned by many who should be in a good position to speak from experience. Almost every Occidental trading in the Far East has decided views on the subject, and these are, as a rule, unfavourable to the commercial morality of the Japanese. The European and American merchants who are established in the Treaty Ports of Japan are continually uttering complaints, which find their way into Consular Reports, of obligations neglected, debts unpaid, claims unsatisfied, contracts unfulfilled, and judgments of the Courts nullified by combinations of native Traders' Guilds for the purpose of that very Occidental operation known as "Boycotting." A certain amount of suspicion attaches to these lamentations owing to their origin. They proceed from people who have every reason to desire that industrial and commercial circles in the West should be deterred from *direct* dealing with the Japanese—and, thanks to the efforts of the native merchants, seconded and encouraged by their Government, the tendency is all in the direction of *direct* trading—and what better deterring agent could be found than the bogey of the "dishonest Japanese trader"? Moreover, the complaints come from merchants who are not, as a rule, really in direct touch with the Japanese mercantile classes, but, almost invariably, deal with them through the intermediary of a *Bantō*, the Japanese equivalent of the Chinese *Comprador*, the native *employé* who acts as a go-between, and is not always as scrupulous as he should be. He does not hesitate, at times, to manipulate his employer's business with less regard for its success than for sundry little speculations of his own, and sometimes throws the blame of losses, without compunction, on the shoulders of the Japanese factors, or retailers, to whom he sells, or of the producers, or their agents, from whom he buys. To this must be added the fact that the Occident hears but one version of the state of commercial morality in the Far East, that put forward by its own merchants.

Little, or nothing, is known, in the West, of the many
heartless swindles perpetrated by Occidentals in Eastern
Asia in the days, not further back than the 'sixties, when
the yellow races were still as children in matters of international commerce, and in knowledge of the products of
Occidental industry.   We seldom, if ever, hear of the
crazy steam-ships, the rickety machinery, the faulty rifles,
the unsound goods of all kinds that were sold, in those days,
at exorbitant prices, to buyers incapable, at the time, of
detecting the frauds.   To this day, there must be instances
of unfair dealing on the part of some of the foreign merchants, unless the Occidental mercantile class in the Far
East be *entirely* composed of absolutely blameless, high-
minded men—in which case it would present a marked
contrast to every other commercial community in the
world—but these instances are not paraded before our
eyes.   The native trader, or producer, may suffer by them,
but he is, so far, practically inarticulate as regards venti-
lating his grievances before the Western public, whereas
the Occidental merchant in the Far East can, and does,
give vent to his indignation and his grumbling in the
columns of newspapers, and in the pages of magazines and
of Consular Reports.

Whilst carefully weighing these conditions, militating
against the absolute accuracy of the Western merchant's
sweeping condemnation of Japanese commercial methods,
it must be stated that there is, unfortunately, a solid basis
of truth under his exaggerated censure.   There are Japanese
merchants, manufacturers, and bankers who rank as high
in morality, and in strict adherence to the fairest methods,
as any in the West, but they are, as yet, in a minority.
There is a valid reason for this lamentable fact in the
comparatively recent date of the raising of the Japanese
commercial man's status to the plane of respectability,
hardly attained by him in Old Japan.   Until the Great
Change, in 1867-8, the Japanese nation, apart from the
outcast *Eta* and *Hi-nin*, was divided into four great classes:

Shi, the military, administrative, and literary class, *Nō*, the agriculturists, *Kō*, the craftsmen, and, last and least, *Shō*, the traders. Some of the trading class accumulated great wealth, especially by lucky speculations in rice, and by judicious banking for *Dai-miyo*, or feudal lords, but they were accounted of the lowest class of citizens for all that. A few succeeded, by dint of munificent donations for public purposes, in obtaining honours of some sort from the Government of the *Shō-gun*, a way of acquiring rank not unknown in the West, but the distinctions conferred did not alter the fact that they belonged to the despised class of traders—again a parallel to Occidental conditions. It is easy to understand how, in a nation of warriors, those men who devoted themselves to commerce were looked down upon, especially when it is remembered that even in the British Isles, that owe their prosperity to commerce, there are, to this day, thousands of families, often such whose very name betrays them—Mercers, Bakers, Taylors, Glovers, Smythes, and so forth—whose proud boast it is that they "have never been in trade, you know."

There is but little self-respect in any class that is despised by the bulk of its compatriots, and the traders of Old Japan, placed beyond the pale of respectability, formed no exception to the rule. A few great commercial families, like that of Mitsui, established centuries ago, rose, by honesty, ability, and accumulated wealth, above the level of the general ruck of traders, but the majority never rose, either in methods of business, or in popular estimation, above the standing of the small shopkeeper of the Occident. The Great Change brought an alteration in the division of the people; the four classes were replaced by three: *Kuwa-zoku*, or Nobility (Princes, equivalent to British Dukes, Marquesses, Earls, Viscounts, and Barons), *Shi-zoku*, or Gentry (the former *Samurai*, or two-sworded class), and *Hei-min*, or Common People. The last class included the farmers, large and small, the artisans and the traders, thus, for the first time,

lumped together under a common designation. The effect
of this change was not the lowering of the agriculturists
and the craftsmen to the status of the traders, but the
raising of these, as was intended, to a higher level. Not
only *Shi-zoku*, but even members of the aristocracy, did
not disdain to " go into trade," now that the old order of
things had given way to the new, and a marked improvement in commercial aims, methods, and morality soon
became perceptible. The majority of these new recruits
to the ranks of commerce and finance, well-born and
often highly educated, naturally gravitated, and still do
so, towards the higher branches of money-making, towards
banking, insurance, ship-owning and shipbuilding, manufacturing, the exploitation of mines, the management of
railways, and wholesale export and import business conducted on a large scale. It has thus come to pass that
the commercial world of New Japan is divided into two
classes : the great companies, representing that joint-
stock enterprise for which the Japanese have so rapidly
acquired a marked aptitude, and the first-rate private
firms, on the one hand, and the large number of manufacturers in a small way and petty traders, on the
other. Of the first class, it may be declared with assurance that it displays quite as high a standard of integrity,
fully as much energy and perseverance, and as great a
spirit of enterprise, considering the obstacles to be surmounted, as the corresponding class in the Occident. It
enjoys the further advantage that its members have been,
as a rule, carefully and practically trained for their work,
and have acquired a theoretical knowledge of the first
principles underlying all commercial operations that is
seldom found amongst Occidental men of business. There
is, of course, danger in this theoretical knowledge when it
is allowed, as is sometimes the case in Japan, to convert
business men into *doctrinaires*, riding their hobbies at the
fences of common-sense. Political Economy has nowhere
more ardent votaries than in Japan, in accordance with

the curious rule, obtaining throughout the world, by which the poorer nations supply the greater number of students of "the Dismal Science," whereas the people who own the greater part of the world's wealth hold it, and add to it, without bestowing more than a passing thought on the principles, first enunciated by a man of their own race, that are supposed to govern the economics of the globe.

If the majority of Japanese commercial men were like the members of the class just described, we should hear but little complaint on the part of the Occidentals trading in their midst. Unfortunately, the greater number belong to the second category—the petty traders, not always without capital, for some of them are, for Japan, wealthy, but almost always without any broad conception of business, mere hucksters, taking a greater delight in a momentary gain of a few *Yen* than in the undertaking of a transaction likely to result in a steadily increasing trade to the tune of thousands. If these petty traders were to be classified according to Carlyle's division of the English people, one ought, following the testimony of the irate Occidental who deals with them, to place them amongst the knaves, but this would be a grievous error. Rogues some of them may be, and cunning rogues at that, but the great majority are simply *fools*. In their narrow-minded folly, they are bent on squeezing the utmost amount of immediate profit out of a customer, regardless of the fact that they are thereby losing the chance of future steady and lucrative trade. They share with the Dutch of former times the fault of

> "Giving too little
> And asking too much."

It is surprising that such quick-witted people as the Japanese unquestionably are should not have recognised, long ago, the futility of thus "killing the goose that lays the golden eggs." And, verily, the majority of the traders of Japan look upon the Occidental as a goose,

else they would not impute to him such absolute imbecility as is implied in many of the commercial transactions they blandly propose to him.   Fortunately, their
little schemes for plucking the foreigner are generally, as
the French say, "stitched with white thread," and the
too evident snare is spread in vain in sight of the wary
bird.   Occasionally, however, the attempt succeeds ; the
Occidental is caught, either through his ignorance of the
local conditions, or because circumstances combine to place
him at the mercy of the Oriental schemer.   Thereupon
great rejoicing ensues, and the attempt is repeated, need-
less to say, hardly ever with success, as the foreigner
"once bitten" is, to a certainty, "twice shy."

Nobody deplores this folly of the petty trader more
than the Japanese authorities themselves, and they are
making strenuous efforts to put a stop to it, by exhorta-
tion in the Reports of their Consular Officers, and by
providing an excellent commercial education, at small cost
to the students, for the training of a generation of merchants of broader views.   There is no better-organised,
no better-equipped institution of its kind in the world
than the Commercial High School in Tōkio, where a
complete course of instruction, theoretical as well as
admirably practical, is given.   In one large hall of this
School, that has counterparts in the chief commercial
cities of Japan, a number of bays, or recesses, are labelled
with the names of the principal mercantile centres of the
world, and in each of these a number of students, who
have been well grounded in theoretical knowledge, taking
the parts, respectively, of bankers, importers, exporters,
brokers, insurance agents, and shipping agents, carry on
an active, simulated international trade in strict accordance with the business usages of the places at which they
are supposed to be dealing.   The various steps of every
conceivable commercial transaction are accurately gone
through, from the comparison of samples, obtained from
the School Museum, to the giving and receipt of orders,

the making out of invoices and bills of lading, of policies
of insurance and freight - notes, and to the drawing, and
sometimes the "protesting," of bills of exchange, even to
disputes as to quality and packing, giving rise to instructive correspondence in several languages, with the necessary
dictation, shorthand, and type-writing, and "code" telegrams. When will London, the commercial metropolis of
the world, have a Commercial School like that of Tōkio,
or, indeed, a Commercial School of any kind worthy of
the name ?

The flourishing State Institutions that supply an excellent
commercial education in Japan should be the most effective
agencies for the purification and enlightenment of the class
of small merchants whose overreaching rapacity has been
described. Unfortunately, as fast as the students graduate
at these schools, they are absorbed into the staff of one or
other of the great banks, or companies, or important private
firms that need no reformation. The minor houses of business, that most require their skilled supervision, offer no
inducements to tempt them, and they are seldom possessed
of sufficient capital to be able to establish themselves on
their own account. Thus the small fry of Japanese trade
continue to wallow in the mire of commercial ignorance
and short-sighted greed, and the Occidental trader, sooner
or later, suffers at their hands. He raises, in his wrath, a
hue and cry against all Japanese mercantile people indis-
criminately, and the perfectly sound, honest, native firms
are made to bear, in the public opinion of the West, the
odium properly attaching only to the "shady" minor traders.
The mischief is deserving of the closest attention of the
Japanese themselves, for it increases daily in importance,
as the business relations with the Occident become closer
and more numerous, and the efforts of the Japanese to
establish *direct* trade with all parts of the world gain in
intensity. Of course, the Occidental merchant in Japan
could protect himself by resolutely declining to do business
with any native firms not of the highest standing, but this

T

presupposes conditions that are seldom in existence—an intimate acquaintance with the reputation and character of native traders, only to be obtained by *direct* intercourse with them, without the intermediary of the *Bantō*, and necessitating a knowledge of the Japanese language very rarely possessed by Occidental merchants.

As to the Western manufacturer, or merchant, at home, he has not the safeguard his compeer in Japan might employ, had he the energy to do so, for the man in the Occident, eager to sell his wares in Japan, is prone to enter into business relations with Japanese firms without sufficiently searching enquiry into their standing. Most of the great Japanese houses have branches, or agencies, in the chief commercial centres throughout the world. In dealing with these the Occidental at home runs no risk. The danger begins for him when he has executed an order, duly paid for—*first* orders generally are—from a Japanese company, or firm, about which he knows nothing, or very little. How is he to know that he will be incurring great chance of loss by executing that tempting second, or third, order received from the "*Dorobō Kuwai-sha*, Limited," of Ōsaka, or from Messrs. Katari, Kanenaki & Co., of Yokohama, who write such plausible letters in such quaint English? Well, there are Imperial Japanese Consulates in the West, and from any of these trustworthy information as to the probable genuineness of an order from Japan, and the standing of the firm giving it, may be obtained. The Consular Official giving the information will, naturally, not undertake any responsibility regarding it, but he may safely be trusted to do his utmost to safeguard the honour of the national commerce by preventing transactions, as far as lies in his power, that would, in his judgment, end in loss of money to the foreigner, and of reputation to the Japanese.

Time works wonders, and, in the course of years, we may see a new generation of Japanese merchants in every way worthy of the great commercial future that lies before

their country. This desirable end will be attained,
partly by the spread of commercial education, partly by
combination amongst foreign merchants to resist any
questionable practices on the part of Japanese traders,
partly by an inevitable revolution in the foreign business
methods in the Far East—no more "go-between," direct
dealing with the native merchants, and the study of the language and the customs of the country—but chiefly by
the efforts of those Japanese who are wise enough to
recognise the present evil. Unfortunately, many Japanese,
even amongst the most highly educated, still suffer from
the national morbid hyper-sensitiveness, the consequence
of centuries of insular seclusion, to such a degree that they
resent honest foreign criticism, however gently administered,
as an insult to their race. This "touchy" disposition often
leads them to be somewhat lukewarm in certain much-
needed reforms, simply because attention has been drawn
to them by foreign observers. The fact that the candid
friend is a foreigner makes the question, in their eyes,
a national one, to be regarded not, as it shoud be, in
the light of *true* patriotism—ready to accept disinterested
criticism and advice from any quarter, and to give it due
consideration for the national welfare—but with a spirit
of wrong-headed "Chauvinism," rejecting censure and
counsel simply because they come from a foreign source.
I am well aware that several of my statements in these
pages will prove anything but pleasant reading to some
of my Japanese friends. A moment's reflection will
convince them that a plain statement of *the truth* about
their country is a far better way of serving its interests
than the fulsome, indiscriminate adulation that has been
lavished, from some quarters, on everything Japanese.
They know me too well to question my love for their
nation—my whole life bears witness to it—and I venture
to think that the greatest proof thereof I can give is
the attempt to furnish the Occident with an impartial
account of Japanese virtues and defects, in the hope that

the latter may be remedied. No nation is perfect;
strange as it may seem to some of my Readers, even the
British nation is not without its faults. Foreign criticism
is apt to be galling, but the Japanese themselves have a
proverb of which I would remind them: *"Riyō-yaku
kuchi-ni nigashi"* — "the best medicine is bitter in
the mouth."

· The strictures I have passed on the petty traders of
Japan must not be held to apply to all of them indis-
criminately, but chiefly to *a large number* of those who
enter into business relations with Occidentals, either in
Japan, through the *Bantō*, or directly with firms in the
West. The majority of the retail traders, the shopkeepers and small producers, are good, honest, marvellously
industrious · people, content with a small margin of profit.
Their wares are often sold in *Kuwan-kōba*, or bazaars,
at absolutely fixed prices, "every article marked in plain
figures," and the same excellent system is being gradually
adopted in some of the principal shops in Tōkio and in
some of the larger provincial towns. In the other retail
establishments throughout the country the immemorial
Oriental custom of bargaining still flourishes, every transaction occupying an unconscionable time, to the accompaniment not, as in China, of loud protestations and
violent gesticulation, but of much bowing, of expressions
of deep regret at inability to offer, or to accept, a
certain sum, and of numerous cups of tea and pipes of
tobacco. It is when the small trader launches out into
international transactions that his cupidity appears to
become unduly excited. He is brought face to face with
the prospect of sudden immoderate gain, for, in his
eyes, every foreigner seems a very Crœsus—an impression strengthened by the lavish manner in which some
American travellers fling their money about—and he
loses his head and becomes foolishly rapacious. Unless
the foreigner be wary, he may be made to pay dearly
for the mischief wrought by other Occidentals who have

run to extremes, in former transactions, either by un-thinking compliance with first demands of an extravagant nature, or by attempts to beat down the price below a fair limit, so as to show that they are "not going to be taken in" by the vendor, whom they have exasperated by the process, not unknown in London and Paris shops much frequented by ladies, of causing the greater part of the stock to be displayed before them—and ultimately purchasing a mere trifle.

The most powerful lever in the hands of the Japanese who would regenerate their trading class is the feeling of national honour, so highly developed in every other direc-tion amongst their countrymen. There is an expression, current in Japanese commercial circles, that has found its way into the language of the people at large, de-scribing any disgraceful action as likely to *noren-ni kakari,* "to hang to the curtain," that is drawn, at times, before the front of a Japanese shop, and bears the name and trade-mark of the firm—in other words, likely to be a blot on the scutcheon. Let the Japanese once thoroughly understand that unfair commercial methods, excessive greed, and failure to meet engagements, will inevitably tarnish not only the sign-board of the peccant firm, but the glory of the national flag, and public opinion will brand the transgressors, and will establish and maintain a standard of commercial morality as high as any in the world.

The importance of this subject will be readily appre-ciated when the phenomenal strides are considered by which Japan is progressing towards the status of a great industrial country, selling its manufactures far beyond its borders. Ōsaka, always a busy commercial centre since the great Regent Hideyoshi, commonly known as the *Taikō Sama,* made it the seat of his government, in A.D. 1583, bids fair soon to deserve the name, already applied to it, of "the Manchester of Japan." Hundreds of tall chimneys stand hard by its many canals, belching forth clouds of black smoke to disfigure the fair surroundings, and to gladden the hearts of Japanese holders of shares in cotton-mills earning, on an average, dividends of twelve *per cent*. When the good Emperor Nintoku, who is said to have reigned from A.D. 313 to 399, had, in the kindness of his heart, remitted all taxation for the space of three years, to lighten the burdens of his impoverished people, the Civil List was reduced to such a low ebb that the rain leaked through the roof of his Palace at Naniwa, the modern Ōsaka, and the sovereign and his consort went about in wofully shabby raiment. So out-at-elbows did the whole Imperial Court appear, that the farmers, beginning to prosper in the absence of taxation, respectfully offered voluntary contributions, which the Emperor declined with thanks. At last the Empress, who had outdone all records of feminine self-sacrifice by actually wearing the same dress for three years in succession, could bear the strain of Imperial penury no longer, and approached the Emperor on the subject, not at the hour of curtain-lectures, but at a moment equally propitious, in the West, for the discussion of domestic economy, and the suggestion of new gowns and other urgent necessities—at breakfast-time. The Emperor led her on to the leaky Palace roof and, by way of reply to her representations, pointed to the columns of smoke peacefully ascending from the chimneys of his contented subjects all over the countryside. Then, being an early Japanese Emperor, Nintoku broke into poetry, and composed the following lines, sung to this day by every Japanese man, woman and child, who still bless the name of the good Emperor :—

> "*Takaki ya-ni*
> *Noborité mireba*
> *Kemuri tatsu ;—*
> *Tami-no kamado-wa*
> *Nigiwai-ni keri.*"

Which, being interpreted, means :—" Having ascended a

high place and looking around, lo! the smoke is rising;—
the kitchen-hearths of the people are busy." The Sage
Emperor, as he is called, was happy. Like gallant
Henry IV. of France, who wanted every family in his
kingdom to have "a fowl in the pot," Nintoku gauged
the prosperity of his subjects by the state of their
larders. But the Empress refused to be comforted by
the Sovereign's verse. To his assurance that they were
now prosperous, and that there could be nothing to grieve
for, she replied: "What dost thou mean by prosperity?"
The Emperor answered, saying: "It is, doubtless, when
the smoke fills the land, and the people freely attain to
wealth." His Consort retorted, with truly feminine per-
sistency, by again calling attention to the holes in the
dilapidated roof, through which the rain dripped on to
the Imperial bed-quilts. The courtiers caught it in
troughs, and were obliged constantly to shift their sleep-
ing-places so as to find a dry spot. At its best, she said,
the Palace had always been a mere barn, unplastered,
with rough pillars and rafters, and untrimmed thatch,
owing to her husband's desire—"a fad," we may be sure
she called it—to dispense with the forced labour, usual
in the erection of Palaces in those times, as he was unwilling to call the peasants away from their fields.
Although neither the *Kojiki* nor the *Nihongi* mention
the fact, we may assume that the Empress ended with
a renewed appeal, for an inspection of her three-year-old
gown, "absolutely coming to pieces." "Call you this
prosperity, forsooth?" she queried. The Emperor gravely
answered: "When Heaven sets up a Prince in authority,
it is for the sake of the People. The Prince must, therefore, make the People his first care. For this reason the
wise sovereigns of antiquity cast the responsibility on
themselves if a single one amongst their subjects was
cold and starving. The People's poverty is none other
than Our poverty; there is no such thing as the People's
being prosperous and yet the Ruler in poverty." And

the Emperor summed up his argument in words tersely
rendered by Sir Edwin Arnold in his charming verses
" The Emperor's Breakfast ":—

> " Thou and I
> ˙ Have part in all the poor folk's health,
> The People's weal makes the King's wealth." ⁂

Great must be the joy of good Emperor Nintoku's ghost
if it revisits the land he made happy by his benevolent rule !
For smoke curls up in dense clouds from his good City of
Naniwa, now the thriving, bustling Ōsaka, pouring forth
out of hundreds of chimneys higher by many yards than
the upper gallery of his Palace of Takatsu-no-Miya, from
which he had watched the blue spirals wafted up from the
cooking-hearths of his happy subjects, and the modern smoke
means the production of wealth undreamt of in his day.
The multitude of spindles in the great mills of Ōsaka are
spinning Indian cotton into yarn of the coarser " counts,"
to be used in the country, or exported, either as yarn, or
woven into cheap fabrics, to China and to Korea. When
the canal is cut, as it assuredly will be, through the isthmus
between North and South America, the Japanese mills will
be able to obtain, rapidly and cheaply, supplies of the " long-
staple " Sea Island cotton of the Mississippi estuary, and
will spin and weave the finer " counts " in the production
of which Lancashire still rules supreme. As it is, the
Japanese cotton industry, like all other manufactures by
steam power in Japan, a thing of yesterday's creation,
flourishes apace. What is needed for the development of
this, as of Japan's other industries, of her mineral wealth
and her carrying trade, is the one thing the country cannot
supply in sufficient quantity—Capital. Japan is not a rich
country in the sense of accumulated wealth, nor is she so
very poor as many Occidentals have described her. Other-

---

* Sir Edwin Arnold, " The Emperor's Breakfast," in Part I of *Pictures
of Ancient Japanese History,* by T H Asso, Chief Inspector of Machinery,
Imperial Japanese Navy Tōkio, Maruya & Co., 1890.

wise she could not have waged the costly war with China, as she did, without borrowing a single cent beyond her frontiers. But for the due development of her natural resources, of the abundant wealth latent in her new possession, Formosa, and for the most profitable employment of her sons' great technical aptitude, and of the patient, skilful labour of her masses, she must look to foreign financial aid. No more promising field could be found for the investment of Occidental capital; the directions in which it could profitably, and *safely*, be employed are innumerable.

Safety, that is the important consideration in the matter of the investment of Western capital in Japanese enterprises, and it is the one point on which the Occidental mind is not at ease. With curious perverseness, the great bulk of Occidental capitalists and investors allow their judgment to be warped by the doubts and fears of the very people who, claiming to be experts, were so wofully wrong in their forecast of the result of the war with China that they ought to hide their diminished heads in confusion. It is these prophets of evil who discourage the would-be investor by their vague hints at the "serious crisis" that, according to them, seems to be the normal condition of Japanese affairs. It is they who talk, with bated breath, of the possibility of a revolution that might sweep away, in its blind fury, every vestige of the new civilisation of Japan, and who even, in some cases, attribute nefarious designs, and the power to execute them, in certain circumstances, to the members of the old ex-feudal nobility, probably the quietest and most inoffensive body of aristocrats in the world. These doubters are of the kind who predicted victory for the rebel forces in SAIGŌ Takamori's great insurrection in Satsuma, in 1877,—and were, as usual, in error. In spite of the falsification of all their prophecies of disaster, they continue to shake their heads ominously at every kaleidoscopic change in the composition of the Japanese Cabinet, at the resignations, and threats of

resignation, that fill such a large space in the career
of high Japanese officials, at every petty squabble in
the Lower House, at each one of the "deadlocks," the
blind alleys into which the Parliament at Tōkio so often
blunders.

The Occidental capitalist notes the opinions of these
"experts,"· decides to refrain from risking his money in a
country offering, apparently, so little security—and invests
his hundreds of thousands in gold-mining ventures that are
often mere gambling, or in one of the rotten Republics
that parody civilisation in Central and South America, or,
perchance, in one of the heavily over-capitalised, strenuously
"boomed" companies floated, at home, by wily promoters
and their mercenaries, the "guinea-pig" peers. The small
investors follow the capitalist's lead, with great danger to
themselves, for they are, as a rule, unaware that the rich
man does not intend, as they do, to leave his money permanently at the disposal of the particular enterprise it
suits him, for the time being, to support. With touching
confidence they take their cue from the men in whose
experienced hands they are mere counters in the financial
game; the capitalists look with scant favour on the investment of their monies in Japanese undertakings, and the
small fry are not likely to take a different view. Yet the
day is coming when foreign capital will flow into Japan,
for the shrewd men of business of the West will inevitably
penetrate behind the screen of misrepresentation and mis-
understanding erected by interested, or ignorant, persons;
they will see the magic figures 12, 15, even 20, *per cent.*
shining alluringly on the horizon, and they may be trusted
to go in search of the tempting profits with an earnestness
and a vigour recalling the Quest of the Holy Grail. They
will have to be prepared to accept Japanese co-operation
in their enterprises, the natives of the Island Empire being
haunted by visions of future subjection in that "Bondage
to the Bondholder" that has played such an important
part in the history of modern Egypt, and determined not

to wear the golden chains of financial servitude. It is a laudable resolve, but it leads the Japanese to extremes of distrust of foreigners. It is difficult to conceive how a nation so acute as the Japanese fail to see that their ill-concealed fear of foreign domination through close financial and commercial intercourse must inevitably lower their prestige in the eyes of the world. They are never tired of repeating that they are ready to welcome foreign capital, but when they are requested to remove some of the restrictions under which its employment would be circumscribed they reply that it cannot be done; they must surround themselves with all manner of safeguards, lest they be reduced to the servile condition of the Egyptians—*toujours* the Egyptians !—whose country is managed for them, admirably managed, it is true, but none the less managed by aliens. The Japanese who express this view, and they are in an overwhelming majority, do not understand that, by their argument, they are placing themselves on the same moral and intellectual plane as the *Fellahin* of Egypt, a parallel not very flattering to the self-esteem of a proud nation.

Sooner or later, but, probably, ere long, the Japanese, taught in the wholesome school of financial necessity, will abandon their absurdly exaggerated fear of Occidental absorption "by force of capital," and will admit the foreign investor to a share in the proprietorship, and, consequently, in the management of the numerous profitable undertakings requiring capital from abroad. Legislation to this end is being framed by some of Japan's wisest minds; it will rest with her ablest, strongest statesmen to get it passed in a lucid interval of her Parliamentary debates, and to enforce it in the face of much brawling opposition by cheap "patriots" and much argument by timorous Conservatives of the old school. On one point the Japanese ultra-national spirit may be expected to hold out for a very long time: the law forbidding the owning of land by aliens. The great difficulty in the way of the removal of this serious disability is the Japanese principle that the ownership of the land is vested in the Emperor, as representing the nation, but this is mere theory, as the actual holders of the soil, especially the peasants, look upon the acres cultivated by their forefathers for generations, and for which they pay taxes, as absolutely their own. It would be a bold Government indeed that attempted to act on the assumption of national ownership, and to take the peasant-farmer's land from him. The fact that aliens may not own land would seem, *primâ facie*, to oppose an almost insurmountable obstacle to the investment of foreign capital on a large scale, but those behind the scenes in matters Japanese know that it is as easy to run a *jin-riki-sha* through a Japanese law as to drive the proverbial coach-and-four through a British Act of Parliament, and it is an open secret that very valuable land is really owned by various foreigners in the names of Japanese "men of straw." An experienced Japanese lawyer, preferably one who has been called to the English bar—they are, by this time, fairly numerous—will, for an appropriate fee, devise the necessary safeguards for the interests of any Occidentals seriously contemplating investments in Japan, and several of the best Banks in the Empire are prepared to do the same, all restrictive legislation and Treaties notwithstanding.

As to the best form the investment of foreign capital should take, that can only be ascertained by careful enquiries conducted, on the spot, by properly qualified investigators, who should possess an intimate acquaintance with the country and the people, and, especially, a practical knowledge of the language. These qualifications apply equally to investigators into the commercial, industrial and financial possibilities awaiting Occidental enterprise in China and Korea. Here Britons and Americans are at once confronted with the unpleasant fact that Germans, Frenchmen, Russians, Dutchmen, Italians, and even Austrians and Hungarians, are far better equipped for the purpose of fruitful investigation, and of the ultimate commercial struggle, not only by their superior technical training, by the habits of methodical work and discipline acquired in their time of military, or naval, service, and by their natural capacity for adapting themselves to local conditions and native customs, but by the excellent facilities for acquiring the languages of the Far East provided by their respective Governments. In the English-speaking countries, whose Far Eastern interests outweigh by far those of all other nations, it is much easier to acquire a knowledge of Syriac or of Chaldee than of Chinese, Japanese, or Korean. Almost every British, or American, school-child can locate the Brook Kedron—not one in a hundred thousand knows that the Sumida-gawa flows through Tōkio.

Although local investigation is absolutely necessary, two or three of the most important modes of remunerative employment for foreign capital in Japan are at once apparent. The fertile Island of Formosa would well repay the efforts of the planter of tropical, and sub-tropical, produce. In Japan itself, the manufacture of machinery, of machine-tools, and of chemical products would, undoubtedly, prove fairly remunerative, textile manufactures have proved lucrative, the railways are earning satisfactory dividends, the employment of electric power for many purposes has reached a high degree of development, and the enormous extent of coast-line offers, in its numerous bays and inlets, remarkable facilities for the establishment of shipbuilding yards. At a meeting of the Japan Society, held on the 8th of May, 1895, in the Discussion on the excellent Paper on " Japanese Shipping," by Francis Elgar, LL.D., F.R.S., late Director of Dockyards at the British Admiralty, a member of the Society's Council, it was stated by Mr. Martell, the Chief Surveyor to Lloyd's Register, that a ship of three thousand tons could be built, and well built, in Japan for three thousand pounds sterling less—*a pound sterling a ton less*—

than in any other country, although the estimate included the cost of steel plates imported from England, and of the salary of a British engineer to superintend the work.* Since Mr. Martell's statement, the ship has been built at the great saving he indicated. Shipbuilding and ship-owning are amongst the most important enterprises of the present and of the future in Japan, a country in every way adapted, by its geographical position, its coast-line, its natural products, and the aptitudes of its population, to develop a great carrying trade in the Pacific, and to extend it to other seas. The great "Japan Mail Steamship Company" (*Nippon Yu-sen Kuwaisha*) already owns one of the largest fleets in the world. The mines of the Japanese Empire, producing excellent coal, the best copper in the world, and many other minerals, including gold, will, certainly, be worked to much greater advantage when Occidental capital facilitates more scientific prospecting, the employment of the best machinery and modes of treating the ores, and the improvement of means of communication.

If Japan and its dependencies offer a vast field for Occidental enterprise, if Korea, with its fertile soil, its forests, and especially its undoubted mineral wealth, awaits the vivifying influence of foreign capital, how much greater is the prospect of remunerative investment offered by the huge Empire of China! "Prospect" is the right word, for we must look far ahead for the time when the Middle Empire will absorb millions of Occidental capital and return an annual harvest of thumping dividends. This is not the view taken by the public, who, apparently, anticipate that Western enterprise, once it has obtained a footing in the interior of China, will find that mysterious region a perfect commercial Eldorado. Those who hold this comforting belief should moderate their sanguine expectations; their children may live to see them realised. Undoubtedly, a great deal of money will be made in China, or in supplying

* Cf. "*Transactions and Proceedings of the Japan Society*," Vol. III., Part V, London, Kegan Paul, Trench, Trubner & Co., Limited, 1897 (Illustrated.)

the wants of Occidental undertakings in that country, within the first quarter of the twentieth century, but, unless the unforeseen happens in politics, a great part of such wealth will be merely transferred from one set of Occidental pockets to another, from shareholders, in the first instance, to "Syndicates," and, afterwards, from shareholders to contractors and employés.

Whilst I am writing these pages, enquiries, written and verbal, pour in upon me, from all sides, as to the value, in my opinion, of this or that "Concession," or the prospects of this or that "Syndicate." To all I make answer: "The Concession in question is worth just as much as the paper on which it is written, *plus* the market value of Chinese official autographs, and the price the document might fetch as a curiosity, *or* it may be worth more millions than even the sanguine promoters of the 'Syndicate' have estimated in their most hopeful forecast." With this oracular utterance, I light another cigarette by means of a spill twisted out of a strip of newspaper, containing the latest telegrams anent "The Far Eastern Crisis," all bearing, directly or indirectly, on the prospects of various "Concessions," and I return to the writing of this book. But the enquirers are not satisfied; they return to the charge, and clamour to know what mystery lurks in that potent "*or*." And I explain that the great "Concession" is to be appraised just according to the pressure that its holders can bring to bear on the Chinese Government to keep it to the strict fulfilment of its engagements. In other words, the value of the "Concession" depends on the strength and energy, and on the willingness to exert them in support of the enterprise, of the Government of the State whose subjects hold it. That Government must be prepared, if the Concession is to have any real value, to enforce its fulfilment "even at the cost of war"—and war not with China alone, but with the European Power, or combination of Powers, that would certainly back up China in her resistance—moreover, it must be ready to undertake, or at least to superintend and protect, the reform of Chinese methods of administration, without which any Occidental undertaking must prove abortive and disastrous.

The *crux* of the matter is the difficulty of discovering the most potent factors in the Government of China, and the best means of coercing them into compliance with the terms of the " Concession," and into honest administrative methods. For coercion will have to be employed before thousands of officials will give up a system that enriches them. A few are honest men, sincerely anxious to eradicate the cancer of official corruption that is eating up the vitals of the Empire, but they are powerless against the vast majority, who thrive on ill-gotten gains. The support, *vi et armis*, of the honest few against the rascally majority of their colleagues must be the first task of any Power that would ensure for its subjects the enjoyment of the fruits of the " Concessions" they have obtained.

I have devoted so much space, in former pages of this Chapter, to the consideration of commercial conditions in New Japan because, in that country, foreign capital may be invested with full confidence in the stability of the Empire, and in the continuance of the nation in the path of social progress and economic development. The word "stability" used in connection with modern Japanese institutions may cause those to smile who note the "quick-change acts" continually performed by the states-men of the Island Empire, the rapid shifting of the political scenes, the recurring alterations in the names of public Departments and in the titles of officials, the hot and cold fits that come over the feverish young Parliament, so young that it is, naturally, subject to all the ailments of childhood. But all these phenomena are mere bubbles on the surface of the molten mass that is gradually cooling down into a sound, solid, homogeneous whole. Who can tell who the *real rulers* of Japan are ? Certainly they are not the clever, energetic men who form the Administration. *They* may decide in matters of detail, often invested with undue importance, not only by foreign observers, but by the people themselves. Behind the administrators is an unseen controlling power that shows its supreme wisdom by intervening only in moments of grave national import, an irresistible, intangible, unknown influence that steps in at the right instant to check dangerous impulses, to guide the national policy into safe channels, and to bend the popular feeling into concurrence with the Imperial Will that gives this beneficent force its mighty sanction. As long as this guiding influence presides over the destinies of Japan, no serious harm can endanger the nation's true welfare, from without or from within, the stability of the Empire is assured, and the current of progress must continue to flow.

Far different is the state of unfortunate China, a prey to internal dissensions, arising through the sufferings of an oppressed people, and the squabbles and intrigues of an official class united, almost to a man, in one respect only—their determination to enrich themselves by every kind of extortion and peculation. Until that class is driven from office and replaced by honest, capable administrators, dealing justly with the people, no Occidental enterprise can prosper within the borders of the huge Empire. Until that great regeneration takes place, all schemes for *material* improvements are but the building of castles in the air, all talk of profitable railways from " Something - king " to " Somewhere - fu " is but mere twaddle. Let the holders of brilliant " Concessions " remember *by what means* those precious documents were obtained, and they will be able to gauge the integrity of the officials at whose mercy their railways and their mines would be worked. It cannot be too often repeated that in the early reform of the Government of China— reform drastic, unhesitating, complete—lies the only hope of the realisation of the golden dreams of those who would derive profit from the development of China. The

U

task is beyond the power of private, or corporate, initia-
tive. A State alone, and a mighty one, can undertake the
tremendous task, and it can only hope to succeed completely by calling in the co-operation of powerful allies.
The aim is worthy of the effort. Those whose strong
endeavour is crowned with success will deservedly reap
the glory—and abundance of Almighty Dollars.

CHAPTER VII.

FIGHTING POWER.

FERVENTLY as we may hope that the problems of the Far East will be solved by peaceful means, there seems but a faint prospect of these pious aspirations being fulfilled. The New Far East was born amidst the thunder of battle; it appears but too probable that a great deal or "villainous saltpetre" will be burnt before the countries of Eastern Asia subside into conditions offering reasonable guarantees of prolonged peace. And it is likely that the, almost inevitable, struggle will involve not only purely Asiatic Empires, but the great Occidental Powers as well, at all events to the extent of that "unofficial warfare" that has been so much in vogue, all over the world, in the latter half of the nineteenth century—a kind of "war 'on the cheap'" which, like most things attempted on that plan, comes very expensive in the long run.

A glance at a map, showing the enormous coast-line of China, the Korean peninsula, and the islands and islets, nearly two thousand in number, that compose the Japanese Empire, makes it at once evident that the issue of any conflict in the Far East must depend on Sea Power. In Eastern Asia, as in every other part of the world, the country with a great extent of sea-board is always at the mercy of any power stronger at sea. The Japanese understood this great fact from the very inception of their modern navy; Captain Mahan,

U.S.N., had no more eager students of his great work on Sea Power than the keen sailors of Japan, who took his axioms to heart so earnestly that the admirably-planned combined naval and military strategy which gave them the victory over China might serve as a series of "Practical Exercises" in illustration of the American naval author's theories. China, too, heard Mahan's message to the maritime powers and made efforts, very considerable ones for her, to profit by the warning, but she went about it in the bad old Chinese way, and the end of the nineteenth century finds her practically without a navy, whilst Japan occupies the position of the paramount naval power in Eastern Asia. As to Korea, her "Imperial Navy" consisted, after the war between Japan and China, of a Naval Academy without teaching staff or students—before the war there had been an attempt, under American influence, to organise such an institution—and of three Admirals, of the Right Wing, Left Wing, and Centre respectively, who commanded—nothing at all, the few small steamships flying the Korean flag being, in reality, cargo and passenger-boats. Each Province has, _traditionally_, a fleet for the protection of its coast, the Capital having two squadrons allotted to it, but these Armadas do not belong to the category of "fleets in being." They exist only in the imagination of the inventive _Yangban_ who makes out the pay-sheet for the remuneration of the three Admirals, who are subject to the supreme control of the President of the Board of War. Judging from the system in vogue, from time immemorial, in the Korean army, it may be assumed that these pay-sheets include the names of the whole complement of every ship in the various non-existent squadrons. They may be skeleton crews of phantom ships, but a dead Korean, or even one who never lived, is often counted on the "effective strength" in the matter of pay, only his Commanding Officer draws it for him, to avoid confusion and mistakes.

In estimating the reasons that place Japan in the foremost rank as a naval power in the Northern Pacific, other data besides the number and fighting-value of her ships, and the efficiency of their officers and crews, must be taken into consideration. The organisation for war of Japan's naval forces is as nearly perfect as any system, planned with the clearest foresight, and carried out with minute thoroughness, can be; the conflict with China put it to a severe test, from which it emerged triumphantly. To this perfection in organisation must be added the possession of several completely-equipped dockyards and arsenals—in well-fortified positions of great natural strength—and of the sinews of naval warfare—*coal*. Of this essential munition of war Japan possesses an abundant supply, of excellent quality, her principal mines being most conveniently situated, on the seaboard, thus facilitating rapid coaling. When, on the 30th December, 1897, I was "interviewed" on Far Eastern questions by a representative of Reuter's ubiquitous Telegram Agency, I laid great stress on the vital importance of this point, and many of the newspapers that published the "Interview" the next morning—not without misgivings, I dare say, as it contained the apparently incredible statement, from my lips, that Britain was likely to occupy Wei-hai-wei, on its evacuation by the Japanese, who would be found to have acted merely as a "warming-pan" for us —headed the column with the line: "Mainly a Question of Coal."

At that time, I pointed out, nearly the whole available stock of steam-coal in Asiatic waters was in the hands of Britain and of Japan. Had hostilities broken out in the Far East in the winter of 1897–8, the ships of all the other Powers would have been, in a short time, at the mercy of the two States that held the coal. Circumstances so entirely favourable to them are not likely to recur. The countries whose ships were then obliged to have recourse to British coaling-stations, wisely dotted along the great ocean routes between Europe and the Far East, or to the coal-mines of Japan, are now no longer entirely dependent on coal stored under foreign, and probably unfriendly, flags. Realising the fact that their ships moved in Asiatic waters only by the good will of Britain and of Japan, and that their communications with their Far Eastern dependencies were thus precarious, Russia and France had long ago determined on a policy that would free them from this disadvantage. Russia "marked down" the coalfields of Manchuria and of Pe-chi-li as the chief sources of supply for her constantly increasing fleet in the Northern Pacific, until such time as the Great Siberian Railway's completion would place the output of the rich stores of coal, known to exist in Siberia, at her disposal. France made great, and successful, efforts to develop the coalfields of Tong-king, the chief wealth of that costly part of her Indo-Chinese Dominion. Germany conceived the plan of securing a foot-hold in Shan-tung, a Province reputed to contain coal suitable for naval purposes, and cast covetous eyes on Kiao-chau, an excellent harbour in that district. The schemes of the three Powers were put into execution with determination, and with that paramount condition of success: a clear knowledge of the object aimed at. Russia, France and Germany knew what they wanted—and got it. At their newly-acquired naval stations in the Far East they are accumulating large stores of coal, whilst preparing to develop to the fullest extent the mining resources of the territories they have so cleverly managed to get under their control. Every day brings them nearer to complete independence in this vital question of coaling, and, in the meantime, Russia is making experiments on a grand scale with liquid fuel, obtained from her great oilfields in the Baku region, and is causing several of her new warships to be fitted with contrivances enabling them to generate steam by the combustion either of coal or of mineral oil, and in every country of Continental Europe men of science are devoting their energies to the development of electric motive power, in the fond hope of freeing the shipping of their countries from its bondage to coal and thus depriving Britain of one of her greatest advantages in the struggle for supremacy at sea.

Meanwhile, "Old King Coal" continues to rule the ocean, but his sovereignty in Eastern Asia is no longer synonymous with British preponderance. The first ten years of the twentieth century will see the other European Powers, and a new factor in the Far Eastern problem—the United States of America—provided with ample reserves of coal, a great part of it drawn from mines under their own flags, stored in strongly-fortified harbours at strategical points in Eastern Asia. The situation thus created will intensify the regret with which patriotic Britons will view the policy, if it deserve that name, that allowed precious years to be frittered away, during which their country held the trump card of the international game. They will look back with sorrow to the time when Britain could command peace and orderly progress in the Far East by simply denying coal to ambitious disturbers—and neglected to make timely use of the enormous advantage she enjoyed. The Japanese coal-mines are, of course, independent of British control, but it is certain that, in case of hostilities, Japan would declare coal to be contraband of war, and would reserve her supplies for the needs of her own navy, so that Britain's opponents could not reckon upon replenishing their bunkers from that quarter.

The wisdom that presides over the naval system of Japan is well exemplified in the types of vessels composing her fleet. The main idea prevailing in their selection is the defence of the national interests by *offensive* operations against the enemy's fleets—Nelson's own plan, as valid to-day as it was in his time. In the case of Japan, these operations are intended to be carried on at no very

great distance from the base of operations at home, a
fact that ought to bring comfort to those timid minds that
are haunted by visions of Japanese squadrons attacking
Occidental ports, and her warships are, consequently, not
built for the storage of the large quantities of coal that
must be carried by vessels intended, like those of the
British Navy, to fight thousands of miles away from their
own coasts. Much of the space thus left at the disposal
of the designers is utilised, to the best advantage, by the
provision of more guns and of a larger reserve of ammunition, all-important considerations in modern naval
actions, when victory falls to the side that can pour the
heaviest continuous hail of projectiles on to the enemy.
The ships, free from the necessity of carrying coal and
stores for long voyages, can be built comparatively smaller,
and, therefore, "handier," and require smaller comple-
ments to work them. In one of the most important
attributes of modern warships the vessels of the Japanese
Navy take high rank in the world's fleets—they are
amongst the swiftest of all the fighting ships afloat. And
they are *fighting* ships in reality as well as in name,
owing to the wise system that replaces every ship, the
moment she begins to fall behind the times, by a fresh
one, embodying the best "up to date" features that experience, and a careful survey of the progress of foreign
navies, can suggest. In the Japanese "Naval Returns"
the honest course is pursued of plainly indicating the ships
that can alone be relied upon to do effective service in
war ; "wash-tubs," "foot-baths," crawling "cruisers,"
"Noah's Ark" battleships, and the rest of the obsolete
craft that are, in navies that we wot of very near home,
annually paraded in "Lists of Ships in Commission,"
and patched up and tinkered at great expense, have
no place amongst the "fighting ships" of Japan.
They are relegated to the category of ships that can
"neither fight nor run," and are made to end their
days in useful, if subordinate, employment, as training-

ships for Boys and for Cadets, receiving-ships, gunnery and torpedo school-ships, surveying-vessels,
stationary store-hulks, and for purposes of coast and
fishery-police.

Admirably armed and equipped, kept in the very pink
of condition—their engines, especially, tended with extreme care—the splendid warships of New Japan—majestic
battleships, swift cruisers, "lightning-speed" torpedo-boat
destroyers, and torpedo-boats—all possess a boon precious
above any advantage of build, of armour, of speed, or of
artillery: they are manned by officers and crews who
are *sailors*, every inch of every one of them! Not only
have they proved themselves to be imbued with the
most ardent patriotism, animated by heroic gallantry,
capable of chivalry towards fallen foes, endowed with remarkable powers of endurance, wonderfully obedient to
discipline, and skilful to the highest degree in all that
pertains to modern naval warfare—they have shown the
world repeatedly that they possess, besides all these
qualities, to be found in the *personnel* of several other
navies, that scarcely definable *something* that makes the
British sailor the glorious fellow that he is, that *something*
that I must call the "Bluejacket Spirit." It is hardly to
be described in words; object-lessons alone could make
it manifest. In order to explain it to my non-naval
Readers, I would have to take them to some great naval
roadstead in foreign parts, where men-of-war of half a
dozen nations are lying at anchor, and I would bid them
watch officers and men of the various navies at drill—
at gun-drill, boat-drill, small-arms drill, cutlass-drill, gym-
nastics, torpedo-drill—at any of the many exercises that
fill the life of that "Jack of all Trades," and Master of
All, the modern man-of-war's man, who is "Sailor and
Soldier too" (in many navies, including the Japanese, the
Marines have been abolished, their duties being performed
by the Bluejackets,) and often engineer, mechanic, and
electrician besides. Especially should the various ships'

companies be watched at heavy-gun-drill. Under the various flags a general average of excellence will probably be found to prevail. In all, or nearly all, the ships' batteries one will note the swift execution of commands, the steady, mechanical, almost automatic, motions, performed in silence, that constitute perfect drill. But under two ensigns only something far beyond mere precision and discipline will be noted, an indescribable spirit that rings out in the calm, strong voice of the Officer of Quarters, and illumines his keen face, a spirit that shines in the eyes of the gun's crew, from the bronzed, bearded Petty Officer, the Captain of the Gun, to the rosy-cheeked First-Class Boy acting as Extra Powderman. It quivers in the strong limbs of the brawny Seamen-Gunners, it is in the elastic "skip" of their bare feet, as silent, nimble, sure of their work, they serve the huge gun. Under their control, the great piece of ordnance, with its complicated mechanism, so intricate, yet obedient to a child's touch, seems to become a living thing. The contrivances that load, and train, the great cannon, that lay, and fire, and sponge it, are purely mechanical; they can be managed by any well-trained, intelligent men, but, in order to achieve the best results, a dash of the Bluejacket Spirit must enter into the composition of the gun's crew. It is that animating spirit one finds at work in the men who sail under the white ensign of St. George, and in those over whom the sun-flag of Japan shakes out its folds in the breeze. See those men at any sort of work, afloat or ashore, you will find the same alert intelligence, the same brisk, unhesitating movements, the same spruce appearance, the same pride in their work well done, the same "joy of living," of being hale and hearty, smart and "fit." Put the Bluejackets of Britain and those of Japan to any unusual work, set them to build a landing-stage out of spare spars and odds and ends of timber, to throw up earthworks, to paint a shed, to work a sewing-machine, to fell a tree or to ride a bicycle, to scale a cliff or to

mind a baby, they will enter upon the unaccustomed
duty with a rattling, rousing energy, a rapidity of understanding and a handiness in execution, that do one good
to see. Real live men, and, what is more, real live Bluejackets, the sailors of Britain's Royal Navy, with the
glorious traditions of centuries to inspire them, and those
of Japan's brand-new naval service are imbued with the
spirit I have attempted to describe. And of such is the
Kingdom of the Sea.*

Japan possesses all the elements of Sea-Power: swift,
powerful ships, adapted to the work they are intended for,
numerous good harbours, excellent coal in abundance,
capital facilities for the repair of her vessels, and the
necessary plant, constantly augmented and improved, for
building new ones. Her naval organisation is wise and
efficient, her administrative services are thorough and
honest; her naval officers are gallant, dashing, and scientifically trained, and the armament they control is of
the latest and best pattern. Strong in ships, strong
in guns, Japan is stronger still in the factor without
which ships and guns are useless—"the Man behind the
Gun."

The careful forethought, the adaptation of means to
the end to be achieved, the study of minute details, and

* The "Bluejacket Spirit" may also be observed, in full activity, in the
crews of United States warships, especially of those having a large infusion
of the Anglo-Saxon-Celtic element, either American-born, or imported, by
expiration of service, or by the quicker way of desertion, from the British
Royal Navy American Naval Officers, who are, by their gallantry and
technical skill, as well as by their kindly courtesy, an honour to the naval
profession, are apt to be rather sensitive on this point They will assure you
that their splendid men are *Americans.* "Why, certainly! That Signalman
hails from New York. The Quartermaster over there is a Philadelphian;
every man has the State he belongs to entered against his name on enrolment.
That Gunner's Mate very like a Seaman-Gunner you were shipmate with,
years ago, in H M S. *Goshawk?* Impossible, he is entered in the ship's
books as from New Jersey!" But there is a twinkle in the Gunner's Mate's
bright eyes, and the soft accent of the old "West Country" round about
"Plymouth, Eng ," is perceptible through the twang acquired under the Stars
and Stripes Recruiting officers at Brooklyn Navy Yard, as elsewhere, do not
waste time in investigating a smart man s statements as to his nationality.

the general earnestness and thoroughness that distinguish
the organisation of the Japanese Navy, the absolute
efficiency of which reflects the highest honour on the
British Naval Advisers and Instructors, and the French
Naval Constructors and Engineers, who nursed it through
its infancy, are equally evident in the military system of
Japan. The history of the war with China, in 1894–5,
is one long chain of instances of the efficiency of the
Japanese land and sea forces, co-operating with such
complete unity of purpose and direction that it is difficult
to determine which of the two services deserves the
higher praise. This much is certain, that the lessons
learnt from the foreign Instructors who guided the first
steps of the Army of New Japan—British officers at the
very outset, then, for a number of years, a French *Mission
Militaire*, Italian artillerists in the gun-foundry at Ōsaka,
and, lastly, German Military Advisers—have been turned
to the best advantage. Japan possesses not only the
most powerful navy in Eastern waters, but also the
most formidable mobile land force in the Far East, indeed
in the whole of Asia, if we take into consideration the
circumstances that render the continual presence in India
of a large British garrison, both European and Native,
necessary, and therefore immobilise the greater part of what
would otherwise be the strongest army east of the Red
Sea. I purposely lay stress on the mobility of the Japanese
army, and upon the fact of the greater portion of the
British army in India, including the native troops, being
required permanently in that Empire and on its frontiers,
because therein lie considerations of the utmost importance
in the solution of the problems of the Far East. Japan
can, when her interests demand it, land a couple of Army
Corps, each thirty thousand strong, perfectly armed and
equipped, on the mainland of Asia within three weeks of
the issue of the order to "Mobilise," and, thanks to her
insular position, to her trained reserves at home, and to
her efficient navy, she can do this without exposing her

coasts to the risk of successful invasion, and in the
confident knowledge that, holding command of the comparatively narrow seas between her shores and the continent, her lines of communication with the expeditionary
corps would remain secure, unless her opponent happened
to be a naval power of the first rank, possessing dockyards
and reserves of coal in Eastern Asia.

With what skill this force would be directed, how
accurately the co-operation of its various units would be
timed, how smoothly the Commissariat and Medical Services
would work, how gallantly the highly-trained officers and
the docile, hardy rank and file would fight, all this admits
of no doubt in the minds of the military experts who have
studied the performance of the Japanese army in the war
with China. Of course, if arrayed against an enemy more
formidable than the Chinese, the army of Japan could
scarcely be expected to obtain such overwhelming results
with such slight losses, but it would, undoubtedly, give an
excellent account of itself in the face of any foe, however
formidable, and it looks forward to the possibility, nay, to
the probability, of such a conflict with perfect confidence ;
not in a spirit of overweening conceit and of depreciation
of its likely opponents, but with a firm belief in the capacity
of its leaders, the efficiency of its organisation and the skill
and gallantry of its men. The military leaders of Japan
are well aware that there is no finality in matters pertaining
to the art of war, and they are continually striving to
perfect the admirable fighting-machine they have created.
They are, especially, devoting their attention to the increase
and improvement of the Cavalry, numerically the weakest
arm in a mountainous island country, breeding small horses
(ponies, rather, notorious for their vicious propensities)
and affording scant space for the manœuvres of mounted
troops, even in the plains, owing to their being intersected,
over large areas, by the innumerable channels for the irri-
gation of the rice-fields, and the narrow, raised causeways
between the plots.

The importance of the Japanese army as a thoroughly efficient, "up-to-date" force, comparing favourably, in everything but numbers, with the great armies of Continental Europe, is now well understood by Occidentals. The "Fighting Power," on land, of the Chinese Empire is, on the contrary, the subject of much discussion even amongst those who know the country and the people, and is, naturally, a mystery to the general public. The general impression is that the Chinese are arrant cowards, an idea strengthened by the unanimity with which large bodies of "Braves" fled, panic-stricken, on many occasions during the war with Japan, abandoning strong positions almost without firing a shot at the enemy, often numerically inferior, and by the excess of prudence, to use no stronger term, that caused certain Chinese Captains, at the battle off the Yalu, to take their ships out of harm's way early in the action. The Military Mandarins directing their troops from a dignified seat, placed in a sheltered spot well in rear of the fighting line ; the Chinese Cavalry who rode into action at Ping-yang under umbrellas of yellow oiled paper, fanning themselves vigorously, whilst servants brought up the rear, carrying the troopers' Winchester repeating carbines ; the General who, after the crushing defeat at that place, begged the Japanese Commander-in-Chief to allow him another twelve hours' respite "as it would be so inconvenient to surrender in the rain, and the weather might clear by the morrow;" the *Tao-tai* of Wei-hai-wei, Niu Chang-ping, who, at the capitulation of that fortress and of the fleet under its guns, requested Admiral Itō to be good enough to return the warship *Kuang-ping*, "because she really belonged to the Squadron of the Viceroy of Kwang-tung (Canton), who had nothing to do with the war," and, if she were kept by the Japanese, he, the *Tao-tai*, "would have no excuse to offer to the aforesaid Viceroy;" perhaps the Japanese Admiral, sympathising with Niu in his trouble, would kindly return her hull, keeping her armament ; the Viceroy would not "look-see"

NEW JAPAN.

A Sergeant of Infantry of the Line, in Field Service Order, as in the early part of the War against China (1894).

Drawn by KUBOTA Beisen.

too closely, and no awkward questions would be asked! All these grotesque incidents of the war, and many more, as well as other manifestations of pigtailed pig-headedness following immediately after that grand, but wasted, object-lesson, made a deep impression on the Western mind. Of the follies perpetrated *after* the war, the following is a typical specimen :—On the 24th of August, 1896, the *Peking Gazette* published a Report by His Excellency TsÊNG Ch'i, Tartar General and Military Governor of Hei-lung-chiang, which gives an excellent insight into the working of the Celestial official and military mind. The Report begins with remarks on the futility of the antiquated armament—bows and arrows and old fashioned muskets—of eleven thousand out of the eighteen thousand Tartar troops, officered by Manchus, under his command (the remainder were armed with "up to date" Mauser rifles). The General's condemnation of the old-fashioned arms as "worse than useless in actual warfare," and his fulminations against their use as "like child's play . . . . good enough against *Nien-fei*, Red Turbans, and other rebels, but useless against foreign troops" (the Japanese) "armed with most superior weapons, that sent their bullets to a considerable distance" (one is irresistibly reminded of the Curate's threatened "really hard knock" in *The Private Secretary*,) might emanate from an earnest military reformer. They inspire a feeling of hopefulness in the future of an Empire whose military leaders begin to see the error of their old ways, but this feeling is soon dispelled, for in the next few sentences General TsÊNG Ch'i expresses the fear that the arming of *all* his troops with "new far-carrying rifles" would not be feasible, because, as he plaintively remarks, "the exchequer is *too empty* to pay the cost."

However, the gallant and ingenious Tartar General devised a remedy for the absurdly inadequate armament of his men. After delivering an address on the subject to the Manchu officers under his command, he "proposed to

them"—I am quoting the *Peking Gazette*—"to use the
t'ai-t'siang, or two-men 'gingal,' apportioning *three* men
to each gun, *i.e*; one man to carry the gun at the muzzle"
(letting it rest on his shoulder, presumably,) "one man
to fire it, and a third with the ammunition and armed
with a sword to guard the other two while at work. As
the 'gingals' now lying in the Tsi-tsi-har Arsenal are of
the old-fashioned make, which require the lighted rope
fuse, and are, therefore, useless in rainy weather, Memorialist" (that is, General Tsêng, reporting to the Throne,)
"proposed to manufacture new *t'ai-t'siang*, after the
Kiang-su pattern, loading by the breech with cartridge.
This innovation being unanimously approved of by the
said Manchu Commandants, Memorialist would now ask
the consent of the Throne to arm the troops of the Hei-
lung-chiang with the *t'ai-t'siang*, and proposes to raise the
funds necessary for manufacturing them and the ammunition required for them." Thus far the Report in the
Peking Gazette, which remains ominously silent as to
the ways and means the General proposed to adopt
in order "to raise the funds necessary for manufacturing." A very slight effort of the imaginative
faculty enables one to form an idea of their nature.
The Report was laid at the foot of the Throne, and
the Imperial Rescript thereon consists of the one word:
"Noted."

The occupant of the Dragon Throne "noted" the
scheme of reform in armament evolved from the fertile,
and very Chinese, brain of General Tsêng; the Occident
noted many similar instances of Celestial military inepti-
tude, adding them to its previous knowledge of Chinese
timorousness in the field, and was more than ever convinced of the unfitness of the Chinese for war. So general
did this conviction become that it caused Occidentals to
forget the desperate resistance offered by Chinese troops
on several occasions during the war with Japan, especially,
it is true, when they were in some "tight place," whence

flight was impossible. It made them overlook the gallant conduct of General Tso Pao-kwei, who fell at Ping-yang, killed by the third bullet that struck him, whilst cheering on his men, and the stout defence of Wei-hai-wei by the heroic Admiral Ting. Little was known in the West of the valour displayed by many Chinese sailors at the battle off the Yalu, when the crews of some of the Celestial battleships were, in their ardour, fighting with one another at the ammunition hoists for supplies of projectiles and cartridges for their respective guns. Individual acts of courage disappeared in the midst of the general *débâcle* of cowardice, corruption and imbecility, and the popular feeling of the West towards China's fighting power, at the close of the war, was one of well-justified contempt.

With that strange inconsistency that frequently characterises it, British public opinion, having pronounced the Chinese to be arrant cowards, began immediately to form plans for a brilliant era of progress and prosperity in China, to be secured by a powerful defensive force, on sea and land, composed of those very men whose lack of courage had been so bitterly derided. What magician was expected to transform them, by a wave of his wand, from an unwarlike rabble into capable, brave soldiers and sailors? The British Officer was—nay, is, for the belief is still widely prevalent—the wizard credited with such superhuman powers. If anyone ventured to call these powers in question, he was triumphantly referred to "Chinese Gordon" and his "Ever-victorious Army." Now, far be it from me to write a single word that might appear to be intended to minimise the grand achievements in China of that pure-hearted hero, but, surely, his glory is sufficiently great to be able to dispense with the halo of exaggeration which has formed round the story of his exploits in the Celestial Empire. Dispassionately considered, his great work in China amounts to this, that he formed, trained and led a force of native soldiers with which he completely defeated the *Tai-ping* rebels, who

v

had overrun some of the fairest provinces, and had shaken
the Empire to its very foundations. But it must not be
forgotten that his opponents were a mere horde of badly-
armed, worse-equipped, peasants and "coolies," without
drill or organisation. They had degenerated, in the course
of nearly fourteen years of civil war, from a band of
enthusiasts—inspired partly by racial feeling against the
Manchu dynasty, partly by discontent at the appalling
misgovernment, partly by religious mysticism, a sort of
ill-digested rudimentary Christianity, that developed into
a travesty of the Faith, comparable to the *Hau-hau*
"religion" of the Maori insurgents, in New Zealand, in
the 'sixties—from the nearest approach to an army of
patriots that China had seen for two centuries, to an
immense horde of robbers. Moreover, the vast majority
of the population, who had sided with them, in the
beginning, in all the districts they conquered, had become
heartily sick of the degenerate *Tai-ping* "liberators,"
their plundering and their atrocious cruelties, and, consequently, afforded all possible aid to the Imperial troops.
In these circumstances, and against such foes—brave,
without doubt, but absolutely without organisation or
plans—the European weapons, drill, discipline (such as it
was,) and tactics introduced by Gordon could not but
prevail, but the force he had created would, had it been
pitted against the army of even a small European state,
have speedily lost its claim to the proud title of "Ever-
victorious." The error into which the British public
fell in estimating the value of Gordon's "Army" is again
prevalent whenever the question of the reorganisation of
China's Fighting Power is discussed.

That British officers would rapidly convert the Chinese
armed rabble into *the semblance of an army* admits of
no doubt. The result of the untiring efforts of the
numerous German Instructors formerly in the pay of some
of the Viceroys, and of the British Instructors at one time
employed to train the *personnel* of the navy, proves that
the Chinese readily acquire the rudiments of the naval

and military arts, but it also shows that they can very
seldom proceed beyond the elementary stages. They
easily learn the drill necessary for the performance of
simple evolutions, they acquire the manual, firing, and
bayonet exercises in a relatively short time, they can be
trained, without any great difficulty, to serve the most
modern types of guns, and to use torpedos, but they do
it all in a purely mechanical way, correctly enough, but
"woodenly." Their hearts are not in the work. They
obey the foreign Instructor—not always with a good
grace—they repose in him a relative confidence rarely
accorded to any of their officers of their own race;
they will follow him into action *if they must;* they
will even, under his command, quit themselves creditably in the fight, but only *creditably.* They may
respect their Occidental leader, they do not love him;
he ever remains, in their eyes, the tiresome pedant who
is so absurdly particular in matters of detail; who insists,
for instance, on the screwing up, or down, of the sights
on a heavy gun, and on the judging of distances to something more accurate than a *li* or two, who "fusses" about
a missing machine-gun, and actually will have guns and
rifles cleaned that must, inevitably, become dirty again
when they are fired. They humour his curious whims in
order to escape punishment, but the spirit of emulation is
not in them. Train them, drill them, arm them as you
will, put them into uniform, stiffen their backs and ex-
pand their chests, teach them to march, to ride, to shoot
—they will remain a mere collection of armed men, not
an army. Unwarlike in temperament, inwardly despising
their profession, themselves despised by their civilian compatriots for following it, they will never be fit to stand
up against Occidental troops until their national character
has undergone a complete change. When the science of
war has been studied by a future generation of Chinese
native officers, of higher character than those hitherto
employed, when the navy and the army become "respectable" services in the eyes of the people, above all, when

the naval and military administration is cleansed of the corruption and jobbery that reign supreme — *then* the British Instructor may convert all the excellent *physical* material handed over to him—the endurance and the strength, accompanied by wonderful patience and cheerfulness—into a *real* Navy, into a *real* Army, worthy of the name. For the present, and for a long time to come, China cannot produce Fighting Power, by sea or land, that could, even under the tuition of the wonder-working British Officer, successfully resist the forces either of her strong neighbours, Russia or Japan, could array against her. The fact is a disappointing one for Britain; it would be *so* convenient if a new Chinese Navy—built, of course, in the United Kingdom, provided with British officers "lent" by the Admiralty, and receiving thumping salaries from China, and commanded by that most genial and breezy of Commercial Travellers, "our Lord Charles Beresford,"—with a still more thumping salary—if such a navy, in conjunction with a reorganised Chinese Army, officered, in the higher ranks, by scores of British officers, "seconded" from their regiments, or on half-pay, or even "retired," and of others, perchance, from the Militia, but all in receipt of handsome pay and "allowances" from the Chinese exchequer—could overawe Russia in the Far East and keep her peacefully within her borders! It is a pleasant dream, nothing more. China cannot, under her present misrule, afford the luxury of such forces. Even if she could, their existence would, indeed, be highly obnoxious to Russia, and to her friends, but it would not terrify them in the least. They would increase their armaments, and continue to pursue their policy undisturbed. Russia knows the Chinese so thoroughly that she has no dread of Celestial forces, even if commanded by British officers.

Although Russia has so accurately gauged the military inefficiency of the Chinese, she has taken steps to provide herself, in the future, with a large, and practically inexhaustible, force of Chinese soldiers, trained and com-

manded by Muscovite officers. One of the first outward
and visible signs of the supremacy of Russian influence in
China was the arrival at Peking, about the time of the
occupation of Port Arthur by the Tsar's troops, of a
Colonel of the Russian Staff, to take up the position of
Military Adviser to the Chinese Government. The gallant
Palkovnik proceeded at once to take charge of the instruction of the large force of sturdy Northern Chinese
and hardy Hu-nan men—the " fighting cocks " of China—
assembled in entrenched camps in the region round Peking,
and appears to have then become engulphed in space.
At all events, but vague rumours of his whereabouts have
since reached the outer world. Enquiring tourists are
not encouraged in the vicinity of any spot where Russia's
plans are being carried out, until the execution of the
schemes devised in St. Petersburg has become an accomplished fact, not to be upset by any amount of descriptive
reporting, nor by a hail of " paper bullets " from the
British press. I happen to know that the Russian Military
Adviser and his Staff of Instructors are carrying on their
work unremittingly, and I venture to predict that they
will achieve success. Half-Asiatic themselves, the Russians
have a remarkable facility for understanding the character
of the Chinese people, with whom they easily ingratiate
themselves. The Chinese soldier finds in the Russian an
officer whom he understands, and the feeling that springs
up between them is far nearer to the ideal relation
between the officer and his men—so tersely laid down
by the great Skobeleff: "a father to the Privates, an
elder brother to the Non-Commissioned Officers "—than
could ever be the case were the Chinese under British
leaders, who appear to them a strange, uncanny race,
whose motives and customs, whose very amusements, are
beyond Celestial comprehension. Gradually, and surely,
Russia is training for her own purposes a Chinese army,
instructed, at no cost to China, by Russian officers, a force
that is destined to play a great part in the future history
of Asia. It will, we may be sure, be practically trained

to fit it for the end in view; not for a contest with Occidental troops—the Russians know their Chinese allies, or, rather, vassals, too well for that risky experiment— but to overawe those amongst the Chinese who, feeling the promptings of the spirit of reform, might attempt to break the fetters that Russia is helping to rivet more tightly, and for garrison and police duties in the occupied territories, and along Russia's enormously extended lines of communication overland, thus freeing many thousands of Russian troops for that struggle against white men that Chinese soldiers would be unequal to. For the purposes indicated, Chinese troops, trained and commanded by Russians, would be perfectly serviceable.

There is another nation, a Far Eastern one, that is called upon by its manifest destiny to play a great part in the reorganisation of China's Fighting Power by sea and land. Several Japanese officers have already been engaged by the Viceroy of Hu-nan, the most anti-foreign Province, as Military Instructors, and more will follow. The Japanese have everything in their favour, as compared even with the Russians, in the competition for the creation of new, and *real*, naval and military forces in China. Their officers, accustomed to a very moderate scale of pay, and of living, will make but slight demands on the impover- ished Chinese exchequer; they understand the Chinese nature as no Occidental can, and they enjoy the inesti- mable advantage of being able to convey their meaning, by means of a few strokes of a pencil, to any Chinese able to read his own language. Moreover, the Chinese have good reason to respect the prowess of the Japanese. A Chinese navy and a Chinese army, trained and led by Japanese—truly, the forecast is calculated to give cause for grave reflection! And its fulfilment is within the bounds of probability, in spite of Russia's efforts, and of Palace Revolutions and other "alarums and excursions." But the time is not yet, and, meanwhile, the Fighting Power, by sea and land, of the Far Eastern Empires is summed up in one word—Japan.

CHAPTER VIII.

THE YELLOW PERIL.

THE first illustration to this Chapter boasts of high parentage. It is a reproduction of the allegorical drawing, by Professor H. Knackfuss, from a design due to the pencil of His Majesty William the Second, German Emperor and King of Prussia—the famous *Kaiserbild* that caused such a sensation, throughout the world, on its production in 1895, a sensation heightened when the original was sent to St. Petersburg, as a gift from its Imperial designer to the Tsar. "*Les petits cadeaux entretiennent l'amitié*," and His Germanic Majesty was, at that time, particularly anxious to assure his powerful neighbour of the warmth and sincerity of his friendship. In order to prove his desire for that good understanding with Russia that was ever a cardinal point in Bismarck's policy, and to take another step towards that reconciliation with France which it is the Emperor's laudable ambition to achieve, in order, besides, to obtain a triumph over British diplomacy and prestige in the Far East that would earn plaudits from the Anglophobe majority of his subjects, Kaiser Wilhelm had just joined Russia and France in bullying Japan out of the Liao-tung Peninsula, now in Russian hands. This extraordinary reversal of Germany's policy of intimate friendship with Japan—a policy pursued for many years, right up to the close of the war with China, with the most beneficial results for German trade—was put down, by the world at large, to a *coup de tête* of the preternaturally

active young monarch. Some, with a certain claim to
being behind the scenes, ascribed the sudden change of
front to the influence of Herr von Brandt, a clever
diplomatist who had represented Germany for years at the
Courts of Peking and of Tōkio, and had made himself
conspicuous at both by the energy with which he "pushed"
the commercial interests of his country, especially in the
matter of government contracts tendered for by compatriots.
In accordance with the good old Prussian custom, whenever any subject becomes of great importance to the
German Empire the Sovereign summons those who are
reputed to have particular knowledge of the question, and
hears from them "verbal reports," intended to inform the
Imperial mind—a practice that might be imitated, with
advantage, nearer home. It was alleged, in 1895, that on
the occasion of Herr von Brandt's audience, to which he
was summoned immediately after the original Japanese
terms of peace became known, he drew such an appalling
picture of the danger Europe would incur if Japan were
allowed to obtain a footing on the mainland of Asia that
the Emperor resolved to reverse his Asiatic policy, and to
join Russia and France in coercing Japan. It is an interesting story, this, of the "expert" setting forth his views
so eloquently as to infect the monarch with the "Yellow
Fever" that has periodically attacked Occidental thinkers
ever since the publication of the late Dr. C. H. Pearson's remarkable work, *National Life and Character : a Forecast,*
but it makes too great a demand on our credulity.

The German Emperor is known to be frequently
swayed by sudden impulse, but we may be sure that, in
a matter of such moment as the policy of Germany in the
Far East, he would not have lightly jeopardised the
rising commerce of his subjects with Japan, nor the paramount influence Germany had obtained in that country,
without grave cause. Great as Germany's interests in
the Far East undoubtedly are, her chief concern must be
her position towards her powerful neighbours in Europe.

Russia's traditional policy in Eastern Asia was approaching fruition, the Japanese victories over China had "forced" the fruit so rapidly that the Chinese pear, prematurely ripe, was on the point of falling into the lap, not of the patient Muscovite, who had waited for it so long, but into that of the unexpected new-comer, Japan. Russia had to act quickly, in order to warn off the intruder and to spread her own apron under the tree. She inaugurated the "Intervention of the Powers"; her bond slave, France, had to follow suit. Britain, to her everlasting honour, and ultimate profit, refused to be a party to the dirty trick, for such it was, that deprived Japan of her lawful, and dearly-bought, spoils in order to hand them over to Russia. Germany knew all along what aims Russia was pursuing. She was well aware that Japan would not be allowed to keep the most important fruits of her victory, and if she showed ostentatious sympathy, during the war, with the Japanese, whom she looked upon as her pupils in military science, "show-pupils," too, Germany, or, at all events, her statesmen, did not hesitate to throw over Japan the moment it became necessary to propitiate Russia. The German Emperor, therefore, when he joined the intervening powers, forming, in Asia, a new, and apparently unnatural, Triple Alliance, acted in accordance with the dictates of a cool, calculating policy, leading, in the first place, to a cordial understanding with Russia, in the near future, to territorial acquisition in China (the Kiao-chàu *coup* was not quite the unpremeditated affair the general public believed it to be,) and, ultimately, to the detriment of Britain—all things devoutly wished for, especially the last, by the great majority of Germans.

Having openly cast in his lot, at the proper time, with Russia and France in the Far East, the German Emperor was in need of a justification, especially in the eyes of his bewildered subjects, up to that time so enthusiastic for the cause of Japan. As they read the staitling news of the New Triple Alliance, the good Germans shook their heads, and muttered into their beer-glasses—not too loudly, for like the "bhoys" of "Slattery's Mounted Foot," renowned in song, they are fond of

> " Playing rebel tunes
> *Cautiously* on the dhrum."

, And their muttering was to the effect that this was another of their Emperor's playful ways of startling the world—"*wieder ein Kaiserstreich !*" Some went so far as to show one another, in corners, a pamphlet entitled *Caligula*, a learned and laboured classical joke, chuckling over its pages until the shadow of a passing *Schutzmann* sent them, hurriedly and with beating hearts, in different directions. The public opinion of Germany had to be brought into line with the Imperial policy ; what better argument could be employed for this end than that of fear ? The dissatisfied must be brought to recognise that their Sovereign's wisdom had saved the nation from imminent danger—so the "Yellow Peril" bogey was brought out and plainly exhibited, like a yokel's turnip-and-sheet "ghost," to scare the lieges. This artifice of state-craft was admirably suited both to the German national character, predisposed to take a deep interest in great racial problems, to be worked out in the distant future— a period the matter-of-fact Briton, constitutionally averse to looking beyond the tip of his nose, leaves to take care of itself—and to the Kaiser's idiosyncrasy. To pose as the Saviour of Christendom from the impending Yellow Peril is an attitude that commends itself strongly to the Emperor's highly-developed dramatic instinct. From the moment he adopted it a process, not infrequent with him, commenced in his impressionable mind, by which he rapidly persuaded himself that he actually *was* the Champion of Christendom against the caitiff Paynim.

Under the influence of this belief, a sincere one, for no one can justly accuse him of insincerity in any of his actions, the Kaiser designed the drawing he commissioned Professor Knackfuss to carry out, the striking pictorial allegory reproduced, by special permission, as an illustration to this Chapter. Its authorship, the gracious manner in which permission to use it was, unhesitatingly, granted, and, above all, the fact that the fee charged for the permission was contributed, by His Majesty's desire, to a charitable institution enjoying the Imperial patronage, forbid any criticism of the artistic qualities of the famous drawing, but an examination of the meaning it is intended to convey throws a strong light on the Kaiser's position towards Far Eastern affairs. There is more in the picture than meets the eye.

On the brow of a high cliff stands an Archangel, probably Michael, the namesake, and patron, of that *deutscher Michel*—typical of the Teuton as John Bull is of the Englishman—who, as was proclaimed in one of the Kaiser's famous oratorical outbursts, has planted his shield firmly on Chinese soil. With flaming sword in hand, the Archangel is exhorting a group of female personifications of the principal nations of Europe, and pointing towards the approaching Peril, separated from them by a river, unspecified, but presumably the Danube, flowing, with a great bend, through the valley far below. Germany, tall and buxom—all the ladies are of the well-nourished type dear to the allegorical artists of the Fatherland—the eagle with open wings on her helmet recalling the headgear of the Kaiser's own magnificent *Gardes du Corps*, leans forward, eagerly listening to the archangelic summons to arms. Clad in a coat of mail, but gloveless—her fists unmailed—with drawn sword, and grasping her shield, she is evidently "spoiling for a fight." Somebody must have said "Kiao-chau."

Russia, in Scythian scale-armour, avoids being mistaken for an armadillo, or, rather, a pangolin, by wearing an appropriate bear's skin on her head and back. Armed with the Cossack lance, she leans, in touching amity, on

Germania's shoulder, a sight so irritating to France, carrying a pike, and wearing the Phrygian cap of the Republic, that she—Gallia—absolutely refuses to look again in their direction, but prefers to gaze at the Peril. France shades her bright eyes with her hand; at least, that is her apparent attitude. Personally, I fancy she is arranging her "fringe," disturbed by the wind on that bleak, Gustave Doré-esque cliff. For it is a male Peril that approaches.

In the second rank, Austria, her corselet blazoned with the double-headed eagle, appears unarmed, a poor compliment, on the part of the Imperial artist, to the army of his most trusted ally; perhaps a gentle hint that the said heterogeneous force might, with advantage, be strengthened and generally improved. Hungary is absent; probably, the Asiatic origin of the Magyars, their cousinship, albeit many times removed, to the Peril, made it seem unadvisable to invite Pannonia to ascend the cliff. She might, very likely, have "had words" with Russia, or might have quarrelled with Austria and dissolved partnership with her there and then. Austria's attitude amongst the group is remarkable. She holds Britannia's irresolute hand by the wrist, to feel if her cold blood yet pulsates, and is evidently urging her to make up her mind and to join the League. Britannia, our own beautiful, familiar Britannia, has stepped straight off our handsome bronze coinage—we now see it was not a bicycle but a shield that she had been seated on—but she carries a spear, instead of her usual trident. Where is that symbol of maritime supremacy? Can it be that its presence would have reminded Germania too painfully of certain aspirations so difficult to realise, of warships painfully "crawling" Eastwards, and of a certain grand National Subscription for the Building of Battleships and Cruisers, that produced £79 10s. 5d. in the course of a single fortnight? Britannia wavers; her lovely face—a reminiscence, may-be, of sweet English-girls seen at Cowes—is pensive. She knows that Peril well, you see; she has done a good deal of business with him in the past, and, naturally, feels reluctant to use her spear against an old and valued customer. So Austria has been deputed to persuade her; strangely enough, for Austria, who has earned the nickname of "the China of Europe," has, practically, almost no interests in the Far East. Here again, the picture speaks clearly to the few who know that, on more than one occasion, to Austria has the task been allotted of approaching Britain on subjects of prime interest to the Triple Alliance, and especially to the "predominant partner," Germany. Italy stands next to Britannia, bareheaded, clad in a Roman corselet, her Legionary's sword *sheathed* by her side, perhaps an allusion to the nicks chipped on its edge, blunted on Abyssinian steel on the fateful day of Adowa. Last of all stand two more typical figures, one—perhaps Portugal—almost entirely hidden, clasping the hand of another whom we see plainly, and who may be Spain, carrying two javelins. Judging by the revelations of the war with the United States, their points are probably of tin. It is noticeable that America is not represented. She was evidently, at the time, still clad in that Monroe gown, so old-fashioned that she could not think of appearing in it before all those smartly-dressed ladies. In the heavens the Cross is shining above the group, its radiance forming a St. Andrew's Cross, the badge of Russia, the instrument of the martyrdom of one of her Patron Saints.

And the Peril? He is approaching, in the midst of a fiery glory, bursting through a storm-cloud, seated on a dragon, an unmistakable Far Eastern dragon, the cloud itself rising from the flames of a burning city. The dragon seems an ill-chosen mount for a conquering Mongolian Peril, as the expression "His Majesty mounted the Dragon" means that an Emperor of China has departed this life. However, there is no accounting for tastes; Monsieur de

Rougemont used, he said, to ride turtles; the Yellow Peril ˆ
mounts a dragon. *Chacun à son goût.* Fair cities lie
between the bank of the river and the cliff, their spires,
and domes, and castles exposed to the fate of the burning
town beyond, if only the storm-cloud reach them. Strangely,
the Peril himself is not ferocious in appearance. He sits,
cross-legged, in calm contemplation, with folded hands
and placid countenance, a Peril a child might play with!
Indeed, there is something about him that reminds one
irresistibly of the sweet *Jizō*, the gentle god whom the
Japanese have told off to be the playmate of little children's
souls in the other world. And no wonder, for the Peril,
as depicted by the Imperial Designer, is none other than
the Lord Buddha, the incarnation of Goodness and Wisdom,
the self-forgetting founder of the beautiful creed of Gentleness and Pity, the Lord of whom it is written: "For the
Lord Buddha loved all created things, even the lowliest
insect."

The German Emperor is a wonderfully versatile, remarkably clever man; there is hardly a science, an art, or a
sport, in which he does not take a lively interest, and in
which he has not attained a certain degree of proficiency.
That he is a clever designer is shown by the composition
of the *Kaiserbild;* his bright, quick intellect is evident in
the grouping and the details. But "even Homer nods," and
—I trust this is not *Majestätsbeleidigung,* an unmannerly
offence I hold in contempt—even the Kaiser is not infallible, especially in matters of the Far East. Hence his
mistake in selecting, as the personification of the "Yellow
Peril," the figure of the founder of Buddhism, at the present
time the least aggressive religion in the world. This error
in symbolism apart, the Kaiser's meaning is plainly conveyed by the picture he designed. His Majesty foresees
a time, within measurable distance, when a struggle for
the survival of the fittest must take place between the
peoples of Europe, if not of the White Race all over the
world, and the Yellow Men, and he exhorts the nations

of the West to unite against the common foe. In case
his spokesman, the Archangel with the flaming sword,
should not make himself clearly understood, the German
Emperor himself appeals, in the margin of the drawing,
to those he would rouse to common action against the
impending Peril. Here is his Imperial Message, traced in
his own characteristically bold, clear writing :—

And, to emphasise the international character of the proposed
League, the appeal is translated into French : "*Nations
européennes ! Défendez vos biens sacrés !*" and into English,
very freely, as : " Nations of Europe ! Join in the defence
of your faith and your home !" The whole is authenticated
by the Imperial sign manual, " Wilhelm, I.R.", and the
origin of the picture is told in the words written in the
left-hand corner : "*Nach einem Entwurf' Seiner Majestät
des Deutschen Kaisers, Königs von Preussen, Wilhelm II.,
gez. v. H. Knackfuss, 1895.*" ("Drawn by H. Knackfuss,
1895, from a Design by His Majesty William II., German
Emperor, King of Prussia.") To point the moral of his
allegory, the German Emperor presented the original drawing to the Tsar ; surely, a plain sign to the rest of the
world that, whilst willing, and ready, to take a prominent
part in the New Crusade, His Germanic Majesty looked,
and looks, upon the Autocrat of All the Russias as the
natural leader in the movement to repel the Peril that
must cross his frontier first.

There are elements in the Kaiser's composite character
that escape the casual observer, even amongst his own
subjects. The British public has hardly been able to form
a just estimate of the young monarch owing to the wave

of indignation that swept over the whole British Empire
in January, 1896, in consequence of his famous telegram
to President Kruger; "an insult to Britain," people called
it at the time; "ill-advised," they said, later on, and so
it was from the point of view of the Briton, who forgets,
or ignores, that this very "wire" did more to establish
the Emperor's popularity with the bulk of the German
people than any other act of his reign. Fortunately, time
and the whirligig of international politics have soothed
the Briton's wrath, actors no longer hustle one another in
their hurry to get down to the footlights first and say
something sarcastic about the German Emperor; music
hall "stars" no longer write to managers that they have
secured "a good new song; real *good*, with spicy *encore*
verse about the German Emperor; bound to fetch 'em!"
Now that the Briton can contemplate, with unruffled
nerves, the Kaiser's acts—his fine speeches must ever
remain amusing mysteries to the Briton, they are intended
for home consumption—he cannot fail to discover three
leading features in the Sovereign's character: that he is
exceedingly clever, that he is thoroughly German, and
thoroughly earnest in all he does. A closer study will
reveal another important characteristic — the strain of
mysticism that tinges many of his conceptions. It is this
mystic inclination that explains the fascination of the
Imperial mind by glimpses of a future struggle for existence between the Christian Occident and Far Eastern
Heathendom, from which the Cross is to emerge triumph-
ant, thanks to the keen swords of modern Knights of the
Holy Grail. King Arthur is the chivalrous Emperor's
pattern—none can deny his chivalry, which has captivated
even the bitter press-men of the Boulevards—and we have
no reason to complain, for the prototype is a thoroughly
British one.

Of what nature is this "Yellow Peril" against which
the Emperor warns us, that danger about which so much
has been spoken and written? It has formed a leading

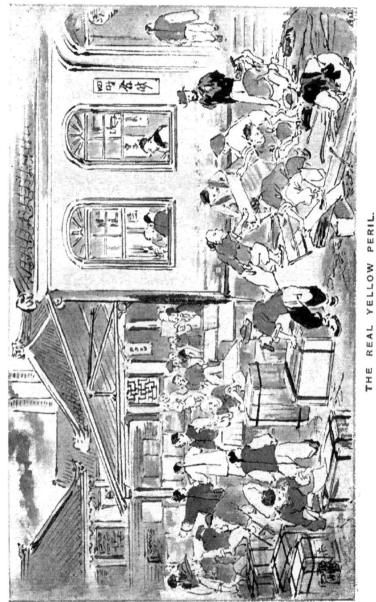

THE REAL YELLOW PERIL.

China Awakened. A Forecast.

Drawn by KUBOTA Beisen.

topic of discussion in every Occidental country. Volumes have been written about it, some grave, some gay; some wise, some silly. To the latter category belongs a farrago of absurdities embodied in a "bluggy" novel published, in 1898, under the title of *The Yellow Danger*, the work of a writer who has not taken the trouble to "get up" even as much information about the Far East as may be gleaned from a School Board Geography Primer. To most of the minds preoccupied with this question, the Peril menacing Occidental civilisation is the possible irruption into Europe of a countless multitude of Chinese, armed, equipped and trained on the Western plan, who would bear down all opposition by reason of their vast numbers, and would spread ruin in their track. This spectre may be easily laid. The passages relating to China in the Chapter on "Fighting Power" will serve to exorcise it, at all events for many years to come.

There is, however, a *real* "Yellow Peril," one that it behoves us to keep in view, to study, and to prepare to meet as best we may. It is indicated in the second illustration to this Chapter, the reproduction of one of the twelve drawings the famous Tōkio artist, KUBOTA Beisen, has specially designed, from notes· supplied by myself, for this book. I recommend this picture of the highly probable future to the notice of those worthy people who pray, night and morning, for the "awakening of China." Were we mindful only of our own interests; did not philanthropy, which knows no distinction of race, or of nationality, fill the hearts of some of us; did greed, lusting after the fortunes to be made out of an awakened China, not animate others; did these opposite feelings not combine to sway the minds of many more, we should fervently pray that the Celestial Empire might continue in its lethargic slumber for evermore. Once the many millions of China call in the, hitherto despised, aid of Western science, they will not for long be content to employ it chiefly for the benefit of the Occident.

w

The busy factories, such as the one Kubota has prophetically depicted, where docile, intelligent Chinese will
work in swarms, for fifteen hours out of the twenty-four,
under the skilled guidance of Occidentals, will, in due
course, be succeeded by similar establishments conducted,
on their· own account, by scientifically - trained Chinese.
Imagination falters at the contemplation of the prospect.
What chance will the workers of the Occident, striving
daily to do less work for higher wages, have against the
teeming millions of Chinese, sober, docile, marvellously
thrifty, intelligent and skilful, working, unremittingly and
cheerfully, for pay that would keep them in comfort, but
on which no Occidental could live ?   The enormous industrial development of New Japan, and the competition,
in many cases successful, it has entered into with the
Occident—not only in Japan itself, but in markets hitherto
considered as virtually reserved for the products of Europe
and America—supply an object - lesson that teaches us
what the Far East can do when thoroughly aroused.
But the economic condition of New Japan, the gradual,
but relatively enormous, rise in the cost of living, and, consequently, in the price of labour, the spirit of combination
amongst the workers—an entirely new phenomenon in
its present form — leading to strikes and "lock-outs,"
all these point to the conditions that will exist, in
course of time, in China to mitigate the severity of her
competition with the Occident. These palliatives, however,
still leave the power of competition of Japan but slightly
diminished.   In China, the country of slow movement,
they will take much longer to come into play, and, when
they do, the new industries of China, enjoying all the
advantages imaginable—extremely cheap, intelligent, easily-
directed labour, scientifically-trained management, abundant
coal, iron in plenty, home-grown raw material of almost
every kind, widely-ramified water-transport on great rivers
and long canals, numerous ports and, by that time, an
extensive railway system—will still be in a far better

position to produce well and cheaply than their old-established rivals in the Occident.

Here is food for reflection for the Occidental industrial classes, high and low, especially for those who contribute their labour. If a correct appreciation of the industrial possibilities of the New Far East—possibilities that will be probabilities next year, and certainties within this generation—could be brought home to the Occidental workers, Capital and Labour would, if not entirely bereft of reason, cease their internecine strife. Here is a question for our Socialists, of various shades, to consider. How do they propose, if any of their social systems be put into operation, to cope with the competition of the Yellow Multitudes, to whom Socialism is as naught? If they could but realise the imminent danger that threatens them, the workers of the West would, provided a spark of sense is in their brains, abandon their present tendency towards working less, and, by many accounts, less well, for increased wages that render some industries barely profitable. They, and their employers, would apply their minds to solving the great problems of profit-sharing by co-operation, and strive to introduce a more rational, healthier, more economical standard of living for master and for man. In Britain and in her Colonies the two great causes of the workers' thriftlessness — drink and debased "sport"—would have to be kept in check, in order to face the new conditions. Truly, if the well-grounded fear of overwhelming Far Eastern competition cause the West to set its industrial fabric in order, the "Yellow Peril" may yet prove a blessing in disguise.

CHAPTER IX.

RUSSIA, FRANCE AND GERMANY IN THE FAR EAST.

HATS off, everybody ! Hats off to a Power that knows what it wants—and gets it. The great Russian Empire knows with perfect certainty what it desires, and it obtains it, by hook or by crook, by fair means, if possible, if not, then by foul, but *it gets it.* What a painful contrast to Britain's so-called "policy" in China in the last thirty years of the nineteenth century ! The British nation, uncertainly treading paths that lead to humiliation —or to nowhere—has been feebly fumbling for a line of direction, abandoned almost as soon as it is found ; distracted by conflicting advisers, misinformed by interested, or ignorant, counsellors, led away on unimportant side-issues, tricked by superior diplomacy, flouted by Asiatic arrogance, baffled at every turn, chuckling over illusory successes—truly, the spectacle of Britain struggling in the meshes of the Far Eastern net, uttering threats she does not carry out and exacting pledges she allows to be broken with impunity, may well cause the Oriental to doubt her strength. In the case of Russia, he sees plainly the one thing that he respects above all others : power, animated by the will to use it. We in the West, accustomed for many years to look upon Russia as a "Colossus with feet of clay," can hardly conceive the degree of awe with which the peoples of the Far East have watched, and continue to watch, the giant strides wherewith the Colossus marches, ever forward, on their continent. The feet may be of clay, but they are planted with firm step wheresoever the Colossus listeth.

That is the point that impresses Orientals so deeply, the calm way in which Russia pursues her policy in Asia, undeterred by remonstrance or bluster, steadily making for the goal she has had in view for generations. And how wisely she proceeds! She never uses force when other methods, thoroughly understood by her Semi-Asiatic mind, will answer her purpose, but, when stern measures are needed, employs them with a ruthlessness, prompt and complete, that impresses the unreformed Oriental far more than our half-hearted, philanthropic attempts to gain his friendship by "regenerating" him. In nine cases out of ten, the Chinese does not want to be "regenerated"—to become "civilised," like unto ourselves, would appear to him a disaster—but he is heartily afraid of a beating, and the Power that wields the scourge is the one that looms largest in his eyes. Russia omits nothing that may contribute to increase this feeling of awe in the hearts of the Chinese—the Japanese, safely guarded in their island home by their powerful navy, look upon Russia's advance with less trepidation. The Government at St. Petersburg is mindful of the necessity for upholding this prestige of power, even in the selection of physically imposing individuals to represent her in the Far East. The biggest Finns in the Imperial Navy are shipped in her Asiatic Squadron, the tallest foot-soldiers, not serving in the regiments of the Imperial Guard, are sent to Vladivostock and to Port Arthur; even the diplomatists and the Consular officials acting in Eastern Asia are, as a rule, tall, well set-up men, as imposing in appearance as they are suave in ordinary intercourse, astute in negotiation and cunning in intrigue.

There is no service in the world whose members are more carefully chosen, more thoroughly trained, or so certain of being rewarded in exact accordance with the results they achieve, than the Diplomatic and the Consular

Corps of Russia in the East. (The officers of both services are interchangeable; a very wise provision.) In the land of jobbery and patronage, where Officers of the Guards, of noble birth, look down upon those of the Line as hardly belonging to the same army, in the country of nepotism and Palace back-stairs intrigue, two services, and two only, are free from these evils—the General Staff, and the Diplomatic and Consular Corps serving in the East. The privileges of the "well-born"—they are worth having, in Russia, as they include immunity from being flogged by the Police—count for nothing in the selection of the instruments that do the Tsar's work in Asia; fitness alone is taken into consideration. Even the despised and hated Jew is enrolled into this select *service d'élite* if he be considered likely to render efficient service. His name is "russified," and he is required to become "converted" to the Greek Orthodox Faith, but once the "off" or the "eff" is tacked on to his name, and he conforms with the outward practices of the Russian Church, no enquiry is made into the soundness of his orthodoxy. He goes to work, and to work well, in the ranks of a service that includes Armenians of the same mental calibre as himself, quick-witted Poles, and plodding, learned Germans from the Baltic Provinces, all labouring strenuously, side by side with real Russians, towards one common end. As to the means these absolutely efficient officials employ, they are calculated to make the average British diplomatist's hair stand on end "like quills upon the fretful porcupine," for they include everything calculated to be of service, "from pitch-and-toss to—constructive—murder." It is the nimble *rouble* that is pitched and tossed—into the itching palm of the Mandarin, and if an inconvenient person disappears rather suddenly from the scene—well, it only shows how very unhealthy it is to oppose the "manifest destiny" of a great Empire. It is not always convenient to kidnap undesirable people, as was done in the case of Prince Alexander of Bulgaria. Those who

RUSSIA'S ADVANCE IN THE FAR EAST, 1858 TO 1898.

Drawn, under the direction of the Author, by H. J. Evans.

saw, as I did, the long benches outside the handsome building of the Russian Legation at Bucharest, in the days when the late Gospodin Hitrovo was Minister, filled with rows of bravos "waiting for a job"—rascaldom from every part of the Balkan Peninsula, bristling with weapons—know what "shady" individuals can be of use, at times, in the furtherance of a policy of Orthodox Christian civilisation.

No detail is considered too petty for deep consideration by Russia's agents in the East. Every scrap of information is received, checked, tabulated, not—as with us—to lie forgotten in a dusty pigeon-hole, but to be instantly referred to when required, emendations being added, whenever necessary, to keep the information up to date. These *renseignements* embrace every subject that can be considered likely to prove useful in the work of the particular agency that collects them. They are gleaned, partly locally, partly at other agencies, that transmit them to headquarters on the banks of the Neva, whence they are disseminated to the offices likely to make good use of them. A case in point occurs to me as I write. At a certain, politically important, centre in Asia, a vacancy in the representation of Britain had just been filled up. The appointment of the new incumbent of the post had been gazetted, and he was on his way to take up the duties. The Russian representative on the spot enquired, in conversation with a colleague, the Consul of another European Power, whether he knew anything of "*ce nouvel Anglais qui nous arrive.*" No, the *cher collègue* knew nothing at all about Her Britannic Majesty's new representative. "Ah!" said the Muscovite, lighting another *papiros* of fragrant *Samsun krepki,* "I do. He is a very clever and energetic official, a soldier, formerly a Captain in the Royal Blankshire Fusiliers, tall, thin, and athletic. He is a bachelor, a good shot and, *mirabile dictu,* speaks three European languages and two Oriental ones! He is not a hard drinker, but he is an inveterate smoker.

His pet fad is collecting postage-stamps. *C'est bon à noter.*" "You know him, then?" was the rejoinder. "Not in the least. But I have heard," said the Tsar's officer, who had received a despatch from Russia that morning giving him all these particulars, and many more important ones, about the man against whom he was soon to be pitted in the diplomatic struggle, an unequal one from the outset, for the Russian, admirably backed up by his Government, had all the chances in his favour as against the unfortunate British officer, considered by his own Foreign Office as a *sentinelle perdue*, to be communicated with, and heard from, as rarely as possible. "No news, good news" is an adage of much comfort to the Downing Street Permanent Official.

The men who work for Russia in the Far East enjoy advantages over their colleagues of other nations—and especially over their British antagonists—that spring from racial causes. The *educated* Russian is an excellent linguist. I lay stress on the word "educated," because it is a common fallacy that *all* Russians speak several languages. In comparison with the vast population of the Empire, the linguists are few, but they excel in the languages they acquire. Not only do they learn the tongues of the Far East with greater facility, and speak them more fluently, and with a far better pronunciation and intonation, than Britons, who seldom lose their insular inflections—I know Englishmen who, after a residence of years in Ōsaka, persist in calling it "Osahka," or even "Osahker"—but they have the inestimable advantage of being able to learn the languages *before* proceeding to the Far East, in the excellent, practical School the Russian Government maintains for the purpose. France, Germany, Italy, the Netherlands, even Austria-Hungary, all possess special Schools for the same purpose. *Britain does not.* Comment is superfluous. Besides the priceless boon of a facility of tongues, and a readiness to make use of them rare in Britons—I know some Britons who know two or three foreign languages, theoretically, remarkably well, but you might live with them for a year and not be aware of their knowledge; they never practise, and consequently speak falteringly, with an atrocious accent—the Russians possess an inborn faculty, due to the Asiatic strain in their blood, of adaptation to Oriental surroundings. The Russian can feel perfectly at home amongst Asiatics—the Briton, except in very rare cases, never does. The Russian *understands* the Far Eastern, and especially the Chinese, mind—to the average Briton it mostly remains a sealed book. I have known many Britons, Englishmen in particular, who have spent the best years of their life amongst Asiatics, and possess a wide knowledge of their language, their institutions, their manners and customs, but who are as totally ignorant of the processes of the native mind, the true feelings of the native heart, as on the day they left Mincing Lane, or "the sweet, shady side of Piccadilly."

Their sympathetic intuition stands the Russians in good stead. Not only do they thoroughly understand the Far Easterns, but the latter understand them. They can appreciate Russia's aim, they understand Russia's methods, her virtues and her vices, not so very unlike their own. We, on the contrary, are a standing puzzle to them, as they are to most of us. Our objects appear to them vague and illusory, our methods queer and wrong-headed, our amusements sheer lunacy, our virtues pale and negative, our vices incomprehensible. (I am dealing, of course, only with the opinions of the Oriental whose mind has not undergone the influences of education of the Occidental type.) When the British Minister makes representations, however serious, to the *Tsung-li-Yamên*, bringing forward cogent reasons and lucid argument, he often leaves the Chinese negotiators, half cunning, half pigheaded, wondering at His Excellency's speeches and at the motives of the Government that

instructed him. When Gospodin Pavloff retires, in high
dudgeon, from the Conference Room, after thumping the
large round table, so as to make the little saucers of
sweetmeats dance, wherewith the Chinese Board of Foreign
Affairs regale their exasperated interviewers, the wise men
of the *Yamên*—the angry words and threats of the Tsar's
representative still ringing in their ears—understand perfectly
well what he requires of them in furtherance of his
country's plain policy. They believe in the reality of his
menaces, for they know the Tsar has the power, and, if
he must come to extremities, the will to execute them—
and the members of the Board, too, for the matter of that
—and, in accordance with the concluding words of Chinese
Imperial Rescripts, they "Tremble and Obey."

Russia's methods are not always of the violent type.
Her arguments are frequently persuasive, nay, seductive.
A Russian official, who had long experience in China, once
said: "There is but one way to negotiate with a Mandarin:
hold a thousand *rouble* note in your left hand, and take
two turns of his pigtail round your right." Much as the
Chinese corrupt official — there are a few incorruptible
ones—likes to be offered "temptations," he, none the less,
entertains, in common with all his countrymen, a profound
respect for the man who dares to browbeat him successfully. He shares this feeling with the Russian. A Muscovite *isvostchik* who was soundly drubbed by an irate
"fare" he had upset in the snow, climbed on to his
little perch on the sleigh, rubbing his bruised shoulder,
with the exclamation of involuntary admiration: "*Mala-
dietz!*" ("What a fellow! There's a man for you!")

Just so the Chinese, who looks up to the man who
carries a big stick, *and uses it* on occasion. It is in
this respect that Britain commits a grave error in her
dealings with China. Her "big stick"—the splendid fleet
she keeps in Far Eastern waters—is well in evidence; the
mischief is that no one in Eastern Asia believes that she
ever intends to use it.

Russia has, I have endeavoured to explain, an admirable staff to do her work in Eastern Asia. These devoted men spend laborious days, and nights, in working, on lines I have indicated, to obtain, as far as in them lies, the realisation of their country's ardent desire. What is it, then, that Russia wants? To the mind of the average, Non-Russian, and Non-French, observer, there would seem to be but one possible answer to this question. Russia's great want is, of course, some *real* civilisation : *education* for the besotted, illiterate, superstitious, dirty and unhealthy millions of " the Black People," the good, poor, suffering masses of the huge Empire, whose virtues are all their own, whose vices are all those of the system of alternate repression and neglect under which they vegetate ; *sanitation*, both *material* and *moral*—a stiff broom to sweep the filth not only, materially, from the reeking St. Petersburg tenement-house and the peasant's log-hut, but also, morally, from the hundreds of Government offices where thousands of underpaid *Tchinovniki* batten on the people, robbing the poor and the rich, the *muzhik* and the Tsar ; *peace*, to allow of the development of her marvellous resources ; *toleration*, to permit her people to worship God in the way that seems to them the best ; and, last, but chief of all, *liberty*, just a little liberty to begin with, in a mild, tentative sort of way, merely the right of the subjects to their own souls and bodies, the right to speak, to read, to write, to lie down at night unhaunted by the ghastly fear of an enemy's malicious denunciation, of the midnight police-raid, the exile " by Administrative Order " and—Siberia. Surely, that is what Russia wants, with a wide re-opening of that " window facing Europe " that Peter the Great first opened, and that has now been shut for some years, and bolted and barred by the Procurator of the Holy Synod, Gospodin Pobedonostzeff, partly a Russian pinchbeck imitation of the Grand Inquisitor Torquemada, partly a weak replica of General Booth. A little of the fresh, free air of heaven, let in to vivify the

stifling, grovelling masses, surely that is Russia's pressing
need ?

Not a bit of it, at least not in the opinion of the vast
majority of the Russian people. A small, a very small,
proportion of the population may sigh for all, or for
some, of these _desiderata,_ but that proportion is either in
the mines, working in chains, probably, or breaking its
heart in the drearmess of " internment " in an unsavoury
Yakut _ulus_ out in the _taiga,_ the Siberian "bush," or in exile
in Switzerland, or in a London suburb, or living a hunted
life in Russia itself. An infinitesimal fraction of it lives
in Palaces, talks treason — an average number of the
Times contains two or three columns of treason, from the
Russian Censor's point of view—in whispers, over glasses
of tea-and-lemon, and sometimes does the most daring
things, deeds to subvert an Empire—such as pinning
pathetic appeals, or threatening manifestos, to the Tsar's
arm-chair. But all of them together are as a drop in
the great ocean of the Russian majority that asks for
none of those things which seem to us so essential, knows
them not and does not feel the want of them.

What, then, does the Russian majority want ? Its
plausible friends in our midst assure us that it only
wants to get to the sea, to the real, open sea, not to
narrow waters like the Baltic, ice-bound in almost every
port in winter, nor to " closed seas" like the Black Sea,
where Turkey could "bottle up" the Russian fleet by
closing the Bosphorus, just as a possible future Nelson
might seize the narrow straits between Denmark and Scandinavia, and "bottle up" the Tsar's Baltic Squadron. Russia,
they say, wants to get access to an ocean open the whole
year round, not rendered impassable by ice for several
months, like the White Sea, nor to be forced only by
powerful ice-breakers, like the Pacific at Vladivostock.
With this craving for an outlet to the free ocean every-
one must needs sympathise. One cannot expect that a
nation of nearly one hundred and thirty millions will for

ever remain content to be confined within a bottle with four narrow necks, three of them ice-bound every winter, and the fourth at all times at the mercy of a foreign, and probably hostile, Power. Russia's irresistible impulse towards the open sea is but natural; it is justified, and no power on earth can permanently arrest what is moving with the momentum of an elemental force. Britain's business is to see to it that Russia reaches the sea only at such places, and under such conditions, as will involve the least damage to British interests.

But Russia wants more than mere access to the open sea. Russia wants to rule, in the first place, over China; *absolutely* over Manchuria, Mongolia and Northern China proper, then over Chinese Turkestan as far as the Pamir table-land; *indirectly* over the whole of China. No "Spheres of Influence" for Russia, or, rather, one vast "Sphere of Influence," Russian influence, to wit, conterminous with the borders of the Chinese Empire. And Russia knows that once she has firmly established her rule, call it "Suzerainty," "Protectorate," "Influence," or what you will, over China, she will be the mistress of three-fourths of Asia, together with her partner, France, and that is what Russia wants. Nor does her ambition stop there. She wants to rule over Asia, and to control Europe too, ay, and as much of the rest of the globe as she can place under her influence. Russia wants as much of the world as she can get hold of, because Russia believes, firmly, implicitly, that it is her "manifest destiny" to be a World-Power, a greater Rome, a stronger and more Imperial Britain. "Russia first, and the rest nowhere!" That is the idea implanted in every Russian mind, the wish imbedded in every Russian heart, but not in the manner of theoretical Chauvinism, that sentimental patriotism that makes the people of every great nation desire to see theirs placed first amongst the Powers; no, this Russian patriotism is more of the ardent, irresistible, Japanese type; it is more than a national feeling, because it is *a religion.*

To absorb new territory means, to the Briton, to secure a large space where he can find fresh customers for his wares, and grow produce to sell "at home," or in other countries; a place where his superabundant sons, and daughters too, sometimes, may make new homes for themselves and become self-supporting; he even looks upon it as a convenient "dumping-ground" for his ne'er-do-weels, the scapegraces who are supposed to undergo an instantaneous and complete moral reformation the moment they land in the dependency, where half-a-dozen whiskey-bars face them on the wharf. To the Frenchman, the conquest of a "Colony," so-called, means the opportunity of a number of people to live at the public expense, with the additional delights of being invested with authority, and having an official title and a uniform. Moreover, it is flattering to the nation's self-esteem; there is a dash of heroism and romance about it. To the German, the seizure of another "Colony," also so-called, for it attracts but few colonists, means very much the same as to the Frenchman, with this difference, that the German makes an honest and determined effort to trade there, and that he can enjoy himself to his heart's content by ordering the natives about in sharp, barrack-yard tones.

Each nation has its own ideal of enjoyment. The Briton is happiest when he can do "as he jolly well pleases"; the Frenchman is glad when he can make someone else do what he, the Frenchman, likes; the German, especially the Prussian, rejoices when he can make somebody do what that somebody does not like. All three nations look upon colonies and dependencies with favour, although from opposite points of view. The Russian regards his conquests in quite another light. To him they are not only regions promising a rich harvest of profit, they are lands where he will continue his holy mission—the Russification of the World. Gradually he goes to work, ruthlessly "russifying" by force, where force is the best method, operating persuasively, with great tact, where violence would fail. Above all, he encourages the native to become a Russian, especially in the matter of religion, by holding out social inducements, a line of conduct the Briton never adopts, save in a half-hearted manner. Ask anyone just returned from a British settlement in Africa whether the converted, "civilised" Negro, or Kaffir, is made welcome in white society. In India, the British are more friendly to the native who remains faithful to his own customs, his traditions, and his creed, than to the "civilised" native, who wears European clothes and has taken his B.A. degree at an Indian, or even at an English, University.* Not so the Russian. He takes to his heart the Turkoman who has abjured Islam and changed his name from Ali Khan to "Alikhanoff." He makes much of him socially, gives him a commission in the army, if he be a fighting chief, confers decorations upon him, invites him to the Court of St. Petersburg and makes him feel, generally, that he is a Russian like himself, provided always that he has submitted to the process of "russification." He must be made much of, for he is a useful tool in the great work of making Russia Mistress of the World. Yes, Russia the World-Power, that is the idea. As it happens, a somewhat similar idea with regard to Britain has its seat in every British brain. Hence the trouble in the present and the future.

In her plans for the subjugation of China, Russia has, of course, the devoted assistance of her "dear friend and ally," France, who supports all her efforts diplomatically, and aids her with what is much more important—money. Russia's wonderful railway across Asia, the great Trans-Siberian Line, is being built with French capital, and the

---

* An exception to this rule is made when the native plays high-class cricket with consummate skill. In such case, the white community in India condescend to intimacy with him. The rest of the British race make a demi-god of him.

greater part of the industrial enterprises that are developing, at a prodigious rate, the resources of Russia, in Europe
and in Asia, derive their funds, and much of the energy
and of the scientifically-trained skill with which they are
being conducted, from France. I have it on the authority
of one of London's leading financiers, a man well known
for the accuracy of his information and the prudence of
his statements, that the amount lent to Russia, in one
way or another, by French investors reached, in 1897, the
enormous total of *three hundred million pounds sterling.*
This immense sum includes the French capital invested in
industrial undertakings in the Russian Empire, but a great
part of it represents money lent to the Russian State.
Now, what has France, as a nation, got in return for this
extraordinary display of confidence? The individual investors in the Russian Funds receive their interest regu-
larly—Russia is scrupulously careful to keep up her credit,
and during the Crimean War she paid the interest due to
her creditors even amongst those who were fighting against
her—and many of the Russian undertakings financed in
Paris earn dividends, but what has the Republic received
in exchange for all this French money? *Two kisses.* The
Tsar kissed President Faure on both cheeks at their meeting
in St. Petersburg. That is at the rate of one hundred and
fifty millions sterling *per* kiss. Our Metropolitan Police
Magistrates value them, on occasion, at a considerably lower
rate, as sundry fines, reported in the press, do testify.

Signs are not wanting that the French people are
beginning to chafe at the one-sided nature of their alliance
with Russia, but it is a fact that, were the compact to
terminate in Europe, it would endure for years to come,
if Russia so desired, in the Far East. The motive of this
strange "union of hearts" is, on the part of the French,
not love for Russia but hatred, blind hatred, of Germany
and of Britain. The former feeling is easily accounted
for—such a crushing defeat as proud, sensitive France
suffered in 1870–71 must rankle for many years. Her

animosity against Britain is more complex and less logical.
Jealousy is at the bottom of it, and unreasoning spite, as
some of France's worthiest and wisest men—those whose
warning voices are drowned in the popular clamour—
sorrowfully admit.   The French are straining every nerve,
to carry out, in Asia as in Africa, that policy of expansion
that was devised by her regenerators to restore the nation's
confidence in itself, so rudely shaken by her collapse under
the blows of Germany.   It was necessary to show the
French people, unnerved by the disasters of the war and
the horrors of the Commune, that victory would yet follow
the tricolour, that the bells of Notre Dame could still
peal for triumphs achieved by French arms.   The victories
were over Tunisian soldiery, Annamite and Tong-king
rabble, faint-hearted Malagasy, and brave, but ill-equipped,
Dahomeyans, it is true, but they were triumphs all the
same, very similar to many of those the British army
achieves in various of our "little wars," and they gave
back to the French that belief in their own prowess that
puts life into nations.   Unfortunately for the peace and
concord of two great peoples, near neighbours who ought
to be close friends, the French policy of expansion beyond
the seas brought them, and still brings them, into perilous
contact with Britain's outposts throughout the world.   The
same thing occurs in the case of Germany's attempts to
found a "World-Empire."   It is, naturally, extremely galling to the Frenchman, or the German, who enters territory,
he has "marked down" for his own—the black, brown, or
yellow owner is not consulted in the matter—to find a
Scotchman there selling something.   So the Gaul and the
Teuton unite in vituperation of "perfidious Albion," and
repeat the phrase so often that it has passed into an
article of belief.

Animated by these unfriendly feelings towards Britain,
France has lost no opportunity, in the last decade of the
nineteenth century, to exert her influence in the Far East
against Britain's interests.   And her influence is great,

X

especially in China, owing to the proximity of her Indo-Chinese possessions, of whose vast extent the average Briton has but a faint notion, and to the number, the energy and the indomitable courage of the Roman Catholic Missionaries, of French nationality, whom she protects in China. The *rôle* of France in the Far East is, indeed, an important one. She is gradually, but surely, extending her paramount influence in Yun - nan and Kwang-si. Her Missionaries, every one of whom acts as an " agent in advance " to further her interests, penetrate into the most remote districts, her engineers are making surveys on Chinese soil for the railways that are to open up communications with the trade-routes in her Indo-Chinese dominion, in competition with the British railway from Upper Burma into China, about which we have been talking, talking, talking, and writing, writing, writing so much — and doing so little. The Consular Agents of France travel through Southern China from end to end, and so do her officials from Tong-king, who have a peculiar way of enjoying their " leave season." Their pastime in that holiday period often consists in sailing on the waters of the Yang-tsze, or clambering in the passes and gorges of Yun-nan and of Sze-chuen, accompanied by large escorts of their Annamite and Tong-king soldiers, fully armed and equipped, and by French officers, in uniform all the time. The Chinese authorities look on in a dazed sort of way, and make no protest. If Britain attempted a similar course of action the *Tsung-li Yamên* would worry our Minister about it to the verge of exasperation. But France is the friend of Russia ; China feels the two halves of the Russo-French nut-cracker closing on her, North and South, and is helpless and powerless to resist the steady, unrelenting pressure.

To add to China's troubles, Germany, after many years of close commercial intercourse, and of great influence, due, chiefly, to the fact that she posed as the disinterested friend, has driven her wedge into the Celestial Empire.

She has secured, at Kiao-chau, an excellent harbour and coaling-station for her China Squadron, that is to be a powerful one when the Kaiser's aspirations to sea-power proceed towards realisation. The "Mailed Fist" expedition raised a smile at its grandiloquent "send off," and its slow progress across the seas, but it achieved important moral effects. The interview Prince Henry of Prussia had with the Son of Heaven, an interview obtained from the Government at Peking by threats it knew were meant to be carried out, convinced the Mandarins that they had to deal with a Power that would "stand no nonsense." That is the object to be aimed at in all relations with China. Russia, and her ally, France, and Germany, who sides with them when it suits her convenience, have inspired the ruling class of China with a terror that is worth, to these masterful Powers, a whole cartload of Treaties and Conventions. What use Russia and her subservient partner intend to make of their power in China is plainly evident. Russia aims at supreme control, and will let France, whose thrifty people have supplied her with the sinews of war, have a share of the spoil. Germany's object is a different one. Her lust is not so much after territory in the Far East. She required a base for her operations, a *Stützpunkt,* and she has got it, and an excellent one, at Kiao-chau. There she can, under her own flag, lay her plans for the Far Eastern phase of the commercial and industrial contest with Britain she is waging, with remarkable success, all over the world. Russia's industries cannot, for many years to come, supply the markets of Northern and Central China with all the manufactures they require. She will not object to Germany's sharing in the business if British products can thereby be ousted.

Russia remains the chief factor of the situation, and the White Tsar holds the future of China in his hand, unless a stronger Power exerts its might and wrests the supremacy from him.

CHAPTER X.

BRITAIN'S CLEAR COURSE.

THE course is clear that lies before Britain in the Far East. It is plainly marked on the chart of history. Every rock ahead, every shoal is clearly indicated by the survey of experience, every current is traced, so that the pilot may steer with unerring confidence. Yet, at the close of the nineteenth century, the good ship *British Policy* is stranded, high and dry, at the mouth of the Pei-ho, and on a coast that her captain ought to know better than a shipmaster of any other nation.

"Ah!" I hear the Reader exclaim, "now for an indictment of the conduct of Britain's affairs in the Far East!" And, according to his particular political convictions, he prepares to approve or to blame. If he be an opponent of the policy of the Marquess of Salisbury, or one of the "Revolted Tories," whom the Far Eastern Crisis drove into mutiny, he will applaud when I state that the interests of Britain are indeed in jeopardy in Eastern Asia, that she has lost the proud position of absolute paramount influence that was hers for so long, that the efforts made to retrieve her vanished prestige have been inadequate, and that the small successes incidentally gained, and paraded with much solemnity, have been, to a great extent, illusory. "There!" he will say, "I knew it! Such a miserably weak, vacillating, futile policy was never seen before!" But, desiring to be strictly impartial, I am compelled to give heart

of grace to his political opponents, the stalwarts of the
Unionist Party, by affirming my conviction that, had
his side been in office, they would have fared just as
badly—or worse. Whatever party might have been in
office during 1897 and 1898, the results of its Far Eastern
policy were, almost inevitably, foredoomed to be inadequate for the maintenance of Britain's interests and
prestige. "The stars in their courses" were fighting
against us, it might appear, so persistently did ill-luck
attend one after another of the honest and strenuous, but
ill-directed, efforts that were made to keep British policy
on a successful course. Those who guided these efforts
were but reaping the results of years of ignorance and
neglect on the part of remote predecessors, who be-
queathed to successive Secretaries of State incorrect information, antiquated and futile methods, and inadequate
means of carrying out even these. An inexorable fatality
that attends a wrongly-conceived policy drives it from
bad to worse, and Britain's course of action towards
China, having acquired a twist in the wrong direction in
the 'seventies,—under the entirely erroneous impression that
China was a valuable and potent ally in case of need—
went on increasing its deviation from the true line from
year to year. Blunder followed on blunder, all arising
from the original error, and each mistake, more serious
than the last, whittling away a large slice of that prestige,
that respect for our power, and that fear of our anger,
that forms the foundation of our position in China. In
the meantime, new factors were being introduced into the
Far Eastern situation, at first hardly noticeable, or treated
by us with good-humoured contempt, but growing apace
until they became the formidable elements we must now
take into consideration at every step of our Far Eastern
action.

In the last twenty-five years of the century, great
Powers have appeared on the scene in Eastern Asia, for
the first time, with whom we have now to reckon, but

our policy and our methods have not been adapted to meet the changed conditions. Where we stood alone face to face with the Far Eastern peoples, almost the only great Occidental Power they knew, we are now surrounded by active, well-equipped competitors, carrying out policies, based on sound knowledge, by modern means suited to the end in view.

Had those in charge of Britain's policy, in the eventful years 1897 and 1898, cast off the old methods, had they taken a leaf out the book of our chief opponent in Asia, Russia, and acted with the firmness the situation demanded, would such a course have been crowned with success? I venture to say that the result would have been but little more satisfactory—or, rather, but slightly less unsatisfactory—than has actually been the case. This seems, at first sight, a paradox, for, surely, the complete change of our policy and methods from effeteness to vigour, from futility to efficiency, must have surmounted all obstacles in our way? Not necessarily; the *real* cause of the failure of our policy lies deep indeed. The whole nation is responsible for its existence, not only the Ministers who bear the blame. It behoves every patriot to examine its nature and to strive with might and main to remove the defect. The cause is lack of sufficient *Strength*.

Powerful as Britain undeniably is, supreme as she is at sea, the growth of her defensive, and of her offensive forces —in modern war the terms are, in our case, practically synonymous—has not kept pace with the expansion of her world-wide Empire, nor with the power to harm her of her possible foes. This lamentable fact has never been more apparent than during the crisis in the Far East. Had Britain opposed the machinations of Russia, and of France, at the critical moment, with a firm declaration that any attempt on their part to coerce China into an attitude opposed to our interests, any encroachment on Chinese territory calculated to imperil the integrity of the

Chinese Empire, any slamming of the "Open Door," would be resisted by force of arms, she would have been taken at her word. It would have meant *War*. Truly, we spoke of the contingency of war. A Cabinet Minister flourished the words "even at the cost of war" in a famous speech, but it was only in a Pickwickian sense, and the attempted "bluff" fell flat. It did not cause Russia to deviate from her course by a hair's breadth; it did not, in the end, cause China to respect our power one whit the more. The Briton has a good conceit of the national might, but the sane man would be hard to find who would have advocated an attempt on the part of Britain to oppose by force of arms the policy in the Far East of Russia and France, possibly supported, openly or covertly, by Germany, in 1898. I am aware that this statement may be opposed by some who proudly point to our superiority in fighting power, and in coal resources, in Far Eastern waters. "Why," they say triumphantly, "we could, unaided, drive the fleets of our antagonists off the China seas, and our indisputable command of the lines of maritime communication would prevent our opponents from reinforcing their troops in Eastern Asia, and from forwarding fresh supplies of stores to their strongholds in those regions, save by the long and difficult overland route, by the way of Siberia, almost impracticable for purposes of war until the great Trans-Continental Railway is completed."

Those who reason in this way overlook the fact that the struggle would have to be fought out not in the Far East only, but in Europe itself. The die would be cast, not in the Yellow Sea, but in the English Channel; the decisive naval action would be fought in the Straits of Dover, or off the Canaries, or near the Azores; the pitched battles on land would take place not in the vicinity of Peking, but in the forests of Finland, or on the plains of Northern France. Those who talk glibly of the certainty of Britain's overcoming, in the end, the united might of

Russia and of France base their forecast entirely on our undoubted superiority at sea to either of the allies, and, in all likelihood, taking into consideration the excellence of our naval *personnel*, to both of them combined. They forget that the defeat of their naval forces would not necessarily involve for Russia and France the absolute national ruin that would attend the destruction of Britain's sea-power, were such an eventuality imaginable. The British navy could, no doubt, destroy the maritime commerce of both our opponents; they would not be staggered by the blow, for France's merchant shipping is small in importance relatively to her population and her coast-line, whilst Russia's mercantile fleet might be swept off the seas without crippling the nation to any appreciable extent. Granted that, in such a conflict, Britain had driven the hostile flags off the ocean, hostilities might be indefinitely prolonged, the protracted state of tension working incalculable injury to her industries, for, victorious at sea, she would lack the powerful land forces requisite to deliver what Sir Charles Dilke has called "the counterstroke" against the huge armaments within her enemies' frontiers. France can be really conquered only at Paris, Russia only at Moscow. To overcome these giants one must strike at the heart. For such an enterprise against two great nations in arms Britain lacks the requisite military strength, the hundreds of thousands of *trained* soldiers, led by Generals experienced in handling, scientifically, vast bodies of men. She can find *men* in abundance, even men with some sort of military training, strong, hardy, brave as lions, but she cannot, as yet and for some time to come, place in the field a homogeneous force, practically, and constantly, organised, equipped, and trained for war—in one word, an *Army*—large enough to undertake operations against the immense fighting-machines of great Continental Powers like Russia and France.

The Man in the Street has some inkling of this fact, as may be inferred from the eagerness with which he catches at the idea of an alliance, or, rather, alliances, that would provide Britain, in his opinion, with the military power in which she is deficient. Not that he will openly admit that the deficiency exists; in his heart, filled with intense, and justifiable, pride of race, misgivings as to Britain's power on land struggle with the conviction that one Briton is a match for any three foreigners. But the idea of alliances is a soothing one, and the degree of the attraction it exercises on the public mind may be gauged by the readiness with which every indication of a probable co-operation of foreign nations is acclaimed by the masses. It is taken for granted by nearly every Briton that the assistance of Japan's powerful navy and excellent army is assured to Britain in the event of hostilities in the Far East. The wish is father to the thought, but it would be unwise to look upon such an alliance as a foregone conclusion. The interests of Britain and of Japan in Asia being so largely identical, common-sense points to combined action in case of need as inevitable, yet there are obstacles in the way that are not sufficiently appreciated by the British nation. There exists in Japan a very considerable party opposed to the idea of any foreign alliance, holding that the wisest course for the nation to pursue is an opportunist policy, keeping aloof from engagements that might prove embarrassing, and profiting, as occasion arises, by the rivalries of the various Occidental Powers. Another large, and influential, section of the population is in favour of co-operation with Britain in the Far East, but demands a compact, guaranteeing immunity for Japan from the risks attending, in the opinion of this party, an alliance with us. The Japanese are keen students of modern history, and they note, with feelings of pardonable uneasiness, the fatality that seems to pursue nations which throw in their lot with Britain, and help to fight her battles. Without going back to the days of the Crimean war, and considering the fate of Shamyl and his undaunted Circassians, the Japanese find food for reflection in the

case of the Swazi nation, who stood by the British in
many a ' hard-fought tussle in South Africa, and were
"rewarded" for their assistance by. being handed over to
the tender mercies of "Oom Paul" and his Boers, and in
the doom of the Jaalin, and other "Friendlies," destroyed,
root and branch, by the Khalifa's savage Baggara for the
unpardonable sin of having borne arms for Britain. Such
"awful examples" are well calculated to alarm the cautious
Japanese, who seek for guarantees that they would not be
abandoned to the vengeance of Russia and her ally, should
Britain, in the event of combined action with Japan
against their common foes, retire · prematurely from the
contest, patching up a hasty, and inconclusive, peace for
the sake of her commerce and her industries, crippled by
war on a vast scale.

Finally, there are Japanese, and they are in the
majority, who doubt not only Britain's earnestness in the
protection of her assailed interests in Eastern Asia, which
are almost entirely parallel with those of Japan, but are
even sceptical as to her ability to defend those interests
by force of arms. They admit the great strength of our
navy, whilst criticising some of its shortcomings—especially
the want of a perfect system of Reserves for adequately
supplying the *trained* officers and men required to fill
up the vacancies caused by the large number of casualties
inseparable from modern naval warfare—but to say that they
are not impressed by our land forces is to state the case
very mildly. Accustomed to look upon the German army
as the criterion in all military matters, they compare ours
with the Kaiser's great machine of "Blood and Iron,"
with its perfect, simple, well-lubricated gearing, that
obeys, silently and swiftly, with unerring accuracy, the
impulsion of the master-minds trained in Moltke's school,
and the result is not in favour of our complicated and
costly military system, with its many anomalies, its waste
of energy and of wealth. Warriors to a man, holding
the militant professions in almost superstitious reverence,

they fail to understand the spirit of a nation that cheers itself hoarse over the deeds of heroism of its sailors and its soldiers—and pays a certain small minority of its sons to do its fighting for it. The Japanese who read the account in the London newspapers of the wildly enthusiastic reception accorded by the populace to the battalion of Grenadier Guards returning from the admirably-planned and executed capture of Omdurman, noted, with feelings of pained astonishment we can hardly appreciate, the answer given by a stalwart Corporal to an energetic reporter, who enquired : " Well, how was it ? " " We've fairly earned our pay ! " quoth the Guardsman, and his comrades within earshot assented heartily. " *Our pay !* " These words in the mouth of a conquering hero have a strange ring in the ears of the Japanese, who cannot conceive why the patriotic British remain the only European nation that refuses to enter in its Statutes the assertion of every man's bounden duty to be trained for the defence of his native land.

To these considerations, inclining the Japanese to underestimate Britain's Fighting Power, must be added the influence of the constant carping criticism of all British methods dinned into their ears for many years past by Occidentals from every country of Continental Europe, and — until recently—from America, repeating their dismal prophecies of the decline of Britain's power, many Japanese swelling the Anti-British chorus with echoes of Anglophobe ravings heard in their student-days in Paris, in Berlin, in Vienna, in St. Petersburg, or in Chicago. The most severe blow to that British prestige which alone can make an Anglo-Japanese co-operation possible has been given by Britain herself. The vacillating, weak policy pursued by her Government during the troublous times in China, in 1897 and 1898, served to intensify the feeling, so actively fostered amongst the Japanese parties just enumerated, that Britain's hand had become palsied, that her resolution.

had forsaken her. The Japanese friends of Britain waited anxiously for a sign that the old British spirit was awakening, that the lion had not lost his might in his long lethargy. Twice, or thrice, they thought the moment had come. Brave words were uttered by British statesmen, British warships, ominously ready to translate those words into deeds, cruised on mysterious errands, and the rulers of Japan's policy thought another day would bring that startling proof of Britain's virility which would silence her detractors amongst their own people and would irresistibly lead to the alliance they feel in their hearts must come for the mutual benefit of both nations. Alas ! Their hopes were shattered. The brave words were followed by paltry deeds ; the great warships returned from their aimless yachting cruises—and Russia went marching on. Once only did Britain rise to the highest level of patriotic determination, standing firm as a rock in defence of her interests—but that was not in the Far East, not in the face of Russia and her ally ; it was in Africa, and the possible foe was *France alone,* for the extraordinary compact between the Autocrat and the Republic, uniting them so closely in Asia, does not, apparently, extend to the region of the Upper Nile. Britain's firmness of front had some effect on the minds of the peoples of Eastern Asia, but, on second thoughts, it only increased the impression, actively propagated by Britain's enemies, that Africa would, in future, absorb all her energies, and that she was content, with that end in view, to relinquish, almost without a struggle the paramount position she had won for herself, and so long maintained, in the Far East.

If the alliance of Japan with Britain is thus not the matter of absolute certainty it is so generally thought to be, still less ground is there for the comforting belief, so prevalent towards the close of 1898, that the co-operation of Germany in the Far East is assured to Britain in her opposition to the schemes of Russia and of France. The

German Emperor cordially desires, there is no doubt about it, a *rapprochement* with Britain all over the world, but with this proviso—an all-important one—that his reconciliation with us shall *in no wise endanger the traditional good understanding with Russia* that is the key-stone of German policy. Moreover, the German people see the Kaiser's improved relations with Britain with no favourable eye. The bitter antagonism of commercial rivalry—the deepest cause of international animosities—inspires them with a jealous dislike of Britain that no Imperial change of policy can eradicate.

There remains one possible, nay, a probable, ally to be considered—the United States of America, whose interests in the Far East are, to a great extent, identical with those of Britain and of Japan. Were Britain involved in a struggle with Russia and France in the Far East, and, consequently, all over the world, America might be trusted to extend to her relative in difficulties if not active assistance, at all events a neutrality of as benevolent a character as that shown towards America by Britain during the war with Spain. And that is really, for some years to come, all that Britain needs from America, merely sympathy that will ensure the uninterrupted supply of the food-stuffs from across the Atlantic necessary to the existence of the population of the British Isles. Those supplies are sure to come, alliance or no alliance, for dollars are to be earned, by selling corn to famished people, and no mortal power exists that can prevent an American from earning dollars wherever they can be acquired. As to *active* co-operation, the excellent navy of the United States would be a useful ally, but not an indispensable one, whilst, with regard to operations on land, America has no regular troops to spare for operations beyond her own territories, soon to be so vastly increased. Men she could supply by tens of thousands, but persons in military uniforms are not necessarily soldiers, a fact often lost sight of by the English-speaking public on both sides of the Atlantic.

The average Briton; seeing the alliances he had fondly cherished as either existent or imminent fade into problematic visions under the search-light of dispassionate enquiry, may well feel uneasy, and ask the question so often propounded: "Can we not come to an understanding with Russia?" That would, indeed, be a glorious solution of the Far Eastern imbroglio! Britain, Russia, France, Germany, America and, of course, Japan, each working peacefully in its own clearly-defined "Sphere of Influence" to the ultimate benefit, not only of itself—the prime consideration in national policy—but of Eastern Asia—the vision is millennial! Unfortunately, it is not likely to commend itself to Russia, who holds the trumps of the game in her hands. Why should she abandon the advantages she has won by her perseverance, her boldness and her skill? To induce her to relinquish these, or any of them, we must either offer her compensation, or frighten her into dropping the cards. What can we "trade" with Russia that will equal in value what we ask her to abandon? A survey of the map of the world yields no answer to the question. The one equivalent we might, a few years ago, have offered her we have deliberately thrown away. As long as we remained the ally of the Ottoman Empire, we could always hold out as a bait to Russia our withdrawal of support from her coveted prize. Since we have assumed, mainly for religious and sentimental reasons, an attitude of uncompromising hostility towards the Sultan, now our bitter enemy, we can no longer use Turkey as a pawn in the great diplomatic game of chess. Russia knows that she can now work her will in Turkey, both in Europe and in Asia, without troubling herself about our interference. It is with Germany and with Austria-Hungary she will have to deal for the inheritance of that "Sick Man" who is such an unconscionably long time in dying—not with Britain.

As to frightening Russia into abandoning her prey in

Eastern Asia, Russia is not easily terrified. She has, it is true, no wish to fight us yet awhile — the great Siberian Railway is not yet completed. In the meantime the Peace Conference, to which the Powers are coming, each with a revolver in the hip-pocket and a Bowie-knife in the boot, will agreeably fill up the "wait" before the rise of the curtain on the Great Drama of the Future of the Far East. If Britain is to be prepared to play her part worthily in that epoch-making performance, she has no time to lose. Her cue is "*Strength.*" Let Britain make herself strong ; absolutely, undeniably, evidently strong, not only on sea, but on land. This may necessitate a departure from her traditional military system. It probably will. "What ? Universal Compulsory Service in the Navy or the Army ? Impossible ! Un-English !" I think I hear the outcry, but I know of something still more Un-English : it is called Defeat, likewise Humiliation.

Let Britain be strong, not with the arrogant strength of the bully, but with the calm force of the strong man armed, determined to keep what he has worked for and won. Let her but show her determination to increase her power, by land as well as on the sea, to proportions commensurate to the World-Empire she has to guard from jealous competitors ; let her but give an earnest of her resolve to defend it against all comers, and the effect will not be slow in making itself felt. Japan will, with one accord, become the valuable and trusty ally of her natural friend, Britain, strong enough to command confidence and respect. China will turn from her Muscovite "Protector"'s heavy yoke and seek regeneration at the hands of Britain—whom she will trust when she once more fears her wrath—of America, soon to be an Asiatic Power, and of Japan, best fitted of all to undertake the task. Germany, France, Belgium, all the industrial nations of the world will work with might and main at the development of an untold wealth of resources. Russia, kept within due bounds by the counterpoise of an immensely strong Britain, will find abundant occupation in exploiting the natural riches of her vast Asiatic Dominions. Peace, prosperity, and the dawn of a brilliant era will come to the New Far East.

THE END.

INDEX.

—•◦•—

Y

PRINTED BY CASSELL & COMPANY. LIMITED LA BELLE SAUVAGE, LONDON, E C

30.704